COMPUTER AUGMENTED TEAMWORK: A GUIDED TOUR

Robert P. Bostrom
Richard T. Watson
Susan T. Kinney

VNR VAN NOSTRAND REINHOLD
New York

Library of Congress Catalog Card Number 92-15663
ISBN 0-442-00277-7

Manufactured in the United States of America.

Van Nostrand Reinhold
115 Fifth Avenue
New York, New York 10003

Chapman and Hall
2-6 Boundary Row
London, SE 1 8HN

Thomas Nelson Australia
102 Dodds Street
South Melbourne 3205
Victoria, Australia

Nelson Canada
1120 Birchmount Road
Scarborough, Ontario M1K 5G4, Canada

Library of Congress Cataloging-in-Publication Data

Computer augmented teamwork : a guided tour / edited by Robert P.
  Bostrom, Richard T. Watson, Susan T. Kinney.
      p.   cm.
    Includes bibliographical references and index.
    ISBN 0-442-00277-7
    1. Research—Data processing.   2. Operations research—Data
processing.   3. Technology—Data processing.   4. Universities and
colleges—Research.   I. Bostrom, Robert P.   II. Watson, Richard
Thomas.   III. Kinney, Susan T.
  Q180.55.E4C66   1992
  658.4'036'0285—dc20   92-15663
                                                       CIP

Contents

Section III   **Task-Oriented Team Technology   139**

Part A   **Self-Constructed Technology   141**

Chapter 8   **GroupSystems   143**

Chapter 9   **An Overview of the GDSS Research Project and the SAMM System   163**

Part B   **Self-Constructed and Acquired Technology   181**

Chapter 10   **Flexible Facilities for Electronic Meetings   183**

Foreword

It is a special event for me to see this book come to fruition, thanks to my friends at the University of Georgia. They picked up my pieces and carried them forward to completion in an expedient and clever way.

It is quite commonly accepted that computers have changed the nature of organizational work. The impact of group support technologies, however, will be far more fundamental. Whereas computers in the 1960s served primarily to automate manually performed functions, the group support technologies of the 1990s will be the foundations on which totally new forms of organizations will be built—organizational forms that we can barely imagine.

Group support technology has been creeping into the research community since about 1978. After gaining momentum in the mid-1980s, the field has become one of the most active areas of research. Now it is also becoming an active area of commercial development.

The subject of information technology support for groups is complex; there are a variety of perspectives and approaches to research, all of them valid. It presents a vast hunting ground for researchers with diverse perspectives—each hunting with carefully fashioned equipment of his or her own making, and often for a different species of beast. There is, then, an air of mystery that cloaks this new arena of research and makes it extremely appealing to hunters and tourists alike.

This book takes you on an expertly guided tour of an exciting and intriguing landscape, and thereby represents a significant contribution. Both newcomer as well as experienced researcher will benefit from reading this book, for it will introduce them to what is thus far known about computer-augmented teamwork. I commend the authors for their work and strongly recommend this book to the reader. Welcome to the safari!

Gerald Wagner
Milagro, Inc.

The Contributors[1]

Mark J. Abel (MARKABEL©ASHLAND.INTEL.COM)

To contact his coauthors at US West, write to them at US West Advance Technologies, 4001 Discovery Drive, Suite 280, Boulder, CO 80303.

Mark Abel is a senior staff engineer in Intel's Architecture Development Lab in Hillsboro, Oregon, where he is leading the Network Architecture group and helping develop Intel's computer-supported collaboration vision. Prior to this position, he was a member of the technical staff at US West Advanced Technologies and was also manager of Broadband Applications with the US West Compass Broadband Trials Program. Mr. Abel helped initiate and carry out the TeleCollaboration research project at US West Advanced Technologies. Before coming to US West, he was with the Xerox Palo Alto Research Center in Portland, where he was involved in the pioneering Portland-Palo Alto collaboration-over-distance project. He has a bachelor's degree in electrical engineering from the University of Michigan and a master's degree in electrical engineering from Stanford University.

---

[1]The address of only the first author of each chapter is given.

Fran Ackermann (CIHS05©VAXA.STATHCLYDE.AC.UK)

Fran Ackermann is a research fellow in the Department of Management Science at the University of Strathclyde. She became interested in methods for supporting decision-making groups using computers while working in the Department of Management at Bath University, England, with Professor Eden. To be able to explore group decision support systems in detail she undertook and completed a part time Ph.D. in this area, looking at how one particular GDSS compared with the literature and other research findings. She has worked with a considerable number of client groups at all levels from both the public and private sectors on both messy problem solving and strategy formulation, implementation, and control. Current interests in the GDSS area include the role of facilitation and the link between DSS and GDSS.

Robert Anson (RISANSON©IDBSU)

Computer Information Systems and Production Management Department, College of Business, Boise State University, 1910 University Drive, Boise, ID 83712.

Robert Anson, assistant professor of Computer Information Systems at Boise State University, holds a B.A. from the University of Washington and an M.B.A. and Ph.D. in management information systems from Indiana University. His major research interests involve group facilitation and facilitation in computer-supported environments. He has been involved in developing facilitation training programs for the GSS environment. Currently, he is creating a proposal to develop an advanced, multimedia group room at BSU for groupware research and pedagogical applications.

Lynda M. Applegate (LAPPLEGATE©HBS.HBS.HARVARD.EDU)

Loeb House, Room 25, Soldiers Field Road, Harvard School of Business, Harvard University, Boston, MA 02163.

Lynda Applegate is associate professor at the Harvard Business School. She received a Ph.D. in business administration from the University of Arizona with a major in management information systems and a minor in quantitative methods. Before joining the faculty at the Harvard Business School, Dr. Applegate held a number of management positions and previous faculty appointments at the University of Michigan, the University of Washington, and the University of Arizona. Dr. Applegate is an active consultant and teaches regularly in corporate executive programs. Her research and recent publications focus on the role of technology in organization restructuring and the design and implementation of management support systems. She has served as an invited speaker and presented papers at international conferences on information systems research and is a member of the National Academy of Management and the Institute for Management Science. Since arriving at Harvard, she has taught courses on management information systems, organization design, management control, and managerial economics in the M.B.A. program and research methods in the doctoral program. She also teaches in the Harvard Business School Executive Education Program.

Robert P. Bostrom (BBOSTROM©UGABUS)

Department of Management, College of Business, University of Georgia, Athens, GA 30602.

Robert Bostrom is associate professor of management and the program director of the

Collaborative Work Support Systems Research Project at the University of Georgia. He is also president of a small consulting company that provides consulting, training, and meeting facilitation services. He holds a B.A. in Chemistry, M.B.A. from Michigan State University, M.S. in computer science from SUNY at Albany, and Ph.D. in MIS from the University of Minnesota. His overall research mission focuses on improving organizational systems through the effective integration of human/social and technological dimensions.

Stephen Bulick (BULICK©USWEST.COM)

Stephen Bulick is a member of the technical staff in the Intelligent Customer Assistance Group at US West Advanced Technologies in Boulder, Colorado. He received a B.A. in English literature from Washington and Jefferson College in 1970 and a Ph.D in information science from the University of Pittsburgh in 1980. He joined AT&T Bell Laboratories in 1978 to develop information systems for the Bell Labs Library Network, where he was responsible for its on-line catalog and various other information retrieval systems. In 1985 he moved to Bell Communications Research to pursue interests in network-based multimedia information retrieval and then to US West in 1988 to work on real-time multimedia communication. He is the author of a number of technical papers and one book, and his current interests center on various aspects of multimedia, including communication, information retrieval, writing, and document architectures. He and his wife live in Boulder with their two young daughters.

Laku Chidambaram (CBADLCH©HHCCVM)

University of Hawaii at Manoa, Department of Decision Sciences, 2404 Maile Way, Honolulu, HI 96822.

Laku Chidambaram joined the University of Hawaii in 1989 and is assistant professor of decision sciences at the College of Business Administration (C.B.A.). He received his Ph.D. from Indiana University with a double major in management information systems (MIS) and international business. He also holds an M.B.A. from the University of Georgia and has worked as an international trade consultant. Recently, he was involved in establishing the Electronic Meeting Room at the C.B.A. for conducting group behavioral research and studying computer-supported communication in a global setting. His current research interests include group decision support systems, cross-cultural computer-mediated communication, and multinational information systems. He is also a co-principal investigator in an extensive study of international telecommunications management in multinational corporations. His articles have appeared in refereed journals, books, and conference proceedings. Dr. Chidambaram has taught various information systems courses at the undergraduate and graduate level. In 1991, he was awarded the C.B.A. Teaching Excellence Award.

Wynne Chin (CHIN©ACS.UCALGARY.CA)

Wynne Chin is associate professor, Management Information Systems, in the Faculty of Management of the University of Calgary. He previously taught at Wayne State University and at the University of Michigan, where he was presented with an award for teaching excellence. In 1989, he was honored with a Doctoral Fellow from the Society of Information Management. His background includes academic degrees in biophysics from the University of California at Berkeley, bioengineering from Northwestern University, and an M.B.A. from the University of Michigan. His primary research interests include user acceptance of new information technology. In particular, he specializes in the role that individual attitudes and social structure play in influencing the diffusion of such technologies during implementation. His other interests include methodological issues in information systems research, the use of social network analysis and latent structural analysis, office automation, and end-user computing.

Stephen Coffin (SCOFFIN©USWEST.COM)

Stephen Coffin was born in Bangor, Maine, and received a B.A. from Wesleyan University and a Ph.D. in experimental/physiological psychology from Stanford University. He spent nine years at Bell Labs, working first on the design of computer-based operations support systems for the telephone business, then on the design and development of personal computers, add-on boards, and software. He was three years at US West Advanced Technologies, working on multimedia and user-interface software. He is the author of two books on the UNIX Operating System.

Doug Corey (DOUGC©USWEST.COM)

Doug Corey is technical director of the Input/Output Technologies Group in the Applied Research Division of US West Advanced Technologies. His group is involved in exploring multimedia telecommunication services with emphasis on what the services provide, how they work, the user interface, and how they can be carried on the telephone network. Mr. Corey was previously with Tektronix, Inc., in Beaverton, Oregon, where he was the software engineering manager for an advanced line of computer-based instrumentation. Before that, he was with Bell Laboratories in Whippany, NJ, where he worked on software for electronic loop multiplexing equipment, portions of the No. 5 ESS switching system software, and the COSMOS main distributing frame management software. Earlier, he was with Bellcomm, Inc., in Washington, DC, where he worked on mission planning and analysis for the Apollo and Skylab manned spaceflight programs. Mr. Corey holds a B.S. degree from Washington State University and an M.S. degree from New York University in electrical engineering.

Paul Cornell

Paul Cornell is the manager of Behavioral and Environmental Research at Steelcase Research and Development. He is involved in researching and designing a variety of forward-looking furniture to house technology. The goal of this work is to determine how the design of furniture affects the environment and technology on behalf of productivity in our working life. He has a Ph.D. in industrial and operations psychology from Pennsylvania State University. Before joining Steelcase he was with Burroughs (now Unysis) in a group that designed displays, keyboards, and software applications.

Alan R. Dennis (ADENNIS©UGABUS)

Alan Dennis is assistant professor of management information systems in the Terry College of Business at the University of Georgia. He received a bachelor degree in computer science from Acadia University (Nova Scotia), an M.B.A. from Queen's University (Ontario), and a Ph.D. in management information systems from the University of Arizona. Before entering the Arizona doctoral program, he spent three years on the faculty of the Queen's School of Business and was a winner of the AACSB National Doctoral Fellowship. He has published articles in a variety of journals, including *Communications of the ACM; Academy of Management Journal; MIS Quarterly; Journal of MIS; Small Group Research*; and *IEEE Transactions on Systems, Man, and Cybernetics*. His current research interests include electronic meeting systems, systems analysis and design, and business process reengineering.

Gerardine DeSanctis (DESANCTIS©UMNACVX)

Gerardine DeSanctis is associate professor of management information systems at the University of Minnesota. She holds a Ph.D. in business administration from Texas Tech University. Since 1984 she has worked with an interdisciplinary team investigating the design and implementation of group decision support systems. Texaco, Inc., and the Internal Revenue Service are involved in cooperative studies of GDSS impacts with the University of Minnesota, based on prototype systems developed by Dr. DeSanctis and her colleagues. She currently serves as associate editor for *Management Science* and *Information Systems Research* and is a senior editor for *Organization Science*.

Gary W. Dickson (DICKSON©VX.ACS.UMN.EDU)

Information and Decision Sciences, University of Minnesota, 271 19th Avenue South, Minneapolis, MN 55455.

Gary Dickson is professor of management information systems at the University of Minnesota. He holds a Ph.D. in business administration from the University of Washington. He has been active in numerous initial developments in the MIS field, including establishing the first doctoral program and research center. He was the founding editor of *MIS Quarterly* and the chair of the first International Conference on Information Systems. He has conducted research programs in the areas of decision support systems, the management of the information systems function, managerial graphics, and group decision support. He has published extensively on these topics.

Colin Eden

Management Science, Strathclyde Business School, University of Strathclyde, Livingston Tower, 26 Richmond St. Glasgow G1 1XH.

Colin Eden is head of the Department of Management Science at the Strathclyde Business School in Scotland. He qualified as an engineer and obtained his doctorate in production scheduling. He became a professional operational research analyst and then management consultant prior to becoming an academic. He has been at the forefront of developments in cognitive mapping, with two books discussing its role in organization: *Thinking in Organizations* and *Messing About in Problems*, published in 1979 and 1983, respectively. He has written over 70 papers and has consulted with numerous large organizations and community groups in relation to strategy development.

R. Brent Gallupe (GALLUPEB©QUCDN)

School of Business, Queen's University, Kingston, Canada, K7L 3N6.

Brent Gallupe is associate professor of information systems in the School of Business, Queen's University, Canada. His Ph.D. in management information systems is from the

University of Minnesota. His current research interests include group decision support systems, end-user computing, and the evaluation of information systems. His work has appeared in journals such as *Management Science, MIS Quarterly, Journal of Applied Psychology*, and *Information and Management*.

Joey F. George (GEORGE©ARIZMIS)

Joey George is assistant professor of MIS at the University of Arizona. He earned his bachelor's degree at Stanford University in 1979 and his Ph.D. in management at the University of California at Irvine in 1986. His research focuses on information systems in the work place. His current research investigates the effects of electronic meeting systems (EMS) on the group work process and its outcomes, EMS in non-American cultures, and the effects of extensive computerization in organizational work groups.

Abhijit Gopal (GOPAL©ACS.UCALGARY.CA)

MIS Area Faculty of Management, University of Calgary, 2500 Univ. Dr. N.W., Calgary, Alberta T2N 1N4.

Abhijit Gopal has a degree in economics from the University of Madras, India, a degree in law from the University of Bombay, India; an M.B.A. from Bowling Green State University; and a Ph.D. in management information systems from the University of Georgia. He has also worked for several years in the advertising industry, both as a copywriter and in the audiovisual production facility of a major advertising agency. He joined the University of Calgary in 1990. His research is in the area of group decision support systems and is aimed at understanding how to implement these systems in organizations. He is also involved in research in end-user computing and telecommunications. His experience in advertising and its management has given him a keen interest in the use of information technology to improve individual and group processes in organizations.

Paul Gray (GRAYP©CLARGRAD)

Information Science Department, Claremont McKenna College, Claremont, CA 91711.

Paul Gray is professor in, and in 1983, founder of the Programs in Information Science at Claremont Graduate School in Claremont, California. He was the project leader for the 2 million IBM grant awarded to Claremont for the management of information systems. His publications include 7 books and 66 papers. His work on telecommuting led to a award of a NATO Systems Science Prize. He is president-elect of the Institute of Management Sciences in 1991-1992 and president 1992-1993. He is past president of Omega Rho, a national honorary society. He previously served as secretary and as vice president-at-large of the Institute of Management Sciences and as a member of the Council of the Operations Research Society of America. He is on the editorial board of six journals and is also the book review editor for the *Journal of Information Systems Management*. He is editor-in-chief of the scholarly journal *International Information Systems*, which began publication in 1992. Dr. Gray's current research interests center on supporting group decision making and cooperative group work. He holds a Ph.D. from Stanford in operations research, M.S. degrees from Michigan and

Purdue, and a B.A. from New York University. His experience includes 18 years in industry and research institutes. He has been a professor at Stanford, Georgia Tech, USC, SMU, and the Claremont Graduate School. He served as a department chair for 10 years as well as a manager in industry.

Stephen Hayne (SCHAYNE©ACS.UCALGARY.CA)

Stephen Hayne received his Ph.D. from the University of Arizona in 1990 and is currently an assistant professor at the University of Calgary. His dissertation addressed the distributed data-base design process using group design as a method to reduce the time and difficulty of data-base modeling. He has taught courses on software engineering, telecommunications, and data-base systems management. He has received several research grants to investigate group support systems and expert systems. His current research interests involve building systems that use graphics to support group work, including the incorporation of traditional activities such as gesturing, as well as studying the effects of conflict and cooperation on group support systems.

Alan R. Heminger (HEMINGER©IUBACS)

Alan Heminger is assistant professor of MIS in the Decisions and Information Systems Department at Indiana University. He received his Ph.D. in MIS at the University of Arizona in December 1988 and joined the faculty at Indiana University in January 1989. In 1987, he was selected as a Doctoral Fellow by the Society for Information Management (SIM) for his work in the operational implementation of a GDSS system at an IBM facility. He has also carried out research in public goods problems as they affect users of computer networks. Since arriving at Indiana University, he has continued his research into the use of GSS. In addition to his other academic duties, he served as the director of the Computer Based Organizational Support (CBOS) program at the Institute for the Study of Developmental Disabilities (ISDD) from January 1989 to July 1990. In 1990, he initiated a project and has worked with others from the ISDD, the Linton-Stockton School District, and the Indiana University School of Business to design and create Comments, a GSS that can support any combination of same- or different-time or place meetings. Current research includes the use and further development of this system.

Starr Roxanne Hiltz (ROXANNE©EIES2.NJIT.EDU)

Computer & Information Sciences, New Jersey Institute of Technology, Newark, NJ 07102.

Starr Roxanne Hiltz is professor of computer and information science, New Jersey Institute of Technology, and a member of the faculty at the Graduate School of Business, Rutgers University. She also directs the Collaborative Systems Laboratory at New Jersey Institute of Technology. From 1986 through 1990, she directed the Virtual Classroom project, with major funding from the Corporation for Public Broadcasting. This project created software and evaluation tools for computer-mediated communication in education and applied these tools in a wide variety of courses. A forthcoming book will draw heavily on experiences and observations of on-line learning derived from that project. She received her Ph.D. in sociology from the Graduate Faculties of Columbia University and her B.A. from Vassar College. Present research interests center on the development and application of social science methodologies to the study of the impacts of distributed group support systems. An active ACM member, Dr. Hiltz served as vice chair (1979–1981) for what was then called SIGSOC and has subsequently been rechristened as SIGCHI (Computer-Human Interaction). She serves on the editorial or advisory boards of *Organizational Computing* and the *Social Science Computer Review*.

Robert Johansen

2744 Sand Hill Road, Menlo Park, CA 94025-7097.

Robert Johansen, senior research fellow and director, New Technologies Program at Institute for the Future (IFTF), has worked for nearly 20 years in the fields of telecommunications and computing. He has focused on the business, social, and organizational effects of new systems. Working with vendors, he has assisted them in understanding their information needs and opportunities, in making judgments about which media are most appropriate for them to use, and in tracking the effects of new information systems. A social scientist with an interdisciplinary background, he holds a B.S. degree from the University of Illinois and a Ph.D. from Northwestern University.

Lola J. Killey

Lola Killey is the systems project coordinator for the Cognitive Science and Machine Intelligence Laboratory at the University of Michigan. She is actively involved in its groupware and collaborative systems research. Ms. Killey is also responsible for the operation and planning of the computing and audiovideo environment at the laboratory. Her interests include distributed systems, groupware architectures and applications, multimedia systems, and user-interface management systems. She received her B.S. in electrical engineering from Purdue University in 1980 and an M.S. in electrical engineering from the University of Michigan in 1986. She previously worked at the Industrial Technology Institute, participating in international and national standards developments in computer networking. She has published articles on image processing, communications protocols, and collaborative environments.

Susan Tucker Kinney (SKINNEY©AC.WFUNET.WFU.EDU)

Susan Kinney earned a B.A. in psychology at Auburn University, an M.Ed. in psychometry from Georgia Southern University, and a Ph.D. in business administration from the University of Georgia. Dr. Kinney is assistant professor of management at the Babcock Graduate School at Wake Forest University. Her current research interests include human factors and organizational impacts in telecommunications, cross-cultural communication, and computer-supported collaborative work. Her publications include conference proceedings; book chapters; and cases in the areas of mental health, communication, and group support systems.

Kum-Yew Lai

Kum-Yew Lai is a research scientist at the Center for Coordination Science of the Massachusetts Institute of Technology. He obtained his undergraduate and master's degrees at MIT and is currently doing graduate work at the Wharton School of the

University of Pennsylvania. Prior to his position at MIT, he was assistant treasurer at DBS Bank, Singapore.

Paul Licker (LICKER©ACS.UGALGARY.CA)

Paul Licker is professor of management information systems, in the Faculty of Management of the University of Calgary. Before coming to Calgary, he taught at Virginia Commonwealth University; the University of Ottawa; and the University of Pennsylvania, where he earned a Ph.D. in communications. His dissertation work concerned the boundaries between communicative and noncommunicative acts. His primary teaching and research interests are in the management of information systems functions, group decision support systems, systems analysis and design, and human communication. He is the author of numerous research articles and two books: *Fundamentals of Systems Analysis with Application Design* (1987) and *The Art of Managing Software Development People* (1985). His textbook in MIS, called *MIS for Managers*, is due to be published in 1993.

Robert Luchetti

Robert Luchetti is principal of Robert Luchetti Associates, Inc., of Cambridge, MA, a multidisciplinary architecture, interiors, and industrial design firm. Mr. Luchetti holds a master's degree in architecture from the Graduate School of Design at Harvard University and a B.A. in environmental design from the University of California at Berkeley. He has extensive experience in the planning and design of office environments. He was one of the winners of the competition sponsored by the French Ministry of Culture for New Office Furniture in 1983, along with Philip Stone of Harvard. He has completed a number of advanced concept office environment projects with the Steelcase Corporation and such clients as IBM, Travelers Mortgage Services Company, Hewlett Packard, and the University of Michigan.

Lisbeth A. Mack

Lisbeth Mack is an associate partner with Andersen Consulting in Chicago. She holds an M.B.A. from the University of Michigan and has extensive experience with systems design and implementation, project management, and team facilitation. While with the Center for Strategic Technology of Andersen Consulting, she has pursued research projects involving CSCW applications for computer systems design teams, emphasizing human-computer interface design and the development of the overall teamwork environment.

Thomas W. Malone (MALONE©EAGLE.MIT.EDU)

Sloan School of Management, Massachusetts Institute of Technology, Cambridge, MA 02139.

Thomas Malone is the Patrick J. McGovern Professor of Information Systems at the MIT School of Management and the director of the Center for Coordination Science. His research focuses on (1) how computer and communications technology can help people work together in groups and organizations and (2) how organizations can be designed to take advantage of the new capabilities provided by information technology. Before joining the MIT faculty, Dr. Malone was a research scientist at the Xerox Palo Alto

Research Center (PARC), where he designed educational software and office information systems. He is on the editorial boards of *Human Computer Interaction*, *Management Science*, *Information Systems Research*, and *Organizational Science*. His background includes a Ph.D. from Stanford University and degrees in applied mathematics, engineering, and psychology.

William Benjamin Martz, Jr.

Ben Martz graduated from the College of William and Mary in 1981 with a B.B.A. In 1985, he received his M.S. from the University of Arizona and entered the Ph.D. program. He received his Ph.D. with a concentration in management information systems in 1989. His experiences with electronic meeting systems include the design and coding of software for work groups, the facilitation of groups using group work software, and the coordination of the implementation of work group software in an organization. His current interests include support for group problem solving in an electronic environment, electronic work group software for a distributed environment, and group-oriented analysis and decision techniques. He is currently employed by Ventana Corporation as its vice president for research and development.

Jay F. Nunamaker, Jr. (NUNAMAKE©ARIZMIS)

Department of Management Information Systems, University of Arizona, Tucson, Arizona 85721.

Jay Nunamaker is head of the Department of Management Information Systems and professor of MIS and computer sciences at the University of Arizona. He received his Ph.D. from Case Institute of Technology in systems engineering and operations research. He was associate professor of computer science and industrial management at Purdue University, before joining the University of Arizona in 1974 to develop the MIS program. He has written numerous papers on group support systems, the automation of software construction, performance evaluation of computer systems, and decision support systems for systems analysis and design, and he has lectured throughout Europe (including Russia), Asia, and South America.

Gary M. Olson (GMO©CSMIL.UMICH.EDU)

Machine Intelligence Laboratory, University of Michigan, 701 Tappan Street, Ann Arbor, MI 48109-4948.

Gary Olson is professor of psychology and director of the Cognitive Science and Machine Intelligence Laboratory at the University of Michigan. His current research interests are in the areas of collaboration technology and human-computer interaction. Specifically, he is working on computer support for collaborative activities, such as software engineering, design, policy formation, decision making, writing, and education. His Ph.D. is in psychology from Stanford University, and before joining the University of Michigan he was on the faculty at Michigan State University. He has published numerous articles and chapters on basic and applied cognitive psychology and has served on many national committees.

Judith S. Olson (JSO©CSMIL.UMICH.EDU)

Judith Olson is professor of computer and information systems in the Michigan

Business School and professor of psychology at the University of Michigan. Her current research focuses on human-computer interaction, relating to the design and evaluation of software for human problem solving in business, both in individual settings and for group work. Before joining the Michigan Business School she was on the faculty of the Department of Psychology at Michigan and served as a technical supervisor for human factors in systems engineering at Bell Laboratories. Her Ph.D. in psychology is from the University of Michigan. She has numerous publications in journals and books in the fields of her interest and has served on many national committees.

Carol Pollard (POLLARD©ACS.UCALGARY.CA)

Carol Pollard has academic degrees in information science and psychology and an M.B.A. and a Ph.D. in MIS from the University of Pittsburgh. Dr. Pollard is presently an assistant professor of MIS at the University of Calgary. Her present research interests are the development of strategies for the successful adoption, diffusion, and use of group support systems in organizations as well as the social and organizational impact of emerging technologies on work flow. Her research has been presented at national and international conferences and published in *MIS Quarterly*. In addition to her research and teaching activities, she has been a consultant to organizations on the evaluation of group processes and applicability of group support systems and the use of total quality management techniques.

Marshall Scott Poole (MSPOOLE©UMNACVX)

Scott Poole is professor of speech communication at the University of Minnesota. He received his Ph.D. from the University of Wisconsin and has served on the faculties of the University of Illinois and the University of Michigan. His research interests include social impacts of technology, group and organizational communication, conflict manage-ment, and communication research methods. He has written or edited numerous books and articles on these topics. He recently founded the NCR Communications and Coop-eration Technology Laboratory at the University of Minnesota.

K. S. Raman (RAMANKS©NUSVM)

National University of Singapore, Department of Information Systems and Computer Science, Lower Kent Ridge Road, Singapore 0511 K. S. Raman is senior teaching fellow and coordinator of the information systems program in the Department of Information Systems and Computer Science, National University of Singapore (NUS). Before joining NUS, he was group EDP manager of Sime Darby, a large multinational conglomerate in the Asia-Pacific region. His teaching and research interests include management infor-mation systems, decision support systems, group decision support systems, adoption of IT in small businesses, and government policy and IT diffusion. He is on the editorial boards of *MIS Quarterly* and *International Information Systems*.

John Rohrbaugh (JWR26©ALBNUVMS)

The University at Albany, State University of New York, Center for Policy Research, 135 Western Ave., Milne 300, Albany, NY 12222.

John Rohrbaugh is an associate professor in the Rockefeller College of Public Affairs and Policy, the University at Albany, State University of New York. He earned his Ph.D.

in social psychology at the University of Colorado at Boulder. As the director of the Decision Techtronics Group at the Rockefeller Institute of Government, he is responsible for the development of decision conferencing in New York State. However, his research interests span the larger field of small-group processes and decision making in management teams. He has published articles on related topics in *Decision Support Systems*, *Journal of Applied Psychology*, *Management Science*, and *Organizational Behavior and Human Decision Processes*. He also serves on the editorial board of *Informatization* and *Public Sector*.

Jill Schmidt (SCHMIDT©USWEST.COM)

Jill Schmidt is a member of the technical staff at US West Advanced Technologies, where she works in applied research on multimedia communications and new interaction paradigms. She received a B.S.E.E./C.S. in 1985 and an M.S.E. in 1986 from Johns Hopkins University in Baltimore, Maryland, and has worked for AT&T, designing and developing data communications equipment. She currently resides in Louisville, Colorado.

Murray Turoff

Murray Turoff is professor of computer science and of management at the New Jersey Institute of Technology. He also directs the MIS major for the joint Rutgers/NJIT Ph.D. in management. Dr. Turoff received his B.S. from the University of California in math and physics and his Ph.D. from Brandeis University in physics. His prior positions were with IBM, the Institute for Defense Analysis, and the Office of Emergency Preparedness in the Executive Offices of the President. For two decades Dr. Turoff has been active in research and development associated with the utilization of the computer to aid and facilitate human communications. Credited as "the father of computer conferencing," he designed the first computer conferencing system while working in the executive offices of the president of the United States in 1969. Turoff serves on the editorial boards of *Technological Forecasting and Social Change*, *The Journal of Management Information Systems*, and *Organizational Computing*. Current activities include research and consulting on the design of interactive systems, technological forecasting and assessment, planning and policy studies, office automation, management information, and decision support systems. Dr. Hiltz and Dr. Turoff, who are married, are most proud of their jointly authored book, *The Network Nation: Human Communication via Computer*, which won the 1978 award of the Association of American Publishers as the outstanding technical publication of the year (Addison-Wesley, 1978; fourth printing, 1982).

Joseph S. Valacich (VALACICH©IUBACS)

Joseph Valacich is assistant professor of decision and information systems at Indiana University. He received a B.A. in computer science and M.B.A. from the University of Montana and a Ph.D. from the University of Arizona in 1989. Dr. Valacich worked for several years in the information systems field as a programmer, analyst, and product manager. His research interests are in group decision behavior, focusing primarily on the design and investigation of group support technologies on group and organizational processes and performance. His publications on these and related topics include an edited book and articles in *Management Science*; *Communications of the ACM*; *IEEE System, Man, and Cybernetics*; and *The International Journal on Man-Machine Studies*.

David Van Over (DVANOVER©IDUI1)

David Van Over is an assistant professor at the University of Idaho. He received his Ph.D. from the University of Houston in 1988. He taught at the University of Georgia for three years before taking his current position, where he teaches systems analysis and design and telecommunications. His research interests include collaborative work support systems, organizational uses of telecommunications, and decision support systems.

Douglas R. Vogel (VOGEL©ARIZMIS)

Douglas Vogel is assistant professor of MIS at the University of Arizona. He has been involved with computers and computer systems in various capacities for over 20 years. He received his M.S. in computer science from UCLA in 1972 and his Ph.D. in business administration from the University of Minnesota in 1986, where he was also research coordinator for the MIS Research Center. His current research interests bridge the business and academic communities in addressing the impact of MIS on aspects of interpersonal communication, group decision making, and organizational productivity. Dr. Vogel is especially involved in University of Arizona electronic meeting system research.

Richard Watson (RWATSON©UGABUS)

Richard Watson is an assistant professor in the Department of Management at the University of Georgia. He studied mathematics and computing at the University of Western Australia, where he completed a B.Sc. and Graduate Diploma. He undertook a master's of administration at Monash University In Melbourne, Australia. His Ph.D. in management information systems was awarded by the University of Minnesota. Dr. Watson joined the faculty of the University of Georgia in 1989. His current research interests are group support systems, executive information systems, and information systems management.

K. K. Wei (WEIKK©NUSDISCS)

K. K. Wei is a lecturer in the Department of Information Systems and Computer Science, National University of Singapore (NUS). He received his Ph.D. from the University of York in England. His teaching and research interests include group decision support systems, human computer interface, and data base.

Sylvia Wilbur (SYLVIA©CS.QMC.AC.UK)

Queen Mary & Westfield College, University of London, Department of Computer Science, Mile End Road, London E1 4NS England.

Sylvia Wilbur is senior lecturer in the Department of Computer Science at Queen Mary & Westfield College, University of London, specializing in data communications and computer-supported cooperative work. She holds a B.A. (Oxford) and an M.Sc. (Kent). Currently, the focus of her research is support for real-time remote collaboration, with emphasis on requirements for multimedia support services. Recent research contracts have included the Cosmos project (1986-1989), and TMPI (Theories of Multiparty Interaction), funded by British Telecom (1989-1992). She chairs a European Working Group on Multimedia Support for Remote Collaboration and is a member of IFIP WG8.4.

Bayard E. Wynne (WYNNE©IUBUS)

Indiana University, Business School, Bu 560-D, 10th & Fee Lanes, Bloomington, IN, 47405.

Dr. Wynne is professor of decision and information systems in the Graduate School of Business Administration at Indiana University. A former corporate officer of Fortune 500 firms and board member of a smaller firm for years, Dr. Wynne has focused his research on management issues and the practice of management by individuals and groups in the context of interacting organization and information systems. Business strategy, innovation, technology transfer, team development, and problem solving and decision making are areas of active interest to him. Active internationally, Dr. Wynne researches, teaches, or trains doctoral students; publishes; and consults in these areas. His professional activities as founder, officer, or merely participating member of societies span engineering, psychology, management, planning, and the management sciences. His spare-time, avocational interests are competitive ultramarathon bicycling, mathematical recreation, and reading.

Introduction—The Tour

We are proud to offer you this carefully designed tour package—an opportunity to behold the landscape of current developments in a new approach to an old problem—the low quality of many team meetings. Many organizations are now considering traveling along a path that will lead to the adoption of team technology, an assembly of information technologies designed to improve the performance of group work. Keeping in mind the many demands on your time and resources, we have created this whirlwind excursion that takes you on a guided tour of major research sites studying computer-augmented teamwork. Just as one might choose to take a grand tour of Europe (15 countries in 20 days), so we offer you the chance to experience these many different research spheres in fewer than 400 pages. If something really intrigues you, we provide maps of where to go, whom to see, and what to ask for as you travel on your own. We have designed this package to meet the needs of each of you: the seasoned tourist, the first-timer, and the armchair traveler.

Some of you are seasoned travelers, who have experienced firsthand many of the places to which we will take you. Indeed, you are the historians and the progenitors of these emerging cultures. However, you may want to look beyond your own islands of inquiry in order to understand the evolution of this society as a whole.

For many of you, this is your first trip abroad. You want the grand tour so that you get an overall appreciation of the breadth of team technology. You may be considering an individual move that will offer you new places to explore and a fresh direction for your career. Alternatively, you may be the front-runner for your organization, looking for the right contacts to lead your business team into this field.

The rest of you are our armchair travelers. You are content to live vicariously through the experiences of others. We offer you the safety and security of staying at home while we take you on a visual and visceral junket through this exciting, new territory.

We are your travel agents. We will take you on a leisurely cruise through these archipelagos of research, pointing out clusters of islands whose inhabitants have similar cultures based on shared foundations and philosophies. We will show you what makes each culture distinct. We will point out the loosely constructed catwalks between close islands and the fresh construction of the strong bridges that will eventually provide easy access to all the islands. We will introduce you to the scientists and scholars who have lived with and helped shape the culture; who intimately understand the language, values, and beliefs of the inhabitants; and who will serve as your tour guides.

These islands are at different stages of development. Some are established, and others are just emerging. Some have shown success in funding large, ambitious projects, whereas others are more modest in scope. All appear to have bright futures in a global society that is looking for ways to improve teamwork.

Bon voyage!

ACKNOWLEDGEMENT

The challenge of bringing together these researchers and their ideas was first embraced by Jerry Wagner. It was his vision of the benefits of sharing our work with one another and with the rest of the world that led to this book. We commend his foresight and thank him for giving us the opportunity to bring this project to fruition.

GETTING PREPARED FOR THE TRIP

The premise of this book is that people have an inherent need to work together and that humankind benefits from collaborative endeavors. Some of the advantages gained by joint efforts include a larger body of shared experiences and knowledge from which to draw, the generation of a greater number of problem-solving approaches and solutions, and a greater understanding and increased commitment by group members. In the organizational context, recognition of these factors has led many enterprises to place increased reliance on teamwork.

Furthermore, powerful forces are pressuring businesses to make constructive use of the power of teams. The complexity and rate of change of the global business environment create many intricate problems. An organization can flourish or flounder based simply on its ability to get its product to the market quickly and to respond flexibly to unanticipated change. Only teams have the pooled expertise and wherewithal to solve and rapidly implement solutions to complex problems. Only highly coordinated, interlinked groups can respond rapidly to many market exigencies. Computer-supported teams are the answer to many of today's and tomorrow's problems.

The reality of organizational teamwork right now, though, is quite different. Problem analysis, idea generation, information sharing, decision making, and the many other subsets of communication and task completion are still being carried out much as they always have been. Employees run into one another in the hall or talk over dinner or sit for long hours in what often are perceived as perpetual meetings. There is accumulating evidence to suggest that meetings are a major misuse of human resources. Ineffective meetings are estimated to cost one Fortune 500 corporation $71 million per year (Mosvick and Nelson, 1987).

The costs of ineffectual meetings are almost certainly going to escalate as we move to a post industrial society. Managers already spend some 30 percent to 80 percent of their time in meetings (Mintzberg, 1973; Mosvick and Nelson, 1987; Monge, McSween, and Wyer, 1990). All of these problems are compounded as organizations grow. Structures and responsibilities have to be redefined and rules must be made to handle increasing complexity. Teams in these larger organizations may now find themselves spending twice as much time in meetings as previously (Monge, McSween, and Wyer, 1990). They are also finding it more difficult to keep the creative team spirit that originally helped make the organization a success.

Technology can support group work in four ways: structuring group processes, supporting communication, providing enhanced information processing, and providing modeling capabilities. However, the focus of technology-supported teamwork should not be just on the hardware and software that provide these capabilities. Rather, we advocate a sociotechnical perspective that balances people, technology, and the organizational context in which the two intersect.

The sociotechnical perspective portrays the use of technology as a social practice that emerges over time. Exogenous or input variables, such as technology and task, form a context in which a team develops. Team outcomes are not directly affected by exogenous variables but rather by how the structures introduced by these variables are appropriated and used by the team. In investigating the effects of team technology, it is the structures the technology promotes in the team and the appropriation process that are important, not the features of the technology per se. Thus, the adaptive power of group social processes determines the effective appropriation of team technology. This sociotechnical emphasis is reflected throughout this book in discussions of technology development and use (e.g., technology structures that promote team development), research issues (e.g., importance of the facilitator role in the selection and appropriation of technology), and theoretical perspectives (e.g., Adaptive Structuration Theory). Different research sites focus on different parts of a complex sociotechnical system—a team.

THE WORLD MAP

To provide a framework in which to understand how all of these pieces fit together, we partition the research into clusters based on common research themes and common characteristics of the technology. Our model (see Figure A-1) illustrates the theme

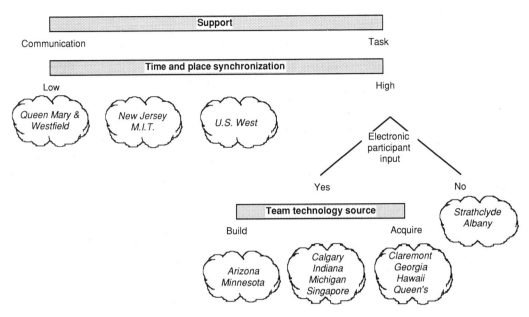

FIGURE A-1.   Team Technology Research Clusters

continuums we chose. It is important to note, however, that this grouping of research is not definitive. The model is an approximation of the relationship among research sites, and there may be other variables that, if used as a basis for clustering, would present a different spatial relationship. Also, many of the sites are either involved in a variety of studies that fall in different places on our dimensions or are in transition to another location. Nevertheless, we find the model a useful way of segmenting research centers.

At the highest level, it is useful to make the distinction between the degree to which researchers choose to focus on communication support versus a focus on task support. In communication support the emphasis is on facilitating the transfer of information among group members. At the other end of the continuum, the focus is on providing a set of computer tools to carry out a task-based agenda for achieving team goals. Although communication support is an integral part of all of these systems, most of the authors of this book are currently concentrating on task support. Neither focus excludes the other, but what varies is the degree of emphasis given to each. Unfortunately, one of the byproducts of focused research can be a lack of awareness of developments across the broader front. This book brings together the work from the many streams so that readers may gain a holistic appreciation of team technology today.

Researchers also can decide whether to conduct their studies in proximal (same-place) or dispersed (different-place) settings and synchronously (same time) or asynchronously (different time). We found that their support focus mapped quite well with their choice for time and place synchronization. The greater the focus on communication support, the more likely researchers were to examine teams operating in different places at different times (i.e., low time and place synchronization). Researchers at New Jersey Institute of

Technology (NJIT), Massachusetts Institute of Technology (MIT), Queen Mary and Westfield College (QMW), and US West Advanced Technologies are all examining the work of dispersed teams using self-constructed systems that users enter through connected workstations. Conversely, the rest of the sites mainly have a task focus and tend to set their studies in the more traditional same-time/same-place context (i.e., high time and place synchronization).

Task-oriented team support can be further partitioned according to whether the system permits electronic input directly from the users (through keyboards or keypads) or user input is captured by a support person, the approach used by the universities of Strathclyde and Albany. Support people are provided to capture the users' ideas for model building, decision making, and other group functions. These sites use the term *decision conferencing* to describe this facilitator-driven, technology-supported method of team support. They have an action-oriented focus to research because they primarily study industry groups who are solving highly salient problems within an organizational context.

The largest cluster of research sites represented in this book are those that focus on task support and have group members key text directly from their workstations into the system. In these task-based settings, a facilitator may manage the technology and lead the process, or the users may function independently from a facilitator.

This final group of researchers can be further categorized by whether they developed their own group support software, acquired it from other developers, or use both self-developed and acquired technologies. The universities of Arizona and Minnesota are examples of sites that have developed their own software. The University of Michigan, Indiana University, the University of Calgary, and the National University of Singapore are all developing their own software and using systems that they have acquired from other universities or from a commercial source. The last group, Claremont Graduate School, the University of Georgia, Queen's University, and the University of Hawaii, are all primarily using acquired software.

CITY MAPS

Section 1 of the book provides background information for your tour. It starts with a broad overview of the area by Johansen, followed by illustrative cases by Bostrom and Anson and Applegate. Johansen (Chapter 1) develops two useful frameworks for understanding and evaluating team technology. The first focuses on the needs of business teams, independent of technology. The second expands on the time and place dimensions introduced in our model. It is used by Johansen to categorize technology and demonstrate how technology might be used to meet the needs of business teams now and in the future. These two models provide a structure for thinking about the various examples of computer-augmented teamwork in this book.

Johansen points out that the two key technology environments are same time/same place and different time/different place. Bostrom and Anson (Chapter 2) discuss a tutorial case of a same time/same place meeting. The tutorial provides an opportunity to participate vicariously in an actual meeting from both the participant and facilitator perspectives. It highlights the benefits and obstacles of team technology, the importance of meeting design, and the facilitator's role in a successful electronic meeting. The case (IBM Computer Conferencing) in Chapter 3 provides background information for those not familiar with computer conferencing systems. The introduction preceding this case presents an overall framework for managing and researching the diffusion of teamwork technology, and the case describes an instance of the development and assimilation of this technology.

To get the most out of your tour, we would strongly recommend reading Section I first, especially those with little background in this area. After gaining familiarity with this background material, you will be ready to explore any of the other three sections of the book. Each section has an introduction that will point out the key features of the chapters, providing a detailed overview of the material.

Sections II, III, and IV follow the pattern outlined in our model. Section II contains contributions by those researchers who are focusing primarily on communication support and whose studies also tend to look at different-time/different-place meetings. Section III represents the side of the continuum where the research focus is predominantly on the support of task-related activities in face-to-face meetings. It contains three subsets based on whether or not the group support system used by the researchers is self-constructed, acquired, or both. Section IV examines two sites that specialize in using information technology to help live groups solve complex problems. In contrast to the other sites, participants do not interact directly with the computer; rather support personnel collect participant data and enter them into the computer.

Each of the chapters in Sections II, III, and IV was developed with a template provided by the editors. Although presented in different formats with different emphases, the chapters contain similar information. Each chapter details the research infrastructure (facilities, resources, staff, etc.) in terms of its history, status, and future growth. Each research site describes the technology it has developed or acquired and how the technology has been used in research, teaching, or service. Future technology development efforts are also described. Summaries of and insights gained from completed research and future research directions are outlined. Many of the project outputs (papers, books, etc.), along with references to foundation work, are contained in the Bibliography at the end of the book.

A QUICK GUIDE

At the end of the book there are a series of indexes that will enable you to locate quickly key information in this book. Each index covers a particular topic and lists the chapter or chapters in which more information may be found. The Geographic Index lists research centers by nation. The key concepts or themes of each chapter are listed in the Theme Index. The Education Index provides access to chapters describing educational applications of team technology. The Product Index contains details of all products discussed in this book. The Video Index catalogs videotapes on team technology.

CUSTOMS

Up to this point, we have deliberately avoided the acronym avalanche frequently associated with information technology. Many different labels describing team technology (we counted over 25) are in use and no one designation has emerged as the most accepted. Some of the more common ones include group decision support systems (GDSS), group support systems (GSS), computer-supported cooperative work (CSCW), groupware, electronic meeting systems (EMS), decision conferencing, collaborative work support systems (CWSS), electronic communities (EC), distributed group support systems, and collaborative systems. Some of the appellations are more closely associated with communication support than task support. They include computer conferencing, computer-mediated communication systems (CMCS), group information system technologies (GIS), TeleCollaboration, and computer-assisted communication (CAC). Although GDSS is still very much in use, we are beginning to see a movement away from strict reference to decision making as these technologies are proving to be beneficial across a much wider span of group tasks. In the following chapters, many of these terms are used to describe the systems in various institutions. We made no attempt to force uniformity of terms. Regardless of the name, the computer-based technologies discussed in this book are all designed to improve the performance of task-oriented teams.

Section I

Introduction

The purpose of this section is to provide the necessary background information, both conceptual and experiential, to make your tour of the various research sites a great success. The conceptual information is presented through a series of conceptual maps developed in the three chapters in this section. The primary vehicle for conveying the experiential information is through the two case studies.

Maps were essential equipment for early explorers. They helped to chart a new course and guided the next round of exploration. In an information age, language and conceptual maps are instruments for navigating uncharted territories. Thus, conceptual maps or frameworks are important tools for exploring emerging teamwork technologies. Such frameworks also provide a focal point for exchange and inquiry. A good framework illuminates an area both by what it describes and emphasizes and by what it doesn't. Because they undergo challenge, modification, integration, or replacement, frameworks foster the evolution of our understanding. The following frameworks are introduced in chapters 1 through 3 (the number in brackets indicates the chapter in which the framework is discussed):

1. **Team Performance model**—focuses on the developmental needs of business teams [1].
2. **Groupware time and place model**—maps current and future technology by a focus on time and place [1].
3. **Meeting model**—defines meetings in terms of outcomes, agendas, roles, and rules [2].
4. **Meeting cycle model**—describes the three phases of meetings: pre-, during, and post- [2].
5. **Facilitator role**—is defined in terms of functions and activities performed during the meeting cycle [2].
6. **Meeting design**—targets mapping technology to meeting activities [2].
7. **Technology benefits**—categorizes potential benefits according to technology features [2].
8. **Diffusion of teamwork technology**—highlights diffusion as a series of tasks: innovation development, assimilation, and institutionalization [3].

These frameworks are necessary for understanding and gaining insights from each of the tour stops. Additional conceptual maps, available at many of the tour stops, build on these base frameworks.

Johansen develops models 1 and 2 as a means of matching team technology (model 2) to stages of team performance (model 1). He also discusses current and future technology in terms of model 2. Bostrom and Anson develop frameworks 3 through 7 in their tutorial case presentation of an actual face-to-face, computer-supported meeting. These frameworks are part of the basic toolkit used by a facilitator to design and run an electronic meeting. Applegate develops the technology diffusion framework in her introduction to her teaching case and uses the case to illustrate its application and importance.

It would be difficult to understand the information provided in the different chapters without having some experience of teamwork technology. Chapter 2 and the case in Chapter 3 add this experiential dimension. They also provide excellent teaching or training tools for those using this book in a classroom. The case (IBM Computer Conferencing) provides information on a different-time/different-place system (computer conferencing) and an example of the management of the technology diffusion process primarily through the assimilation and institutionalization phases.

Let us reiterate our recommendation in Introduction to read this section first, especially chapters 1 and 2, and to read chapter 3 if you are interested in technology diffusion or want more background on teamwork technologies and their use. This recommendation applies especially to those with little background in this area. After grasping this background material, you will be able to explore any of the other chapters and gain a rich set of insights from your journey.

Chapter 1

An Introduction to Computer-Augmented Teamwork

Robert Johansen

Institute for the Future (IFTF)

Groupware and *collaborative systems* are two on a growing list of terms used to describe the general area of computer-augmented teamwork. Other similar terms such as *computer-supported collaborative work* (CSCW), *shared systems*, *work group computing*, and *coordination technology* are also used, as is the current Silicon Valley catchphrase "the transition from the personal to the *interpersonal* computer." I use *groupware* for simplicity's sake and because it is the most common term now used in business communities to describe such systems. It is too early, however, for a single word to capture the diversity of computer-augmented teamwork.

More than a new technology or a new class of products, computer-augmented teamwork is a *perspective* on computing and telecommunications. This perspective is based on the premise that the user is a collaborative work group rather than an individual—as in personal computing—or an aggregation of unallied users—as in time-share computing. There are both electronic and nonelectronic forms of groupware. Electronic groupware typically involves shared computing and telecommunications resources that are used collaboratively by teams.

The primary reason that computer-augmented teams are worth studying is that this is an emerging technology that is linked to clear and pressing user needs, the needs of business teams. Business teams are small, cross-organizational, time-driven, task-focused, cohesive work groups. Business teams are part of the evolving organization of the future that includes flatter hierarchies, network style, and international flavor.

For the past few years, IFTF has been tracking the emergence of groupware and studying it as an area for application. IFTF is an independent research group in Silicon Valley that focuses on identifying and evaluating emerging information technologies. Our first approach was to identify options from a user point of view.[1] Currently, we are tracking start-up companies that are creating groupware products, researching market dynamics, and conducting pilot tests of various forms of groupware in several large companies. In the process of this ongoing work, we have found two models particularly useful in understanding and evaluating groupware prospects. The first model focuses on the needs of business teams, independent of technology. The second categorizes the basic options for groupware technology that might be used to meet the needs of business teams. These two models provide a structure for thinking about the various examples of computer-augmented teamwork in this book. These models and their applications to teamwork are discussed in Johansen et al. (1991).

UNDERSTANDING TEAM NEEDS

When your user is a collaborative team rather than an individual, it is crucial that you understand the nature of team needs. Fortunately, there is a considerable body of experiential research on the processes of team building and managing operational teams. After reviewing this literature, we concluded that the Team Performance model (Drexler, Sibbet, and Forester, 1988) most effectively summarizes the basic dynamics of business teams.[2] Figure 1-1 depicts the model and its basic stages: orientation, trust building, goal and role clarification, commitment to action, implementation, high performance, and renewal.

In our own research, we have found that businesspeople quickly understand and identify with this model and start talking through it after just a few minutes of exposure. Team Performance provides a basic structure within which they can discuss the needs of their team at different stages in their work. It separates the general stages that teams go through and is also flexible enough to allow for the unique characteristics of different teams.

For example, it is well known that Japanese business teams tend to emphasize activity that falls within what the model delineates as orientation and trust building. Japanese companies are willing to invest great amounts of time in developing these basic allegiances, even though orientation and trust building are not directly related to the generation of quick results. Yet as a result of this early investment, Japanese teams typically have little trouble in making commitments and moving to implementation. In contrast, American teams, often frustrated with long introductory processes that do not show immediate returns, frequently feel compelled to move to the commitment and implementation stages as quickly as possible. Prematurely in the implementation mode,

---

[1] The results of this analysis are contained in Johansen (1988). Others at IFTF working on the groupware project team include Paul Saffo, Alexia Martin, and Robert Mittman.

[2] For further information on the use of the model and the questionnaire developed for it, contact Graphic Guides, 832 Folsom, San Francisco.

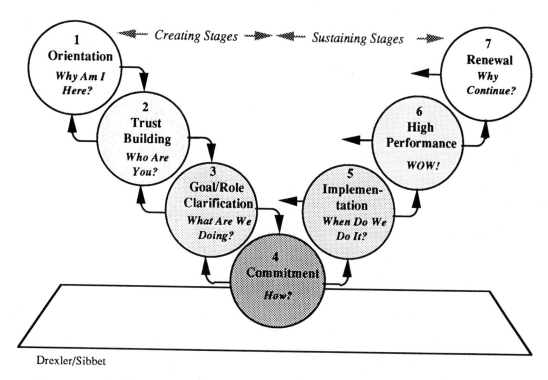

Drexler/Sibbet

FIGURE 1-1.   Team Performance Model

many American teams discover that team members do not trust one another or are not oriented to the task in compatible ways. Thus, they have to take a remedial cycle through orientation and trust building.

The Team Performance model provides a simple, nonthreatening way to articulate the activities of teams that are often not thought about consciously. Once the stages are identified, it is easier to ask whether or not the needs of each stage have been met. As such a discussion ensues, it is easy and useful to begin a consideration of groupware options.

GROUPWARE OPTIONS

Through our discussions with prospective users of groupware, we were able to develop the model in Figure 1-2. This map, inspired by DeSanctis and Gallupe (1987)[3] is a way of introducing options once the basic needs of a team have been identified through a tool

---

[3] Our version was modified in discussions with various user groups and other researchers. Christine Bullen at MIT and Ken Lyon at Procter & Gamble were particularly helpful in this refinement process.

	Same Time	**Different Times**
Same Place	*Need:* *Face-to-Face Meetings* e.g. Copyboards PC Projectors Facilitation Services Group Decision Rooms Polling Systems	*Need:* *Administrative,* *Filing and Filtering* Computer Labs e.g. Shared Files Shift Work Kiosks Team Rooms Group Displays
Different Places	*Need:* *Cross-Distance Meetings* e.g. Conference Calls Graphics and Audio Screen Sharing Video Teleconferencing Spontaneous Meetings	*Need:* *Ongoing Coordination* e.g. Group Writing Computer Conferencing Conversational Structuring Forms Management Group Voice Mail

FIGURE 1-2.   Business Team Needs and Groupware Solutions

like the Team Performance model. Specific team needs are associated with each cell in this simple matrix.

Same Time/Same Place

Face-to-face meetings are the most natural form of team communications for most people and probably will remain so for at least the foreseeable future. For example, orientation and trust-building activities almost always need to take place in a same-time/same-place mode. The immediate feedback offered by face-to-face meetings, coupled with the opportunities at informal meetings to get to know others in subtle ways, are important characteristics for teams to consider. Face-to-face contact is also likely to be important at the renewal stage, when the team needs to reexamine its work and generate excitement for the next round of activities. In short, same-time/same-place meetings have great value for any team, especially when done well (although many of them are not). Same-time/same-place meetings are often costly, however, in both time and travel expenses.

Groupware tools for face-to-face meetings range from low-cost copyboards and overhead projectors to high-investment team rooms. Simple copyboards provide the ability to make a paper copy of whatever is written on a whiteboard or (with some machines) a flip chart pad. Overhead projectors can provide a platform for the display of personal computer images.

A special team room can be built to allow each participant to communicate through workstations simultaneously. For example, International Computers Limited (ICL) has developed an experimental modular room called The Pod that emphasizes careful interior design geared toward cohesive team behavior. The University of Arizona College of Business and Public Administration has developed a host of software tools for same-time/same-place environments and has several prototype rooms. Some of these tools have now been adapted by IBM, and other companies. The University of Minnesota has a system called SAMM that focuses on the needs of small collaborative teams. There are now more than 100 same-time/same-place groupware systems, most of them in university or research and development (R&D) settings. There is also a growing number of commercial products (discussed in later chapters).

Same-time/same-place groupware will finally come into its own in the 1990s, although there are strong cultural barriers to overcome. In most U.S. businesses today, conference rooms are decidedly low-tech, perhaps furnished only with a flip chart pad, a whiteboard, and an overhead projector. Some rooms have slide projectors, VCRs, or audio conferencing units, but most do not. Furthermore, the people in charge of these austere conference rooms are rewarded for saving money, not for innovating. Businesspeople assume they must meet in the old-fashioned way, without technology. But this belief will give way, gradually, to a recognition of the value of electronic tools, chiefly a written record of what was agreed on during the meeting, anonymous discussions, simultaneous input of ideas, and voting or ranking of alternatives.

Low-tech tools will be most common in the short run, such as the copyboard or personal computer (PC) projector systems. A significant minority of rooms, however, will be equipped with terminal devices (ranging from a keypad to a full keyboard) for each participant. This book's group support system (GSS) software index lists tools that can be provided. A key question is unresolved, however: Is this a product and/or a service? Once this question is answered, such rooms will become practical for many businesses. I think it will be concluded that both products and services are involved. "High-touch" characteristics will be critical for such rooms, with an emphasis—in the short run at least—on human facilitators. Furthermore, I think such systems are on the verge of becoming practical and that this emergence will occur over the next five years.

Same Time/Different Place

Often it is not possible to get a team together for a face-to-face meeting, so meetings via electronic means are a practical alternative. The goal is not to replace travel with telecommunications, as predicted in the 1970s, but to permit a more selective use of face-to-face meetings—for example, during critical stages in the life of a team, such as kickoff meetings or after key milestones have been accomplished. Same-time/different-place groupware is likely to be most useful for the goal and role clarification and commitment stages, assuming that orientation and trust building have been done well. Same-time communication permits immediate feedback, which is important for goal clarification and commitment because team members can see whether their proposals are being accepted and can understand who is signing up to do what. However, it may not be necessary for everyone to be present at the same place. Also, during the implementation stage, periodic same-time/different-place meetings can provide regular reviews of progress.

Same-time/same-place software can often be used for same-time/different-place meetings with appropriate communication connections. Groupware tools for same-time/different-place meetings also vary from low-tech to high-tech. At the modest end of the scale is the telephone, probably the most practical building block to consider. Coupled with a digital conference call bridge, the telephone provides voice connections as well as the potential for exchanges of facsimile and even screen images from personal computers. Often, conference calling plus some document exchange is all that is necessary for a team to meet productively. Not surprisingly, conference calling in North America is growing rapidly—even when it is not marketed. At the other end of the cost scale is full-motion video teleconferencing, which is finally being seen as a practical option. The installed base of two-way motion video rooms has grown substantially over the last few years, the price of coders and decoders has dropped dramatically, and the cost of transmission has entered the realm of reason. Although still not cheap, two-way video teleconferencing has certainly become cost-justifiable for many team applications. Increasingly, such rooms also contain computer-based tools for team support. For example, both Bell Communications Research (Bellcore) and AT&T Bell Labs are working on more advanced systems for same-time/different-place communication. Both are exploring foundation technologies to support such meetings, including network environments and applications. Advanced efforts like these are discussed later in this book (see Chapter 7).

Same-time/different-place groupware over the next five years is likely to be steady, with significant increases in the scale of activity but little change in basic functions. Conference calling in North America is already growing at a rate of 15 percent or better with no marketing, and the capabilities of digital conference calling bridges mean much better sound quality and parallel PC images. Conference calling may seem boring to many computer people, but it is a critical building block with considerable momentum. Video teleconferencing, which has been an emerging technology for almost two decades, finally has an installed base of two-way video rooms (over 2,000 rooms in North America) and people are using the medium in practical ways. In addition, the synergies of motion video and personal computing will be developing over the next five years, meaning drastic reductions in costs. In short, same-time/different-place meetings are crucial to the life of business teams and have a very high probability of success on a large scale over the next five years.

Different Time/Different Place

Different-time/different-place needs focus on the implementation and performance stages of the Team Performance model. At this stage, today's business teams often do not have time to get together in person and probably cannot even arrange for same-time/different-place meetings. The convenience and flexibility of different-time/different-place communication are attractive as a way of coordinating disparate and fast-paced team efforts. Such tools can also be critical for coordinating teams.

Groupware tools for different-time/different-place exchanges are typically extensions of existing networks such as local-area networks (LANS), other private networks, or public networks. Electronic mail is a particularly attractive building block for such efforts. Computer conferencing (the variation of electronic mail in which messages are stored by topic or by group) is another form of a groupware capability, as is group writing, in which the participants contribute to a document at different times and the software remembers who made what changes at which time. Such group writing tools can also be used to support teams of programmers for joint software development.

At the other end of the spectrum, different-time/different-place groupware will build on the considerable electronic infrastructure that is already here. In particular, electronic mail and voice mail provide very attractive building blocks for group-oriented services. Both "horseless carriage" or "paving the cowpaths" products: They simply automate what used to be done with conventional media. Now that large systems are in place, however, it is possible to extend the concept and add group capabilities for communications, project management, and other group functions. Person-to-person systems can evolve into groupware. Given the time demands on most business teams, the flexibility of different-time/different place groupware will be attractive indeed.

Different Time/Same Place

Physical space
shared electronic space

The different-time/same-place cell in the matrix is the most difficult to understand. At the present time, there are few examples of groupware applied in this way. However, it suggests important team needs that are not implied by the other cells. A key factor in discussing this cell is the definition of *same place*. One definition refers to the exact same physical place, such as an office that is used by different people at different times. Bulletin boards in an office are a simple same-place/different-time tool, but electronic systems could also be used to store information and communicate to people who use the office at different times. Another definition involves the same metropolitan area. This is interesting because experience with video teleconferencing suggests that metropolitan area uses were actually more common in the early days than were long-distance uses. I suspect that groupware will evolve in a similar fashion. Thus, a team that is spread around a campus or in different offices in the same metropolitan area could have one form of different-time/same-place needs.

Another definition of *same place* could refer to a team room, assigned at the beginning of a team's life. Team rooms are an example of same place/different time: They are "club rooms" assigned to teams, often with electronic aids of different sorts to facilitate group memory, chart progress toward team goals, and otherwise assist a team in getting its job done. Over the next five years, I expect that team rooms will become increasingly common (particularly in companies where open offices are the norm) and that many of them will be equipped with various forms of groupware. Groupware can be used for shared filing and the storage of tools and displays (e.g., graphics or videos), which can be used by the team members at different times in the same team room. Another example is shift work, in which a team of people must hand off to another team, to keep a manufacturing line going, for example, or to continue a process of international currency trading.

Few current products are focused on different time/same place. I know of several large private companies who are using team rooms in this fashion, but most of this work is exploratory. However, many of the groupware facilitares that support same-time/same-place meetings are being used like a team room. One example is a university that evaluates its MBA curriculum by running a series of cumulative student meetings. Eden and Ackermann (see Chapter 19) provide another interesting example. They have supported large planning and decision-making groups (with as many as 200 participants) by running smaller subsections of the group and then merging their outputs. I suspect that other creative ideas will be generated, even though we have trouble imagining them today.

FUTURE DIRECTIONS

Groupware in its many forms will not be an instant success; it will have a long period of introduction. However, within the next five to ten years, groupware will be something that we simply will expect all computers (and telephones) to provide. Figure 1-3 summarizes my judgments about likely future directions. The uncertainties include how long groupware will take to mature, what its path(s) of development will be, and who will make money from whatever occurs.

One obvious group of winners will be the network providers. No matter what tools teams use, their members will have to be linked somehow. Local private networks will have an early advantage, but long-haul carriers stand to benefit greatly as well. Look for providers of all kinds of networks to develop joint ventures and incentives to introduce groupware tools. Network providers will usually not supply the end products; instead, they will derive their profits from the network traffic that is generated—and there will be *lots* of traffic.

The safe course, for both users and vendors alike, will be to build on the existing telecommunications and computing infrastructure. Groupware that requires the creation of its own infrastructure will be interesting to watch but highly risky. It will be far more attractive to add a little groupware to an existing infrastructure than it will be to add a lot of groupware when the user has to create new infrastructure.

For the Team Performance model (Figure 1-1), the safest zone for investment is implementation. Groupware that helps teams implement ideas to which they have already committed themselves, probably in the different-time/different-place mode, will be the most successful. Next most attractive will be the goal and role clarification and commitment stages, probably in the same-time/different-place mode. Same-time/same-place groupware is attractive but will be a hard sell in the short run.

Looking across the map in Figures 1-2 and 1-3, I suspect that we soon will see a melting down of divisions among the four cells. For example, many of the tools listed in this book's GSS software index already span two or more cells. In fact, the most used groupware will be those that cut across two or more of the cells. For example, same-time/same-place groupware will be even more useful if the discussion can be

	Same Time	**Different Times**
Same Place	• Low-tech computer aids for conference rooms commonplace. • High-tech, high-touch computer-assisted tools financially practical and used. • Portable and desktop tools for team support grow rapidly.	• Team rooms are commonplace, with electronic aids. • Shift work groupware (e.g., international traders, factories) commonplace. • Shared work environments and telework centers grow, though gradually.
Different Places	• Greatly increased use of conference calls. • Conference calls with PC graphics and image commonplace. • Video conferencing continues gradual growth, with some use of computer aids, with an emphasis on portable units and—eventually—desktop video.	• E-mail and voice mail include strong group features. • "Total Quality" and workflow support groupware commonplace. • Text filtering and "information refineries" commonplace in a few sectors.

**STRONG INTEREST IN LINKAGES ACROSS THE ABOVE CELLS
STRONG MOVE TOWARD ANY TIME/ANY PLACE CAPABILITIES**

FIGURE 1-3.   Probable Future Groupware Developments (Mid-1990s)

carried over to the user's different-time/different-place medium, or electronic meetings could be held to connect a computer-assisted meeting room with people who are not able to be present face to face. Ultimately, any-time/any-place groupware will be the norm, building on ultralight computers and cellular networks. One goal of this book is to make the researchers working in each cell aware of the ongoing work in all the other cells.

One disappointment with the current state of groupware is that people doing the most creative work in each of the four cells in the Figure 1-2 map are often ignorant of work going on in the other three cells. Such overspecialization is understandable in the early stages of a field, however, and it is likely to disappear over the next five years. It is interesting to recall that Doug Engelbart (1990), one of the early groupware pioneers, had a system (NLS) in the late 1960s with capabilities touching on all of the four time and place cells in Figure 1-2. For same time/same place, Engelbart had a team room where the moderator had a full workstation and each of the participants had a mouse and screen. For different time/different place, there were shared journals and group writing capabilities. For same time/different place, there were screen sharing and remote multimedia (including audio and full-motion video). Finally, same-place/different-time capabilities were found in Engelbart's Augmentation Research Center at Stanford Research Institute so that team members could use the center at any time of the day or night, even if other team members were not present simultaneously. Engelbart's broad vision is now becoming practical—even necessary.

There are larger waves of change that will call for groupware capabilities. For example, "total quality" methods are increasing in U.S. companies, fueled by Edwards Deming, Joseph Juran, Philip Crosby, and others. Such programs emphasize customer orientation, an enterprise-wide view, emphasis on process rather than outcomes, decisions driven by data, and long-term orientation. Groupware (primarily different time/different place) can assist teams in implementing quality methods. I suspect that a distinct class of groupware products will emerge to service this rapidly growing market. Other types of enterprise-wide workflow process support will also become common.

Text filtering and what John Clippinger has called information refineries are also likely within a five-year time frame, at least in specialized market segments. Large information companies are already using early versions of such systems. Tom Malone's work at MIT on text filtering and his ambitious notions of the Information Lens and the Object Lens (see Chapter 5) are also likely to be translated into commercial products. Such ideas are different-time/different-place oriented, but they are certainly beyond the horseless carriage. They imply the ability to do things that were not possible to do before: intelligent navigation through large text and data bases. Such systems can also serve to link teams with teams and to coordinate the activities of varied teams within an organization.

Over the next five years, the focus of groupware creativity will shift gradually from inside, small teams to the complicated connections across teams. I do not expect this shift to occur quickly or easily, but it will occur—beginning with specialized business segments that have pressing needs and the financial resources to experiment.

The surest thing in groupware is the importance of business teams. We are entering an age of organizational experimentation and redesign in which teams will be a basic— perhaps *the* basic—organizing unit. Flatter organizations will depend on teams to get things done; the remaining hierarchies will still provide basic business functions, but teams will be most important in most companies.

Peter Drucker's (1988) article "The Coming of the New Organization" set a new *Harvard Business Review* reprint record while trumpeting business teams as a wave of the future. Literally millions of business teams have pressing needs for communications and computing support, whether or not the computer and telecommunications industries choose to help them. Of course, the reality of the team-based organization is still more a matter of public relations than practical experience. We know we will have teams, but we do not know how team-based organizations will evolve.

Meanwhile, the international nature of business is another sure thing—meaning that many teams will cross national boundaries. Furthermore, alliances and customer or supplier links will mean intercompany, as well as international, collaborations. Corporate boundaries will often be difficult to draw and even more difficult to protect. The desires for interoperability with other collaborators will be tempered with concerns about security.

On another front, companies will be looking for ways to avoid long-term commitments to employees wherever possible. Temporary workers, for example, will continue to grow in number since they allow a corporate work force to be increased or decreased quickly, depending on business needs. As for health care benefits, there are strong incentives for employers to shift as many of these costs as possible to employees. The sure thing here is caution about commitments. Analysis of labor trends indicate that the old career-long marriage between employer and employee is giving way to a series of one-night stands. Temporary teams, often connected by groupware, will be commonplace.

The telecommunications and computing infrastructure will continue to improve, although not in an easy, regular fashion. Rather, there will be fits and starts, as well as disappointments, on the way to the workstation of the future. Thus, it is a sure thing that the technology will become more powerful and more portable, but it is not clear just what it will do for users.

The connection between same-time/same-place and different-time/different-place groupware in Figure 1–3 is the central axis for groupware as it currently exists. The quest here is for the familiarity of same time/same place with the flexibility of different time/different place. The sure thing is that this connection will remain central to the evolution of groupware products and services for the foreseeable future. The most promising electronic infrastructure for groupware is available in the different-time/different-place domain (electronic mail, voice mail, local-area networks, public networks, etc), but the cultural familiarity is with face-to-face meetings.

In short, it is a sure thing to expect increases in complexity—with occasional notes of stability and predictability. Anybody's sure things will be debatable, but most people's lists will have at least one thing in common: They will be short.

Computer-augmented teams are inevitable. Business teams are here to stay and they need tools to help get their jobs done, whether or not the computer and telecommunications industries choose to help them. Although the process of introducing this perspective is likely to take some time, there are real opportunities that are not to be denied. This book provides a sampling of these emerging opportunities.

Chapter 2

The Face-to-Face Electronic Meeting: A Tutorial

Robert P. Bostrom,

University of Georgia

Robert Anson,

Boise State University

INTRODUCTION

Why should you be interested in electronic meetings? Because meetings are a very time-consuming feature of a manager's or professional's organizational life and, as numerous studies have borne out, a major time-wasting feature (see the introduction to this book). Without doubt, improving meeting productivity should be viewed as a major strategy for improving organizational productivity, and the introduction of computer technology into the conference room is an emerging approach. It makes the information-processing power of computers available to groups.

The purpose of this chapter is to present a concrete picture of what a face-to-face electronic meeting is like and how group support systems (GSS) technology can help. We will try to paint this picture from three perspectives. First, you will enter an electronic meeting in process as a participant. Second, we will step back to describe electronic meetings and their facilitation. Finally, a case study of an actual electronic meeting is presented, and its formal evaluation provides a graphic illustration of the benefits of GSS.

OVERVIEW OF ELECTRONIC MEETINGS

An Electronic Meeting

Top elected officers and permanent staff members of an international professional association participated for three days in an electronic meeting. The purpose of this annual meeting was to update the three-year strategic plan for the association and to develop a budget for the upcoming year. This planning and budget meeting was facilitated by the authors using an early version of GroupSystems from the University of Arizona (see Chapter 8).

Picture yourself as an association officer in a regular meeting, working on the budget for the coming year. The meeting's outcome is to develop a balanced budget by identifying $500,000 in cuts. You, the other officers, and the staff are seated around a horseshoe-shaped table. The discussion switches from one suggested cut to another, and no agreement is apparent. A couple of people dominate most of the discussion by monopolizing the floor and attempting to influence the group's direction. When new budget cuts are introduced, they are criticized as soon as they are offered. You have been in this type of meeting before!

Now add personal computers to your picture, as in Figure 2-1. A color monitor and a keyboard are in front of each person, with two 5-foot display screens at the head of the conference table. All computers are linked to one another for exchanging and aggregating information. Software provides support for generating, organizing, and evaluating ideas

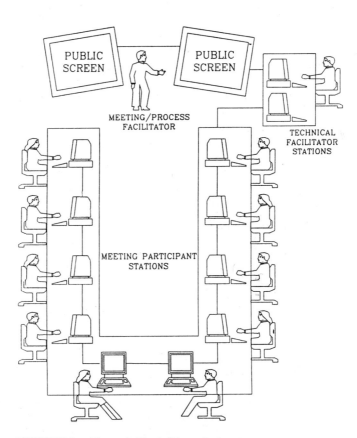

FIGURE 2-1.   Electronic Meeting Room Setting

and judgments. A technical facilitator runs the software and provides the brief instructions needed to operate the system. A second facilitator, who assists the group leader, helps the group work systematically through each step of the budget process. This is an electronic meeting.

Earlier, your group had electronically brainstormed criteria to evaluate budget cuts. A moment ago everyone finished ranking the items generated during the brainstorming session, which took a few minutes. Now a public screen is displaying the list of combined rankings for the group (see Figure 2-2). Discussion is focused on the criteria the group considers most important, and these are shown on the screen.

Pointing to the ranking distribution displayed, you point out to the group that the opinions seem to be widely dispersed, perhaps because some criteria are ambiguous. Discussion then turns to what is meant by the third, first, and last criteria—those with the largest SQR scores (a dispersion measure). After clarifying the meaning of these criteria, the group decides to rank the criteria one more time. This second ranking produces a higher group consensus on the relative importance of the criteria in terms of identifying the most appropriate budget cuts. You remember past meetings in which people would have simply gone on talking past one another, each speaker being unsure about whether others understood or agreed with his or her position.

Now that you have had a chance to experience briefly an electronic meeting, let us step back and define an electronic meeting and discuss how to facilitate one. We will revisit this meeting during the discussion and end the chapter with its detailed description.

LIST OF ISSUES VOTED ON

ISSUES IN RANK ORDER

....

Direct Benefit to membership
Cost/Resources
Contractual-required by law
Revenue Potential
Image and Credibility of the Association
Member involvement
Support Long Range Plan (LRP)

....

TABULATION OF VOTES-NUMBER OF TIMES IN POSITIONS

	1	2	3	4	5	6	7	RANK	SQR
Direct B	3	1	3	1	1	–	–	49	38
Cost/R	2	2	3	–	1	1	–	46	30
Contract	3	2	–	–	–	3	1	40	57
Revenue	– –	2	1	3	3	–	–	38	12
Image an	1	1	–	3	1	2	1	33	34
Member i	–	1	–	1	3	2	2	25	25
Support	–	–	2	1	–	1	5	21	42

(RANK is a function of the number of votes weighted by ranking position.
SQR is a measure of Ranking consensus.)

FIGURE 2-2.   Sample Output from Ranking Activity Voting Topic: Ranking Budget Criteria

What Is an Electronic Meeting?

We view an electronic meeting as a goal- or outcome-directed interaction between two or more people (teams or groups) that can take place in any of four environments (same/different time and place, as defined in Chapter 1). Each of these environments creates different conditions that affect GSS design and usage. Most GSS research and discussion has focused on the face-to-face environment (same time, same place). Although this chapter will discuss a face-to-face electronic meeting, the principles discussed in this section apply to all environments.

Our model of a meeting, presented in Figure 2-3, is focused on outcome. It depicts a meeting as a sociotechnical systems change process. In other words, a meeting is an interaction that transforms a group's present problem into its desired future (accomplishing specific outcomes) through a series of action steps (agenda) utilizing a set of resources (people and technology).

Action steps can be described in terms of a core set of generic activities. That is, an agenda or agenda topic can be broken down into a number of basic information-processing activities (see Figure 2-3). For example, to accomplish a particular topic, a group might *generate* information, *organize* the information into alternatives, *evaluate and*

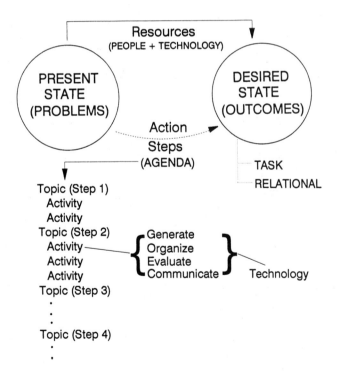

FIGURE 2-3.   Goal/Outcome-Directed Meeting

select alternatives, and discuss (*communicate*) their actions. These generic activities can be used to describe an agenda for any meeting task. GSS tools and other meeting technology can also be classified by the generic activities they support, for example, generate.

Our meeting model (Figure 2-3) also depicts two general types of meeting outcomes that a facilitator helps a group accomplish: task and relational. From a task outcome perspective, a meeting brings together a set of resources (primarily people) to accomplish a task. The task provides the "content," or "what people will be interacting about," of the meeting. Many tasks can be accomplished in a meeting: create a strategic plan, solve a problem, make a decision, share information, resolve a dispute, negotiate a contract, and so on. This fact has led some authors to develop task (McGrath, 1984) and meeting type taxonomies (Mosvick and Nelson, 1987).

From a relational outcome perspective, a meeting is a relationship between people. The foundation of meeting relationships is how people feel about themselves, one another, the meeting process, and the meeting task (Bostrom, Anson, and Clawson, 1993). The relational outcome of a meeting is to create and maintain positive emotions that will lead to constructive relationships among participants that promote working together effectively. Practicing facilitators in both GSS (e.g., Bostrom, Anson, and Clawson, 1993) and non-GSS (e.g., Doyle and Straus, 1976; Kayser, 1990) environments emphasize the importance of positive feelings and relationships. Yet little GSS research has focused on relational outcomes, especially at the emotional level.

In most meetings, some combination of both task and relational outcomes must be achieved. Even when task outcomes are strongly emphasized, good relationships need to be developed and maintained for a group to work effectively (Chidambaram, Bostrom, and Wynne, 1991; Johansen et al., 1991). In other cases, the group development outcome is paramount, regardless of whether or not task outcomes occur.

Facilitation Activities by Meeting Stage

There is still much to be learned about how best to apply GSS. A significant question is how to plan effectively, coordinate, and direct—to *facilitate*—the work of group members while using GSS. The technology itself provides some facilitation, such as the activity structuring provided through a particular software tool. Still, GSS must be used appropriately to take advantage of these capabilities. In addition, GSS does not address other areas of a group's functioning, such as the design of the meeting or managing verbal communications. These and other facilitation activities must come from people. An integration of good computer tools with effective human facilitation can lead to a more effective meeting than either by itself.

There are two general facilitation roles in electronic meetings. The *technical facilitator*, or *technographer*, must be technically competent to ensure that technical difficulties do not interfere with the content of the meeting and that participants are properly trained in using the technology. The role of the *meeting/process facilitator* requires the application of group facilitation skills. The two facilitation roles may both be performed by one person or split between two people (as in the association's meeting). Two people are usually preferable to keep technical and process responsibilities separate. For a detailed discussion of the facilitation role in GSS environments see Bostrom, Anson, and Clawson (1991, 1993).

Meetings rarely die—they just keep rolling along in a cycle of premeeting, meeting, and postmeeting activities (Oppenheim, 1987). The actual meeting is only one phase of this three-phase cycle. One cycle of activity frequently sets the scene for the next. What occurs in the meeting phase is strongly influenced by premeeting activities, which in turn are affected by postmeeting planning activities of the previous meeting.

These three phases provide a useful means of categorizing important facilitation-related activities (Bostrom, Anson, and Clawson, 1993; Bostrom, 1989). Facilitation is viewed as a set of functions or activities carried out during these phases. Facilitative functions may be accomplished by group members or leaders or by an external facilitation specialist. Although one person usually has the formal responsibility of being the primary facilitator for a particular meeting, facilitation must be shared by all attendees. (Throughout this chapter, we use the term *facilitator* to designate this primary facilitator.) All other participants and the GSS are viewed as secondary facilitators. Facilitation-related activities for each phase are reviewed below.

It is important to design or plan a meeting before it convenes. The facilitator works with the group leader and/or members to develop a meeting design. We use a three-step mapping methodology to accomplish these tasks (Bostrom and Anson, 1991). Our model is illustrated in Figure 2–4 for the association's budget development meeting.

The first step is to define the business issue (cut half a million from the budget) and map it to the desired outcome (develop a balanced budget for the coming year). This is a critical step because it is the basis for all other design activities.

The second step is to develop the meeting agenda. Agenda development involves creating and linking generic information-processing activities to accomplish the meeting outcome(s). We introduced four activities in Figure 2–3 generate, organize, evaluate, and communicate. Figure 2–4 illustrates how they are used to create an agenda for our budget development case. The first two steps involve generating and evaluating criteria to select the "best" budget cuts. (This is the portion of the meeting described earlier.) Steps 4 and 5 depict the generation and evaluation of budget item changes, and in step 5 the actual balanced budget is created. A review of agenda development approaches is found in Bostrom and Anson (1991).

The additional advantage of the generic activity model is that it can be used to classify GSS tools and other meeting technology. Most GSS can be thought of as a set of independent software tools that can be linked and can pass data to one another. These tools support meeting activities in the same sense as word processing or spreadsheet packages are tools to support individual work activities. Each GSS tool, however, is designed to support a given group activity such as generation or evaluation. Thus, the software tools of a given GSS, such as GroupSystems, can be classified as shown in Figure 2–5 (for a detailed discussion of GroupSystems tools see Chapter 8). This classification framework can be used by the facilitator to select appropriate GSS tools and other techniques for the meeting (Bostrom and Anson, 1991).

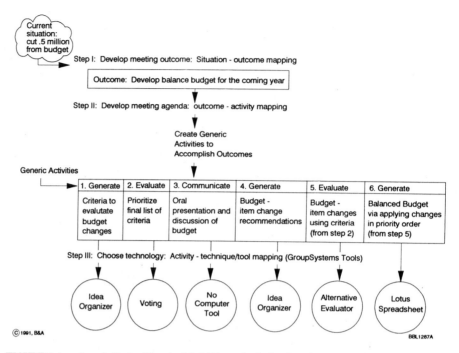

FIGURE 2-4.   Agenda Design Mapping Model Example: Budget Development Session

The third step in the design process involves matching the appropriate technology, GSS tools or manual techniques, to agenda activities. For example, if we look at Figures 2–4 and 2–5, we can see that there are a number of GroupSystem tools that we could use for our first generate. We chose Idea Organizer (IO) to generate the criteria. Using IO, each person individually and simultaneously entered his or her criteria in one area of the screen. Another screen area was used to provide further definition of each criterion. The group's entries were then displayed on the public screen, which was used to orient group discussion for organizing and consolidating individually entered criteria into a single common list. The IO tool was also used in step 4 to generate budget changes. The selection of IO was based primarily on the need to generate only a small number of alternatives and to let people have access to what everyone else had generated. (A detailed discussion of tool selection parameters is beyond the scope of this chapter; see Bostrom and Anson, 1991, for details.)

Once the outcomes and agenda are established, meeting participants can be selected and informed about meeting preparation. Participants' roles (facilitator, decision maker, etc.) and ground rules (e.g., no-attack rule) need to be established. Although critical to the success of the meeting, this premeeting stage is often neglected or underemphasized in practice (e.g., Mosvick and Nelson, 1987). In fact, one of the biggest benefits of the introduction of GSS is that it forces people to pay careful attention to meeting design (Watson et al., 1991).

MEETING ACTIVITIES	GROUPSYSTEMS TOOLS
GENERATE (CREATE, LIST, IDENTIFY)	ELECTRONIC BRAINSTORMING (EBS) TOPIC COMMENTER IDEA ORGANIZATION GROUP WRITER GROUP OUTLINER GROUP DICTIONARY POLICY FORMATION
ORGANIZE (STRUCTURE, REFINE, CLUSTER, RELATE, CATEGORIZE)	EBS (by keyword) IDEA ORGANIZATION GROUP MATRIX GROUP OUTLINER
EVALUATE (SELECT, ELIMINATE) QUANTITATIVE	VOTE (RANKING, ETC.) ALTERNATIVE EVALUATION QUESTIONNAIRE GROUP MATRIX
QUALITATIVE	GENERATE TOOL, GROUP MATRIX
COMMUNICATE (PRESENT, DISTRIBUTE, DISCUSS, EXCHANGE, EXPLAIN, CLARIFY)	ANY GENERATE TOOL WITH ACCESS TO INDIVIDUAL RESPONSES CAN BE USED (E.G. TOPIC COMMENTER)
GROUP PROCESS TEMPLATE (COMBINATION)	STAKEHOLDER IDENTIFICATION (GENERATE, EVALUATE)

© 1990, B & A   III-2a   UGA18

FIGURE 2-5.   GroupSystems Activity Tool Mapping

Both task and relational outcomes must be accomplished during the meeting. A meeting is usually divided into three phases: open/setup, during, close/wrap-up (Bostrom, 1989). During setup, the facilitator must clarify and get agreement on outcomes, make roles and rules clear, and establish a positive group environment. During the meeting, the primary responsibility of the facilitator is to help the group adapt and execute the agenda to accomplish the task outcomes (e.g., develop an action plan), making sure that the group uses the technology appropriately (Bostrom, Anson, and Clawson, 1993). The facilitator must also ensure that a positive environment and constructive relationships are developed and maintained. During closing, facilitators usually summarize the meeting, detailing each point that requires future action (who will do what and by when, who has agreed to what, etc.).

After the meeting, the immediate dissemination of results reinforces the agreements made and maintains momentum into implementation (Mosvick and Nelson, 1987). Monitoring implementation is generally left to those given this responsibility. The role of the facilitator, especially if he or she is not a member of the group, is minimal in this post-meeting stage. The facilitator may, however, be asked to evaluate the meeting and to suggest changes for future meetings.

THE ASSOCIATION'S ELECTRONIC MEETING

Now that you have seen some conceptual models to understand electronic meetings and how to facilitate them, let us return to the association's electronic meeting. The goal here is to illustrate an electronic meeting through the detailed discussion of the association's meeting, highlighting the benefits and obstacles involved.

The international professional association officers' group includes volunteer and elected members drawn from business, government, and academic institutions around the country. The group meets six to seven times per year. One of these meetings is devoted to updating the three-year plan for the association and developing a budget for the coming year. This particular planning and budget meeting was electronically supported through GroupSystems. A total of 14 participants (including 9 officers and 5 permanent staff members) were involved. Only 2 of the permanent staff were active participants; the other 3 had support roles. This was a very important meeting because $500,000 needed to be cut from the budget. Since each participant represented a different set of interests within the association, there was a great deal of conflict about where cuts should be made. We assisted in planning the meeting agenda and provided both process and technical facilitation.

The meeting format developed by Bostrom (1989) and the agenda design model (Bostrom and Anson, 1991) were used as guides for premeeting and meeting activities. Premeeting preparation consisted of a short demonstration of the software for two of the group leaders, plus a few hours of face-to-face and telephone discussions. The facilitators helped the group leaders define meeting outcomes, design an agenda (using the process outlined previously—see Figure 2-4), and define group leader and facilitation roles. Three officers assumed the role of group leader during different parts of the meeting. Each group leader had the final authority for clarifying the content of topics being addressed and directing the facilitators to move the group along from one activity to the next.

The group followed the agenda developed before the meeting to a great extent. However, some changes were made along the way to accommodate the evolving needs of the group. The agendas for updating the long-range plan and developing the budget will now be reviewed in depth.

The Long-Range Planning (LRP) Process

The long-range planning process involved three activity sequences, repeated through four cycles (see Table 2-1). Each cycle corresponded to one of four sections in the long-range plan (LRP).

The first activity in the sequence used the Topic Commentor (TC) tool to generate suggestions for modifying and adding to the list of objectives within a given section of the prior year's LRP. TC was chosen because a structured generation process was needed. TC provides a series of windows or frames (i.e., the structure) into which participants post their comments. In this situation, each window represented a current objective, and one additional window was set aside for new objectives. Members entered suggestions individually at their computer stations. After everyone had finished entering, the suggestions were displayed on the public screen for review by the group. Modifications that were

TABLE 2-1   Long Range Plan (LRP) Procedure

LRP Section	Activity	GroupSystems Tool	Time (min)
Association growth and support section	Enter objectives suggestions	TOPIC COMMENTER (TC)	13
	Group review of suggestions	TC/Public Screen	5
	Prioritize final objectives list	VOTING	9
Education services section	Enter objectives suggestions	TOPIC COMMENTER (TC)	5
	Group review of suggestions	TC/Public Screen	4
	Prioritize final objectives list	VOTING	9
Public Affairs section	Enter objectives suggestions	TOPIC COMMENTER (TC)	6
	Group review of suggestions	TC/Public Screen	25
	Prioritize final objectives list	VOTING	8
Finance section	Enter objectives suggestions	TOPIC COMMENTER (TC)	5
	Group review of suggestions	TC/Public Screen	12
	Prioritize final objectives list	VOTING	3
Relative importance of LRP sections	Prioritize list of LRP sections	VOTING	6
	Review ranked list	VOTING/Public Screen	4
		TOTAL	114 mins

accepted by the group were made directly to the public display listing (by the technical facilitator) to create an ongoing final record. The process facilitator helped the group systematically review and agree on changes to be recorded. Next, the Voting tool was used by each individual to rank the objectives. The ranking option of Voting forced participants to choose explicit priorities. The combined rankings were then reviewed by the group.

Four cycles of generating, reviewing, and prioritizing the objectives within each LRP section took an average of 26 minutes per section. Finally, the Voting tool was used to set priorities for the four LRP sections themselves. The entire process of reviewing and updating the LRP took less than two hours. Printed transcripts of the comments and evaluations entered into the system were distributed to the members for reference during the subsequent budget review.

The Budget Review Process

The major task facing the association officers was to produce a balanced budget. The process involved the review and acceptance or modification of each line item in the budget proposed by the permanent staff. The review process took 11 hours overall; however, 40 percent of this time was spent orally reviewing the budget proposed by the staff. The overall agenda was introduced in Figure 2-4 and shown in detail in Table 2-2.

The first step involved developing a list of criteria with which to evaluate recommendations proposed by the permanent staff. Two GroupSystems tools were used to carry out the three activities associated with this step. (You participated vicariously in this portion of the meeting earlier in this chapter.) The final list of criteria is shown in Figure 2-2. The process of articulating and ranking the criteria took only 35 minutes because of both the technology and the overall design of the meeting. Since the group had already

TABLE 2-2   Budget Review Procedure

Budget Task	Activity	Group Systems Tool	Time (min)
Develop criteria to evaluate recommendations for change	Generate criteria	IDEA ORGANIZER (IO)	3
	Group review/ consolidate list	IO/PUBLIC SCREEN	22*
	Prioritize final list of criteria	VOTING	10
Review budget proposed for staff	Oral presentation	None	270*
Generate recommendations to change proposed budget	Enter budget-item change recommendations	IDEA ORGANIZER (IO)	60
	Group review to consolidate duplicate entries	IO/PUBLIC SCREEN	13
	Group review of changes for clarification and shared understanding	IO/PUBLIC SCREEN	20*
Evaluate recommended changes	Rate each change recommendation using criteria	ALTERNATIVE EVALUATOR	60
	Group review of combined ratings and testing of alternative weighting of criteria to create a prioritized list of changes to be made in the budget	ALTERNATIVE EVALUATOR (Mostly discussion)	50*
Apply recommended changes to budget	Recommended changes made to budget spreadsheet in priority order to achieve balanced budget	Public Screens (one displaying results from step 4; the other showed the LOTUS budget spreadsheet)	150*
		Total time	658 min
		Non-electronic*	512 min
		Electronic	146 min

updated its LRP and developed a mission statement, selecting what was important to the organization, that is, criteria, was straightforward.

In the second step, the director of finance and the secretary/treasurer orally clarified the budget they had proposed. The discussion of the budget took four and one-half hours.

In the third step, once the evaluation criteria had been formulated and the proposed budget had been discussed, group members spent the next hour individually generating recommendations for changing the proposed budget. The IO tool was used to support the generation of recommendations. (The reasons for this choice were discussed previously.) Each entry consisted of the budget line item number and the suggested change, plus any further elaboration of rationale for the recommendation. The group first checked this list briefly to eliminate duplicate items, then reviewed each of the 45 recommended changes to clarify their meaning. Evaluation was explicitly postponed until the next step. This entire process lasted three and one-quarter hours.

The fourth step involved individually rating (on a scale of 1 to 10) each recommended change according to the extent to which it addressed each of the six criteria. The individual multicriteria assessments were automatically summarized by the Alternative Evaluator (AE) tool. (There was no choice in tools here: AE is the only tool that handles multicriteria evaluations.) The criteria weightings used were based on the priorities set in step 1 (see Table 2-2). After the combined ratings were displayed, participants suggested a number of alternative schemes for weighting criteria, and a number of these were tested. This behavior occurred because the participants' preferred budget cuts did not show up on the top of the combined-rating list. After about 30 minutes of "what ifs," one participant reminded the participants that they had agreed on a set of criteria weights in step 1. Everyone realized that the group did have a "shared frame," and the meeting moved on.[1] The final list of recommendations, which was sorted using an agreed-on set of criteria weights, was printed and displayed on a public screen for use in the next step. This evaluation and sorting process, which would have been impossible to perform in a regular meeting, was completed in just under two hours.

In the final step a LOTUS spreadsheet of the entire budget was displayed on a second public screen. Changes were made to the spreadsheet one at a time, starting with the recommendations having the highest priority in the list displayed on the first public screen. The spreadsheet had the bottom-line net balance figure in view at all times. Thus, the impact on the net balance could be seen as each recommended change was made to the spreadsheet. Of the 45 recommended changes, 19 were incorporated into the budget unchanged, 4 were modified by the group as they were entered into the spreadsheet, 21 were dropped, and 1 was referred to the staff for further work. The final budget spreadsheet was produced in two and one-half hours. With one item unresolved, the budget was nearly balanced.

---

[1]This is one of the general rules of facilitation: Always try to establish a larger, shared frame, especially when conflict exists. In this case, developing the criteria first expedited the evaluation and selection process and then minimized the amount of conflict and potential negative behavior that could have ensued.

BENEFITS AND OBSTACLES OF ELECTRONIC MEETINGS

GSS Benefits

Before presenting our evaluations of the association's meeting, we would like to introduce a general framework for looking at GSS benefits that provides a structure for our evaluation. Attributes that create an electronic meeting context include anonymity, simultaneity, process structuring, electronic recording and display and expanded information-processing capacity. These attributes, shown in Table 2–3, represent our synthesis of the literature's identification of GSS attributes and their potential benefits. Table 2–3 implies that when GSS is used appropriately, a number of potential benefits can occur. For example, simultaneous input allows for more equal participation (i.e., reducing dominance) and contributions directed to areas of expertise and interest. Anonymity creates a context in which participants feel less threatened because the group focuses on the information rather than the contributor. These attributes both overcome common dysfunctional behaviors (e.g., dominance) and provide new capabilities not available in traditional meetings (e.g., ability for all to talk at the same time).

Evaluation of the Association's Meeting

We evaluated the meeting in a variety of ways: through our observations, formal pre- and postmeeting surveys, and telephone interviews with members in the week following the

TABLE 2–3   GSS Features and Their Benefits

GSS Features	Potential Benefits
Simultaneous Input/Simultaneity	Opportunity for broader, equal and more active participation
	Participation and contribution at own level of ability and interest
	More input in less time
	Reduces communication dominance by the few
Anonymity	Less individual inhibitions
	Focus on idea rather than contributor
	Enhanced group ownership of ideas
Process/agenda Structuring	Provides framework and process structures
	Facilitates agenda control and completion
	Improved topic focus
Electronic Recording and Display	Immediate display of data
	Complete and immediate meeting minutes
	Enhanced group memory
	Easier modification
Extended Information Processing Capacity	Automates complex tasks
	Creates easy accessibility to information, others' ideas and other software tools

meeting. Responses to the technology, the facilitation, and the meeting overall were very positive across all research media.

The presurvey showed that the participants did not enter with biases against the use of computers or against meetings in general. The participants were involved in an average of 5.6 meetings per week and had very positive attitudes toward this involvement. They also had a positive attitude toward computers and were typically frequent computer users. Only one group member requested an assistant for typing. The typist was used for the first two days but only for entering textual information; the member voted without the typist's assistance.

Two postmeeting surveys were conducted. The first asked for perceptions of the technology and its effects on meeting outcomes. On a seven-point scale (with 7 representing a very positive response), the technology was perceived to be very easy to use (mean: 6.4) and appropriate for the meeting (6.4). Participants also felt that it improved the quality of meeting outputs (5.9) and contributed to greater efficiency (6.3) and acceptance of group outputs (6.0). These results confirmed that the technology itself was viewed as playing an important role in accomplishing the meeting outcomes.

A second survey contained 25 pairs of questions. Each pair prompted the participant to contrast this meeting with previous association meetings on a specific dimension. The participants responded by marking, on adjacent seven-point scales, their perceptions of this and previous meetings of the group. The electronic meeting was rated significantly more effective than previous meetings in all areas. The magnitude of the differences is noteworthy. The mean scores for the electronic meeting were from 0.9 to 2.7 scale points higher, and 17 of the 25 differences were statistically significant (and the other 8 all approached significance).

In terms of meeting outcomes, the participants indicated that compared to past nonelectronic meetings, the electronic meeting

- Was more satisfying, relevant, effective, and efficient
- Had more healthy interpersonal relations
- Had participants who were more confident that outcomes were the best and who were more responsible for and committed to the outcomes

In terms of the meeting process, participants' responses indicated that in the electronic meeting

- Issues were dealt with more systematically and examined more constructively
- Group behavior was more goal-directed
- Leadership and coordination were handled better
- Participants stayed more focused on relevant issues, felt more comfortable in expressing ideas, and thought that their contributions were better amplified

The survey results provide very strong support for using electronic rather than traditional meetings for this group.

The participants' actual comments provide additional support for the survey findings. During the week following the meeting, we conducted open-ended telephone interviews

TABLE 2-4   Interview Comments on GSS Technology

Anonymity

Allowed the input of ideas that people would have hesitated giving otherwise. Individuals could try out ideas and see the group's reaction without letting other believe they were committed to the ideas.

Allowed the evaluation of ideas on their merit.

Anonymity was very important in itself. There would have been more stray sniping without it. Even nonanonymity would have been better than a manual meeting, however, because ideas, once posted to the public screen, were at least one step removed from the individual.

Simultaneous Input

Allowed the group to put more ideas on the table faster and reach consensus more rapidly.

Faster to obtain ideas, develop shared ideas, ranking, and consensus.

Means for Structuring the Meeting

Approach to working on tasks was far more organized compared to last year.

Provided the opportunity to look at entered information more closely and systematically.

Electronic Recording and Display

Critical ideas were not lost as in past meetings, so that people could focus on the problem.

All thoughts were discussed by the group, and nothing was lost; there were opportunities for discussion.

Expanded Information-Processing Capacity

Technology made some almost impossible takes possible, such as ranking and determining the degree of importance to group.

People were able to assess easily others' positions and thinking on issues, to see how many other people were thinking the same thing, and to know that support for their position existed.

TABLE 2-5   Interview Comments on Facilitation, Group Dynamics, and Meeting Outcomes

Comments Related to Support from Process Facilitator

Facilitator did not limit opportunities; help cut through when the group got bogged down; facilitated the pace of the meeting.

Wording of questions is critical; the wording of questions can tend to lead to predetermined answers, which was a problem in the first issue dealt with in the meeting.

Facilitator is the key, knowing the right question to ask and importance of preplanning for session.

Comments Related to Meeting Outcomes and Group Dynamics

Hostile reactions were directed more at the group instead of individuals, resulting in less personal conflicts.

This [budget review] was the most straightforward, nonturf process that I have seen in the last six years. It took roughly one-half the time normally needed.

The documented outputs can eliminate the need to prove decisions to higher-up group of officers [in the next cycle of the budget review process.]

Some turf differences still came out, although these were crucial to the discussion. Both sides were expressed, and majority decision process gave means of resolving disagreements. Without the technology it would have been more tense given the nature of the task.

Broader participation (fewer quiet members) than previous meetings, including more opportunity for permanent staff to have input.

Want to use the technology next year.

with nine of the participants. Tables 2–4 and 2–5 display representative comments from these interviews. The comments are stated in the participants' own words. We organized these comments into three sections: (1) the five GSS support attributes (described in Table 2–3), (2) process facilitation comments, and (3) meeting outcomes and group dynamics.

Some additional themes highlighted by the participants include the following:

- "Politicking" was significantly reduced.
- Conflicts were constructively resolved.
- The stress level of members was significantly reduced.
- The meeting was less dominated by the top officers.
- The technology was flexibly adapted to the group's needs.
- Overall, the meeting accomplished more in less time than could have been accomplished without the technology.

These comments, along with the survey results, support the claims made earlier that GSS helps to improve meetings in five general ways (See Table 2–3). *Anonymity* made it easier for people to contribute ideas and to focus on the merit of the ideas expressed. *Simultaneity* made eliciting ideas and judgments more efficient. *Structuring* helped to make the problem-solving approach more organized and the examination of information more systematic. *Electronic recording and display* prevented ideas from getting lost along the way. *Expanded information-processing capacity* made it possible to gather and evaluate the group's position and thinking. Furthermore, participants' comments emphasized the importance of the facilitator in moving a group through its work. Major overall improvements in how the members worked together were noted by both the officers and staff.

Perhaps the bottom-line statement that illustrates the success of this electronic meeting is that all participants wanted to use the technology for their next meeting. They decided to hold another meeting supported by GroupSystems in the following fall. A preliminary examination of surveys from the second meeting shows equally positive results.

Potential Obstacles

This case demonstrates how the use of GSS can result in a very productive face-to-face meeting. However, not all GSS researchers have concluded that GSS produces these benefits. Some research results are contradictory (Dennis et al., 1988; Dennis, Valacich, and Nunamaker, 1991). There are indications that many of the negative and contradictory research findings may be due to research design problems (e.g., artificial groups and tasks, small group sizes, and poor fit between task and technology), the use of different GSS products, and the absence of a facilitator role. Where these obstacles have not intervened—when real groups and tasks were involved and effective facilitation was provided—the findings suggest that GSS can dramatically improve meeting productivity (Dennis et al., 1988; Dennis, Valacich, and Nunamaker, 1991).

Although it does appear that GSS features can help resolve group problems and enhance group productivity, there are potential dysfunctional aspects of the technology that facilitators need to be aware of. For example, the screen size limits how much information can be laid out at any time in front of an individual or group. Ease of scrolling between screens alleviates this problem somewhat, but paper printouts are often still needed to give users access to a total view. Multiple public display screens or enlarged terminal screens could offer additional support.

Our experience has shown that using a keyboard does not inhibit most participants. However, on occasion we bring in typists to help input text for participants with deficient typing skills (as we did in the association case). Similarly, participants are able to learn to use most GSS software without prior training. Instruction is provided when each tool is used for the first time. Participants regularly comment on how easy it is to use.

In the final analysis, GSS technology may contribute a number of benefits to collaborative work. However, whether or not this potential is realized depends on how a GSS is used and to what tasks it is applied. Matching the GSS technology to the group, the task, and the desired outcome(s) is one of the most critical areas of concern. There are some group or task situations in which GSS technology, especially in its current state, may not help (DeSanctis and Gallupe, 1987). For example, overly simple tasks or tasks assigned to small (two- or three-person) groups may be accomplished more effectively in a regular setting. However, there has been little research into the bounds of contingencies in which GSS may be effectively used.

As demonstrated in the association case, effective facilitation of the group process and the technology is critical. The facilitator must work with the group or its leader to select and implement appropriate GSS tools. If the meeting is designed poorly, the technology's added efficiency can easily lead a group away from its goals even more rapidly than in a traditional meeting. Similarly, GSS can make a good facilitator better, but it cannot, currently, make a poor facilitator look good. It is the integration of good computer tools with effective human facilitation that leads to more effective meetings.

Meetings in Different GSS Environments

In this chapter, we have focused on face-to-face (i.e., same time and place) meetings. However, GSS and other collaborative technologies have expanded the types of environments so that meetings can occur at the same time but different place and different time but same or different place (see Chapter 1). Let us focus on how the association meeting could have been carried out in these other electronic environments.

Given the appropriate communication network connections, the meeting could have been easily carried out in a same-time/different-place mode. Some type of audio and/or video connection could have been added to support communication. When one moves to a different time, a shared group space is required for the participants to access at different times. In current communication-oriented systems (e.g., electronic mail, teleconferences, and bulletin boards), this shared space provides some structure (e.g., topics), which is used to organize and facilitate discussions. This communication space lacks the process structuring, outcome-directed shared space found in most same-time/same-place GSS. In these environments, the meeting agenda would be the primary shared space. Thus, in an any-time/any-place GSS, such as VisionQuest, the participants log into the system to find a menu of meetings (called dialogues in VisionQuest). In the association case two would be listed—long range plan and budget development. The selection of one of these would then lead to an electronic version of the agenda shown in either Table 2-1 or Table 2-2. Once at the agenda, the participants would initiate the execution of a particular tool, for example, to generate criteria.

Anytime/any-place systems need to support both task accomplishment and communication. Thus, communication-based systems such as EIES (see Chapter 5) add functionality to support this type of task- or agenda-activity-based processing. Similarly, task-oriented GSS are adding communication features and/or providing links to communication-based systems. The availability of an any-time/any-place systems creates more meeting design alternatives because the facilitator can combine different environments to accomplish meeting outcome(s) and agenda that unfold over time. For example, the association's long-range planning meeting could have used a combination of different time/different place followed by same time/same place. The suggested updates to the plan could have been generated in a different-time/different-place mode, followed by a face-to-face meeting to discuss, select, and update the plan.

Three facilitation issues become apparent as we move from same-time to different-time environments: (1) availability and richness of communication channels, (2) immediacy of feedback, and (3) means of coordination. In different-time environments, the facilitator has to rely more on the GSS to enrich communication, gather and assess feedback, and monitor and coordinate activities (e.g., agenda). Very little is known currently on what mechanisms (tools, features, etc.) are needed or how to apply them to facilitate effectively in non-same-time/same-place environments. This is a very rich and challenging research area (Bostrom, Anson, and Clawson, 1993).

CONCLUSION

The group support systems (GSS) discussed in this book are intended to improve the effectiveness and efficiency of meetings. They are designed to amplify the positive aspects of working in a group (incorporating multiple viewpoints and sources of information, establishing group consensus and cohesiveness, etc.) and to reduce the negative aspects of group meetings (topic wandering, domination by some members, inhibitions about contributing openly, inefficiencies because only one person can speak at a time, etc.). The association case demonstrated how the use of GSS can result in a very productive face-to-face meeting.

Our own experience points to two key factors that influence the effectiveness of a GSS. First, the GSS used in a meeting should provide the flexibility to adapt to specific group needs regardless of which approach is chosen to perform a task. Second, technical and process facilitation plays a central role in the productive use of a GSS. The facilitator must effectively match the technology to the group and its task and then help the group to use the system appropriately to accomplish its task.

We are at a very early and exciting point in GSS development. As reflected in this book, the level of GSS activity is building. More researchers are starting to explore the area, and organizations are starting to install and use GSS regularly. The next five years should see a rapid dissemination of GSS technology (see Chapter 1).

Chapter 3

A Case Study in the Assimilation of Technology Support for Teams

Lynda M. Applegate

Harvard Business School

For the past decade researchers in both the business and academic community have spent considerable time, intellectual (and sometimes physical) effort, and dollars studying the potential of technology support for teams. As can be seen in this book, the research spans the globe, from Singapore to London, and spans the potential technology applications, from facilitating group communication to support of specific group processes and tasks. Much of this research has focused on design of new groupware technologies or evaluating the influence of the technology on the group process in laboratory environments, often using students as subjects. Recently there has been increased emphasis on the study of the transfer and assimilation of group technologies into organizations. This is a critical area of research since we must first understand the challenges of moving these technologies from the research lab to organizations before we can fully explore the benefits of computer-augmented teamwork within organizations. It is only then that we will begin to recognize the true profits from our collective research efforts.

This chapter presents a case study on one company's experiences with the transfer and assimilation of technology to support cooperative work. From its birth in the early 1980s the Thomas J. Watson Research Center, the history of the diffusion of computer conferencing throughout IBM is traced. The case ends in 1987 with a group of IBM researchers pondering the final stage of the process—the institutionalization of computer conferencing within the formal organizational system. The case, which illustrates the process of diffusing technology support for teamwork in an organization, enables a focused discussion of the challenges of institutionalizing the technology through the development of formal structures, policies, and control processes.

The IBM case study is one of nine cases on computer-augmented teamwork that are available through Harvard Business School. These cases address a broad range of group technologies including electronic meeting support systems, computer conferencing, and executive information systems designed to support management teams and organizational coordination and control. Teaching notes that suggest approaches for teaching the cases and additional information on each company's handling of the management challenges in the case are also available. In addition, videotapes and software are available for several cases. (The appendix to this chapter contains a list of materials and ordering information.)

The remainder of this chapter describes a general framework for understanding the diffusion of technology innovation in organizations. The IBM case is then discussed in relation to the framework.

A FRAMEWORK FOR UNDERSTANDING DIFFUSION OF TECHNOLOGY INNOVATION[1]

The theoretical foundations for understanding the development, assimilation, and institutionalization of technology support for teams within organizations can be found in the general literature on the diffusion of technology innovations. Figure 3-1 summarizes key frameworks from previous research. Figure 3-2 presents a general framework that I developed. It characterizes the diffusion of technology innovation as a series of tasks or stages that describe the process of innovation development, assimilation, and institutionalization. Although some have faulted stage models for failing to depict the "chaotic" nature of true innovation (Epplie, 1984; Quinn, 1986), these models have proven useful for research and practice as long as sequential passage from stage to stage is not assumed.

Innovation Development

The framework in Figure 3-2 focuses attention on the introduction and assimilation of technologies that are "new to the world" rather than just "new to the organization." [2] Because of the revolutionary nature of these new technologies, responsibility for identifying, developing, and selling the innovations often lies with an organizational unit outside of those that contain the eventual end users. Kanter (1988) has found that although idea generation is most effective when there is close connection with future users, structural isolation during the idea development phase is an important asset. She points out that the

---

[1]The framework discussed in this section was originally described in Applegate (1991). Due to the complexity, only the major elements will be discussed in this chapter.

[2]This distinction was proposed by Dorothy Leonard-Barton in a personal conversation.

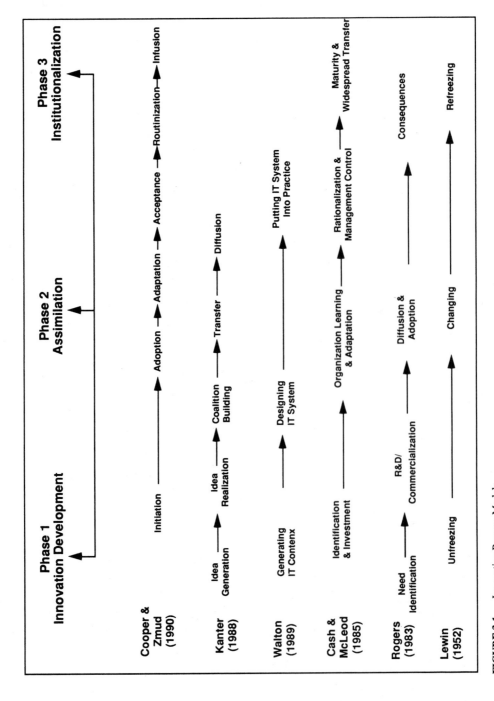

FIGURE 3-1. Innovation Process Models

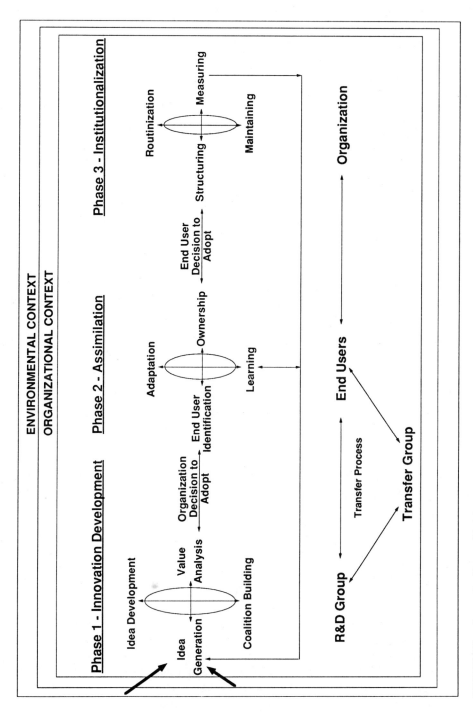

FIGURE 3-2.   Innovation Process Model

37

innovation development process is intensely creative and demands flexibility, experimentation, and freedom from existing biases. Many of the most innovative companies rely on separate organizational units for innovation development. These can be either internal or external to the organization and either permanent or temporary.

Transfer

A number of factors have been associated with success and failure in the transfer of new technology from these separate R&D units to organizational end users.

R&D and End-User Linkages

The need for structural isolation during idea development notwithstanding, Kanter (1988) found tight linkages with potential end users, other stakeholders, and power groups within the target organization to be critical. An R&D group, she stresses, must balance an outward focus on procuring information and resources and stimulating demand for the innovation with an inward focus on buffering the group from outside interference. Sophisticated boundary management is needed during the innovation development process to maintain a balance between isolation and linkage with external users and power sources. (Gladstein and Caldwell, 1985).

Once it has been developed, a new technology can be transferred from R&D to end users either directly or through a bridging mechanism called a *transfer unit*. The transfer unit can be a formal group whose primary responsibility is to move new ideas into the organization, or it can be a parallel organization created to transfer a specific innovation. If a transfer unit is not used, the R&D group must work closely with each new user group to ensure successful transfer and assimilation of the technology. The R&D units must carefully balance the opportunities for learning and networking that come from a direct transfer with the time and effort needed to ensure a successful transfer. Some groupware technologies are easier to transfer in some organizations because of close alignment among the team, task, and technology and a facilitative organizational environment. These technologies almost seem to "diffuse naturally." Others are more difficult and will require significant attention. In the latter case, an R&D unit may decide to use a formal technology transfer unit to assist with the transfer process.

Use of a transfer unit makes the introduction and assimilation of a new technology a two-step process. First, the R&D group must successfully transfer the technology innovation to the transfer unit. Then, the transfer unit must successfully transfer the innovation to the end users. To manage the assimilation process effectively, a transfer unit must thoroughly understand how to use the new innovation, what to use it for, how to teach others to use it, and how to manage the change process. Clear delineation of the roles and task responsibilities of the R&D group and transfer unit is critical. As the transfer process unfolds, these roles and task responsibilities change. Often responsibility is concentrated in the R&D group early in the transfer process and shifts gradually to the transfer unit. Occasionally, often because of political rivalries, an R&D group has difficulty relinquishing control to the transfer unit. Kanter (1988) has found that uncertainty and political controversy decrease the effectiveness of a transfer unit dedicated to transferring new innovations from R&D to end users. Applegate and Wishart (1988) describe the functioning of a formal technology transfer unit in a large organization and illustrate the uncertainties and political controversies that can arise during the transfer process.

Management Sponsorship

The presence of strong power figures willing to champion and support an innovation has been identified as critical to successful assimilation. However, the definition of what constitutes an effective champion remains elusive. Leonard-Barton and Deschamps (1988) argue that the characteristics of an effective management sponsor are contingent on characteristics of the organization, end user, task, and type of innovation. For example, their study of a decentralized organization whose work force contained a high percentage of autonomous professionals found that effective champions were often evaluated less on the strength of their formal legitimacy than on the persuasiveness of their message, perceived competency in evaluating the innovation, and position within the informal power and influence systems. They found that end users' skill levels and internal motivation to use the technology innovation were much stronger intervening variables in the decision to adopt an innovation than perceived managerial influence.

End-User Receptivity

Research on the successful introduction of innovation suggests several criteria that can be used in the selection of potential end users. Kanter (1988) found that innovations that minimize the degree of change in organizational, group, or individual processes tend to have the highest chance of success. Unfortunately, innovations that do not lead to some change in the underlying organizational or work processes are often perceived to have little value. Leonard-Barton (1988) suggests that innovations that necessitate major change and adaptation can be viewed as either a problem or an opportunity. Other authors (see, for example, Cash and McLeod, 1988), observing that many strategic technology innovations involve fundamental organizational changes, argue that companies must learn to manage the risks of these major adaptations to reap the rewards.

In the face of change in work or decision processes, it is helpful if end users are experiencing a high level of frustration with the current process and/or perceive a high level of benefit from the use of the new technology. Nadler and Tushman (1980) suggest that change is facilitated when end users, anticipating the innovation, have already begun to loosen formal and informal organizational arrangements to accommodate it. Markus (1984) observes that user resistance to information technology is often due to the introduction of a system whose features conflict with the organizational setting. She found that user resistance was minimized when people welcomed the changes embodied in the system, were indifferent to the changes, or could successfully circumvent the changes. Walton (1989) and Zuboff (1988) found that user resistance could often be traced to the introduction of a system whose features conflicted with the task it was designed to support.

Researchers studying the transfer of technologies to support teamwork have found that the initial organizational end-user teams must be carefully chosen to facilitate alignment of team, task, and technology (Applegate, 1991; Vogel, 1989). Potential misalignments and strategies for dealing with them must be identified before the transfer, and close connections among the R&D unit, transfer unit, and end-user units must be maintained throughout the transfer process to define strategies for dealing with un-anticipated misalignments and to promote shared learning. One of the most frequent problems with the transfer of technology innovations designed to support teamwork (and technology innovations in general) is the tendency for the R&D unit to "throw the innovation over the wall" to a transfer unit or end-user unit. In doing so, the R&D unit makes the implicit (or explicit) assumption that the technology will not need to be adapted to align with the needs of the users or the organization. In effect this behavior says, "It worked for us so any failure is your problem not ours." In fact, the assimilation process requires mutual adaptation of team, task, and technology dimensions in an environmental and organizational context that demands a certain level of support from the research center, especially early in the transfer process.

Assimilation

Walton (1989) and Leonard-Barton (1988) characterize the assimilation of new technology as a process of alignment and mutual adaptation. Leonard-Barton defines this mutual adaptation process as a successive decrease in misalignment among end users, organizational infrastructure, technology, and task. Walton focuses on the development of alignment among business, the organization, and the information technology strategy at the macro level, followed by the development of commitment and competence by end users.

Assimilation of technology innovations to support teamwork can thus be viewed as an adaptation and learning process in which misalignments among environment, organization, team, task, and technology are corrected and end users eventually adopt and assume ownership for the innovation. Failure to correct misalignments frequently results in discontinuation of use or outright rejection unless strong management is able to force compliance. The assimilation process can thus be characterized as one of compliance (external control, or simple adoption) and/or commitment (internal control, which adds individual ownership to the adoption process) (Walton, 1989). Behaviors that signify that a technology has moved beyond externally motivated adoption to true end-user ownership include the ability to end users to identify additional uses for the technology, the ability to describe benefits and added value that result from the use of the innovation, and a willingness to pay for the innovation.

Institutionalization

As a new technology is adopted (ideally with the development of true commitment and ownership) by an ever-expanding base of users, there comes a point at which the benefits (and costs) of the technology extend beyond the local level to the organization as a whole. Although it is difficult to identify the exact point at which this shift from local to organizational impact occurs, most organizations do react at some point to the continued penetration of a technology innovation with attempts to institutionalize the innovation into the formal organizational system. Organizational structures, control systems, and efforts to develop formal policies and standards are often put in place. Cash and McLeod (1985) call this process "rationalization;" Cooper and Zmud (1990) call it "routinization." Lewin, in his widely used model of organizational change, stresses the need for organizations to "unfreeze, change, and refreeze" to accommodate a new innovation.[3]

The challenge in institutionalizing a technology, especially if there is a desire to preserve end-user commitment and ownership and organizational flexibility, is to develop structures and controls that simultaneously support both continued local innovation and adaptation and organizational effectiveness and efficiency.

THE FRAMEWORK IN ACTION

The IBM computer conferencing case provides an opportunity for applying these general principles on the diffusion of technology innovation to the current challenge of introducing and assimilating technology support for teamwork within organizations.

Innovation Development

The IBM computer conferencing system was developed in a research center physically, organizationally, and culturally separate from the parent organization. Watson Center researchers were not pressured to "get current products out the door." Instead, they were evaluated and rewarded on the ability to generate new ideas and technology innovations that could find their way into IBM work environments and IBM products. As such, the organization and culture supported experimentation and finding new ways to deal with current problems.

But how did the IBM research unit maintain "close connection with future users" to ensure that their technology innovations addressed real customer and IBM needs? Prior to computer conferencing this was a source of major difficulty. It is interesting to note, however, that conferencing itself has become an important source of ongoing communication between Watson Center researchers and IBM product development, engineering, marketing, and service employees. There are numerous examples throughout the case that highlight the critical role of computer conferencing in helping to connect the research unit with eventual end users. These quotes from several research center managers illustrate this point.

> We had developed some software a while back that we thought was very helpful so we opened a forum on it. The feedback we got was solid, so we added some of the suggested improvements and put more versions out. One IBM group in Holland was trying to develop a product that was similar to our software. They saw our forum and contacted us. We worked out a joint arrangement with them and now we're working together. And that's just one example; we've had similar experiences with other groups. As a result, IBM will be offering several products that contain the code from our software.

---

[3] In my recent work with companies I have found that many organizations are finding it necessary only to "semi-freeze" to enable the continuous improvement and flexibility required in the 1990s. I call this phenomenon "managing in slush." It is important to note that some level of organizational support and control are usually required for technologies that support organization effectiveness rather than just individual or team effectiveness.

Computer conferences are an excellent test-bed for new products. If you build a version, put it out on a conference, and show that it is useful internally in IBM, you can sometimes convince the marketing people it should be sold to customers.

In the Research Division, we're measured on our ability to get the results of our research efforts into IBM products. Before the conferences I could count on my fingers the number of times someone *asked* for one of our research developments for use in a product. But now, with the visibility of our software in the conferences, it happens regularly. It's refreshing to be asked for your assistance instead of being in sales mode all the time.

Transfer and Assimilation

IBM's adoption of computer conferencing illustrates the gradual, informal diffusion of a general purpose communication technology in which the technology is provided as a corporate resource that end users voluntarily decide to use based on need. No formal technology transfer strategy is employed. Other cases listed in the appendix present other technology diffusion models.

Conferencing within IBM grew out of a frustration with the current methods of communicating information on the new IBM PC product. When the IBM PC was announced, electronic mail and a monthly (paper-based) newsletter were used to distribute information among the research center, product development, and marketing and service groups. A widely dispersed human and electronic communication network was already in place, and there was a critical need to communicate vast amounts of information quickly to meet the corporate objective of rapidly gaining control of the PC marketplace. The initial conferencing application, IBMPC, arose out of this already established need. It offered significant improvement over the limited information-processing capacity of E-mail and newsletters and did not require great changes in work processes or significant time investments by users. The users all had access to the technology needed to participate in IBMPC and knew how to use it. In Walton's (1989) framework, the critical conditions for successful technology transfer and assimilation—access, motivation, and mastery—were all met. There was close alignment among technology, task, and team with the initial set of users and throughout the assimilation.

The research center team members were part of this paper-based network of IBMPC enthusiasts. They developed the technology on their own initiative and transferred it directly within the existing organizational network to the initial end-user group. They informed the widely dispersed network of potential users of the availability of this new technology through the existing communication channels, E-mail and the written newsletter, so little time and effort was needed by the research center team to create awareness of the technology. They maintained their involvement as members of the communication network and continued to adapt the technology to the changing needs of the user base. Initially difficult to use by all but the most computer-literate hackers, early technical adaptations were primarily aimed at improving the user interface to enable broader participation. Later enhancements were designed to deal with the challenges of managing the complexity of the rapidly expanding information content and communication channels.

The diverse nature of the initial set of end users in terms of geographic location and organizational roles and the broad applicability of the technology helped support the continued assimilation of the technology. Participation in the conferencing communication forums increased rapidly. By 1983, less than two years after it was developed, IBMPC contained 800 separate discussion topics (called forums), and 35 geographically dispersed replications of the data base (called shadows) had been created to improve response time. By 1988, at the end of the case, it contained more than 4,000 forums, had more than 40,000 users,[4] and conference-related communications accounted for 5 percent of the capacity of IBM's internal computer netwok. All of this occurred without any formal participation or sanction by IBM management within or outside of the research center. As argued by Leonard-Barton and Deschamps (1988) it would be expected that the high percentage of autonomous, technology-literate, professional users in the conferencing user group would result in a greater reliance on informal networks of influence rather than strong management sponsorship to support diffusion of the technology.

Institutionalization

Six months after the development and initial transfer of the technology, a research center manager recognized the organizational impact of the conferencing technology and appointed one member of the research center team to oversee the technology transfer and assimilation and to begin to formulate policies. The manager explained;

> I asked Dave Chess, who at that time was the Watson Center PC consultant, if he would be interested in assuming responsibility for the IBMPC conference with my support. My intent was to have Chess: (1) review the contributions to the conference to assure consistency with established IBM business practice and to take action, when necessary, including editing and deleting inappropriate comments; (2) enhance the conferencing software to make it easy to use as well as economical in terms of computer resources; and (3) work with other employees throughout the company to establish conferencing standards. Dave is a technical wizard, has great writing skills, and is sensitive to other people. This was the unique blend of talents we needed to accomplish our objectives.

The initial set of rules was developed through a collaborative process with users of the conference.[5] These early rules were the first attempts at institutionalizing the technology within the organization. They represented the agreed-on standards of the conference members and, as such, were local in their scope of control.

Several years later computer conferencing was widely used throughout the company. As detailed in the case, the benefits of the conference were felt everywhere. Despite its growth, the initial set of rules, which were monitored and enforced by the same research center employee appointed in 1982 to oversee transfer of the technology, was the only attempts at formal institutionalization. Concerned that more formal controls may be needed and that the conferences should be formally sanctioned by senior management, the director of the research center hired a lawyer to review formally the conferencing

---

[4]At the time of the case, IBM employed 385,000 people worldwide.

[5]A forum was opened, called "rules," which invited participants to develop collaboratively a set of policy statements that would ensure that their collective interests were met.

communications, to begin senior management education, and to help draft a formal corporate policy statement. The director explained;

> I was concerned that many executives did not fully understand the conferences' roles and benefits. The use of the conference for sharing software has had a tremendous impact on the success of the IBM PC product. [In addition, IBMPC] has come to be used for things we never even envisioned, like product development and sales support. But because of its size, it has attracted the attention of senior managers. Unfortunately all they ever hear are the complaints. I knew that eventually we would want to carry a proposal forward for corporate approval, but we had to lay the groundwork first.
> That groundwork was education.

The case ends at this point, enabling a discussion of how to approach institutionalization of computer conferencing at IBM. The challenge of establishing formal policies that do not destroy the spirit of innovation and voluntary participation that have been critical factors in the success of conferencing is a key point for discussion. The teaching note that accompanies the case provides additional information on how the company addressed this issue.

SUMMARY

The IBM computer conferencing case, along with other cases listed in the appendix, provides an opportunity for studying the challenges of transferring, assimilating, and institutionalizing technology suport for teams. As researchers and practitioners, we are just beginning to understand the issues that must be resolved to ensure that the exciting technologies discussed in this book will be used for maximal benefit in organizations. The possibilities for dramatic organizational transformation provide the needed motivation to persevere.

The difficulty of generalizing formal controls that had evolved naturally in the initial users to the total population is highlighted in the quote from a research center manager, "the rules work for us but will they work for everyone."

IBM Computer Conferencing*

Harvard Business School
Lynda Applegate

Reviewing the progress of internal computer conferencing at International Business Machines (IBM) Corporation at a meeting at IBM's Thomas J. Watson Research Center in Yorktown Heights were Al Weis, director of Computing Systems. Gerald Waldbaum, manager of Advanced Worksta-

---

*Research Associate H. Jeff Smith prepared this case under the supervision of Assistant Professor Lynda M. Applegate as the basis for class discussion rather than to illustrate either effective or ineffective handling of an administrative situation.

tion Projects and Services and owner of "IBMPC," the first and largest IBM computer conference, John Alvord, manager of Advanced Workstation Projects, Dave Chess, advisory programmer, Advanced Workstation Projects, and Gloria Whittico, lawyer, and current administrator of IBMPC. Computer conferencing was becoming a major force at IBM and, though it had yielded benefits, long-term management issues were becoming apparent. This meeting was being held to review solutions to conferencing problems and prepare a recommendation on computer conferencing for corporate approval.

ORIGINS OF COMPUTER CONFERENCING

Computer Conferencing, a form of computer communication that might be characterized as open format electronic mail, originated as a mechanism for facilitating technical discussions among computer experts. The "conference" usually resided on a large computer to which participants could dial in using a terminal or personal computer with a modem. The conference software was capable of transferring computer programs and images as well as messages.

As the number of people with personal computers and modems increased, many existing conferences were opened up to wider participation and new conferences on nontechnical topics were established. By the mid-1980s, a variety of how-to conferences were available on such topics as gardening and woodworking.

The Watson Research Center had been instrumental in the evolution of IBM's computer conferencing. IBM's oldest and most popular internal computer conference, called IBMPC, had grown quickly since its inception in 1981; it contained more than 4,000 separate topic areas, had more than 40,000 users, and conference-related communications accounted for 5% of the capacity of IBM's internal computer network. Initiated to support technical discussions of IBM's Personal Computer (PC) products, IBMPC became, over time, a part of the IBM infrastructure, and as it grew, the Watson Center team continually added structure and control to its management. Heavily used by software developers, engineers, technical specialists, customer support groups, and other IBM professionals, it was considered a model conference at IBM.

Because it was widely known for its computer conferencing expertise, the Watson Center team was often approached with procedural and policy questions. It had begun a program of executive education in 1985 to explain the use and benefits of, and develop standards for, computer conferencing. The program was scheduled to present a set of policy recommendations at corporate headquarters in Armonk, New York, to be reviewed by the corporate director of Information Systems and general counsel.

COMPANY BACKGROUND

Created in 1911 as the Computing-Tabulating-Recording Company, IBM had seen phenomenal growth. Its product line had expanded from office tabulating machines, time clocks, and scales to computer hardware and software, and it was widely regarded as an example of a well-managed company. In 1987, this "blue chip" corporation[1] had annual revenues of $54 billion, and ranked fourth in sales and second in net income among the *Fortune* 500.[2] (See *Exhibit 1* for selected financial data.) As of March 1988, IBM employed more than 385,000 people worldwide, organized into several discrete business units (see *Exhibit 2*).

---

[1]Thomas J. Peters and Robert H. Waterman, Jr., *In Search of Excellence* (New York: Harper & Row Publishers, 1982), pp. 14-15, 145, 198, 238. Also see Thomas J. Peters and Nancy K. Austin, *A Passion for Excellence* (New York: Random House, 1985).

[2]"The fortune 500 Largest U.S. Industrial Corporations," *Fortune*, April 27, 1987, pp. 364-383.

IBM prided itself on its corporate citizenship and strong cultural norms. Three "basic beliefs" permeated the IBM culture:

1. Respect for the individual—caring about the dignity and rights of each person in the organization;
2. Customer service—providing the best service of any company in the world; and
3. Excellence—believing that all jobs and projects should be performed in a superior way.

COMPUTER CONFERENCING AT IBM[3]

IBM was one of the first companies in the computer industry to embrace conferencing in its internal operations. IBMPC and other conferences had been developed in the early 1980s. By 1988, IBM had more than 300 active conferences, which it categorized as "public" and "private." *Public* conferences (about 100) supported the dissemination of nonsensitive information to anyone on the IBM internal computer network. Examples included IBMVM, an information exchange for IBM's "virtual machine" (VM) operating system, IBMTEXT, an information exchange for text processing topics, and IBMARTS, an information exchange for electronic music and music education. Access to *private* conferences (of which there were more than 200) was controlled by the conference owner, as they often contained classified information.

Conferences were usually maintained on a mainframe (host) computer connected to "VNET," IBM's internal computer communications network. Conference owners, reviewers, and contributors communicated with the host via their local computer and VNET. "Shadows," or copies, of conferences were sometimes maintained on local computers to reduce access cost and time from distant locations.

Conferences typically contained "forums" on various topics. "The conference is like a file cabinet, and the forums are the file folders," explained one systems programmer. "The communications from users are in the file folders." A user could read a forum and add or "append," a new item to the contents. Attributes associated with each item in the forum indicated the time and date of creation and identified the appender. (*Exhibit 3* illustrates the computer conferencing system flow.)

That the internal computer conferences had become as much a part of the IBM organization and culture as electronic mail was evident in John Alvord's observation that 1986 "was the first year that the number of computer messages exceeded the number of internal telephone calls in IBM. Also," Alvord added, "the number of envelopes that were physically mailed from one IBM office to another actually declined for the first time in 1986. The electronic office," he concluded, "is definitely here."

Although not quantified, productivity gains for users and support groups were widely claimed. Chief benefits were broad, rapid, paperless distribution of information and extensive sharing of software and skills. "You can get a message around the world in just a few minutes," observed one manager, adding that, "old communication paths were becoming much less important in IBM. There's a lot more personal networking than in the past. Managing communication has become a real challenge."

IBMPC—GROWTH AND EVOLUTION OF A COMPUTER CONFERENCE

IBMPC's evolution was typical of computer conferences. Announcement of the IBM Personal Computer in 1981 had led to what the Watson Center team called "rumor distribution." One person would send a message to a few other people, each of whom would forward it electronically to many

---

[3]Helpful information has been provided by D. Chess and M. Cowlishaw, "A Large-scale Computer Conferencing System," *IBM Systems Journal*, 26:1, 1987.

other users. Thus began a distribution network. Electronic mail, being designed for person-to-person communication, was not an efficient mechanism for sharing general, common information among a large number of people, and as the distribution network continued to grow, pressure mounted for the creation of a conferencing vehicle.[4]

Recognizing that there was a need for technical experts to discuss PC-related topics, and that allowing these experts to share individually developed software programs would improve the use of the newly announced PCs, and concerned that the existing electronic mail "rumor distribution" system was becoming ineffective, Walt Daniels, a Watson Center employee, created a computer conference, which was outlined in an early issue of an internal PC newsletter. Since the conference was viewed as a technical communication vehicle, no rules were in place, and the difficulty of using the system limited participation to "hackers" (computer experts).

By November 1981, Gerald Waldbaum had become convinced that Daniels' efforts had produced a useful tool that should be supported. Waldbaum recalled, "A Watson Center employee who was not a manager set up the conference without management approval,"

> I felt that the nature of this project required managerial support and protection. So I asked Dave Chess, who at that time was the Watson Center PC consultant, if he would be interested in assuming responsibility for the IBM Conference with my support. My intent was to have Chess:
>
> 1. review the contributions to the conference to assure consistency with established IBM business practice and to take action, when necessary, including editing and deleting inappropriate comments;
> 2. enhance the conferencing software to make it easy to use—thus improving the productivity of the conference users—as well as economical in terms of computer resources; and
> 3. work with other employees throughout the company to establish conferencing standards.
>
> Dave is a technical wizard, has great writing skills, and is sensitive to people. This was the unique blend of talents we needed to accomplish our objectives.

One of Chess's first duties was to document IBMPC's submissions process and create its first set of working rules. Chess's rules, completed early in 1982, were still being used, with minor alterations, in March 1988, and had adopted by many other IBM conferences, becoming a "de facto" standard. (A sample of these rules is provided in *Exhibit 4*.)

"We had only one objective," Waldbaum said of the early years of computer conferencing;

> to help the conference survive! We knew it was becoming a valuable part of IBM. It was having a real impact on our software development, our marketing efforts, and our internal user support. The problem was that some people were making inappropriate comments in the forums. We didn't want people insulting others, trying to sell products, or discussing confidential information.
>
> During the early 1980s, Dave looked at every append to IBMPC, because it was important that inappropriate submissions be removed quickly and that the standards be enforced. After his technical modifications made the conference easier to use, it became even more important to constantly check the submissions, because our user community was growing very quickly.

By 1983, IBMPC contained 800 separate forums, and 35 shadows had been created. With the decision that year to label the IBMPC files "IBM Internal Use Only," the conference became the

---

[4]Electronic mail and conferences often have complementary roles. For example, conference participants often have person-to-person electronic mail discussions outside the conference domain.

[5]IBM's four levels of security classification, in increasing order of sensitivity, were: IBM INTERNAL USE ONLY, IBM CONFIDENTIAL, IBM CONFIDENTIAL-RESTRICTED, AND REGISTERED IBM CONFIDENTIAL. All levels higher than IBM INTERNAL USE ONLY were considered "need-to-know," and were subject to appropriate access controls.

first to have a security classification.[5] Waldbaum, whose sponsorship had made him the "owner" of IBMPC, hired John Alvord to create a structure to manage the conference.

What Waldbaum called "the information overload created by IBMPC" was manifestly evident by October 1985; IBMPC had 3,700 forums, and its use had increased tenfold. "We were not enforcing the rules as consistently as I would have liked," recalled Waldbaum, "since Dave and John were very busy and the workload was growing dramatically." Consequently, Waldbaum hired Gloria Whittico, a lawyer working in IBM's PC development division, to (1) enforce the rules consistently by reviewing the submissions, (2) add an informal legal perspective to the management process, and (3) help to sell the idea of conferencing to IBM executives.

Al Weis, the director of Computing Services, viewed this last duty as Whittico's most important assignment. "I was concerned that many executives did not fully understand the conferences' roles and benefits," he explained. "I knew that we eventually would want to carry a proposal forward for corporate approval, but we had to lay the groundwork first. That groundwork was education."

Whittico, the only full-time reviewer associated with a conference at IBM, described the IBMPC environment she would be promoting at the Armonk meeting. "There's no question the IBMPC conference is a benefit to IBM and to our people; they can ask questions and get a response—sometimes in minutes," Whittico observed. "The single most important thing is that you don't have to keep reinventing the wheel. If somebody out there knows the answer, you'll get it. And, believe me, people are using it. If you took the input to IBMPC for an average week and printed it out, it would be two times the length of *War and Peace*!"

"Without IBMPC," observed Chess, the conference's original reviewer and technical developer,

you'd have to search everywhere for specific information. With it, somebody can say, "I want to see everything that's happening with disk drives," and they can have access to the dialogue in seconds. Everybody uses it. Over 3,500 employees actively contribute information, and over 40,000 read it.

The most active users are professional and technical employees in R&D labs, but nontechnical people are using it too. Some of the best discussions have been nontechnical—like marketing techniques, use of computers in education, design of user-friendly interfaces, and future uses of computer technology.

There are so many entries on IBMPC, it's hard to classify completely. But I'd say there are five general categories, (1) appeals for assistance, where somebody wants software to work in a slightly different environment, or just wants to ask a question. (2) tips and techniques, (3) software failure reports and enhancement suggestions, (4) product information and reviews, and (5) reviews of computer programs used inside IBM and suggestions for improving them.

MANAGEMENT OF IBMPC

One of several management issues the Watson Center team saw cutting across the line between policy and technical decisions was information overload. "As the number of appends increases," explained Chess,

you have to do something about the excessive information that accumulates. Some of it is useful, but it can't *all* be. So, what do you archive? One algorithm says, "when the forums get too large, archive the oldest entries in those forums." But that's not always good, since the largest forums are obviously the most popular ones, and you'd be archiving information people were interested in. Another option is, "archive any forum that hasn't been accessed in the last two years." That's a better one, but it may not be sufficient. Gloria and I also tried starting a forum that says, "which of the forums should we archive? You tell us." I liked that option most of all.

As we get more and more appends, there needs to be some sort of indexing or retrieval system so that people can find the information quickly. Scanning the appends in their raw form is quite time consuming. Different conferences approach this in different ways. I know of one that uses a text retrieval facility, so users can search by keywords. Another conference administrator manually extracts the most relevant entries from each forum and puts them in a separate file called "ANSWERS." We are working on several alternatives.

"Dave and Gloria go for consensus," Waldbaum said of the "peer-to-peer" approach to conference management espoused by Chess and Whittico. "Their approach has been very successful with the conference, since it gives people the feeling they're important and involved. In fact, it's worked so well that many of the participants actually help Gloria with her reviewing duties. They send her notes pointing out appends that may violate the rules."

BENEFITS OF COMPUTER CONFERENCING AT IBM

By March 1988, internal computer conferences were embedded in many of IBM's business processes. From engineering and product development through sales and follow-on support activities, users of IBMPC and other internal IBM computer conferences shared their positive experiences.

Engineering and Product Development

Conferences enabled software development and advanced technology departments to test their products internally, often leading to useful relationships with other groups. "We had developed some software a while back that we thought was very helpful, so we put it out on a conference and opened up a forum on it," explained Mark Linehan, manager of a host-workstation communication group that wrote and maintained software.

> The feedback we got was solid, so we added some of the suggested improvements and put more versions out. One IBM group in Holland was trying to develop a product that was similar to our software. They saw our forum and contacted us. We worked out a joint arrangement with them and now we're working together. And that's just one example; we've had similar experiences with other groups. As a result, IBM will be offering several products that contain the code from our software.
>
> Computer conferences are an excellent test-bed for new products. If you build a version, put it out on a conference, and show that it is useful internally in IBM, you can sometimes convince the marketing people it should be sold to customers.

IBM product development processes were also being influenced by the conferences. "There's an official path for requesting new products in IBM," explained a PC programmer in Boca Raton, Florida.

> Marketing reps are supposed to file a request with their marketing headquarters saying, "We have a customer and need a new product or product improvement." Headquarters collects, prioritizes, and sends these to a product planning group where they are re-sorted, sized, and reduced to dollar estimates. Within this multiple stage "meshing" process, the actual customer requirements can get lost.
>
> What we're seeing with the conferences is people going around this process—in a positive way. They'll append to the forum, "here's something my customer needs." Then an internal technical discussion will start and other marketing people will jump in to help refine the description of the product. By the time a formal, "paper," product request form is filed, we're halfway through the process. The old paper system just couldn't keep up; the PC product cycles were just too short. Conferences filled the void.

Waldbaum believed the conferences had improved his organization's software development effectiveness. "In the Research Division, we're measured on our ability to get the results of our research efforts into IBM products," he explained. "Before the conferences, I could count on my fingers the number of times someone *asked* for one of our research developments for use in a product. But now, with the visibility of our software in the conferences, it happens regularly. It's refreshing to be asked for your assistance instead of being in sales mode all the time."

The conferences also made it easier to develop software for use *inside* IBM. One Research Division programmer, who had developed a spreadsheet that would run on a PC and communicate with a mainframe database, uploaded a primitive version of the software to a conference to let other people try it and waited for comments in the forum. "I really got beat up on the first version of the software I put out there," he recalled.

> People said it wasn't very user-friendly. I felt a little funny watching people talk about my work. But, once I saw them using it and commenting on it, I felt *obliged* to fix it. So I started improving it, based on their comments, and putting newer versions out for them to try. It seems to have been a successful effort, since there are now over 10,000 IBM employees using the software. From the feedback I've gotten, it has improved their productivity and been very useful in their jobs.

Sales and Follow-On Support

IBM, being market-driven, took the needs of its customers seriously. "It's important to understand our relationships with customers in IBM," explained a systems engineer in a marketing branch in New York City, who used conferences to support marketing efforts at insurance companies and hospitals.

> They drive us; we don't drive them. So, when they have a need for software, those of us in marketing had better be ready. The conferences are very helpful to me in that regard.
> I'm an infrequent contributor to the forums, but I'm a voracious reader. Every morning, when I arrive at work, I scan several forums to see the appends of the last 24 hours. I find it broadens my understanding of our product line and increases my credibility with our customers. And, on occasion, it has allowed me to make a specific sale.
> For example, a hospital account wanted to use an IBM product called "CVIEW" in a classroom setting. IBM no longer supported the product—it had very few users. There was a technical question in the implementation that I had no idea how to answer, and it wasn't in the documentation. I issued an append to a forum and had an answer within 24 hours. The customer was happy and so was I.
> Another time, a customer wanted to use VSE, an IBM operating system used on smaller machines. Not many internal IBM locations use it because our computers are usually large, so most IBMers don't know much about it. But I appended a question on a forum, and one of the developers in Germany answered me. It solved the problem for the customer and we made the sale.

(One of the engineer's appends and an answer he received are shown in *Exhibit 5.*)

Linehan's group often provided answers to this type of technical question. "A lot of people in IBM don't know where to go to get technical answers," explained Linehan. "Some are in marketing, a lot are in technical jobs at the labs and plant sites, and a few are in service roles. Because IBM is so big, it's very hard sometimes to find the person who knows the answer to a question. In our field, my department is expert, so I allocate a percentage of our time to scanning the forum for our product and answering the appends."

Almost all conferencing participants agreed that it enriched the IBM work environment. "Since we've gotten the conferences, expertise nets have formed all across IBM," observed the Boca Raton programmer. "By that, I mean that people with interests and knowledge in specific fields are being linked together in the conferences, and they're sharing everything from ideas to software."

IBM Work Environment

The sunbelt programmer also believed that the conferences helped employees gain a more global view of IBM, especially with respect to job possibilities.

> IBM doesn't post job openings like some companies, so you have to rely on management for career planning information and for defining the requirements for advancement: education and job experiences. With the conferences, you have a way to talk with other people in the company in other jobs, in addition to relying on your manager for information. There aren't actually any jobs announced in the forum, but you do build contacts through the network. And when you look at the conferences, you get a sense of IBM's entire business. It broadens your viewpoint.

An advisory systems analyst with a psychology background admitted to analyzing the users. "I've noticed that some very articulate contributors are really introverted. And there's a sense of community among the contributors. Most of us have never met, and probably never will," he observed, "but we feel like we know one another."

Occasionally, participants *did* meet one another. "I met one of my best friends that way, recalled Alvord; "he lives in England, and we met for the first time in 1979 after we had corresponded for a couple of years on the conference. In 1980, our two families took a vacation together on a canal boat. That's a human side of computer conferencing that most people haven't experienced."

Benefits in Other Companies

"Conferences could be used in many business settings; there is nothing specific to the IBM environment," observed Waldbaum. "Any large company with a diverse set of operations distributed over a wide-geographic area would benefit. They're an excellent mechanism for distributing information out of a central location, and they also facilitate peer-level communications in a decentralized fashion. That builds an 'esprit de corps' within an organization."

CONFERENCING CONCERNS

Although the conferences' positive contributions throughout IBM were widely acknowledged, a variety of concerns resolved around inappropriate conference use and management sensitivities within IBM.

Inappropriate Conference Use

"Despite the fact that we have guidelines that have been in place for a number of years," Whittico explained,

> there are occasions when someone writes something they shouldn't. I think that people on the conference sometimes forget the normal rules of etiquette we use in personal communication. For example, if we are talking face to face, there are certain things you won't say to me. But, if you're writing anonymously, you may feel less inhibited by social norms. This does not happen often but when it does we want to remove it immediately. We've had a couple of people who were reminded over and over again that they couldn't say certain things in the forums, but they kept on. One person is on a one-year probation now; he can't use IBMPC again until next year.
>
> The areas that we try to control fall into several categories. First, we emphasize that people's comments on the conference should reflect the same levels of professionalism that we require in face-to-face meetings. For example, it is against our culture to swear or become hostile and abusive at IBM business

meetings. By the same token, we prohibit swearing or abusive comments and disparaging comments about IBM or a competitor. We also do not allow people to discuss highly personal matters like setting up dates.

Second, we want to protect confidential information. For that reason, we remove comments that deal with unannounced IBM products and classified or restricted information.

Finally, we are very careful to stay within legal boundaries and to respect the privacy and property of others. For example, though people are encouraged to share software, we do not allow anyone to put copyrighted software on the conference. This includes software that is available on public bulletin boards outside of IBM, has been published in technical journals, or is a product of another company. Since many software ideas start on the conference and end up in IBM products, failure to identify copyrighted software could be a tremendous legal liability for us. This last area is the most difficult for us to control.

Beginning in April 1987, a computer program was used to "sample" append entries for Whittico's inspection. "At first, I read every IBMPC append," she explained,

I'd print them out and take them home at night. It took forever. So, early last year, John Alvord wrote a computer program that lets me pull the most likely candidates for inspection. I look at all appends to certain forums and pull a fair number at random. I also have a list of keywords that *always* trigger a check—right now, I'm using "confidential," "unannounced," "Gloria," and the usual profanity. Sometimes someone will write, "Gloria, are you reading this?" There are about 1,200 appends per day now, and I'm looking at about 700 of them.

Management Sensitivities

The Watson Center team was becoming increasingly aware of the conferences' visibility within IBM, through the growing number of management inquiries. Not all IBM managers supported the use of the conferences. "Every now and then, I hear from managers who are upset that people are wasting time looking at the conference," explained Weis, "Apparently, their people become interested in the conference dialogue and spend quite a bit of time participating. In the managers' view, that's done at the expense of the employees' assigned work."

At times, the distinction between business and personal comments was hazy. "Several months ago," Waldbaum recalled,

one of the conferencing staff employees transferred to another IBM division. Word leaked out before the formal announcement and a comment was made on the IBMPC conference that "pre-announced" the departure. The news spread like wildfire. Pretty soon we saw a number of comments on the forum praising the employee for the good work she had done and wishing her well. A manager called and requested that we remove the comments because they represented an "inappropriate use of the company resources." We disagreed. We believed that this type of communication helped company morale and that the subject of the comments was well within the scope of IBM business. We were sensitive to the manager's concerns, however, and strongly discouraged any future comments.

THE CHALLENGE

Aware of growing management sensitivity, Weis reflected on the importance of the conferences.

Today, IBMPC is well established in IBM. Nobody fully informed would think of taking it down. The increased access to computer terminals across IBM has fueled our growth. The use of the conference for sharing software has had a tremendous impact. IBMPC and many of the other conferences have come to be used for things we never even envisioned, like product development and sales support. But because of its size, it has attracted the attention of senior managers. Unfortunately, all they usually hear about are the complaints.

The Watson Center team believed that the positive aspects of IBMPC and other internal IBM conferences far outweighed any negative aspects, but nevertheless feared that some of the problems with the conference might elicit unnecessarily harsh management reaction. Consequently, the team advocated executive education, and was preparing a recommendation for a corporate position statement on computer conferencing.

In connection with this statement, Waldbaum wondered about the existing conference rules. "We know that our rules work for *us*," he explained, "but will they be applicable for all conferences in IBM? Should a corporate policy statement encompass all decisions, or should some be left to individual managers?" Waldbaum believed that, as the largest and most visible conference, IBMPC should be kept as clean as possible. "But should all conferences come under the same controls?" he wondered.

"Rules have to be enforced consistently and fairly," observed Chess. "You have to put in place no more than you can and are willing to enforce. I think that should be a guiding parameter in all our discussions." (Some of the issues and alternatives the team was considering are listed in *Exhibit 6*.)

SUMMARY

Watson Center team members believed that the success of many internal IBM conferences had been due, in large part, to the strong, voluntary support of the IBM technical and administrative communities, and they worried about losing that support should some of the conferences get "out of control." The team that its presentation to IBM's corporate executives would have to balance the need for control with the need for continued voluntary support from the user community.

"You can make arguments that conferencing activity is risky and should be stopped, but that's throwing the baby out with the bath water, because we know it's a useful and beneficial communication tool for the company," Weis explained. "At the other end, you can let all the conferences run rampant with little or no control, and just hope that everything turns out right. In between, you have various options of centralized and decentralized control."

"Up until now, some of the IBM conferences have been fairly loose in their management," Weis observed. "That's normal when you're starting out with a new technology. But we think it's time to step up to the issues and take a stand, a stand that will ensure that the conferences' benefits can continue while minimizing the problems and risks."

EXHIBIT 1   Selected Financial Data[a] (Dollars in millions except for per share amounts)

	1987		1986		1985	
Gross income		54,217		51,250		50,056
Cost of sales	17,332		16,197		14,911	
Cost of products, services	7,278		6,509		6,192	
Research, development, engineering expenses	5,434		5,221		4,723	
Interest expense	485		475		443	
Selling, general, and administrative expenses	16,431		15,464		13,000	
Other income		1,352		1,005		832
Earnings before taxes		8,609		8,389		11,619
Provision for income taxes	3,351		3,600		5,064	
Net earnings		5,258		4,789		6,555
Net earnings per share		$8.72		$7.81		$10.67
Current assets		31,020		27,749		26,070
Plants, equipment (net of depreciation)		22,922		21,268		19,680
Investments and other assets		9,746		8,797		6,884
Total Assets		63,688		57,814		52,634
Current liabilities		13,377		12,743		11,433
Long-term debt		3,858		4,169		3,955
Other liabilities		3,040		2,004		1,606
Deferred income taxes		5,150		4,524		3,650
Stockholders' equity		38,263		34,374		31,990
Total Liabilities and Stockholders' Equity		63,688		57,814		52,634

[a]Excerpts from the *IBM Annual Report*.

EXHIBIT 2 IBM Computer Conferencing

IBM Organization on January 28, 1988[a]

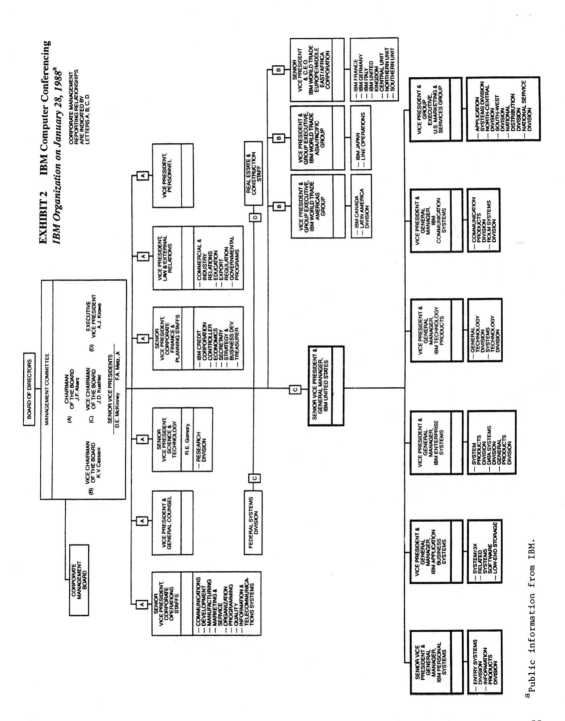

CORPORATE MANAGEMENT
REPORTING RELATIONSHIPS
ARE INDICATED BY
LETTERS A, B, C, D.

BOARD OF DIRECTORS

MANAGEMENT COMMITTEE

(A) CHAIRMAN OF THE BOARD J.F. Akers
(C) VICE CHAIRMAN OF THE BOARD J.D. Kuehler
(B) VICE CHAIRMAN OF THE BOARD K.V. Cassani
(D) EXECUTIVE VICE PRESIDENT A.J. Krowe

SENIOR VICE PRESIDENTS
D.E. McKinney   F.A. Metz, Jr.

CORPORATE MANAGEMENT BOARD

VICE PRESIDENT & GENERAL COUNSEL

SENIOR VICE PRESIDENT, SCIENCE & TECHNOLOGY
R.E. Gomory
— RESEARCH DIVISION

SENIOR VICE PRESIDENT, CORPORATE OPERATIONS STAFFS
— COMMUNICATIONS
— DEVELOPMENT
— MANUFACTURING
— MARKETING & SERVICE
— ORGANIZATION
— PROGRAMMING
— QUALITY
— INFORMATION & TELECOMMUNICATIONS SYSTEMS

SENIOR VICE PRESIDENT, CORPORATE FINANCE & PLANNING STAFFS
— IBM CREDIT CORPORATION
— CONTROLLER
— ECONOMICS
— SECRETARY
— STRATEGY & BUSINESS DEV.
— TREASURER

VICE PRESIDENT, LAW & EXTERNAL RELATIONS
— COMMERCIAL & INDUSTRY RELATIONS
— EDUCATION
— EXPORT REGULATION
— GOVERNMENTAL PROGRAMS

VICE PRESIDENT, PERSONNEL

REAL ESTATE & CONSTRUCTION STAFF

VICE PRESIDENT & GROUP EXECUTIVE, IBM WORLD TRADE AMERICAS GROUP
— IBM CANADA
— LATIN AMERICA DIVISION

VICE PRESIDENT & GROUP EXECUTIVE, IBM WORLD TRADE ASIA/PACIFIC GROUP
— IBM JAPAN
— LINE OPERATIONS

SENIOR VICE PRESIDENT & C.E.O. IBM WORLD TRADE EUROPE/MIDDLE EAST/AFRICA CORPORATION
— IBM FRANCE
— IBM GERMANY
— IBM ITALY
— IBM UNITED KINGDOM
— CENTRAL UNIT
— NORTHERN UNIT
— SOUTHERN UNIT

FEDERAL SYSTEMS DIVISION

SENIOR VICE PRESIDENT & GENERAL MANAGER, IBM UNITED STATES

SENIOR VICE PRESIDENT & GENERAL MANAGER, IBM PERSONAL SYSTEMS
— ENTRY SYSTEMS DIVISION
— INFORMATION PRODUCTS DIVISION

VICE PRESIDENT & GENERAL MANAGER, IBM APPLICATION BUSINESS SYSTEMS
— SYSTEM/3X
— RELATED PRODUCTS DIVISION
— SYSTEMS SOFTWARE
— LOW-END STORAGE

VICE PRESIDENT & GENERAL MANAGER, IBM ENTERPRISE SYSTEMS
— SYSTEM PRODUCTS DIVISION
— DATA SYSTEMS DIVISION
— GENERAL PRODUCTS DIVISION

VICE PRESIDENT & GENERAL MANAGER, IBM TECHNOLOGY PRODUCTS
— GENERAL TECHNOLOGY DIVISION
— SYSTEMS TECHNOLOGY DIVISION

VICE PRESIDENT & GENERAL MANAGER, IBM COMMUNICATION SYSTEMS
— COMMUNICATION PRODUCTS DIVISION
— ROLM SYSTEMS DIVISION

VICE PRESIDENT & GROUP EXECUTIVE, U.S. MARKETING & SERVICES GROUP
— APPLICATION SYSTEMS DIVISION
— NORTH-CENTRAL DIVISION
— SOUTH-WEST DIVISION
— NATIONAL DISTRIBUTION DIVISION
— NATIONAL SERVICE DIVISION

[a]Public information from IBM.

55

EXHIBIT 2 (continued)
IBM Organization Chart—Research Division[a] *(March 1988)*

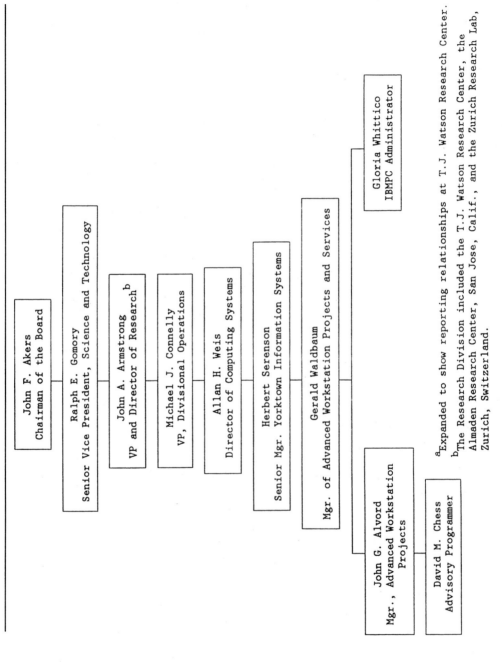

John F. Akers
Chairman of the Board

Ralph E. Gomory
Senior Vice President, Science and Technology

John A. Armstrong
VP and Director of Research[b]

Michael J. Connelly
VP, Divisional Operations

Allan H. Weis
Director of Computing Systems

Herbert Serenson
Senior Mgr. Yorktown Information Systems

Gerald Waldbaum
Mgr. of Advanced Workstation Projects and Services

Gloria Whittico
IBMPC Administrator

John G. Alvord
Mgr., Advanced Workstation Projects

David M. Chess
Advisory Programmer

[a]Expanded to show reporting relationships at T.J. Watson Research Center.
[b]The Research Division included the T.J. Watson Research Center, the Almaden Research Center, San Jose, Calif., and the Zurich Research Lab, Zurich, Switzerland.

EXHIBIT 3   IBM Computer Conferencing
Conference System Flow[a]

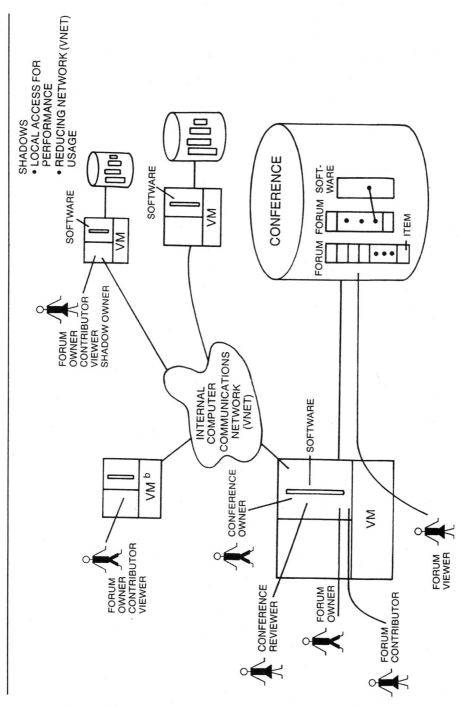

SHADOWS
• LOCAL ACCESS FOR PERFORMANCE
• REDUCING NETWORK (VNET) USAGE

SOFTWARE

VM

SOFTWARE

VM

FORUM
OWNER
CONTRIBUTOR
VIEWER
SHADOW OWNER

INTERNAL COMPUTER COMMUNICATIONS NETWORK (VNET)

VM[b]

FORUM
OWNER
CONTRIBUTOR
VIEWER

SOFTWARE

CONFERENCE
OWNER

CONFERENCE
REVIEWER

FORUM
OWNER

FORUM
CONTRIBUTOR

VM

FORUM
VIEWER

CONFERENCE

FORUM   FORUM   SOFT-
                WARE

ITEM

a Adapted from IBM internal documents.
b "Virtual Machine" operating system.

57

EXHIBIT 4   Excerpts from IBMPC Rules

- The information on IBMPC is for IBM business use only.
- The IBMPC conference is intended for peer-to-peer communications. It is not a substitute for official communication channels.
- Submitters agree that IBM is free to use internally, without obligation or charge, any information or software on IBMPC.
- IBMPC is not to be used for personal (nonbusiness-related) requests for information or for discussion of religion or politics.
- Submissions should be expressed with accepted business courtesy and good taste.
    - —No ethnic slurs, personal insults, obscenities
    - —No "letterwriting" campaigns
    - —Use of sarcasm and irony is strongly discouraged
- Use or copying of submitted information or software must not infringe any patents, copyrights, trade secrets, or similar rights of others. It is the responsibility of the submitter to ensure compliance with this rule.
- Unless special authorization is obtained from Patent Operations management, all authors of submitted information must be IBM employees.
- No copyrighted or third-party proprietary information is permitted on IBMPC without special arrangements.
- IBMPC is not to be used for personal profit. It is not to be used to advertise software, hardware, or books whose sale yields direct financial rewards to you.
- Submitted software and accompanying documentation must be labeled IBM INTERNAL USE ONLY and must not bear any non-IBM restrictive or proprietary legend.
- If you are the author of software which you have developed on your own time and your own equipment, you may put it on the IBMPC conference. By doing so, you are allowing IBM to make unlimited internal business use of that version of the software.

EXHIBIT 5   Sample Append and Answer

The New York City systems engineer appended the following:

DOSVSE FORUM appended at 19:18:24 on 87/08/04 GMT

I'm an SE here in NY supporting multiple 43XX accounts. One of my accounts is installing VM/SP version 4.2. We had our first pass yesterday and ran into some technical difficulties, but we believe those are solved now. The customer and myself have attended the VM Implementation Class and the last offering of the VM for VSE Users Class.

Right now I want to ask a general question. I somebody is running version 2.1.3, is there a reason for them to migrate to version 2.1.6 or whatever the latest version is? Does it buy them anything other than support for new devices? Where does service fit into this—i.e., if someone goes from version 2.1.3 to version 2.1.6, does that mean that all service between the two releases is automatically included?

He received the following response from West Germany:

DOSVSE FORUM appended at 14:28:45 on 87/08/05 GMT

The main reasons a customer would go from version 2.1.3 to version 2.1.6 are because:

A. There are problems on the system where corrections to the code have to be applied. Therefore, the service refresh provided in the latest version would update the entire system and not just a component.
B. The customer wants to take advantage of a new function provided in the refresh. For example in version 2.1.4, VSE provided significant improvements in the Intelligent Workstation Support area so that PCs could have access to temporary storage. There are enhancements in the refreshes that might be of interest. The enhancements are not as extensive as a version or release level, but warrant looking at.
C. Another reason would be the hardware support as you mentioned.
D. All or any combination of the above.

As for having to do a refresh, you can go directly from version 2.1.3 to version 2.1.6. The refresh process works very well.

I suggest that you look at the manual Hardware and System Support Extensions SC33-6184. It will highlight the main differences between the modification levels. It also goes in to detail on the functional aspects. Feel free to contact me directly using electronic mail if you need more help.

Steve

EXHIBIT 6   Issues and Alternatives

Issue	Alternatives
Should we have rules at all?	No rules—local managers have responsibility? Total corporate control—make rules and enforce them? Various alternatives between these two?
Will rules apply to all conferences?	Public conferences? Private Conferences? Determination based on number of participants?
Kinds of data allowed?	Security classifications for public, private conferences? • IBM Internal Use Only • IBM Confidential • IBM Confidential-Restricted • Registered IBM Confidential Copyrighted data? Company Assets? Fear of leaks/losses?
Creation of new forums on existing conferences?	Corporate Approval? Level of management approval? • None • 1st line manager • 2nd line manager • Executive Staff Approvals? • Information Systems • Legal and Patent • Personnel
Creation of new forums on existing conferences?	No approval required? User's manager's approval required? Conference owner's approval required?
Deletion of conferences and/or appends?	By whom? Approvals Required?
Review of Conference conversations?	Pre-Review of post-view?[a] Manager required to be reviewer? Management designee? Legal/personnel approval of reviewer? Different reviews for public/private or small/large conferences?
Communication of rules?	Corporate communications? Via the conference?
Formal agreement to rules?	Physical, written agreement required? Agreement required for each conference, or one for all? No formal agreement?

[a]"Pre-review" referred to the review of appends *before* they were placed on the conference itself. Most conferences used "post-review" procedures, which checked appends *after* they were added to the conference.

APPENDIX

Computer-Augmented Teamwork
Harvard Business School Course Materials

Cases and Teaching Notes

Center for Machine Intelligence:	9-189-135
Computer Support for Cooperative Work	Rev. 3/90

Cases and Teaching Notes *(con't)*

Frito-Lay, Inc.: A Strategic Transition (A)	9-187-065
	Rev. 1/88
Teaching Note	5-191-191
	Rev. 6/6/91
Frito-Lay, Inc.: A Strategic Transition (B)	9-187-123
	Rev. 5/24/91
Teaching Note Rev.	4/15/91
Frito-Lay, Inc.: A Strategic Transition (C)	9-190-071
	Rev. 5/24/91
Teaching Note	5-190-200
	Rev. 6/21/91
IBM Computer Conferencing	9-188-039
	Rev. 12/2/91
Teaching Note	5-192-074
Lockheed-Georgia Company:	9-187-135
Executive Information Systems	Rev. 7/89
Teaching Note	5-189-061
	Rev. 5/31/90
Phillips 66:	9-189-006
Executive Information System	Rev. 11/26/91
Teaching Note	5-189-072
	Rev. 5/2/91
Westinghouse Electric Corporation:	9-189-119
Automating the Capital Budgeting Process (A)	Rev. 2/90
Teaching Note	5-190-151
	Rev. 4/20/90
Westinghouse Electric Corporation:	9-190-068
Automating the Capital Budgeting Process (B)	
Westinghouse Electric Corporation:	9-189-120
Automating the Capital Budgeting Process (B1)	
Westinghouse Electric Corporation:	9-189-121
Automating the Capital Budgeting Process (B2)	
Westinghouse Electric Corporation:	9-189-122
Automating the Capital Budgeting Process (B3)	
Xerox Corporation: Executive Support System	9-189-134

	Rev. 3/28/90
Teaching Note	5-190-182

Notes

Executive Information Systems: Technology Overview	9-189-159
Information Technology and Managerial Effectiveness: Instructors Note	5-190-185

Videotapes

Center for Machine Intelligence: Electronic Meeting Support at GM/EDS	9-891-507
Frito-Lay, Inc.: The Information Revolution (restricted to academic use)	1-891-010
Phillips 66 Company: Executive Information System Interview with president Bob Wallace	9-890-510
Westinghouse Electric Corporation: Automating the Capital Budgeting Process (A1)	9-891-507
Westinghouse Electric Corporation: Automating the Capital Budgeting Process (A2)	9-890-520
Westinghouse Electric Corporation: Automating the Capital Budgeting Process (B)	9-890-521

Software (contact author)

Frito-Lay, Inc.: Decision Support System Demo
(requires access to Comshare EIS software-PC version)
Phillips 66: Executive Information System Demo

To order any of these materials (except software) contact Harvard Business School Publishing Division: Operations Department, Boston, MA 02163. FAX (617) 495-6985. Phone (617) 495-6117 or -6192 (please mention telephone code 126A when placing order).

Section II

Communication-Oriented Team Support

Soon, teams will have more choices about how, when, and under what conditions they choose to communicate with one another. With the introduction of broadband networks, they will be able to choose from several multimedia technologies that are capable of supporting any-time/any-place interaction.

The four chapters in this section cover research that primarily focuses on communication support. In each case, the researchers are working with systems developed to support their research agenda. Although they also study proximal and synchronous groups, it is their use of dispersed, and sometimes asynchronous, teams and their emphasis on communication that distinguishes them from the other chapters. Whereas the most common form of communication support for teamwork is electronic mail, each of these systems goes beyond merely facilitating the flow of information between two dispersed individuals. To varying degrees, they also provide structure to support both the communication and the group processes of all team members. Despite these similarities in their research, their work differs on two key dimensions: media richness and task interdependency.

A medium's richness is a measure of its capacity to facilitate shared meaning (Trevino, Daft, and Lengel 1990). It is influenced by the amount and form of information that a technology is capable of transmitting. For example, a medium that transmits only text is leaner than one that also supports audio and or video information. Of those systems discussed, US West's TeleCollaboration (Chapter 7) is the richest and includes audio, data, and motion video networks to support teams in multilocations. At the lean end, providing communication support primarily in the form of text, are New Jersey Institute of Technology (NJIT) (Chapter 4), Massachusetts Institute of Technology (MIT) (Chapter 5), and Queen Mary and Westfield College (QMW) (Chapter 6).

Task interdependency is an important distinguishing characteristic of the approaches taken by the research in this area. There are three types of task independencies: independent, pooled, and sequential (Thompson, 1967). An independent task can be performed by one person without interaction with anyone else. A pooled task requires two or more persons to interact in order to complete an activity. A sequential task demands that several people perform their respective tasks in sequence. The outputs of one task become the input to another.

Much of the work at MIT and QMW focuses on supporting sequential tasks that can be coordinated by electronic message exchange. Indeed, the MIT research is housed in the Center for Coordination Science, and Wilber and Dollimore describe how Cosmos can be used to coordinate the serial process of reviewing an academic paper. In contrast, NJIT and US West's research is directed more at pooled tasks. For example, NJIT's computer conferencing system, EIES, is used to fuse the collective thoughts of the participants.

Information overload is an implicit consideration of the research covered in three of the sites (NJIT, MIT, and QMW) and could soon be a factor in the other (U.S. West). The human capacity to process information is bounded and overload occurs when this limit is exceeded. Filtering and chunking, techniques for handling information overload, are used by some of the systems described in this section. For example, MIT's Information Lens system provides rules for filtering and sorting messages, and the communication structures of Cosmos are a form of chunking. NJIT'S EIES provides filtering, organizing, and scanning features as well as the capacity to create a hierarchical structure of conference topics. These facilities are all devices for reducing information overload.

The recognition of individual limits for dealing with information raises a number of questions. If one is able to reach quickly a position of information overload with a lean medium such as text, why hasn't this been a problem with the rich interchange used by U.S. West? Is it because all transmissions are real time, so that there is no storing and backlogging of information that one must deal with cumulatively? Is it because these are the early stages of this research, and the sheer number of messages has not been enough to trigger overload? Electronic mail is not a problem when we get five messages a day, but what happens when that number becomes 25 or 100? What will be the effect of getting 25 recorded video messages a day? Are we more able to process information through our visual channels? What if we are connected to five other research sites and are now expected to "come" to all of their meetings? Are we more likely to have information overload with multimedia dispersed groups than with lean media?

We are also seeing a movement by the researchers not only to expand the communication media they are using but also to build up support for goal-directed group tasks. Both MIT, through Object Lens, and NJIT, through EIES 2, have extended their capacity to support task-oriented groups.

Several conceptual models are introduced in this section. NJIT presents two key important concepts in its chapter. First, it introduces the notion that an object-oriented data base is a suitable foundation for developing team technology because it readily supports evolution of a system. Second, it details the Virtual Classroom, a new model for linking teachers and students. An important concept underlying the MIT work is the notion of semiformal computer systems, which occupy the middle ground between high (e.g., a transaction-processing application) and low (e.g., electronic mail) structure. Research at QMW is based on generically defining a communication structure through roles, actions, and types of messages, and these elements are the core of its conceptual model. The US West research is driven by understanding the factors that influence technology adoption, and its chapter discusses some of the key issues that influence adoption.

In summary, we see that there are five important distinctions in the research studies in this section. First, they all focus largely but not exclusively on communication. Second, the technological basis of the various systems varies in its degree of medium richness. Third, they support different task interdependencies. Fourth, they vary in their attention to and method of tackling information overload. Fifth, systems development is moving toward supporting any-time/any-place collaboration.

Chapter 4

Virtual Meetings: Computer Conferencing and Distributed Group Support

Starr Roxanne Hiltz and Murray Turoff

New Jersey Institute of Technology

INTRODUCTION

This chapter begins with an overview of our work on group support systems located within a computerized conferencing system, including the objectives and assumptions on which the research is based. It then expands two key ideas: Conferencing software can be structured in a variety of ways to fit different types of groups and tasks, and asynchronous (nonsimultaneous) communication presents both an opportunity to improve group processes and a design challenge.

The research facilities needed to study the interaction of software structures with the social context in which they are used consists of a tailorable software system. Examples are provided of several of the subsystems developed in such a "laboratory without walls," and the features of NJIT's current system, EIES 2, are described. Major sources of support for the research program are identified.

The second half of the chapter covers highlights of results of several research projects: longitudinal studies of user communities, experimental studies of synchronous group decision making, educational applications in a Virtual Classroom, and current work on distributed group support systems. Finally, plans for future research and development are described.

OVERVIEW

Facilities to support group work do not have to be physical; they can be constructed in software, or "virtual" structures, allowing participants to "meet" and work together through a computer-mediated communication system (CMCS). These systems use computers and telecommunications networks to compose, store, deliver, regulate, and process communication among the group members and between the computer and the group. Among the types of systems that come under this heading are electronic mail, computerized conferencing, and bulletin-board systems. The most common form of CMCS is electronic mail, or message systems that deliver primarily discrete text communications from a sender to one or more recipients by computer networks. Conferencing systems order and maintain a permanent data base of discussions and activities related to a task and are structured to support group work. Conferences have "memberships," and different members may have different roles, supported by software.

Our work on group support systems has focused on computer conferencing. Three main application areas have been of primary importance: medium to large scientific and professional communities (Hiltz 1984; Hiltz and Turoff, 1990); group decision support (Turoff, 1991; Turoff and Hiltz, 1982a); and educational delivery (Hiltz, 1986, 1992). The following are key aspects of our work on the design and evaluation of CMCS:

- The objective of CMCS is to provide an opportunity for a group to exhibit collective intelligence (Hiltz and Turoff, 1978). That is, the results of the group communication process are better than any single member of the group could have obtained alone.
- The major benefits offered by CMCS result from the ability to utilize the computer to tailor the communication structure to fit the nature of both the application and the group (Hiltz and Turoff, 1985).
- CMCS needs to support group communications 24 hours a day and offer the flexibility of being used synchronously or asynchronously. Individuals do not deal with problems only when they meet together as a group. Nor do they operate, in most situations, as only one group. In real organizations groups are very fluid in their nature, and the process is one of overlapping and intersecting subgroups.
- Appropriate communication structures are extremely sensitive to group norms and organizational culture.
- Both individual and group problem-solving requirements imply that one must integrate computer resources as part of the communication process (Turoff, 1971).
- Groups evolve their use of CMCS, and the development of new facilities must be part of a planned feedback process (Hiltz and Turoff, 1981; Turoff and Hiltz, 1982a).
- Human roles, and the computer support of human roles, are key factors in the success of group activities (Turoff, 1972, 1985).
- The privacy and security (as well as reliability) of human communications are essential to the acceptance of the system (Turoff, 1982).

The themes of the importance of structure and the advantages of providing the opportunity for asynchronous communication are expanded in the following sections.

STRUCTURES TO SUPPORT GROUP WORK

Colleagues who worked with us for several years, Peter and Trudy Johnson-Lenz (1982), created and defined the term *groupware*:

> Intentional GROUP processes and procedures to
> achieve specific purposes
> plus
> softWARE tools designed to support and facilitate
> the group's work.

A primary emphasis at NJIT has been the design and evaluation of a variety of such groupware structures to match the requirements of groups with different tasks, sizes, and social characteristics. Aspects of structure include the following:

- Linear vs. tree-shaped conferences. In a linear structure, each item is entered in the order in which it is submitted. All conference entries are at the same level. In a tree-shaped structure, responses to root items are attached. The number of levels may be limited by the software or branch in an unlimited number of hierarchical levels.
- Processing supports. Data bases and facilities to support numerical processing and displays may be integrated with the text discussions.
- Filtering, organizing, and scanning features and/or agents, such as key words, associations, and text searches. These may act on either an individual or group support basis.
- Length limitations. Limits may be set on root conference items, such as 15 lines or 50 lines, in order to encourage concise communications.
- Privileges associated with roles in a conference. These may be set by the software. For example, a conference moderator or leader may have the privilege not only to add or delete members and to read or write comments but also to edit any item or change its key words or to select what special tools or features will be available in the conference.
- Pen names and anonymity. Are they permitted, or are all entries automatically signed with the name of the author?
- Knowledge-type data structures. These allow groups to contribute and gather complex viewpoints according to specialized categories, as in the Delphi Process (Linstone and Turoff, 1975).
- Sequential or ordered steps: The system may require facilities or items to be utilized in a certain order by the group. For example, members of a conference may have to vote individually before being able to view voting results. At the extreme, an agenda may be established that leads individuals through several sequential steps in a problem-solving process rather than permitting free discussion.

Many CMCS have a single structure or set of tools, which may fit some groups and tasks but not others. Structures should be "tailorable," so that different groups and conferences using the same system can each employ a set of tools and procedures that best fits its task. This is the design challenge for the current generation of CMCS.

ASYNCHRONOUS COMMUNICATION

The most misunderstood concept in CMCS is the view that an asynchronous (or nonsimultaneous) communication process is a problem because it is not the sequential process that people use in the face-to-face mode. The approach "How do we make CMCS feel to the user like face-to-face processes?" is incorrect. The real issue is "How do we use the opportunity of asynchronous communications to create a group process that is actually better than face-to-face group communications?"

The primary advantage of using CMCS to support group processes is not that people can engage in the process whenever it is convenient for them. It lies in the very fundamental asynchronous nature of the communication medium. Many of the current design philosophies attempt to maintain the sequential nature of the process that groups go through in face-to-face settings, assuming that this is the correct approach. On the contrary, the potential for real improvement in group processes lies in the fact that individuals can concentrate on the part of the problem they can contribute to at a given time, regardless of where the other individuals are in the group process. In addition, the computer can provide interventions to lessen process losses (Steiner, 1972).

The rigid specification of a group process may conflict with the ways in which specific individuals can best contribute to the task. The resulting opportunity for asynchronous approaches to group problem solving is to free the individual to deal with the problem in ways consistent with his or her cognitive style. The resulting design challenge is to provide the communication structures to allow for synchronization of the group process and the organization of the material for the benefit of the group.

RESEARCH FACILITIES AND SUPPORT

The physical facilities to support the research consist of an adequate number and size of computers to support development work as well as experiments and field trials. Over the years, this equipment has involved a number of minicomputers; currently, we have systems running on Hewlett Packard minicomputers, several SUN workstations, and an IBM AIX workstation. The systems themselves are laboratories without walls, which can be entered from anyplace in the world, using a personal computer, a modem, and a telephone. We also have a small collaborative systems laboratory, with seven workstations, for training experimental subjects.

The Computerized Conferencing and Communications Center at the New Jersey Institute of Technology was established in 1974, based on the following premises about the environment necessary to advance the state of the art in using computers to facilitate group communication:

- The design of the system, the social context of the group, and the nature of the application interact to determine success or failure in the use of this technology.
- Understanding the relationship between the design and the social context requires evaluation of the technology in real-world settings.
- Evolution of the technology must occur, based on feedback from the evaluation of its impact in these field trials.

EIES

Based on these premises, the center established the Electronic Information Exchange System (EIES 1) in 1976 to create an environment for both developing the technology and studying its impact. EIES 1 was made available to groups from industry, government, nonprofit organizations, and academia. EIES 1 averaged about 2,000 users a year from its inception until its current phaseout in 1991. Many existing commercial systems (e.g., Participate) evolved from prototype special communication structures first implemented and field-tested under instrumental conditions in the EIES 1 environment. Many of the features and facilities in other commercial systems can be traced back to prototypes in the EIES 1 environment.

Over 25 special subsystems were developed on EIES from 1976 to 1987. Each represented a special structure and set of tools for specific types of group tasks. Among those worthy of note are the following:

1. TERMS: The Joint Electron Device Engineering Council (JEDEC) uses EIES for selected aspects of its work of promoting hardware and software standardization in microcomputer and large-scale integration products. JEDEC's standardization activities are conducted by a series of committees, which ordinarily communicate only through quarterly face-to-face meetings, with phone and/or mail in between. A great deal of JEDEC's work in reaching standards that will obtain the required unanimous approval of its members involves first reaching agreement on a set of terms and definitions that apply to a given topic. In addition to free-form discussions in conferences, a structured decision aid was programmed to support the process of developing and reaching agreement on such a standard set of terms and definitions (Johnson-Lenz, Johnson-Lenz, and Hessman, 1980). Called TERMS, this system allows any member of a committee to

• Add a proposed term (abbreviation and full name) to a list
• Add a proposed alternative definition anonymously to a list
• Make a comment about the desirability of a given definition
• Vote on each proposed term and definition
• Revote at any time, based on current votes and new alternatives

The set of items contained in the TERMS subsystem for any specific standards effort was called a Glossary and was maintained as a separately organized data base, associated with the group's conference.

2. RESOURCES: This is a data-base subsystem that allows for the mixing of qualitative and quantitative information in specified formats for both creation and retrieval. The unique feature of RESOURCES is that it was designed to handle the problem of a group of individuals gathering and validating entries to a data base. Therefore, all entries are identified by who is contributing them, and it is possible to associate comments with any entry in the data base.

3. REPORTS: This is a group-oriented authoring system that provides the ability to establish outlines of a report and signify different roles for individuals at every major point in the outline. Therefore, one can assign authorship, editing, contributing, and

organizing privileges to different individuals at different places in the planned report. This system follows many ideas in Englebart's (1973; Englebart, Watson, and Norton, 1976) work in collaborative composition and adds very explicit role structures for editing, organizing, and producing the resulting documents.

4. TOPICS: This system (Johnson-Lenz and Johnson-Lenz, 1981) was designed to handle unpredictable information exchange, in which a large group of people (100 or more) are involved in trying to exchange information. Every member of the network is allowed to send three line inquiries to every other member. Each recipient of an inquiry can decide whether to track future responses to the question. Responses can be supplied by any member but have to be limited to one page. There is a human indexer who has the software-supported power to keep all the keys consistent. A human editor has the job of collecting the responses, eliminating duplications, and developing summary briefs. The inquiries, responses, and briefs go into a data base structure for later retrieval.

5. SURVEY: This is a complete system for doing surveys and allows those taking the survey to get summaries of the results (Hiltz, 1979). In one specialized evaluation application, we put up a standardized psychological test and gave the user an assessment of his or her personality type.

6. ZBB and GDSS: One of the most important systems built as part of EIES is an asynchronous version of zero-based budgeting (ZBB) (Bahgat 1986). ZBB has largely been a failure in the face-to-face mode because of the huge amount of communication requirements it normally adds to the already top-heavy budgeting process. The CMCS was utilized quite successfully by about 30 people to allocate $1.5 million of capital budget funding without a single face-to-face meeting of the group. This research demonstrated that an approach to budget planning that was difficult to use in the face-to-face mode could be better utilized in the CMCS asynchronous mode.

7. DECISION SUPPORT TOOLS and PROCESSES: In one experiment, a special structure was created that led the participants through 57 steps, from introducing themselves to one another and receiving their task through agreement on a solution. Among the special tools was a rank-ordering routine to help the group understand its preference structure and real-time alerts whenever a group member changed his or her vote. The various decision support structures experimented with on EIES 1 were generally employed in a same-time/different-place mode.

Another important and unique aspect of EIES 1 is that it includes extensive monitoring facilities for evaluation research. In addition to recording the number and length of each type of communication written and read by each member, it includes the ability to generate a "who-to-whom" matrix of message traffic for each group and a conference participation analysis that gives the number and percentage of comments for each member for a requested time period.

The key observation about all these specialized structures on EIES is that they went through considerable design evolution. Both user participation in design conference discussions and feedback from the users of the prototypes were used to tailor the structures to the needs of the users. Another important finding is that it is possible to use the technology as a tool to better understand individual and group problem-solving processes (Hiltz, Turoff, and Johnson, 1982a).

EIES 2

Approximately five years ago, the Center decided it had learned most of what could be learned from the single central computer environment, which was the foundation of the internal EIES 1 design. The decision was made to begin the design and implementation of a new generation of the technology that would be suitable for a distributed network environment and also incorporate what we had learned about the functionality necessary to support the group communication process.

Following our original philosophy, it was also decided to create this new system as a product, so that it could provide field inputs from a wide variety of groups and applications as well as allowing usage by large populations. There was also the consideration that an outstanding product in this area would provide a degree of financial stability for the research program. EIES 2 operates within the UNIX environment and has been leased or distributed to a number of sites. An additional important factor was the necessity for this new system to serve as our research platform for continued evolution of the technology.

The combination of these factors led to a number of key design decisions that makes EIES 2 a system with a foundation that will allow continued evolution and the incorporation of additional functionality.

- EIES 2 is based on an object-oriented data base and a compiler for the X.409 communication data base specification language. This system allows the evolution of new object types as they are needed.
- EIES 2 internally utilizes X.400 data specifications.
- EIES 2 has its own Remote Operations Server for every User Agent and Group Agent. The ROS design conforms to the X.400 standard.
- The system is written in C, and includes a SMALLTALK Interpreter used as the specification language for the interface and for integration work with other computer resources.

The basic facilities and types of communication objects included and planned in EIES 2 are shown in Table 4-1. Many of these objects should be clear to anyone who has had some experience with CMCS technology (Turoff, 1989; Turoff et. al., 1989). However, ACTIVITIES is a concept that is very new and not explicitly present in other current systems.

Activities on EIES 2

One of the necessities for a CMCS system to service group-oriented objectives is the integration of other computer resources within the CMCS environment. This requirement means that the following types of capabilities must be available:

- Decision support tools collect, process, and display votes, such as weighting, ranking, or yes-no straw votes on options.

TABLE 4-1   EIES 2 STRUCTURE

Object	Explanation
Members	The users of the system
Personal index	To track items
Roles	Privilege collections
Groups	Super members of the system
Membership list	Status of all members
Group index	Shared by all members
Group conference	Owned by group
Group messages	Sent and received to group
Conferences	Topic communication space
Membership list	Status of all members
Conference index	Comment keys
Comments	Entries in a conference
Replies	To higher-level comment
Attachments	Passive file attached to comment
Activities	Executable programs (e.g., voting)
Directory	Of members, groups, and conferences
Interest index	Member interests and message-sending key
Topic index	Group and conference topics
Messages	Private, group, and public
Notifications	Transaction notices
Forms	Structured data collection
Lists	Labeled collections of items
Index entries	
Reference keys	Pointers to items
Filters	Screening terms
Labels	Substitutions for commands or strings

- Members of a CMC system should be able to bring data from other data bases into the communication environment.
- Members must be able to trigger the execution of programs that support the group process and obtain the results of these programs within the conferencing environment.

There are many approaches to integration with the underlying technology. We utilize the metaphor of an activity that can be attached to any communication item, such as a comment or message. This activity, when triggered or accomplished, will execute a program or procedure on the host computer or the network of computers. Unlike EIES 1, in which each special structure for computer support had its own commands and interface, every executable program made available in EIES 2 is an activity, and the basic activity menu (Create, Do, Modify, View) applies to all of them. Some examples of activities that are available or under development on EIES 2 include the following:

1. List-gathering activity: An example of a necessary activity is the ability to collect collaboratively a list of structured items and to treat this collection as one type of list. One list is the table of contents of a document, such as the document the group is trying to create. Another type is a set of tasks to be accomplished. In addition, there could be lists of issues to address, terms to define, alternative criteria for a decision, possible solutions to a problem, and so on.

The person creating an activity has to have control over when certain actions are allowed. For example, if people are contributing to the list, the owner of the activity should be able to do such things as close it to further contributions. The owner should be able to open, at the right time, certain other actions that can take place on an existing list:

- Associate a voting scale with items on the list, which may be of a number of different types, for example, a simple yes-no vote or an arbitrary 1 to 7 scale, which can be used to measure consensus on such dimensions as agreement, feasibility, importance, and so on.
- Allow other text items to be associated with the items on the list, such as in the actual drafting of entries for the table of contents.
- Freeze contributions at any time and edit and reorganize the list.
- Allow selections of responsibility for items on the list, such as in voluntary task assignment.
- Control a person's access to the activity before he or she has made a contribution to it.
- Open the activity to access by others who are not part of the original group developing the contents of the activity.

Many types of activities are possible, both of a very general and a very specific nature. Whatever the nature of a specific activity, it is important that this facility can track its status for both individuals and the group. The leaders of facilitators of a group need to know who in the group has or has not completed a given activity. Also, the system should have facilities for sending automatic reminders to anyone who has not done a particular activity.

The concept of activities within a CMCS is open-ended and represents one of the primary mechanisms for future extensions to EIES 2. What is crucial is that the incorporation of a wide range of tailored facilities to support an application must be provided through a common interface metaphor, with the same command functions and object definitions applying to the whole set. This is the only way that all the members of the group can quickly acquire and learn the tools as they are carrying out the application.

2. Gradebook activity: This is essentially a spreadsheet with privileges, created for the Virtual Classroom project. The rows are student members of the system; the columns are grades. The instructor has the privilege of defining the grades and their weights, entering and modifying grades (numbers in the spreadsheet), and seeing anybody's average at any time. Students have the privilege of seeing their own grades and weighted average and the total for the entire class. When new grades are entered in the Gradebook, notification is automatically sent to the students.

This is a particular collaborative spreadsheet structure for a specific purpose; slightly different spreadsheet activities could be made available for such tasks as budgeting or planning. Allowing different individuals to make different estimates of the same budget items is one such example.

3. Question response activity: This is similar in function to the nominal group technique. Each member of the conference must respond to the question before being able to view the responses of others. This requirement ensures independent thinking on the issue before the participants are influenced by the views of others. It also enforces equal participation.

RESOURCE SUPPORT

The Computerized Conferencing and Communications Center has applied for and received over 20 grants and contracts over the years. Major support ($500,000 or more) has been received from the National Science Foundation, the Annenberg/CPB project, the New Jersey Commission on Science and Technology, the New Jersey Department of Higher Education, and IBM. In addition, substantial awards of funds or equipment have been made by Apple Computer, Hewlett Packard, and the U.S. Department of Defense. Currently, support for research on distributed group support systems is being provided by the National Science Foundation. The center continues to seek support for research and development from public agencies, private foundations, and industry.

Funds for operational expenses such as equipment maintenance, communications charges, and support personnel are also generated by membership and use charges for the versions of the systems operated by NJIT and by software leases and maintenance. NJIT has frequently provided support for operating expenses, when revenues have been insufficient to cover expenses; in the form of matching funds for grants and contracts.

COMPLETED RESEARCH

User Communities

One line of research has been studies of user communities on EIES and other CMCS. The objective has been to describe the nature of social interaction on these systems and the interaction of software features, group size, and task. As part of that effort all the prior work in this area was summarized in a resulting book (Kerr and Hiltz, 1982), which gathered the results of all the efforts in the design and evaluation of CMCS to that time.

The funding for the initial development of EIES came from the National Science Foundation in 1976 for the support of scientific research communities. On-line Communities (Hiltz, 1984) describes the long-term impacts of the system on research and development communities that range in size from 10 to almost 200. This study was followed by a four-system, longitudinal study of "determinants of acceptance of computer-mediated communication systems." The study documented how characteristics of the users, the system, and the task or application interact to influence whether or not invited users will become dropouts (Hiltz, 1989), the extent to which CMCS is "productivity enhancing" (Hiltz, 1988), and user satisfaction (Hiltz and Johnson, 1990).

Synchronous Decision Experiments

Our initial studies of the use of computerized conferencing as a group decision support system used groups that participated at the same time but from different locations. It is not possible to get true control for asynchronous groups, and we wished to discover how communications process and decision outcome varied between face-to-face groups and computer-mediated groups when everything else was held constant (Turoff and Hiltz, 1982a). The three experiments followed a logical progression, as follows.

The first experiment compared the process and outcome of face-to-face versus unstructured computerized conferences. By "unstructured," we mean that the participants were not given any decision support tools to aid either their group process or their ability to analyze the data generated during the process. The subjects were college students, so that the experiment could be conducted in laboratory facilities (one-way mirrors, extensive recording equipment, etc.). Basically, we found no difference in the quality of decision between the two modes but less likelihood that the CMCS groups could reach complete consensus on a decision. We also observed substantial differences in the communication process, as measured by Bales Interaction Process Analysis (Hiltz et al., 1981; Hiltz, Johnson, and Turoff, 1986).

The second experiment in this series moved out into the field for one-day problem-solving exercises. The subjects were managers and staff in business, government, and academic bureaucracies. It replicated all of the procedures for one of the conditions in the first experiment but also introduced two structures to support decision making in the CMCS environment, in a factorial design. The first structure was the designation by the group of a formal leader, with explicit rights and responsibilities for facilitating the group. The second was statistical feedback: the aggregation and tabular display of voting results on the group decision. We observed a strong interaction between these two structures in examining the two main dependent variables, group consensus on a decision and quality of the group decision. Either the human leader or the statistical feedback, alone, improved consensus, but together they did not. Statistical feedback in the absence of a human leader was detrimental to a group decision that exemplified collective intelligence (operationalized as a group decision better than the quality of the decision reached by the "best" group member before discussion) (Hiltz, Johnson, and Turoff 1991).

The third experiment used groups of executives who were attending a training course, employees of an organization with a strong corporate culture. It compared face-to-face groups, computerized conferencing groups for which the participants' names were identified, and conferencing groups for which pen names were used. The tasks used could show "risky" or "conservative" shifts by the participants in order to attain a desirable objective. Contrary to some previous experiments by others employing students as subjects, the use of pen names (a form of anonymity) did not result in any great amount of "flaming" or disinhibition among the corporate users. Pen-named conferences showed consistent, but statistically insignificant tendencies toward less disagreement about the final group choice, more participation, and greater equality of participation. The final group choices were significantly more conservative in the pen-name computer conferences the conservative corporate subculture (Hiltz, Turoff, and Johnson, 1985, 1989).

EDUCATIONAL APPLICATIONS:
THE VIRTUAL CLASSROOM

One type of work that can be done more effectively in teams than alone is learning (Bouton and Garth, 1983; Collier, 1980). A long-term project of the conferencing center has been the design and evaluation of software and appropriate pedagogical procedures to facilitate the delivery of college and high-school level courses on-line. A Virtual Classroom is a teaching and learning environment located in a computer-mediated communication system. Rather than being built of bricks and boards, it consists of a set of group communication and work "spaces" and facilities constructed in software.

Prototypes of Virtual Classroom software features were first created and evaluated within EIES 1 and were then incorporated into EIES 2, mainly as activities. Some of these communication structures resemble facilities or procedures used in traditional classrooms. For example, Personal TEIES is a PC-based front end that resembles a blackboard. Like a blackboard, it allows diagrams to be mixed with text and transmitted to others, who can modify the diagrams. Other Virtual Classroom facilities support forms of interaction that would be difficult or impossible in the face-to-face environment Table 4-2. All are accessed not by traveling to a university but by typing and reading from a personal computer that connects by telephone to a mini- or a mainframe computer operating the Virtual Classroom software. Participation is asynchronous; that is, the Virtual Classroom participants dial in at any time around the clock and from any location in the world accessible by a reliable telephone system.

The objectives of the Virtual Classroom are as follows:

- To improve access to advanced educational experiences by allowing students and instructors to participate in remote learning communities at times and places convenient to them, using personal computers at home, on a campus, or at work
- To improve the quality and effectiveness of education by using the computer to support a collaborative learning process

Collaborative learning is defined as a learning process that emphasizes group or cooperative efforts among faculty and students. It stresses active participation and interaction on the part of both students and instructors. Knowledge is gained through an active dialogue in which those participants share their ideas and information.

The initial evaluation objectives were to describe the nature of the educational experiences and outcomes in this delivery mode, to compare them to the traditional (physical) classroom, and to determine those conditions associated with good or poor outcomes. To explore these questions, it was necessary to observe a variety of courses, students, and implementation environments. The primary research design rested on matched but nonequivalent sections of the same course taught on-line and in the traditional classroom. Although the same teacher, text and other printed materials, and midterm and final exams were used, the classes were nonequivalent because the students were able to self-select the delivery mode. We also looked at some mixed-mode courses and, at some distance, education courses that did not have a matched traditional section.

TABLE 4–2   Some Communication Structures in the Virtual and Traditional Classrooms

Virtual Classroom Software Feature	Function	Traditional Classroom Equivalent
Conferences	Class discussion & lectures	Classroom
Messages	"Private" student-student & student-teacher discussions	Office hours "Hallway" conversations Telephone calls
Notebooks	Individual & working groups composition & storage of documents	Paper & ring-binders word processor & diskette
Document read activity	Scan & read "published" material"	Books & Journals
"Personal TEIES"	Create, modify & share diagrams	Blackboard
Exam	Timed student-teacher feedback with no other communication permitted during test taking	Exam
Gradebook	Teacher may record & change grades and averages; students may access only his/her grades	Gradebook (paper)
Pen-names & Anonymity	Encourage self-disclosure and experimentation	
Response Activity	Force independent thinking & active participation	
Selection Activity	Manage distribution of unique assignments	Circulate sign-up sheets
Directory	Self-supplied description of status and interests; telephone & mailing contact information; last time online; online groups the member belongs to.	

All together, we collected data from a total of 132 students in completely on-line courses, 96 in mixed-mode courses, and 89 in traditional or control courses. Most of the data used in the study were collected with a pre- and postcourse questionnaire. However, we also have behavioral data (including grades and SAT scores, when appropriate or available, and amount and type of on-line activity) and qualitative observations and interviews. Detailed descriptions of the software, methodology, and findings can be found in the book on this project (Hiltz, 1992).

The results of the field trials we conducted between 1985 and 1991 are generally positive; that is, they support the conclusion that the Virtual Classroom mode of delivery can increase access to and the effectiveness of college-level education. The following is a summary of some of the major findings comparing the Virtual Classroom (VC) to the traditional classroom (TC).

• Mastery: There were few significant differences in scores measuring the Mastery of material taught in the virtual and traditional classrooms. In computer science and management courses (Hsu, 1992), grades were significantly better in the VC section, but in others there was no significant difference.

- Student preference: VC students perceived it to be superior to the TC on a number of dimensions:
  —Convenient access to educational experiences
  —Increased participation in a course
  —Improved ability to apply the material of the course in new contexts and express their own independent ideas relating to the material, most likely to occur in mixed-mode courses
  —Improved access to their professor
  —Computer comfort: improved attitudes toward and greater knowledge of the use of computers
  —Improved overall quality, whereby the student assesses the experience as being better than the TC in some way, involving learning more on the whole or getting more out of the course

Although the average results supported these conclusions, there was a great deal of variance in outcomes, particularly among courses. Generally, whether or not these outcomes occur depends more on variations among courses than on variations among modes of delivery. The totally on-line upper-level courses at NJIT, the courses offered to remote students, and the mixed-mode courses were most likely to result in student perceptions of the Virtual Classroom as being better in any of these senses.

It was hypothesized that those students who experience group learning in the Virtual Classroom are most likely to judge the outcomes of on-line courses to be superior to the outcomes of traditional courses. This view was supported by both correlational analysis of survey data and qualitative data from individual interviews. Those students who experienced high levels of communication with other students and with their professor (who participated in a group learning approach to their coursework) were most likely to judge the outcomes of VC courses to be superior to those of traditionally delivered courses.

DISTRIBUTED GROUP SUPPORT SYSTEMS AND COLLABORATIVE SYSTEMS

Our current efforts focus on the asynchronous or distributed group process, whether this is decision making or the production of some sort of group product. This project, funded primarily by the National Science Foundation (NSF), is an integrated program of theory building, software tool development and assessment, and controlled experiments in an area of collaboration technology that we call distributed group support systems. Such a system embeds group decision support system (GDSS) tools and procedures a computer-mediated communication system.

Distributed has several meanings: temporal, spatial, and technological. The central interest of the program of study is asynchronous groups, in which interaction is distributed in time as well as in space. The group members use the system to work together to reach a decision or complete their cooperative work over a period of time, each person working at whatever time and place is convenient. Though we may use more than one computer system for comparison purposes, the chief vehicle for the research is EIES 2. Distributed systems raise special problems of social and technical coordination. The iterative program of research will seek to identify and solve some of these problems.

The primary objective of the project is to build a general theory, supported by empirical evidence, that will enable us to understand how characteristics of the communications mode, structuring of the group process, and software tools interact with characteristics of the group and its task to affect the process and outcome of decision making. The interdisciplinary, multi institutional effort will build on previous GDSS research in "decision rooms," particularly at Minnesota. It aims to extend theory significantly, software tools, and empirical evidence by focusing on the asynchronous environment and comparing it to other conditions for computer-mediated group support. Among those actively involved in the project are Scott Poole of Minnesota and Ronald Rice of Rutgers University.

Building a Theoretical Framework

The first task of the project is to arrive at a theoretical framework that specifies the main variables to be measured and/or manipulated. This theoretical framework, with its associated empirical measures of the variables, will guide the program of research; will enable us to compare the results of different experiments conducted within the project; and will allow us to contrast them to the results of other experiments that have used some of the same variables, particularly at Minnesota.

Our theoretical model started with an expansion of the model proposed by DeSanctis and Gallupe (1987), which asserts that the types of GDSS tools and procedures that will be beneficial depend upon three variables: Communications mode, group size, and task type. The task type classification was developed by McGrath (1984). Two modes of communication were present in the Minnesota framework: face to face (decision room) and dispersed (two or more linked decision rooms). The framework will be expanded and refined as our empirical results and theoretical understanding progress.

Our expanded theoretical framework first adds a third communications mode, asynchronous. Asynchronous use of GDSS tools and processes is in practice a different mode of communication than same-time use. It leads to different communications behavior (such as the tendency toward much longer entries by participants) and to some unique coordination problems (such as what to do about "absent" members who are lagging behind the group). Members meeting at the same time in decision rooms can coordinate their use of the technology in a much more natural or intuitive way than those whose only channel of communication is through the computer. Along with the provision of the tools themselves in a dispersed or distributed environment, there must be facilities for meta communication about when and how the tools will be used and/or for automatic sequencing of the order of use, based on preset criteria.

The effect of a particular group support system on group coordination and decision making can be understood on a theoretical basis only by examining how its use tends to change the process of group communication, and through changes in process, leads to differences in outcomes. The system is a particular combination of the communication medium (same place vs. dispersed, synchronous vs. asynchronous), GDSS tools, and the structuring of process through a facilitator or instructions/agenda, plus the hardware that presents the system to the user.

The theoretical framework that will guide the research is shown in Figure 4-1. We have also developed an initial set of research instruments (questionnaires and planned procedures for measuring process and outcome). These instruments and procedures will be further refined as a result of pilot tests for the first few experiments. Methodologies suitable for the study of decision rooms will need to be modified to be appropriate for the study of distributed systems.

The Experimental Program

The actual experiments in the project are designed and carried out by Ph.D. students, under the direction of the principal investigator and other professionals. The Ph.D. students are recruited primarily from the joint NJIT/Rutgers program in management of computer systems. Interested students first enroll officially in a seminar, where they develop their ideas for a proposal and complete a first draft of the literature review and plans for research. Subsequently, participating students continue to attend the seminar as they further develop their final proposal, begin software development, and conduct pilot studies and then experiments and analysis. Their progress and problems are shared with and discussed by the members of the seminar, as well as with their primary dissertation advisor.

Students first select a task type. Note that besides the classification based on McGrath (1984), we are also interested in variations along the dimensions of difficulty and equivocality. The students then propose a set of tools or processes that are hypothesized to improve the performance of distributed groups undertaking that type of task. The tools are programmed in Smalltalk on EIES 2. The students do some of their own coding, with the advice and assistance of James Whitescarver, the EIES 2 project director at NJIT.

In choosing the experimental design as part of the proposal, one of the variables is generally the use or non use of the special software tools developed. The student then picks one or two other independent variables for manipulation. The most usual design will be a 2 by 2 factorial. Those independent variables not manipulated are either controlled (held constant, e.g., by group size) or measured to be used as covariates. One or more pilot studies are undertaken for each experiment, to test the tools, procedures, instructions, and measurement instruments.

Thus far, four students have decided to join the project and are in the process of writing their proposals. The first experiment, to be conducted by Donna Dufner, will replicate a task (an allocation task called "the foundation") and set of procedures used at Minnesota in several studies. Software coding is almost completed for several tools that replicate some of the functionality in the SAMM system used at Minnesota: the ability of a group to build a common list of options and then to apply several possible voting scales to the items on that list (yes-no, vote for one, or ratings on a scale from 1 to 100). Besides the availability or nonavailability of these tools, the second variable to be

Theoretical Framework: Distributed Group Support Systems

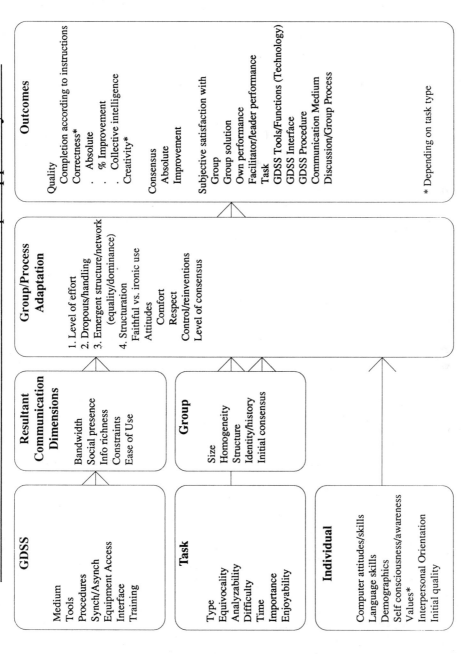

FIGURE 4-1. Theoretical Framework: Distributed Group Support Systems

manipulated for Dufner's experiment is a sequential vs. asynchronous agenda or procedure. The sequential groups will be required to complete each step in the process provided (define the problem, define criteria for a good solution, generate possible solutions, and arrive at agreement on a solution) before going on to the next step. The asynchronous agenda groups will be permitted to work on any step of the process at any time, with the instruction that they must complete all the steps before their task is completed. In both conditions, groups will be given one week to complete their task. Two sets of pilot studies have been completed for this experiment (Dufner and Hiltz, 1991; Hiltz et al., 1991).

Also scheduled to be run shortly as part of this project is an experiment by Ajaz Rana. The task will be peer review (ratings and selection of articles or proposals). A polling activity has been constructed to support this experiment, in which any Likert-type, semantic differential, or nominal scale can be constructed and grouped into an on-line poll to support the group in its efforts to select the "best" article or proposal from a number of options and to identify the strengths and weaknesses of each of the candidates. Group decisions can be compared to expert opinion as a criteria for the correctness of the decision made by the group.

A recently completed thesis deals with the development of a knowledge structure to support collaborative Hypertext (Rao, 1991; Rao and Turoff, 1990; Turoff, Rao, and Hiltz, 1991). Such a framework is intended to allow groups dealing with a complex body of knowledge to contribute their views and information to the group. The existence of a general structure would avoid the problem of having a different system for every type of application area.

FUTURE RESEARCH DIRECTIONS

The research program is tied to both a Ph.D. in management offered jointly with Rutgers (with a concentration in information systems) and a Ph.D. in computer science. As a result, we expect a continued balance in research between the development of the technology and the evaluation of applications. Systematic collection of data from users will be the basis for improvements in both functionality and usability.

With respect to the nature of the applications, the following is a reasonable projection for the next three years because it reflects already funded research projects and thesis work that is currently underway or beginning.

- The development of the technology to service education missions will certainly be a primary component, based on both NJIT's commitment to the use of this technology for education and the focus and resources of the Annenberg/CPB-funded Virtual Classroom project. We intend to continue experiments with gaming supported by the Virtual Classroom; a current thesis will develop and apply a multigroup auditing game (Worell, 1991). Other applications are exploring multimedia courses, which combine the conferencing facility with video (broadcast or taped), audio-graphics real-time conferencing, and/or additional PC-based tools.
- Both the interest of a great many of our management Ph.D. students and our current

NSF-funded three-year effort on Distributed Group Support Systems in the EIES 2 environment mean that software tools for asynchronous group decision support will also be a primary focus of the research program of the center. The products of this R&D will be useful for many managerial applications.

- The concept of Hypertext has always been an integral feature of computer-mediated communications. Conferencing structures may be viewed as specialized collaborative Hypertext structures. We currently have a number of thesis efforts beginning to focus on the concept of evolving Hypertext functionalities with CMCs suitable for the support of Collaborative Composition and knowledge collection efforts on the part of groups. We see this as a core facility for Collaborative Expert Systems, which would be continually updated and utilized by expert groups in an evolving field of knowledge.
- The development of evaluation tools and methodologies to increase understanding of the impact of this technology has always been, and will continue to be, an active endeavor. Determining the real nature of productivity changes and how to measure them in a network of communicating humans is still a fundamental challenge.
- Gaming takes on a new dimension when it is possible for players to participate asynchronously and it also becomes possible to replicate realistic communication constraints. We have explored and documented the benefits of this type of gaming in the management educational environment. Further work will be oriented not only toward education but also toward the possibility of gaming as a decision analysis tool.

These above are the areas that will lead to increased functionality of the EIES 2 system in the next two or three years. As in the past, what happens after that will be greatly influenced by demand and supply. The "demands" are the priorities expressed by the EIES 2 user community for new features and the research questions we are interested in pursuing. The "supply" is the availability of funding (through contracts, grants, or sales revenues for the software) to pay for specific research and enhancements.

Chapter 5

Toward Intelligent Tools
for Information Sharing
and Collaboration

Thomas W. Malone and Kum-Yew Lai

Massachusetts Institute of Technology

If you were to visit our laboratory at the MIT Center for Coordination Science today, you would find students faculty members, and research scientists at work on over a dozen projects involving people working together by using computers. In some projects at the center, researchers are studying how people work together now and analyzing how people might work together differently with new kinds of information technology. In other projects, we are developing new collaborative tools for such tasks as sharing information in groups, making group decisions, and managing projects. Finally, in some of our projects, we focus on developing new theories of coordination that can help build better systems and help organizations coordinate themselves more effectively by using such systems.

This chapter provides a tour of some of our current projects on developing new collaborative tools. More important, it provides a tour through the history that led us to where we are today and a glimpse of where we think we are going. This opportunity to reflect on our history has highlighted for us two key themes that have struck us repeatedly through the course of this work:

1. A small set of simple capabilities (which we now refer to as objects, folders, and agents) are useful in a surprisingly large set of cooperative work and information-management applications.

2. The concept of semiformal systems is a subtle but extremely important guide to creating "intelligent" computer systems that are actually useful to intelligent humans.

In recounting the history of our work, we will attempt to illustrate the implications of these two themes. We proceed as follows: First, we will describe the Information Lens system, an intelligent tool for helping people find, filter, sort, and prioritize electronic messages. This system is one of the primary precursors for current work in the center, and after describing it, we will briefly report on empirical studies of its use. Next, we will describe the Object Lens system, a much more general tool for supporting information sharing and collaboration. One goal of this system is to be "radically tailorable;" that is, nonprogrammers can customize the system for a wide variety of applications including mail sorting (like the Information Lens), project management, task tracking, meeting scheduling, and group decision making. This system is an important vehicle for several of our current projects. Finally, we will provide brief descriptions of several other tools for cooperative work currently under development in our center and suggest the directions to which this work is leading.

INFORMATION LENS: AN INTELLIGENT TOOL FOR MANAGING ELECTRONIC MESSAGES

In late 1984, we began work on the original version of the Information Lens (see Malone et al., 1987, 1988, for complete descriptions). The system was motivated by a desire to help people cope intelligently with the increasingly common problem of large amounts of electronic mail: It helps people to filter, sort, and prioritize messages that are already addressed to them, and it also helps them to find useful messages they would not otherwise have received. In some cases, the system can respond automatically to certain messages, and in other cases it can suggest likely actions for human users to take.

Key Ideas

Four key ideas, together, form the basis of the Information Lens system:

1. A rich set of semistructured message types (or frames) can form the basis for an intelligent information-sharing system. For example, meeting announcements can be structured as templates that include fields for date, time, and place, organizer, and topic, as well as any additional unstructured information. These templates help people compose messages in the first place (e.g., by reminding them of what information to include), and by putting much of the essential information in special fields, the templates enable computers to process automatically a much wider range of information than would be possible with simple keyword methods or automatic parsing.
2. Sets of production rules can be used to specify conveniently automatic processing for these messages. These rules may include multiple levels of reasoning, not just Boolean selection criteria.

3. The use of semistructured message types and automatic rules for processing them can be greatly simplified by a consistent set of display-oriented editors for composing messages, constructing rules, and defining new message templates.

4. The initial introduction and later evolution of a group communication system can be much easier if there is an incremental adoption path, that is, a series of small changes, each of which has the following properties: (a) Individual users can continue to use their existing system with no change if they so desire, (b) individual users who make small changes receive some immediate benefit, and (c) groups of users who adopt the changes receive additional benefits beyond the individual benefits.

System Overview

To provide a natural integration of this system with the capabilities that people already have, the system was built on top of an existing electronic mail system. Users can continue to send and receive their mail as usual, including the use of centrally maintained distribution lists and the manual classification of messages into folders. In addition, the Information Lens provides four important optional capabilities: (1) People can use structured message templates to help them compose their messages; (2) receivers can specify rules to filter and classify automatically messages arriving in their mailbox; (3) senders can include as an addressee of a message, in addition to specific individuals or distribution lists, a special mailbox (currently named "Anyone") to indicate willingness to have this message automatically redistributed to anyone else who might be interested; and (4) receivers can specify rules that find and show messages addressed to Anyone that the receiver would not otherwise have seen (see Figure 5-1). Our primary implementations of this system were in the Xerox Interlisp environment.

Messages

Figure 5-2 shows a sample of the highly graphic interaction through which users can construct messages with semistructured message templates. After selecting a field of a message by pointing with a mouse, the user can point with the mouse again to see the field's default value, an explanation of the field's purpose, or a list of likely alternatives for filling in the field. If the user selects one of these alternatives, that value is automatically inserted in the message text. The user can also edit any fields directly at any time by using the built-in-display-oriented text editor. Users who do not want to take advantage of these message construction aids can simply select the most general message type (Message) and use the text editor to fill in the standard fields (To, From, and Subject) just as they would have done in the underlying mail system.

The templates for different types of messages are arranged in an "inheritance hierarchy," with some message types being specializations of others (e.g., see Fikes and Kehler, [1985]). For example, the Seminar Announcement template is a specialization of the Meeting Announcement template, and it includes an additional field for the speaker that is not present in Meeting Announcements.

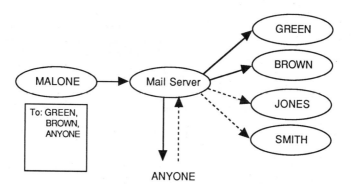

FIGURE 5-1.   Mail Server: The Lens system includes components in the users' workstations and in central server (called Anyone). Messages that include Anyone as an addressee are automatically distributed (via the dotted lines) to all receivers whose interest profiles select the messages as well as to the other explicit addressees.

Rules

Just as the structure of messages simplifies the process of composing messages, it also simplifies the process of constructing rules for processing messages. For instance, Figure 5-3 shows an example of the display-oriented editor used to construct rules in the Information Lens system. This editor uses rule templates that are based on the same message types as those used for message construction, and it uses a similar interaction style with menus available for defaults, alternatives, and explanations.

Figure 5-4 shows some sample rules for performing actions such as moving messages

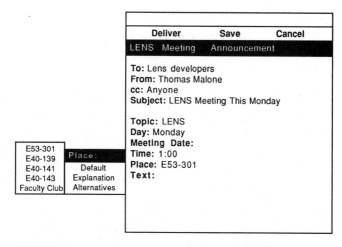

FIGURE 5-2.   Message Delivery: Messages are composed with a display-oriented editor and templates that have pop-up menus associated with the template fields.

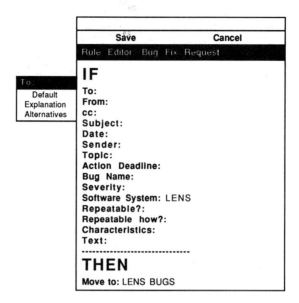

FIGURE 5-3.   Message Processing: Rules for processing messages are composed with the same kind of editor and the same templates as those used for composing messages in the first place.

to specific folders (Figure 5-4a), deleting messages (Figure 5-4b), and automatically "resending" messages to someone else (Figure 5-4c). Resending a message is similar to forwarding it, except that instead of copying the entire original message into the body of a new message, the new message preserves the type and all but the To and cc fields of the original message. Rules can also set characteristics of a message that are tested by later rules (Figure 5-4d).

When the local rules have finished processing all incoming messages, the numbers of new messages that have been automatically moved into different folders the last time the folder was viewed are shown on a hierarchical display of the folder names. To help users understand and modify their rules, a simple explanation capability allows them to see a history of the rules that fired on a given message. In addition to the local rules applied when messages are retrieved to a user's workstation, an individual user can also specify central rules to select messages addressed to Anyone that the user wants to see (see Figure 5-4).

Group Use of Message Types

Users of a system like the Information Lens can take advantage of simple sorting rules, even if they do not use any of the specialized message templates the system provides. But, to the extent that a group of people all use the same message templates, they can benefit even more from rules based on the shared message structures.

One of the important questions, therefore, is how groups of people can develop and evolve a shared language of common message types. One simple solution is to require

(a)	IF		Message type:	Action request
			Action deadline:	Today, Tomorrow
	THEN		Move to:	Urgent

(b)	IF		Message type:	Meeting Announcement
			Day:	Not Tuesday
	THEN		Delete	

(c)	IF		Message type:	Meeting proposal
			Sender:	Not Axsom
	THEN		Resend:	Axsom

(d)	IF		From:	Silk, Siegel
	THEN	Set Characteristic:		VIP
	IF		Message type:	Action request
			Characteristics:	VIP
	THEN		Move to:	Urgent

(e)	IF		Message type:	Request for information
			Subject:	AI, Lisp
	THEN		Show	

FIGURE 5-4.   Sample Rules

everyone to use the same message types, perhaps determined by some central administrator or standards committee. Another, more complicated solution is to let anyone create new message types as long as they also write translation rules, which translate these types into and out of the common language. Lee and Malone (1987) describe one way of categorizing all possible solutions to this translation problem and propose a hybrid solution called Partially Shared Views, which combines many of the best features of the different schemes. Essentially, this solution lets different (and possibly overlapping) groups of people develop and use shared sets of message type definitions (called "views"). When users adopt a view, they can receive messages directly from other users of the view. When they receive a message created in a view they have not adopted, the message is translated automatically into one of the message types they have adopted.

The most interesting case of this automatic translation occurs when the "foreign" message type is a specialization of one already known to the receiver. In this case, the foreign message type is automatically translated into the "nearest common ancestor" type known to both groups. For instance, if you received a Seminar Announcement message and you had not adopted a definition for this type of message, the message would be automatically translated into the nearest parent type, say, Meeting Announcement, that you had adopted. Information from any fields not present in Meeting Announcements (e.g., Speaker) would simply be added into the Text field of the Meeting Announcement message. Then all the rules you had defined for Meeting Announcements would be applied to the incoming message.

Users' Experiences with Information Lens

To see how people outside our own group would actually use a system like the Information Lens, we worked for several years (approximately 1985–1988) with a corporate test site to implement a version of the system in that environment and observe the usage experience. These studies are described in detail in MacKay (1988) and MacKay et al. (1989). In this section we summarize some of the key results.

Can Nonprogrammers Use Rules?

One of the most important questions we had was whether nonprogrammers would be able to use rules effectively. The test site we studied was very advanced in its use of computer technology, and a number of our test users were skilled computer programmers. However, our test sample also included secretaries, managers, and noncomputer scientists. We were happy to find that no one at the test site had trouble understanding how to create and use rules. Even users who had never had any computer programming experience at all told us they found the template-based method of constructing rules to be quite easy to use. For instance, one user, with no computer training, described his first experience with the rule editor as follows: "It's obvious. You just go into the [fields] and type whatever you want."

When Do Users Run Rules?

When we designed the Information Lens system, we expected that people would use rules to sort and process their messages before reading them. However, it was also possible for users to read all their messages first and then apply the rules to sort them into folders. To our surprise, we found that a number of users preferred to use rules in this way. These users said they liked to feel "in control" by seeing all their messages before any rules moved them, and then they could use the rules to file the messages in folders for later retrieval. We called the first kind of users "prioritizers" and the second kind, "archivers" (see MacKay, 1988).

What Kinds of Rules Do Users Write?

In the sample of people we studied most carefully, users created an average of 15 rules each (with a range from 2 to 35 rules per person). The most common kind of rules sorted messages based on the distribution lists to which the messages were addressed. For instance, users often used rules to move messages addressed to a particular distribution list into a folder with the same name, thus creating a kind of computer conferencing system based on electronic mail.

Another important observation was that some of the users who reported the most satisfaction with the system had only a few rules. For instance, one user who was on the verge of being overwhelmed (with more than 30 messages per day) created only two rules: One rule moved messages into a special folder if their Subject field contained the name of a conference this person was organizing. The other rule moved messages into a different folder if they were addressed to this person by name (rather than simply to a distribution list of which this person was a member). This person said that these two rules "changed her life!"

What Did We Learn from Information Lens?

One of the most satisfying experiences a designer can have is the feeling that "things are coming together." Often this means that decisions made about one aspect of the design turn out to have unexpectedly positive consequences later in the design process. Even though we did many things wrong in implementing our prototype versions of Information Lens, we repeatedly had this feeling of unexpected synergy about some of the key design decisions.

In particular, we were genuinely surprised at how useful the semistructured messages turned out to be. For instance, in one of our papers (Malone et al., 1989), we described how adding a few specialized action types to certain kinds of messages greatly simplified the process of designing a variety of different applications such as computer conferencing, task tracking, and calendar management. Even though simple versions of these new applications were relatively easy to do in Information Lens, however, there were some obvious limitations. For instance, it was possible to sort automatically Action Request messages into a "To do" folder, but as in any other folder, the table of contents format for messages would show only the From, Date, and Subject fields. To see other information (such as the Due Date or Requestor), we would have to display each message individually. Clearly this application called for a more general display format for the contents of objects in folders.

As we continued along this line of thinking, we felt ourselves inexorably drawn toward generalizing the Information Lens to include more types of objects (besides just messages), more types of display formats for collections of objects (besides the tables of contents for messages), and more types of agents (besides those used to sort and route messages). As described in the next section, the result of these generalizations became the system we called Object Lens.

We were also struck, in reflecting on our experiences with Information Lens, by the usefulness of letting people structure their messages to a certain degree (e.g., by putting some information in fields) but still include other, unstructured information. For instance, there may well be times when people want to put "I don't know yet" in the Place field of a Meeting Announcement message. In this case, the system can still be useful, though perhaps not as useful as it would be if the field contained the expected kind of information. This thought led us to become more reflective about the benefits of systems that formalize certain items for automatic processing by computers while leaving other items informal for processing by humans. And this notion of semiformal systems emerged in our minds as one of the most important characteristics of the Object Lens system.

OBJECT LENS: A SPREADSHEET FOR COOPERATIVE WORK

In 1987, we began work on the first version of the Object Lens system (see Lai, Malone, and Yu, 1988). Unlike the Information Lens system, which was focused exclusively on electronic messaging, we wanted Object Lens to be a much more general tool for supporting many kinds of cooperative work and information-management applications.

In particular, we had two primary goals in designing this system that differed from the goals of many previous systems to support similar tasks:

1. *Integration.* The system should combine many different applications into a single integrated environment where people use a simple and consistent interface for everything from reading mail to querying data bases and where these applications can interact with one another.
2. *Tailorability.* The system should let ordinary people create and modify these applications for themselves without requiring the help of professional programmers.

To achieve these goals, the system helps people keep track of and share knowledge about various "objects" such as people, tasks, projects, companies, and many other items with which they work. For example, people can use hypertext links to represent relationships between a message and its replies, between people and their supervisors, and between different parts of a complex product. The system also lets people create various kinds of "intelligent agents" to help them organize and respond to this knowledge. For instance, they can use intelligent agents to find electronic messages in which they are interested, to notice overdue tasks, and to notify people of upcoming deadlines.

Semiformal Systems

One of the most important characteristics of Object Lens is that it is a semiformal system. We define a semiformal system as a computer system that has the following three properties: (1) It represents and automatically processes certain information in formally specified ways; (2) it represents and makes it easy for humans to process the same or other information in ways that are not formally specified; and (3) it allows the boundary between formal processing by computers and informal processing by people to be easily changed.

In the past, our computer systems have almost always been at one extreme or the other. At one extreme are very highly structured systems, such as conventional data bases and knowledge bases, with strict requirements about the contents of different kinds of fields and with structured procedures for dealing with the information represented in the system. At the other extreme are very unstructured systems, such as conventional electronic mail and word processing, in which the computer's role is primarily to record, store, and transmit information to other people, not to "understand" or otherwise process the information it stores. The concept of semiformal systems opens up a vast middle ground between these two extremes and suggests how computers can be useful in a much wider range of ways than we have previously come to expect.

Semiformal systems are most useful when we understand enough to formalize in a computer system some, but not all, of the knowledge relevant to acting in a given situation. Such systems are often useful in supporting individual work, and we believe they are especially important in supporting cooperative work, in which there are usually some well-understood patterns in people's behavior and also a very large amount of other knowledge that is potentially relevant but difficult to specify.

Components of Object Lens

In Object Lens, there are three key building blocks out of which users can create their own applications:

1. Semistructured *objects* represent things in the world and links between them represent relationships. Users see and manipulate these objects via template-based interfaces.
2. *Folders* with customizable display formats summarize information about collections of objects.
3. Rule-based *agents* perform active tasks without requiring the direct attention of their users.

In the remainder of this section, we provide an overview of how these three components allow us to expose semiformal knowledge to users in a way that is both visible and changeable. Detailed descriptions of the system's features can be found in Lai, Malone, and Yu (1988) and Malone et. al (1989). Our first versions of this system were implemented in Xerox Interlisp; the current version is implemented in Common Lisp on the Macintosh. To use the mail facilities of the system, the Macintoshes must be linked to a network.

Objects

Figure 5-5 shows a template for an object of type Task. As in the Information Lens, users can insert text in any field. In addition, when users click on a field name with the mouse, a list of likely alternative values for that field appears in a drag-down menu. The

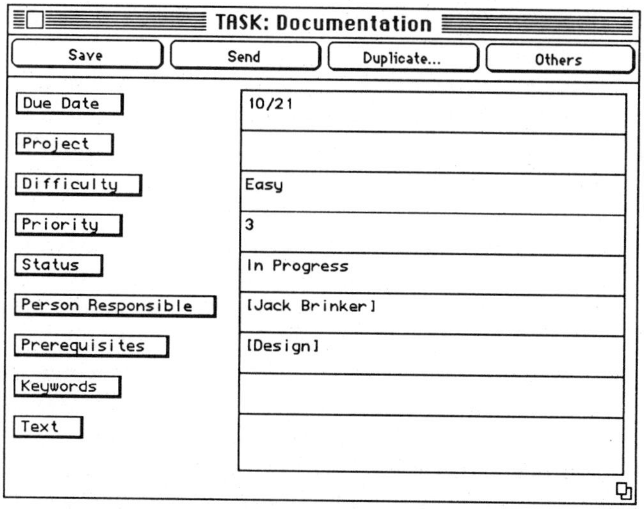

FIGURE 5-5. Edting Objects: Objects can be edited with a simple template editor. Fields can include text, graphics, or links to other objects.

alternatives may be links to other objects (indicated by enclosing square brackets) or just text strings. Selecting one of these alternatives causes it to be automatically inserted in the field. For instance, the figure contains a link to two objects: (1) a Person object called Jack Brinker that represents the person responsible for the task and (2) a Task object called Design that is a prerequisite to documentation. To insert links to objects that are not in the alternatives list, the user simply selects the Add Link action (from the drag-down menu that appears when the field name is selected) and then points to the object to which the link should be made. After a link is inserted, clicking it on with the mouse causes the object it points to to appear on the screen.

Relationships Among Objects

Users can easily see and change the relationships among objects by inserting and deleting links between them. For instance, the Person Responsible and Prerequisite fields of a Task object might contain links to Person and Task objects that represent, respectively, the people responsible for performing the task and the prerequisite tasks that are must be completed before doing the task. Then, for instance, when the user looks at the Task object, it is easy to get more information, such as the phone numbers of the people responsible or the due dates of the prerequisite tasks.

Type Specific Actions

All objects have standard actions (like Save, Send, and Add Link) that can be performed on them. In addition, some object types have other specialized actions that are appropriate only for that kind of object. For instance, messages have actions like Reply and Forward and agents (see below) have a Trigger action that triggers them to start running. In a few cases, the object-specific actions depend not just on the type of the object but also on its state. For instance, messages created on the local workstation have a Send action, and messages received from elsewhere have actions such as Answer and Forward.

Folders

Users of Object Lens can group collections of objects together into special kinds of objects called folders. For instance, folders can be created for groups of people (e.g., project teams or a company directory), tasks (e.g., those completed, those to be done by you, or those to be done by others), messages (grouped according to topic or urgency), and so forth. An object can be added to a folder in three ways: (1) automatically, as the result of a rule action; (2) manually, using the Add Link action on the folder; or (3) manually, by cutting or copying selected links in some object and pasting them into the folder. In all three cases, the folders contain links to the objects, not the objects themselves. Therefore, the same object can appear in more than one folder.

Object Lens provides several different formats for displaying the contents of folders. For instance, the table format shows the values of selected fields from the objects contained in the folder. Figure 5-6(a) shows a folder containing tasks for a project displayed in table format. Users can easily tailor the format of these displays by selecting from a menu the fields they want to have included in the table.

In cases (like this one) in which the objects in a folder are related to one another,

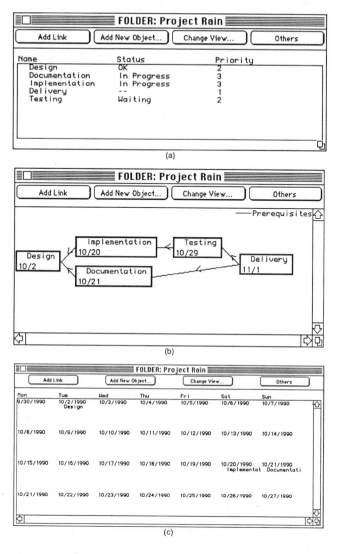

FIGURE 5-6. Choosing Fields: In (a) users can select which fields to display in tables that summarize a collection of objects. In (b) users can choose which fields to be used as edges in a network that summarize the relationships among objects. Finally in (c), users can choose a field containing dates that will be used to display the objects in a calendar.

Object Lens can also display these relationships in a network format. For instance, Figure 5-6(b) shows the same folder but with the display format changed to show the relationships represented by links in the Prerequisites field. In this case, the display resembles a simple PERT chart. It is easy to imagine many more useful network displays, such as organization charts that display employees with Supervisor relationships. At the same time, these network displays can be more sophisticated, such as a *matrix* organization chart that shows *both* the Supervisor and Project Supervisor fields. We have also implemented a calendar display format, Figure 5-6(c), that shows the same folder of task objects indexed by the dates shown in their Due Date fields. Other display formats now being constructed or designed include matrices (e.g. to display trade-off diagrams), outliners, statistical graphs, and geographical maps.

Agents
Users of the Object Lens system can create rule-based agents that process information automatically on behalf of their users. For instance, Figure 5-7 shows an example of a simple agent designed to help a user keep track of tasks to be done. When an agent is

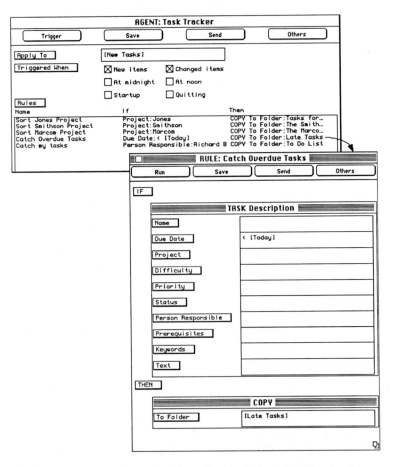

FIGURE 5-7.   Agents: Agents include a collection of rules and specifications for when and where to apply them. Rules describe the objects that satisfy them and specify what action to perform on those objects.

triggered, it applies a set of rules to a collection of objects in a folder. The agent in Figure 5-7 is applied to objects in the New Tasks folder and is triggered whenever a task is added to that folder or a task already in the folder is changed. The agent includes several rules, one of which is shown. This rule finds any tasks with a Due Date before today and copies them to the Late Tasks folder. Some other possible actions include moving and deleting objects from folders and mailing them to other users.

Embedded Descriptions

With the capabilities we have described so far, all rules must depend only on information contained in the objects to which they are being applied. For instance, a rule about a message can depend only on information contained in the message itself. It is often desirable, however, to be able to specify rules that also depend on other information contained elsewhere in the knowledge base. For instance, in the Information Lens system, if a user wanted to specify a rule that applied to all messages from vice presidents, the rule would have to include the names of all the vice presidents in the From field. In Object Lens, it is possible to draw on other information by having descriptions embedded within other descriptions. For instance, the rule shown in Figure 5-8 is satisfied if the message is from any person with a job title that includes "vice president." To apply this rule, the system checks to see whether the string in the From field of the message is the same as the Name of any Person object in the knowledge base that satisfies the description.

Saving and Sharing Knowledge

There are two primary ways for people to save and share information in the current version of Object Lens: (1) They can save any collection of objects in a file, which they (or other people) can load later; and (2) they can mail any collection of objects back and forth to one another in messages. When users load a previously saved file or when they receive a message containing objects, the identity of the objects is preserved. That is, new versions of the objects replace the old versions, any links to objects already in the user's workstation will point to the newest versions of those objects, and the user is notified of these replacements. When users do not want these substitutions to occur, they can easily reinstate the old versions of the objects. We are also currently working on a third way for people to share knowledge: accessing remote data bases via Object Lens.

Creating New Applications in Object Lens

In this section, we give more examples of how the preceding features can be combined to create a variety of cooperative work applications. It should be quite clear that Object Lens provides a set of tools that are only slightly more complex that those in the Information Lens but can empower the user to do much more. We will not reiterate the examples given for the Information Lens, except to illustrate how Object Lens can provide more sophistication in three applications: intelligent message sorting, argumentation support, and conversation structuring.

```
┌─────────────────────────────────────────────────────┐
│ ▤□ ▥▥▥▥▥ RULE: Sort VIP Messages ▥▥▥▥▥▥▥           │
│ ┌──────────┐ ┌──────────┐ ┌──────────┐ ┌──────────┐ │
│ │   Run    │ │   Save   │ │   Send   │ │  Others  │ │
│ └──────────┘ └──────────┘ └──────────┘ └──────────┘ │
│ ┌────┐                                               │
│ │ IF │                                               │
│ └────┘                                               │
│   ┌─────────────── MESSAGE Description ───────────┐  │
│   │ ┌──────┐      ┌──────────────────────────────┐│  │
│   │ │ Name │      │                              ││  │
│   │ └──────┘      └──────────────────────────────┘│  │
│   │ ┌──────┐                                       │  │
│   │ │ From │                                       │  │
│   │ └──────┘                                       │  │
│   │   ┌──────────── EMPLOYEE Description ───────┐  │  │
│   │   │ ┌──────┐          ┌───────────────────┐ │  │  │
│   │   │ │ Name │          │                   │ │  │  │
│   │   │ └──────┘          ├───────────────────┤ │  │  │
│   │   │ ┌─────────┐       │                   │ │  │  │
│   │   │ │ Address │       ├───────────────────┤ │  │  │
│   │   │ └─────────┘       │                   │ │  │  │
│   │   │ ┌─────────────────┤                   │ │  │  │
│   │   │ │ Telephone Number├───────────────────┤ │  │  │
│   │   │ └─────────────────┘                   │ │  │  │
│   │   │ ┌─────────────────┐                   │ │  │  │
│   │   │ │ Network Address │───────────────────┤ │  │  │
│   │   │ └─────────────────┘                   │ │  │  │
│   │   │ ┌───────────┐     │ Vice President    │ │  │  │
│   │   │ │ Job Title │     ├───────────────────┤ │  │  │
│   │   │ └───────────┘     │                   │ │  │  │
│   │   │ ┌─────────┐       ├───────────────────┤ │  │  │
│   │   │ │ Company │       │                   │ │  │  │
│   │   │ └─────────┘       ├───────────────────┤ │  │  │
│   │   │ ┌────────┐        │                   │ │  │  │
│   │   │ │ Office │        ├───────────────────┤ │  │  │
│   │   │ └────────┘        │                   │ │  │  │
│   │   │ ┌────────────┐    ├───────────────────┤ │  │  │
│   │   │ │ Supervisor │    │                   │ │  │  │
│   │   │ └────────────┘    ├───────────────────┤ │  │  │
│   │   │ ┌───────────────────┐                 │ │  │  │
│   │   │ │ Project Supervisor│─────────────────┤ │  │  │
│   │   │ └───────────────────┘                 │ │  │  │
│   │   │ ┌──────────┐      ├───────────────────┤ │  │  │
│   │   │ │ Keywords │      │                   │ │  │  │
│   │   │ └──────────┘      ├───────────────────┤ │  │  │
│   │   │ ┌──────┐          │                   │ │  │  │
│   │   │ │ Text │          └───────────────────┘ │  │  │
│   │   │ └──────┘                                │  │  │
│   │   └─────────────────────────────────────────┘  │  │
│   │ ┌────┐      ┌──────────────────────────────┐   │  │
│   │ │ To │      │                              │   │  │
│   │ └────┘      ├──────────────────────────────┤   │  │
│   │ ┌────┐      │                              │   │  │
│   │ │ Cc │      ├──────────────────────────────┤   │  │
│   │ └────┘      │                              │   │  │
│   │ ┌──────┐    ├──────────────────────────────┤   │  │
│   │ │ Date │    │                              │   │  │
│   │ └──────┘    ├──────────────────────────────┤   │  │
│   │ ┌────────────┐                             │   │  │
│   │ │ In-Reply-To│──────────────────────────── │   │  │
│   │ └────────────┘                             │   │  │
│   │ ┌────────────────┐  ├───────────────────── │   │  │
│   │ │ Previous Version│                         │   │  │
│   │ └────────────────┘  ├───────────────────── │   │  │
│   │ ┌──────────┐        │                      │   │  │
│   │ │ Keywords │        ├───────────────────── │   │  │
│   │ └──────────┘        │                      │   │  │
│   │ ┌──────┐            └──────────────────────┘   │  │
│   │ │ Text │                                       │  │
│   │ └──────┘                                       │  │
│   └───────────────────────────────────────────────┘  │
│ ┌──────┐                                              │
│ │ THEN │                                              │
│ └──────┘                                              │
│   ┌──────────────────── COPY ─────────────────────┐  │
│   │ ┌───────────┐  ┌──────────────────────────┐   │  │
│   │ │ To Folder │  │ [VIP Messages]           │   │  │
│   │ └───────────┘  └──────────────────────────┘   │  │
│   └───────────────────────────────────────────────┘  │
│                                                    ▱  │
└─────────────────────────────────────────────────────┘
```

FIGURE 5-8. Rules: Rules can use embedded descriptions to create complex queries.

Intelligent Message Sorting
of Engineering Change Notices

It was already possible in the Information Lens to sort engineering change notices according to the contents of fields such as Part Affected, Type of Change, and Severity. In Object Lens, it is possible to use additional knowledge to do even more intelligent sorting. For instance, Figure 5-9 shows a rule that uses a doubly embedded description to select all change notices that involve parts for which anyone reporting to a particular manager is responsible.

Argumentation Support

The gIBIS (Conklin and Begeman, 1988) is a tool for helping a group explore and capture the qualitative factors that go into making decisions. Object Lens can be used to create most of the functionality in an argumentation support tool like gIBIS. Elements of a policy analysis in gIBIS are represented as a network containing three types of nodes: Issues, Positions, and Arguments. Each Issue may have several Positions that Respond to it, and each Position, in turn, may have various Arguments that Support or Object to it.

To emulate gIBIS in Object Lens, we first defined these three types of objects: Issues, Positions, and Arguments. For instance, Figure 5-10 shows a sample Position in a discussion about what programming language to use for a new project. This object includes fields for links to Arguments that support or oppose the Position. As in the original gIBIS system, the links between nodes in an argument network can be displayed graphically in a folder with the network display format (see Figure 5-11).

In addition to a shared "live" data base, gIBIS has two other features that would have required new system-level programming to implement: (1) aggregate nodes (the ability to collapse a group of nodes into one aggregate node) and (2) a node index that shows nodes in outline format (with indentations indicating their relations). Even though we did not include these features in our implementation, they would both have been quite consistent with the overall Object Lens paradigm. Aggregate nodes could be implemented with two new actions on folders (one to create aggregates and one to break them apart). An outline format would be a useful addition to the current display formats for folders (tables, networks, and calendars).

Conversation Structuring and Task Tracking

The Coordinator[1] is an electronic mail-based system that helps people structure conversations and track tasks (Winograd and Flores 1986). To emulate the functionality of the Coordinator in Object Lens, three primary system level modifications are required: (1) When users create a new message (it is not a reply to an old one), a new conversation folder is automatically created and linked into the Conversation field of the new message. (2) When users reply to a message of a given type, they are presented with a choice of message types for their reply. The choices are specified in a user-modifiable field called Reply Types. (3) After users select a reply type, the Conversation field in the reply message is automatically filled with a link to the Conversation folder specified in the original message.

---

[1] The Coordinator is a trademark of Action Technologies, Inc.

```
┌─────────────────────────────────────────────────────────┐
│ ▢ ▒▒▒▒▒▒▒▒▒▒▒▒ RULE: Sort Our ECNs ▒▒▒▒▒▒▒▒▒▒▒▒          │
│ ┌──────────┐ ┌──────────┐ ┌──────────┐ ┌──────────┐      │
│ │   Run    │ │   Save   │ │   Send   │ │  Others  │      │
│ └──────────┘ └──────────┘ └──────────┘ └──────────┘      │
│ ┌────┐                                                    │
│ │ IF │                                                    │
│ └────┘                                                    │
│   ▒▒▒▒▒ ENGINEERING CHANGE NOTICE Description ▒▒▒▒▒        │
│   ┌──────┐        ┌───────────────────────────┐           │
│   │ Name │        │                           │           │
│   └──────┘        ├───────────────────────────┤           │
│   ┌──────┐        │                           │           │
│   │ From │        ├───────────────────────────┤           │
│   └──────┘        │                           │           │
│   ┌────┐          ├───────────────────────────┤           │
│   │ To │          │                           │           │
│   └────┘          ├───────────────────────────┤           │
│   ┌────┐          │                           │           │
│   │ Cc │          └───────────────────────────┘           │
│   └────┘                                                   │
│   ┌──────┐                                                 │
│   │ Date │                                                 │
│   └──────┘                                                 │
│   ┌───────────────┐                                        │
│   │ Part Affected │                                        │
│   └───────────────┘                                        │
│      ▒▒▒▒▒▒▒ PART Description ▒▒▒▒▒▒▒                      │
│      ┌──────┐      ┌──────────────────────┐                │
│      │ Name │      │                      │                │
│      └──────┘      ├──────────────────────┤                │
│      ┌─────────────┐                       │                │
│      │ Part Number │     │                │                │
│      └─────────────┘      ├──────────────┤                │
│      ┌───────────┐        │              │                │
│      │ Subsystem │        └──────────────┘                │
│      └───────────┘                                         │
│      ┌─────────────────────┐                               │
│      │ Engineer Responsible │                              │
│      └─────────────────────┘                               │
│         ▒▒▒▒▒▒▒ EMPLOYEE Description ▒▒▒▒▒▒▒               │
│         ┌──────┐     ┌─────────────────────┐               │
│         │ Name │     │                     │               │
│         └──────┘     ├─────────────────────┤               │
│         ┌──────────────────┐                │               │
│         │ Telephone Number ││               │               │
│         └──────────────────┘├───────────────┤               │
│         ┌───────────┐        │              │               │
│         │ Job Title │        ├──────────────┤               │
│         └───────────┘        │              │               │
│         ┌────────┐           ├──────────────┤               │
│         │ Office │           │              │               │
│         └────────┘           ├──────────────┤               │
│         ┌────────────┐        Kevin Crowston │               │
│         │ Supervisor │       │              │               │
│         └────────────┘       ├──────────────┤               │
│         ┌──────────┐         │              │               │
│         │ Keywords │         ├──────────────┤               │
│         └──────────┘         │              │               │
│         ┌──────┐             │              │               │
│         │ Text │             └──────────────┘               │
│         └──────┘                                            │
│      ┌──────────┐    ┌──────────────────────┐              │
│      │ Keywords │    │                      │              │
│      └──────────┘    ├──────────────────────┤              │
│      ┌──────┐        │                      │              │
│      │ Text │        └──────────────────────┘              │
│      └──────┘                                              │
│   ┌────────────────┐  ┌───────────────────────────┐       │
│   │ Type Of Change │  │                           │       │
│   └────────────────┘  ├───────────────────────────┤       │
│   ┌──────────────────┐│                           │       │
│   │ Reason For Change ││                          │       │
│   └──────────────────┘├───────────────────────────┤       │
│   ┌──────────┐        │                           │       │
│   │ Severity │        ├───────────────────────────┤       │
│   └──────────┘        │                           │       │
│   ┌──────────┐        ├───────────────────────────┤       │
│   │ Keywords │        │                           │       │
│   └──────────┘        └───────────────────────────┘       │
│   ┌──────┐                                                 │
│   │ Text │                                                 │
│   └──────┘                                                 │
│ ┌──────┐                                                   │
│ │ THEN │                                                   │
│ └──────┘                                                   │
│         ▒▒▒▒▒▒▒▒▒▒▒ MOVE ▒▒▒▒▒▒▒▒▒▒▒                      │
│   ┌───────────┐   ┌───────────────────────────┐           │
│   │ To Folder │   │ [Our Group's ECNs]        │           │
│   └───────────┘   └───────────────────────────┘           │
└─────────────────────────────────────────────────────────┘
```

FIGURE 5-9.   Linked Objects: Rules can include multiple levels of embedded descriptions that refer to linked objects throughout the knowledge base.

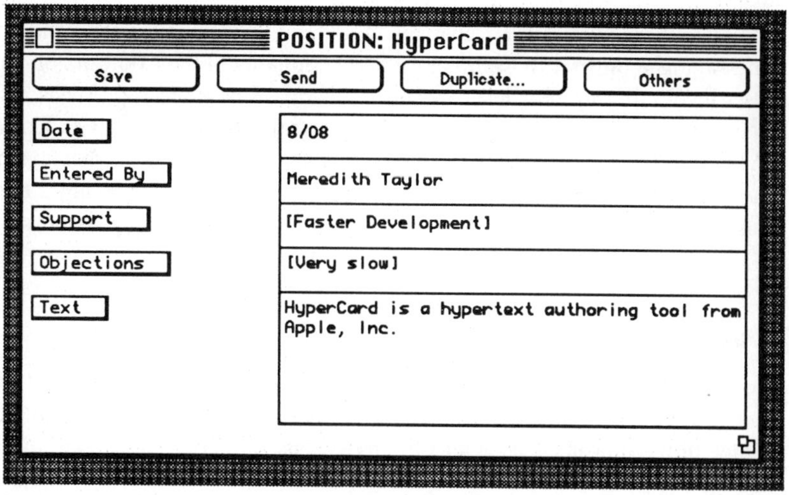

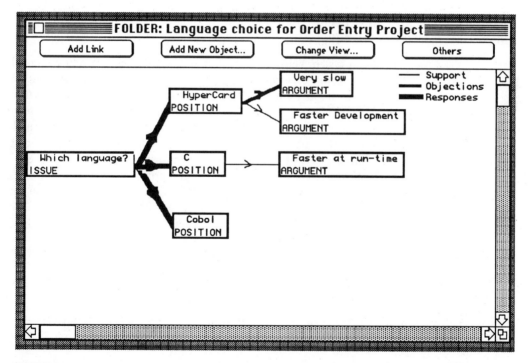

FIGURE 5-10. Positions: A position has links to the arguements that support and oppose it.

FIGURE 5-11. Folder: A network format display of a folder shows the relationships between issues, positions, and arguements, as in the gIBIS system.

After these system-level changes to add conversations (which can be useful in any messaging application), the other main functionality of the Coordinator can be added by user-level tailoring. For instance, one can add 15 new message types and define their reply types to provide the same conversational sequences (such as Conversations for Action) used in the Coordinator. The various kinds of summary displays in the Coordinator can be provided by creating agents with rules that sort messages into folders. For instance, Figure 5-12 shows messages sorted into the Ongoing Matters folder because they contained previous messages in their In-reply-to fields.

OTHER PROJECTS

In addition to these applications of Object Lens, several other current projects in our center involve the development of new tools for information sharing and collaboration. Some of these projects use Object Lens as a starting point; others are based in different environments. But they are all exploring, in one way or another, how semiformal systems comprising some combination of objects, folders, and agents can support collaboration. In the following descriptions, the primary researcher responsible for each project is listed along with the project title.

Answer Garden—A Tool for Growing
Organizational Memory (Mark Ackerman)

The Answer Garden system helps an organization develop a data base of commonly asked questions that grows "organically" as new questions arise and are answered (see Ackerman and Malone, 1990, for more details). It is designed to help in situations (such as field-service organizations and customer hot lines) in which there is a continuing stream of questions, many of which occur over and over but some of which the organization has never seen before. The system includes a branching network of diagnostic questions that helps users find the answers they want. If the answer is not present, the system automatically sends the question to the appropriate expert, and the answer is returned to the user as well as inserted into the branching network. Experts can also modify this network in response to users' problems.

The primary version of this system is implemented in Unix, using C and the X

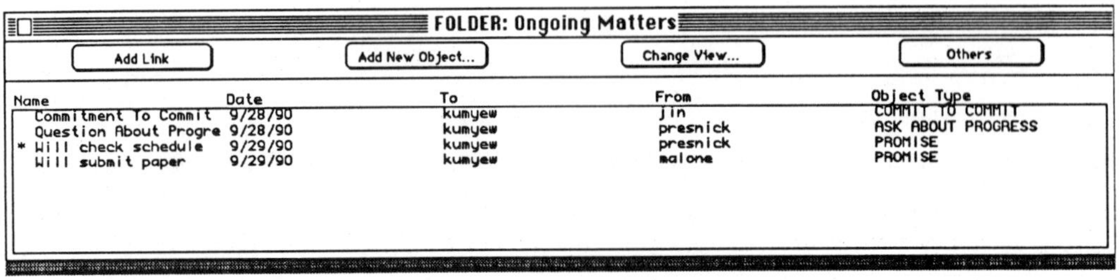

FIGURE 5-12.   Table Format Display Summarizing Messages Like Those Used by Coordinator

Window System, and is intended for large-scale use at a number of sites across a network. The initial data base of questions and answers involves how to use the X Window System itself. We have also implemented a small-scale version of this system in Object Lens. The objects in this version of the system are of several types: diagnostic questions, user questions, and expert answers. Folders contain collections of previous questions and answers, and agents automatically put questions and answers received by mail into the proper folders.

Sibyl—A Tool for Supporting Group Decision Making (Jintae Lee)

Sibyl helps a group keep track of the qualitative elements, such as goals, alternatives, arguments, and counterarguments, involved in making a decision (see Lee, 1990, for more details). This system can have several advantages: (1) The decision may be "better" because it takes more factors into account, (2) a rationale for the decision is available later (for instance, the rationale for a software design decision is available when the program is being modified later), and (3) the arguments and information assembled for one decision can be more easily used for other, similar decisions later.

One version of this system was implemented in the Xerox version of Object Lens; the current version is implemented in the Macintosh version of Object Lens. In this system, objects represent goals, alternatives, and arguments. These objects are linked to one another and summarized in folders. A new folder display format was created to show in matrix form the evaluations of various alternatives for various goals.

HyperVoice—A Flexible Interface for Voice Data Bases (Paul Resnick)

HyperVoice is exploring a different medium for collaboration—shared collections of voice information accessed by touch-tone telephones. For instance, the system could be used for voice bulletin boards (see Resnick and King, 1990) in which people share information without having to type or read. In this system, the "objects" are units of voice, and people can easily skip back and forth on these tracks by using touch-tone telephone buttons. A key idea is that some voice objects are also linked to other voice objects, and again, users can follow these links back and forth simply by pushing touch-tone buttons. This system is implemented on personal computers through a specialized board for the digital storage of voice.

Synapse—A Tool for Integrating Interdependent Plans (David Rosenblitt)

Synapse is designed to help people working on different parts of large projects (such as product design or event planning) coordinate their work by integrating partial plans they have developed separately. Different steps in the plans are represented as objects, and the prerequisites and other requirements for a step are represented as links to other objects. Special (non-rule-based) agents were written specifically for this project to integrate related plans in a way that avoids conflicts and exploits synergies. To do so, the system uses new search heuristics based on the consumption and production of resources. The current version of this system is implemented in the Macintosh version of Object Lens.

CONCLUSIONS: WHAT HAVE WE LEARNED AND WHERE WE ARE GOING

Our experience with all of the applications described has strengthened our belief in the power of the three key components (objects, folders, and agents) as building blocks for a wide variety of applications. The fact that so many applications can be constructed from these components leads us to believe that they may be part of some—as yet unappreciated—level of abstraction out of which radically tailorable systems for information management and collaboration can be built. In a sense, this new level of abstraction may be analogous to data-base management systems: Many people built ad hoc mechanisms for data storage and retrieval before the notion of generalized data-base management systems became established. In a similar way, may people have built ad hoc user interfaces for information-sharing and collaboration applications that may, in many cases, be more easily implemented by using a generalized infrastructure like the one we have described.

Our experience with these applications has also strengthened our belief in the importance of using semiformal systems, in which computers can gradually support more and more of the knowledge and processing involved when humans work together, without ever having to "understand" it all. As we look to the future, we can imagine a world in which people share massively interconnected data bases containing the kinds of semistructured objects we have seen here. The people in this world will be assisted by armies of computational agents that work constantly on their owners' behalf: searching for relevant information, notifying their owners when important things change, and responding automatically to certain conditions in the data base.

A variety of technical challenges remain before such a world can come to pass. Among the most important are issues of scaling: How can we manage globally distributed data bases with millions of interconnected objects shared by hundreds of thousands of users and agents? How can we help numerous, partially overlapping communities of users collectively evolve shared definitions for different types of objects and shared understandings about what these objects mean?

Perhaps even more important than these technical challenges, however, are social and organizational questions: What kinds of information do people want to share in the first place? What kinds of incentives would lead people to contribute to and maintain these knowledge bases? Can systems like these help reduce the tiresome details of successful collaboration without leading to overwhelming, computerized red tape? And for that matter, what makes work satisfying in the first place, and how can systems like these increase this satisfaction?

ACKNOWLEDGEMENTS

Portions of this chapter appeared previously in Lai, Malone, and Yu (1988): MacKay et al. (1988, 1989); and Malone et al. (1987, 1988, 1989). The work described here was performed by many people over a number of years. Here is a partial list of those who contributed to these projects: Steven Brobst, Michael Cohen, Kevin Crowston, Kenneth Grant, Jintae Lee, Wendy MacKay, Ramana Rao, David Rosenblitt, Franklyn Turbak, and Keh-Chiang Yu.

Financial support for this work was provided by Digital Equipment Corporation, the National Science Foundation, Apple Computer, Xerox Corporation, Wang Laboratories, General Motors/Electronic Data Systems, Bankers Trust Company, and the Management in the 1990s Research Program and the International Financial Services Research Center at the Sloan School of Management, MIT.

Chapter 6

The Cosmos Laboratory

Sylvia Wilbur and Jean Dollimore

Department of Computer Science
Queen Mary and Westfield College

INTRODUCTION

Taking a tour of the Cosmos laboratory is not a trip to a quiet research environment. The laboratory is located close to the central office of the Computer Science Department at Queen Mary and Westfield College, and the corridors are busy with students. Of the eight people in the Cosmos team, five are full-time researchers who spend their working days in the large, well-lit room that accommodates the laboratory, at the top of an imposing Victorian building. The other three members are teaching members of staff, who have their private rooms close by and join in whenever they can.

The setting of the laboratory is particularly significant, as the patterns of working life within the department were a direct inspiration for the research. As members of the departmental group, the staff need to cooperate on many shared activities, to exchange information, and to make joint decisions. As individuals, most people are constrained by a tight personal schedule of teaching and research duties that makes it difficult to organize face-to-face meetings for cooperative activities. In this busy environment, a locally developed, electronic bulletin-board system has for some years provided a convenient vehicle for our interactions. Scanning bulletin boards has become an essential component of our departmental culture, and for most people, a high-priority activity.

Each bulletin board is devoted to a specific topic in our working or social lives and is open for public access. The system is used extensively for news broadcasts, griping, information exchange, and public debate of "hot" issues. More focused activities, however, such as decision making, joint authoring, and planning, are almost impossible to achieve on bulletin boards.

The perceived need for improved group support in our own environment was the initial motivation for the Cosmos project. A proposal for a research project, to be carried out in collaboration with four other institutions, was submitted for funding and was accepted in 1986. At the time the work began, the acronym CSCW (Computer-Supported Cooperative Work) had not yet been publicized by the CSCW 1988 conference, and we called our research topic simply "group communication." We scarcely realized what an exciting but complex area we were getting into.

This chapter focuses mainly on the Cosmos laboratory at Queen Mary and Westfield College (QMW), and its work during the period 1986–1989. Official funding for the project ended in November 1989, but work has continued on a smaller scale at QMW and British Telecom, and proposals are in the pipeline for further work with a similar approach and for evaluating the Cosmos software in real-world environments. The chapter begins with an introduction to the project, its goals and objectives, and then goes on to describe the approach that was taken to support structural aspects of group activities. Design concepts, problems, and solutions are discussed, and the language-based approach to configuration presented. Finally, our experiences with the system and possibilities for future work are described.

THE COSMOS TEAM

Cosmos began in June 1986.[1] The name is a short form of *Configurable Structured Message System*, a collaborative project with the broad aim of taking an interdisciplinary approach to the use of E-mail to support structured group activities. Three British universities were involved (London, Nottingham, and Manchester) plus two commercial companies (British Telecom and Computer Sciences Company), with QMW as the lead partner. The team comprised computer scientists, social scientists, and human factors experts. A full list of the academic and industrial partners involved is given at the end of this chapter, together with a short description of their roles in the project.

Three sites participated in the design and construction of the prototype system that was developed; another grouping of three sites contributed to the more theoretical aspects of the work. There were periods when intersite collaboration was closely coupled, whereas at other times interdependencies were less strong. We tried at all times to maintain a cohesive and interactive cross-site team, often communicating on a day-to-day basis.

In common with our interests, and for practical geographical reasons, the five sites relied heavily on the use of E-mail facilities for day-to-day communication. A set of Cosmos bulletin boards was created for research and management-oriented discussions

---

[1]The Cosmos project was funded by the UK Alvey Directorate (project MMI/109) and by the industrial partners British Telecom Research Laboratories and Computer Sciences Company Limited.

and replicated at the three academic sites. A message sent to a local Cosmos bulletin board was automatically forwarded to a board of the same name at the two remote academic sites, whereas the industrial partners made remote connections to their nearest university. Having local copies of bulletin boards encouraged team members to contribute daily to research discussions and helped to reduce the impact of the considerable geographical distances between them.

QMW had the greatest role to play in the collaboration since it led the systems development work, contributed to the theoretical work, and was responsible for overall technical coordination of the project. In providing a tour of the Cosmos laboratory at QMW, the authors gratefully acknowledge the work of our partners in the collaboration and the benefits we gained from an interdisciplinary approach (Wilbur and Young, 1988).

RESEARCH OBJECTIVES

The main objective of the research was to specify and build a system that would support a wide variety of cooperative activities. Our approach has been a human-centred one, in which our goal is to identify the generic components of group communication as a framework for describing group practices in abstract terms. This approach is based on the premise that many work practices in organizations have common underlying structures. For example, a work group may be required to produce a quarterly report, and the procedure for producing this report may be the same every time. The actual people involved may change, the contents of the report will vary each time, but the basic pattern of interactions that are needed for its production vary little. If this underlying pattern can be described in an abstract way within a computer system, actual instances of the activity can be computer-supported for more effective user collaboration. The abstract definition of an activity becomes a machine-interpretable template for a group task, which can be called up for use at any time. An abstract definition becomes a real-world activity by assigning real values to abstractions, for example, by naming users to play roles. An example of the potential usefulness of abstract representations of group work is given later.

The implication of this approach is that a theoretical framework is needed for explicating group-work practices (Bowers and Churcher, 1988). The framework adopted for Cosmos was strongly influenced by theoretical work on human communication, in which the use of language is regarded as a form of action. This perspective emphasises the constructive nature of conversation, which, when we generalise it to E-mail-based cooperation, leads to the concept of *structure* as the key to abstract description of group practices. Hence Cosmos is a *structured* message system, and our objective has been to specify a system that can interpret and support the structural elements of group work.

Our second concern is that Cosmos should be *configurable*, that is, that users should be able to tailor the system to their own requirements by describing in detail the group practices in their organization. The natural approach to this concern is the language-based one, and we have developed two languages called Structure Definition Language (SDL) and Script Language (SL), to be described later.

Although our primary objective has been to specify a system that could interpret SL statements and generally support users in their activities, other strands of research have been woven around this main theme. In the first year of the project, task-analysis methods were used to identify the kind of support that individual users would need at a task level. This led to the development of a conceptual model for Cosmos, which has provided a common basis for the development of three different user interfaces to the system. Although the interaction mechanisms are different for each type of interface, conceptually they are the same, so users should have no difficulty in switching from one workstation to another.

The researchers at QMW have focused mainly on the development of SL and on the design and construction of the prototype system (Dollimore and Wilbur, 1989). In our tour of the Cosmos laboratory, these are the aspects that will receive most attention.

THE COSMOS CONCEPTUAL MODEL

The Cosmos prototype system is designed to support group activities through asynchronous interactions. The real-world model for our design is of a user who participates asynchronously in one or more group *activities* from a workstation screen. Activities are joined or furthered by selecting appropriate icons from the top-level user interface in the Cosmos environment.

A user entering an activity is taken down to a second level in the system, in which specific actions may be taken, such as creating, sending, or viewing messages that contain documents, forms, and so forth. For each activity entered, the user is aided by textual prompts displayed on the screen that indicate what actions are expected next in the context of this task. Messages that have arrived since the last time the activity was entered are presented in labeled *item boxes*, the equivalent of trays or folders, which contain only messages of a specific type. Item boxes are designed to provide a filtering mechanism, to enable messages to be viewed and retrieved by the recipient in an appropriate context. Figure 6-1 shows a user viewing item boxes on a Macintosh screen in the Cosmos laboratory.

When an action has been completed, and a new message is ready to be sent, it will be automatically addressed and delivered to the appropriate person, who will be similarly prompted concerning the next stage of the task. In the example given earlier of a regular quarterly report to which several people contribute, messages exchanged among users will contain the latest version of the report, to which each will add his or her contribution, before it finally returns automatically to the group leader. Other, similar examples may be found in project management, remote tutoring of students, and committee work.

A second aspect of the Cosmos model is the concept of *role*. Roles are contained in specific activity structures and relate to all of the user's behavior in this context. A role in Cosmos, as currently implemented, requires a real user to be assigned to it but could conceivably be played by the system itself in a future version of the software. A message is sent to a role but delivered to the real user(s) playing that role.

The actions to be taken by a role are described in a *script*, which the system can

FIGURE 6-1.   User Viewing Item Boxes on a Macintosh Screen in the Cosmos Laboratory

interpret as a recipe for what the user is expected to do in the context of the group activity. A script contains SL statements. Naturally, since real people always want to have choices and flexibility in their interactions, scripts must offer choices of action at appropriate points. The user is not presented with the entire script, just the actions appropriate to the point the activity has reached, expressed in natural English.

Roles, actions and types of message are all aspects of the generic description of an activity, that is, the *communication structure* from which scripts are derived. An ordinary participant need never be concerned with, or even aware of, the communication structure for his or her activity. The overall model of the system, then, is of an activity space, where the user may choose to switch between the various activities presented. Information is available at any level of the system on which activities are around to join, who the participants of an activity are, and so forth.

GOALS FOR THE PROTOTYPE SYSTEM

Our goal was to design and build a prototype system that would run in a distributed environment, and so the Cosmos architecture has been designed as a set of layered software modules based on a client-server model. These modules may be distributed, if required, in a number of machines interconnected by a high-bandwidth local-area network. In particular, the user-interface component may run on a variety of workstations, using Remote Procedure Call to communicate with the underlying system running on a Cosmos host.

We have built a system that supports collaborators based at different sites, linked by a wide-area network. Each Cosmos host must maintain data about the group activities its users are involved in, and these data must be consistent across all the sites involved. An X.400 Message Delivery Service provides the message transport mechanism.

User interfaces have also been our concern. We have aimed to design and implement several, to suit a variety of terminals and user-interface (UI) technologies, but with a common style as far as is possible. Three interfaces have been developed, one on a Macintosh II, one using the SUN NeWs window manager, and one using a conventional UNIX text-based interface.

SUPPORT FOR STRUCTURE

As already mentioned, the aim of the Cosmos system is to provide support for people who are involved in structured group activities and who communicate through E-mail messages. Our term *communication structure* refers to an abstract structure stored in a computer whose purpose is to support the progress of a joint task.

A communication structure describes the roles of the participants in a joint task in terms of the information each one generates and the order in which this information is exchanged among them. The structure has two main aspects—one is the prescribed sequence of actions expected of each role player in the execution of a task, and the other is the collection of information gathered during the progress of the task. We use the term *messages* to refer to the units of information that people create and exchange. This term follows the normal usage for E-mail and bulletin boards, although our messages can refer to any information used—whether it be large and complex (e.g., a chapter of a book or a project management plan) or small (e.g., a vote or a meeting date), and whatever the type of contents (e.g., a drawing or a spreadsheet as well as plain text).

The definition of a communication structure for a particular activity is a program that defines alternative possible sequences of actions for the successful outcome of the task. Each action prescribes the roles and messages involved in its execution. There are two main actions—to create a message (e.g., an agenda, the minutes of a meeting, a reply, a comment or a vote) and to make it available to some of the other role players. The latter action is done by sending the message as in E-mail to the other role players, who in their turn will receive it.

A structure definition may be used to create a communication structure by choosing people to be the role players, after which each role player will attempt to carry out the actions belonging to that particular role. As the participants perform their actions, the structure accumulates collections of messages and makes them available to the appropriate role players. In some cases it is not appropriate that all the people involved should see all the messages generated. For example in a secret ballot, each voter sees only his or her own vote, but the person counting the votes sees them all without knowing their origin. Another example is remote tutoring, in which the pupils do not see the solutions to problems until after they have submitted their own attempts.

Support for Activities in Cosmos

As we originally approached the design problem, we proposed using stored communication structures as a basis for building software to facilitate the progress of joint activities. We felt that such structures would enable us to write software that knows what actions a particular role player should take next in each activity. But first, we had to consider the fact that a typical user will work in an environment in which many activities are taking place and will typically be involved a number of parallel activities at any one time. This involvement may be active (e.g., editing a journal, writing a paper, chairing a meeting, writing today's news, or replying to personal messages) or it may be more passive (e.g., reading today's news or observing discussions).

Choice of Activity

In presenting each user with the activities available, we wish to distinguish among them on the basis of priority and status (new, in progress, halted, etc.). We do so in Cosmos by presenting the users with a context containing all their current activities and showing which ones currently require actions or contain new messages received from other role players. Information about activities in which they are not currently participating is accessible from a separate context that we call the Cosmos Information Service (CIS).

When a new activity starts, the initiator is expected to give it a name that will be meaningful to the participants. We have found from our experience with bulletin boards that relatively short textual names are best once an activity has started. The CIS provides a source of information about activities that a user might be interested in, including a more detailed description of the purpose of an activity, a reference to its structure definition, and the role players.

An Example of a Structured Activity

An example of the kind of task Cosmos might usefully support is as follows: An editor of a journal has received a paper from an author and has to decide whether or not to accept it. He or she must first forward the paper to a reviewer, or referee, for comments. The scenario might go as follows:

The paper is received from the author by the editor.
The paper is forwarded by the editor to the referee, with a request-for-comments form.
The referee receives the paper and the comments form and reads the paper in due course.
The referee returns the comments form to the editor.
The editor receives the comments and must now decide whether to accept the paper.

The editor creates an editing report, based on the referee's comments and with references
to the original paper.
The report is filed, and an appropriate message is sent to the user.
In Cosmos, each kind of document is defined as a message type.

Support Within an Activity

When the user selects a particular activity, the program prompts the user concerning the
currently appropriate actions. Prompting is provided in terms that can be understood by
the user. Since the new message may often be based on some other message already
created, a suitable general prompt must be presented in this form:

Create a new message <promptString1> based on old messages <name1. . .>

The prompts in angle brackets describe the messages in terms suitable for the particular
activity. For example,

Create a new message "editor's report" based on old messages "author's paper" and
    "referees comments"

This message could be meaningful to users who have messages called "author's paper"
and "referees comments" in their current environment.
    The prompt for sending a message relates the action of sending to the message that
has been created and to the role players who are to receive it. The general form of the
prompt is as follows:

Send the message <promptString1> with <subject of message> to <role1, role2,. . .>
Send the message <promptString> with ?subject of message? to <role1, role2,. . .>
Send the message <promptString1> with ?subject of message? to ?role1, role2,. . .?

Again, the prompts in angle brackets describe the messages suitable for a particular
activity. The words between question marks indicate that the user should input the subject
of the message or the recipient or both. An example of a particular prompt for sending a
message is this:

Send the message "editor's report" with ?subject of message? to "author"

The addresses of the recipients are filled in automatically by the system; this is similar
to the facility for automatic generation of addresses in replies to mail messages that most
mail systems support.
    All the messages that a user receives are available in the context of the appropriate
activity. For example, the author role receives the preceding message in the same activity
from which it is sent. Messages are sorted into several separate groupings within each
activity (item-boxes).
    Figure 6-2 shows a view of a paper-editing activity for a user called Stathis, who is

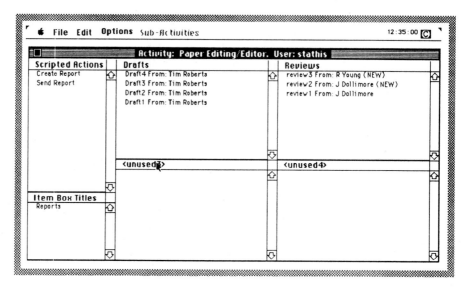

FIGURE 6-2.   View of an Activity in the Macintosh User Interface

playing the role of Editor. At the top left of the screen is shown the list of Scripted Actions that the Editor is expected to take next (Create Report, Send Report). Beneath that is a list of names of new item boxes—in this example, an item box has been created to hold the Editor's report, which will be compiled from documents already available—a draft report from Tim Roberts, and reviews from R. Young and J. Dollimore, which have all been sent to the Editor in messages. Item boxes for these items are shown, each containing a list of message headers. The items are listed in order of arrival, with the most recent ones at the top. The list changes, of course, as the activity progresses.

Users receive messages in the item boxes for their role in each activity. Both the new and old messages are available, but the new ones are indicated. For example, one-line summaries (giving sender, subject, and date) of all the messages in an item box appear in a list, with the new ones at the top and highlighted or colored. The names of the item boxes are taken from the program defining the structure.

In a complex activity, a user may be involved in several parallel threads of work. Thus they can be presented with several prompts at the same time. Nothing happens until the user selects the action corresponding to the prompt. The user is completely free to select any one of the available actions at any time or to do nothing.

The Effect of a User Selecting an Action

When the user selects an action from one of the prompts, an event occurs in the system. In the case of the Create action, the user is given an appropriate software tool (e.g., text editor, drawing program, or spreadsheet program). This work can extend over several interactive sessions, in which case the message being created is saved in the activity environment between sessions. The Create action does not terminate until the user selects the subsequent corresponding Send action.

When a user selects a Send action, the related message is sent to the recipients in an E-mail message. The address of the message (which is automatically generated) contains the name of the activity, the name of the role, and the address of the user playing the role. The message eventually arrives at the destination of each of the recipients and is placed in the appropriate item box within the appropriate activity. The user can choose to read the messages in the item boxes at any time. This does not affect the progress of an activity, but the system notes that this message has been read.

An activity is able to support the ability of the role players to send informal messages to any of the other role players. Informal messages are those that do not affect the progress of the activity.

We also provide an action that enables a user to choose between several alternative future courses of action within an activity. For example, the editor of a paper might decide whether to accept it, reject it, or ask the author to rewrite it. When the user makes such a choice, it affects the future actions of the other role players. For example, if the editor selects Rewrite, the author will be asked to do so and the editor will eventually get another version of the paper.

Personal Mail

Users are given, by default, a personal mail activity for receiving all personal mail messages addressed to them directly. The old messages are stored in an item box in this environment. The Create and Send actions are always available within this activity.

Structured and Less Structured Activities

Some activities have a clearly defined procedure of actions that must be performed to reach a state of completion. Other activities, such as discussions, are quite informal and do not require the ordering of actions to be prescribed. Many activities fall between the two extremes. Some committees have a structure for following an agenda, addressing the chair, or the secretary taking minutes. Alternatively, a committee may adopt an informal structure in which participants interact more freely. Additional tools such as a voting activity may also be useful.

Definition of a Communication Structure

A Cosmos system will always contain some ready-made communication structure definitions, for example, the one that supports the personal mail activity. We have, among others, definitions for such activities as paper editing, show-of-hands voting, expert advice, remote tutoring, and leave-taking. The structure definitions are available for browsing via the CIS, enabling users to read the informal descriptions about the structures and to look at the structure definitions themselves. If there appears to be no structure suitable for their current proposed activity, users can define a new one and add it to the collection. Structure definitions are written in Script Language (discussed later). Programming in Script Language is a little unusual in that the programmer has to supply the prompts and declare suitable names for the item boxes.

Creation of an Activity

Users create activities from the communication structure definitions available in the system. The same definition could be used many times for many different activities. For example, the definition of a structure for a bulletin board or for a committee meeting was generally useful. When an activity was created from a structure definition, the user was invited to provide a textual description of the purpose of the activity for other users to read when they browse through activities in the CIS. The user also provided the name of the activity and some users to play the other roles.

In some activities, all the role players are selected at the start, and in others, they join during the progress of the activity, for example, when their role becomes active. Joining can take place in three different ways: (1) responding to an invitation through personal mail, (2) self-selection, and (3) being required to join. The first case is suitable for tasks that require definite people to play the various roles, as for example, in joint authoring. In a committee meeting, the chairperson, members, and secretary might have been invited, but others could select themselves to attend. The latter might only be allowed to listen. The third case is suitable for situations like examinations.

If an activity is started from within another activity—for example, the chairperson starts a voting activity within a committee—the users in the first activity are automatically bound to the appropriate roles in the new activity. We have not implemented this procedure in our prototype, but we think that if it had been, it would have become the more usual manner for instantiating activities.

When users assume roles, their addresses are recorded for future use in automatic addressing. The activity becomes visible in their Cosmos environment. Although the user who defines a communication structure is expected to supply the prompt strings, and the names for item boxes, we think it would be more effective if the user who instantiates an activity could modify either of these to make them more suitable for the current usage. We have not provided this facility, mainly because all activities at the same site share the same copy of the structure definition.

THE SCRIPT LANGUAGE

The Script Language is so named because we have modeled its design on the notion that the users playing roles in an activity will follow scripts defining the currently appropriate actions (Dollimore et al., 1988). Although SDL is used to define a communication structure as a single entity, Script Language represents the same structure definition as a set of scripts. An instantiated activity has a set of scripts and an environment. The environment changes as the activity progresses and contains the messages created and exchanged and the current position of each role player.

We have developed a translator that does some of the work of converting definitions written in SDL into Script Language definitions. However, the prompts and item box names must be defined after the translation process.

We separate the structure definition into scripts because we want to have a specification of the actions to be done by a particular role available at the role player's site. The user's environment for that activity contains item boxes and the messages in them; it also contains the bindings of other variables to their values and the current position of the user in the various threads in the script. The interaction between the user and the script for his or her current role is mediated by a program we call the Script Interpreter. Figure 6-3 illustrates the relationship among the user, the script interpreter, and the environment. Each user has the services of a separate Script Interpreter process, which uses the script and the environment as a basis for presenting prompts and item box names to the user via the user interface.

Script Actions

When the user sanctions one of the actions suggested by the prompt, the Script Interpreter is responsible for executing the action. We will mention briefly the effects of the Create, Send, Receive, and Select actions already mentioned.

The Create Action

The Create action in a Script is written in this form:

Create <name> { <name1>, <name2>. . .} "Prompt string".

The first name in angle brackets is the name of a variable for binding to the value of the message created. The other names are optional and refer to other messages that the new message might be based on. The "Prompt string" is displayed in the user interface. When

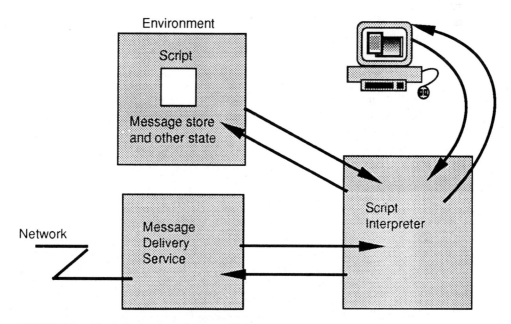

FIGURE 6-3.   The Script Interpreter Interacts with the User

the user decides to perform a Create action, the user interface provides a text editor, drawing program, or other suitable tool. When the user returns from the program provided, the user interface extracts the document or drawing that was created with it, calls the Script Interpreter with the information that a particular Create action has been selected, and then passes the document over. The Script Interpreter stores the document as the value of a variable in its environment. If the user selects the same Create again, the user interface requests the document from the Script Interpreter and again gives it to the user for editing with the appropriate program. Sometimes the Create action specifies that the new message to be created is based on some old messages—in this case, the user interface can request the values of the old messages from the Script Interpreter and make them available to the user.

If the user interface has a multiwindow editor at its disposal, the new and old messages can be displayed in different windows and the user can copy text from one to another.

The Send Action

The Create action in a Script can be written in this form:

Send <message type> to <recipients> <subject expression>

When the user selects a Send action, the user interface informs the Script Interpreter. The latter calls the message delivery service (which will be discussed later) to dispatch the message to the various recipients. If the recipients are specified as role names and the subject expression as a string, the message is immediately ready for delivery. Script writers are allowed to put Input actions instead of roles in the recipient's field or an alternative string in the subject expression.

An Input action in a Script is written as follows:

Input "prompt string"

In this case, the Script Interpreter presents the Input action and its string to the user interface. The user interface uses the prompt string and informs the Script Interpreter of the input from the user.

The message type is used for synchronisation of the Sends in one script with Receives in other scripts. In some cases, the type of a received message can be used to determine the future course of the script.

The Receive Action

The Receive action in a Script is written in this form:

Receive <name> <message types>

This action enables messages of the types specified to be received. The types may be specified as "any" in which case, any message is received. Each user has a separate message queue for each activity in which he or she plays a role. The message delivery service delivers all messages to the appropriate queue, from which they are taken when a Receive action is done. The <name> specifies the variable that holds the received message as its value. The message is then added to the list of messages in the appropriate item box.

We also have an automatic variant of the Receive action, which is done without the user being involved. In this case, the first time the users are aware of the new message is when they see it waiting in an item box. We generally use the automatic variant.

The Select Action

The Select action is provided to enable users to choose a future course of action in the script from two or more alternatives. Here is an example:

```
choice := select {YES, NO}, "Choose from :-",
"Get comments from Reviewers", "End Paper Editing Activity"
export Author
```

In this example, the user is shown the three prompts—the first a general comment about the decision and the other two, the choices. The YES and NO are message types, and the export sends an automatic message of the type chosen to the Author role player.

Item Boxes

The names of the item boxes are declared as *special* variables at the head of the script. The names used are those shown to the user in the user interface. The messages are added to the boxes by using assignment statements in the script. For example, if ReportsList is the name of an item box and Report the name of the variable holding the received message, we just write

```
ReportsList := ReportsList + Report
```

The user interface can request information about the contents of item boxes from the Script Interpreter. When the user browses through an item box, the user interface can request further necessary information from the Script Interpreter.

Parallel Threads in a Script

We provide a construct to enable script writers to specify several parallel threads in a script. For example, after giving a lesson and setting problems, a tutor may have several threads—in the first to receive answers to problems set, in the second to work on notes and problems for the next lesson, in the third to reply to queries, and in the fourth to select when to have another lesson or to finish the course. At this stage the user will see four (or more) prompts, at least one for each thread. Each thread is a sequence of actions and can be specified as optional. A group of parallel threads can terminate without the optional threads being completed, but one of the nonoptional threads must be performed to complete the program represented by a set of threads.

Prompts

When the user selects an activity, the user interface calls the Script Interpreter. The latter gets the script and environment for the user involved and returns the list of currently available actions together with their prompt strings. The user interface can then make as many enquiries as appropriate about the names of item boxes, the messages in them, and the message headers and bodies. It uses the information it gets to display the state of the user's role in the activity.

Each new action by a user results in an updated list of available actions. If the user is idle for a long time, the user interface can request an update from the Script Interpreter, in case the actions of other users have resulted in any changes relevant to this user.

THE SOFTWARE ARCHITECTURE

The software in Cosmos consists of several modules that communicate by means of remote procedure calls. This architecture enables the Cosmos system to be configured in many different ways (Araujo et al., 1988). We have already described the Script Interpreter and mentioned the user interface, the CIS, and the message delivery service.

An Object Server provides a common storage facility used by all of the software modules at one Cosmos host (Dollimore 1988). One of its main purposes is to function as a message store: It contains all of the messages relevant to the users of that Cosmos host. The messages are put there when they are created and when they are received by the message delivery service. The CIS uses the Object Server to store its data base in the form of objects representing users, activities and roles, communication structure definitions, and scripts. It also uses it to store mappings from names to objects, enabling it to provide its information in a hierarchical naming structure for user's browsing.

The Script Interpreter retrieves scripts from the Object Server and uses it to store its environments. When a user takes on a new role, a separate object is created to hold information for this role, that is, the message queue and the script environment. The message queues are references to messages (object identifiers) rather than the messages themselves, so each message (or any other object) is stored only once in each Object Server.

Replication and Message Delivery

The message delivery service takes the messages given to it and delivers them to the Cosmos hosts where the recipients are located. We assume that each user uses one Cosmos host. The message may have been transferred over a wide-area network or it may have been delivered locally over an Ethernet. Message delivery is based on the X.400 Message Delivery Service, and the message has the same identifier in all the hosts to which it is delivered.

To have an activity with participants in separate Cosmos hosts, the data about the activity are replicated from the host where they originated to the other hosts involved. These data change occasionally, for example, when a new user joins, and the changes must be propagated. We have a scheme for replicating these data via ordinary messages.

Scripts are also made available at the participating hosts, but as these do not change during the course of an activity, are sent only once.

The CIS and the Directory Service

The CIS works in conjunction with an X.500 directory service. This interaction is limited to making enquiries about information in the directories. The CIS provides a facility to browse through the information in its data bases, and the browsing has been extended to include information from the directory service.

EVALUATION AND REFLECTIONS ON SYSTEM DESIGN

Development of the Cosmos prototype system has been a larger undertaking than we had anticipated at the start, because it has to work in a distributed environment, supporting collaborative processes between users at remote sites. Thus, data have to be replicated at each site, and messages have to be exchanged by an X.400 Message Delivery Service. So much time had to be devoted to establishing this system that we have had little time left for evaluation.

Toward the end of the project in 1989, several structures were designed for the SL language, based on group tasks such as fixing a date for a meeting, holding a remote tutorial, and editing a paper. These were completed successfully, and the language primitives were found to be adequate for incorporating all the procedural elements that were required for each task.

A major insight that was gained from these exercises was that describing the procedure for what appeared to be a simple task turned out to be surprisingly complicated if all the possible options for behavior were taken into account. This complexity would have been difficult to foresee at the earlier stages of the project, as it was only through the formulation of the theoretical approach and the identification of primitives to describe group structures that we developed a framework for the analysis of group tasks. The implication of this complexity for the Cosmos approach is that the predefinition of group structures is a more difficult exercise than we had anticipated at the outset and should take account of the dynamic aspects of human interaction.

Problems with the Language-based Approach

One of our declared aims was that Cosmos should be a configurable system, and to this end we have developed a language-based approach to enable users to describe precisely their communication structures. Two languages have, in fact, been developed: Script Language, which has already been described, and Structure Definition Language (SDL). Because SDL is an extensible, rule-based notation for the formal description of a wide range of human communication activities, without constraints deriving from the particular implementation environment, it provides a conceptual base for Cosmos. However, only a subset of its features are reflected in SL, whereas SL has capabilities that are not reflected in SDL (such as support for item boxes).

The chief difficulty is that neither SDL or SL is usable by a novice, so to label Cosmos configurable is somewhat misleading. What is needed is a high-level interface to allow ordinary users to describe their group work in familiar terms, perhaps through a graphics-based package, with tools to allow existing structure definitions to be edited and updated.

Reflections on the Overall Design Approach

In the context of the CSCW research community, the *structured communication* approach taken in Cosmos can be likened to the work of Winograd and Flores (1986) in the Coordinator system and more recent work on structured cooperation (Lee, 1990; Shepherd et al., 1990). (Also see Chapter 5). Our approach has emphasized the computer in a mediating role, interpreting descriptions of communication structures and guiding users in their interactions through machine representations of the behavior expected of role players in an activity.

We believe that support for structured asynchronous communication is a valid design concept and that the approach taken by the Cosmos prototype would be useful for real-world tasks for which a well-defined procedure has been established. We do not think it is so useful for activities in which patterns of interaction are hard to predict and subject to frequent change.

Other issues arose during the project that there was no time to address. For example, who should be responsible for defining the actions (i.e., group behavior) for a specific task, and who should be allowed to modify them? How can dynamic modification of an activity and its underlying communication structure be supported while the activity is taking place? How can one instantiation of a structure be linked to another instantiation of the same structure (e.g., for a series of meetings, in which the output from one meeting is input to the next)? The Cosmos collaboration ended in 1989, and effort since that time at QMW has concentrated on making the system more robust for evaluation in real-world situations. Consequently, there has been no opportunity to date to investigate these issues further.

FUTURE PLANS

Our tour has introduced the reader to the Cosmos system and its design approach. At the time of writing, Cosmos activity has paused, although negotiations to evaluate it in a real-world environment are being pursued. A proposal for further collaborative research on structured group work has been submitted for European funding, but the result of this bid will not be known for some time. Meanwhile, we have started to investigate further the major issue that arose during Cosmos—the complexity of interaction in shared group tasks. We are currently exploring issues in synchronous interactivity and are creating a media space to investigate issues in cooperative activity in rich communication environments.

ACKNOWLEDGMENTS

We would like to acknowledge the work of the entire Cosmos team. We are deeply appreciative of their contributions to the project, the intellectual support they have given us, and the pleasure we have had working together. In particular, we would like to thank the following: Professor George Coulouris for his continuous support and innovative suggestions, and Tim Roberts, Paul Buckley, Robert Young, Regina de Araujo, Doug Steel, Stathis Gikas and Tao Sha for their valuable assistance with the research at QMW; also, Peter James and Dr. Keith Dickerson of British Telecom and Paul Wilson of Computer Sciences Company Ltd. for their personal support and loyalty to the project.

COSMOS COLLABORATORS AND AREAS OF WORK RESPONSIBILITY

The following organizations collaborated in the Cosmos project:

British Telecom Research Laboratories, Human Factors Division and Information Technology Applications Division. Investigators: Peter James, Keith Dickerson, Andy Hockley, Bruce Clark, Tony Rubin, Richard Taylor. Responsibilities: User interface style guide and implementation on a SUN workstation; evaluation methodologies.

Computer Sciences Company Limited. Investigator: Paul Wilson. Responsibilities: Contribution to work on communication structures; project publicity; evaluation.

University of Manchester, Department of Psychology. Investigators: John Churcher, John Bowers, Stephen Lee, Martin Lee. Responsibilities: Communication structures; evaluation methodologies.

University of Nottingham, Department of Computer Science. Investigators: Hugh Smith, Julian Onions, Steve Benford, Alan Shephard. Responsibilities: X.400 Message Delivery Service; X.500 Directory Service; contributions to design and software construction of Cosmos prototype.

Queen Mary College, Department of Computer Science. Investigators: Jean Dollimore, Sylvia Wilbur, Peter Johnson, George Coulouris, Tim Roberts, Regina de Araujo, Paul Buckley, Robert Young, Doug Steel, Stathis Gikas, Tao Sha. Responsibilities: Design and construction of Cosmos prototype; definition of Script Language; construction of a user interface for the Apple Macintosh workstation; task analysis and conceptual model work; technical coordination of the project.

Chapter 7

Telecollaboration Research Project

Mark Abel, Doug Corey, Stephen Bulick, Jill Schmidt, Stephen Coffin

US West Advanced Technologies

INTRODUCTION

The US West Advanced Technologies TeleCollaboration research project was an exploration of prototype multimedia communications services for the support of dispersed teams. To provide a testbed and a user community for such services, the Science and Technology Division of US West Advanced Technologies[1] was intentionally dispersed between a headquarters site in Englewood, Colorado, and a smaller site in Boulder, Colorado, from September 1988 through March 1991. The TeleCollaboration project team developed a prototype multimedia environment to support this dispersed organization and iteratively improved this environment through user feedback and observation. This exploratory effort has also been documented in Bulick et al. (1989), Schmidt et al. (1989), and Zigurs, Smith, and Pacanowsky (1989).

The TeleCollaboration infrastructure included 24 multimedia stations (approximately half at each site) in private offices, common areas, and conference rooms interconnected

---

[1]Advanced Technologies is the research and technology arm of US West. Science and Technology is the applied research division of Advanced Technologies. US West is a diversified telecommunications company and parent company of the Regional Bell Operating Company, US West Communications.

by audio, data, and motion video networks. Users were able to place multimedia calls from their desks, participate in multilocation meetings, enter shared audio and video workspaces, look around remote spaces, and generally simulate many types of same-site interaction via the multimedia infrastructure. For the duration of the project, the environment was actively used by about 20 staff members and occasionally used by about 30 other staff members.

The body of this chapter is organized as follows: a description of related work, a brief discussion of the motivations for this work, an overview of the system's technical capabilities, a discussion of the lessons learned from this dispersed organization experiment, and conclusions.

RELATED WORK

Since the mid-1980s, many research organizations have been investigating shared multimedia workspaces and multimedia conferencing. For example, one of the authors, Abel was involved in a predecessor to the TeleCollaboration project at the Xerox Palo Alto Research Center (PARC). The PARC Portland-Palo Alto Experiment developed a pioneering multimedia environment to support a research organization intentionally dispersed between Palo Alto, California, and Portland, Oregon (see Abel, 1990; Goodman and Abel, 1986, 1987). Other efforts focused on similar multimedia technology include the Cruiser project at Bellcore (Root, 1988); the Video Window[2] project at Bellcore (Smoot, 1989); and work by William Newman, Randy Smith, and others at Xerox EuroPARC (Newman and Smith, 1989). Other examples of multimedia conferencing work include Ahuja et al. (1986), Lantz (1986), Ishii (1990), and Pate and Lake (1989).

MOTIVATIONS

The telecommunications industry is planning the introduction of ubiquitous, broadband communications facilities over the next decade (Weinstein, 1987). In addition, the computing industry has begun to introduce workstations and personal computers with multimedia interfaces and capabilities. From a technological perspective, it is therefore an opportune time to investigate the use of multimedia technologies to meet major marketplace needs.

At the same time, major businesses are becoming more and more geographically dispersed because of the expanding global marketplace, the need to be near customers, the need to manufacture goods with the lowest possible labor cost, and the need to attract and retain skilled mobile workers by an attractive work location.

TECHNICAL CAPABILITIES

Technical capabilities include the following:

1. A multimedia "call" (primarily used between offices, akin to a telephone call but with the addition of two-way motion video, default remote camera control, and optional shared windowing)

---

[2]VideoWindow is a trademark of Bell Communications Research.

2. "Look-around" mode (also primarily used from office stations)
3. Impromptu interaction through an always-present video and audio link
4. Video conferencing meetings (primarily between a specially equipped conference room at the Boulder site and a similar conference room at the Englewood site)

Each of these items was designed to simulate a kind of interaction available to co-located colleagues.

Multimedia Call

Used primarily for office-to-office interaction, the multimedia call followed a traditional telephone call model. The sequence of a typical call was as follows:

1. A user initiated a call by selecting a location or user name from a speed-calling list, for example, via a user input on a touch screen, direct manipulation, or telephone.
2. The far end-user's telephone rang, while at the same time the far end-user's video display showed the caller's camera output (so that the called party could see the caller but the caller could not see the called party.[3]
3. If the far end-user answered the phone, connections were established for two-way audio, two-way video, remote camera control (remote camera control allowed viewers to control what they saw at the remote site by controlling the pan, tilt, and zoom of a remote camera), and the option of a shared text and graphics environment.
4. The participants interacted by using the available media.
5. After completing the interaction, the participants "hung up" and the call was torn down, with all facilities returned to their previous idle state.

The telephone model was used because traditional telephone procedures were familiar to most people so that little training was required. The multimedia call was also used to establish meeting connections between the conference rooms because it provided a quick and private communications capability.

Look Around

The look-around option, which was developed to simulate informally dropping by a colleague's office, completed only video and camera control connections. In other words, users could control video switching and cameras to look around a remote location. It was used primarily from office stations. A typical use of this capability was to find a remote colleague or to see if a colleague seemed available for conversation. This model of interaction was originally developed as part of the Xerox PARC Portland-Palo Alto Experiment (Abel, 1990) and has also been explored at Bellcore by the Cruiser project (Root, 1988).

---

[3]This Video Caller Identification was preferred by the TeleCollaboration user community, but it is not the only possibility. Alternatively a system might connect by two-way video only after audio contact has been made. Or a system might only add video after an audio connection is established and both parties specifically allow video.

Always-Available Video Link

An always-present common space to common space audio-video link permitted users to interact with anyone in the shared cross-site space. (The common areas were open areas near researcher offices and labs that provided a comfortable spot for informal interaction.) No user action other than walking in and beginning to speak was required. The linked common area was designed to allow the kind of impromptu meeting and discussion that occurs between colleagues in the hall, at the coffee machine, at the mailboxes, and so forth. This model of interaction was also originally developed as part of the Xerox PARC Portland-Palo Alto Experiment (Abel, 1990). In the summer of 1989, the group extended the shared common space to include a third location, a coffee area at headquarters. The three-way video was provided by split-screen technology, which showed one common area in each quadrant.

Figure 7-1 shows the common space as seen from the Englewood site. The video display was provided by large-screen (45-inch or 60-inch), rear-projection television sets. The audio was full duplex (supported by acoustic echo canceling equipment) and transmitted over high-quality audio links (13 kHz). When users needed to control a camera or change a connection in a common area, they used a touch-screen terminal running an easy-to-use touch-screen interface.

FIGURE 7-1.   Photograph of Shared Commons as seen from Englewood

In addition, the cross-site video also provided a "background connection" for office station users. When not in use for specific interactions, most users with office stations had their office video display show the other site, typically a common area or a split-screen multilocation image. During the course of the business day, this background connection allowed office users to maintain a sense of the comings and goings of their colleagues at the distant site.

Video Conferencing Meetings

This project was not intended to investigate formal teleconferencing. However, meetings are a part of any organization. The multimedia call mechanism described above was used to establish meeting connections, typically between the conference rooms in Boulder and Englewood.

The two conference rooms had large-screen (45-inch), rear-projection television sets for video display. They had full-duplex, open-space audio supported by acoustic echo cancelers and an array of microphones and speakers. The audio was transmitted over standard telephone lines (3.3 kHz). Control in conference rooms was provided by a touch-screen terminal running an easy-to-use touch-screen interface.

The group tried to enhance the feeling of physical proximity in the conference rooms by placing the large-screen television at the correct height at the end of each conference table. This position made each conference room and table appear to be a continuation of the other. Remote camera control was also available in meetings. Remote participants could, for example, zoom in on the board or screen and focus on a particular participant or zoom out to get a view of the majority of the participants, all without interrupting the meeting to ask someone to move the camera. In a typical week, four to five video conferencing meetings lasting an hour or more were held over the link.

INFRASTRUCTURE

The environment was built around the *station,* a collection of equipment that, taken together, provided the end point for a multimedia interaction with another station or with system-wide resources. All stations included a remotely controllable video camera, a video display, audio input and output (e.g., a speakerphone or microphone-speaker combination), and a computer or terminal. Access to computing resources was an integral part of the system. In the long term, we believe that an integrated station will supply many, if not all, of the capabilities embodied in the TeleCollaboration station design. In 1988, the separate components approach was less expensive. Figure 7-2 shows a typical office station, which included a 13-inch video monitor, computer, speakerphone, and controllable camera.

Seventeen of the stations were in private offices, two were in common areas, two were in labs, two were in conference rooms, and one was a mobile station. The mobile station could be moved to other areas of the main site without a full-time video station to allow Boulder lab members to attend meetings remotely. "Plugs" for the mobile station were available in the auditorium and several other critical meeting areas at headquarters. When

FIGURE 7-2.   Photograph of Typical Office Station

the mobile station was not in use for a specific meeting, it supported the coffee area in the three-way common area described earlier.

The network supporting TeleCollaboration was a model of a miniature multimedia telecommunications company, consisting of two semi-independent switching centers (one at each site) connected by a single 45 MBPS facility over fiber between the two sites. Advanced Technologies leased this transmission facility, known as a DS3, from US West Communications. The switching centers at each site actually controlled four internal networks. In other words, the environment employed four networks to simulate what many envision will be a single multimedia network in the future. The four networks at each site were as follows:

1. An analog video network
2. An analog audio network
3. A local area network for shared computing, signaling, and data
4. A hybrid control network (for camera control)

The four networks in Boulder were connected to their counterpart networks in Englewood by channels multiplexed and demultiplexed on the cross-site DS3 (and in one case by standard telephone lines as well). The bridged local-area network provided the primary control channel for the environment.

This environment allowed users to interconnect flexibly any station in the system with any other station(s) and/or shared resource. The software that controlled this environment was written in C and ran on a network of SUN[4] UNIX[5] machines. For more on the technical details of the system, see Bulick et al. (1989) and Schmidt et al. (1989).

LESSONS FROM THE TELECOLLABORATION PROJECT

This section discusses what was learned by using the TeleCollaboration prototype and living with it on a day-to-day basis for two and a half years. Although the project team did some social research and data collection as part of this experiment (Zigurs, Smith, and Pacanowsky, 1989), the primary results of the TeleCollaboration project are anecdotal, or at least qualitative, in nature. The issues presented here include the importance of video, audio quality, adoption of technology, simulating physical space with technology, privacy, document sharing, video eye contact, and remote camera control.

Importance of Video

During the course of this exploratory effort, the researchers, support staff, and management of this research organization worked with ever-present video cameras and monitors. Before the experiment began, many people were skeptical that video would add much to distant interaction, that is, that the video would contribute enough to justify the high cost of intersite video transmission. However, after working constantly with the TeleCollaboration system, most users felt that the video added a dimension of interpersonal interaction and background awareness that would have been unavailable without it. User comments included the following: "I'm more aware of who's around at the other site," "The video makes me feel like we're part of the same group," and so on. Whether video is worth the cost at this time depends a great deal on the application. As the cost for video transmission goes down, it seems clear that video will be applicable to more and more situations. Social scientists claim that two major activities occur in any face-to-face interaction: information transfer, primarily through the audio channel, and interpersonal interaction (e.g., parties deciding that they trust and like each other), often through nonverbal means (Krauss et al., 1977). From this perspective, it seems reasonable to state that video adds a dimension of interpersonal interaction that is unavailable through other media. The results of the Xerox PARC Portland-Palo Alto Experiment also support this assertion (Abel, 1990).

---

[4]SUN is a trademark of SUN Microsystems, Inc.
[5]UNIX is a trademark of AT&T.

Audio Quality

Users will not tolerate poor-quality audio, which was probably the single biggest complaint during this experiment. For example, users seemed to compare their remote experiences to face-to-face meetings. In this case, people preferred full-duplex, full-fidelity, fully bidirectional audio properly synchronized with the accompanying video. Standard half-duplex (i.e., one way at a time) speakerphones do not meet these requirements.

The best solution we encountered for conference rooms or large, open common areas was commercially available dynamic acoustic echo-canceling equipment (which supported full-duplex audio and adapted to various room and line conditions), combined with careful design and tuning of the audio system with the physical environment, for example, microphone placement, speaker placement, and room treatment. Bellcore's VideoWindow supported a full-duplex audio environment by carefully controlling its environment and carefully tuning a set of audio equalizers to deemphasize problem frequencies (Smoot, 1989).

Another method to improve audio is to use human operators to adjust and monitor audio levels constantly, but one of the project's goals was to create a usable environment that required no outside director or operator, so this solution was not acceptable.

Based on the experiences and the responses of the TeleCollaboration project users, any conferencing or multimedia collaboration environment that does not provide adequate audio quality is likely to fail. (In fact, in the TeleCollaboration environment, some users reported that the addition of video made them much more aware and less tolerant of deficiencies in the accompanying audio.)

Adoption of Technology

With any new technology, a critical issue is whether or not users adopt the technology. In the case of the TeleCollaboration technology, important factors in this decision include the following:

1. Users must have a genuine need to communicate with other people and locations available on the network.
2. The system must be convenient to access.
3. The system must be easy or familiar to use.

With a ubiquitous technology like the telephone, most of the people that users need to contact are available on the network. With the prototype multimedia conferencing capability of the TeleCollaboration system, users at the smaller Boulder site were often unable to contact colleagues in other divisions at headquarters because only the research division had TeleCollaboration stations. For any organization that is contemplating installing nonubiquitous multimedia conferencing (or other new networking technology), a needs assessment or survey is probably in order to determine who should be on the network and who needs to communicate with whom.

A key premise of the TeleCollaboration project was that users would have convenient access to stations, starting with their own desktops. The provision of office stations, stations in common areas, and stations in conference rooms covered many day-to-day situations. A mobile station combined with a number of locations with plugs added flexibility. It is the project team's opinion that such convenience of access was critical to the adoption of this technology. Other research indicates that access while traveling would be a powerful addition to on-site access (Reder and Schwab, 1990).

Once the correct people and places were accessible on the system and the users had convenient access to a multimedia station, ease of use came into play. The team explored touch-screen interfaces, direct-manipulation interfaces through a mouse and bit-mapped graphics, and line-oriented command interfaces. Of these computer interfaces, users reported that the touch-screen interface was the easiest to use and easiest to learn for novice users. Another key aspect of the service was its familiarity. For example, users preferred multimedia calling rather than look around because the social protocol of a call was well understood whereas the look-around protocol was not.

Simulating Physical Space with Technology

One of the goals of this experiment was to determine whether it would be possible to maintain a sense of "connectedness" or "community" among members of an organization who are many miles apart.

As discussed earlier, the group extended the shared common space and look-around option (called "video wandering" in Abel, 1990) from the Xerox PARC Portland-Palo Alto experiment. The idea behind these capabilities was to design technology so that it encouraged the sort of everyday, casual encounters that occur between co-located colleagues. Such casual encounters, which might take the form of impromptu conversations, casual greetings, or just casual sighting with no overt acknowledgment, are thought to be as important for maintaining a sense of unity and cohesiveness as more formal, prearranged meetings, and the relationships involved are considered to be as important as the formal relationships defined by organization charts. Various studies show the importance of proximity in forming and maintaining collaborative relationships, for example, Kraut and Egido (1988). In the summer of 1989, the group extended the shared common space to include a third location, a coffee area at headquarters. The team collected many comments to the effect that the connected common spaces and the associated background connection fostered a feeling of community between those at Boulder and those at Englewood. (The look-around option was felt to be less important and less useful.)

Not surprisingly, the group learned that the design of a common space has a great influence on the frequency of casual encounters and on the more general sense of there being interesting activity at the other site to be observed. One important criterion was traffic: The more people used or passed though the common spaces, the more likely there would be an encounter. The desire for more traffic in the Englewood common area was the primary reason the group added the coffee area to create the three-way shared space. More locations could certainly be added.

The project team had more control over the layout of the Boulder site and was able to design it with project goals in mind. For example, a number of shared computers were placed in the Boulder common area to encourage use of the space. In addition, the Boulder common area was situated so that residents must pass through it to go anywhere in the site. Unfortunately, the team had little control over the layout of the Englewood site and was only able to adapt what was already there to project purposes. The layout in the Boulder site seemed to foster interaction and visibility, whereas that in the Englewood site did not.

The team believes that the interaction between the physical environment and technology is a critical variable in the success of TeleCollaboration efforts.

Privacy

As discussed earlier, the system supported a number of modes of interaction, including multimedia calls, teleconferencing-type meetings, impromptu interaction, and background connection. In each of these types of interaction, privacy issues arose.

In multimedia telephony, the team tried to ensure that no one was able to look in on (or listen to) a call in progress. Unlike standard telephone switches, the analog video switch kept users *always* connected to something, so the potential for nonparticipants looking in covertly via video was quite high. This problem was exacerbated by the fact that for most of the duration of the experiment, there was only one video trunk between sites and people tended to watch the cross-site video signal as a default.

For multimedia calls, software prevented covert eavesdropping via video across the link. An intersite multimedia call marked the facilities used in the call as busy. Because most users with office stations watched the cross-site link as a default, the system switched everyone who had such a default to their own site's common area camera for the duration of an intersite call by others. After the intersite call was completed, the users who were switched to prevent covert watching were returned to their default view. Intrasite multimedia calls also marked facilities busy to prevent interception.

Teleconferencing meetings had a similar problem: Participants did not want others watching or listening in. This problem was generally solved by using multimedia calls to establish meeting connections, thereby locking out eavesdroppers and covert watchers.

Encouraging impromptu interaction between the sites while maintaining privacy turned out to be problematic. In particular, the look-around option allowed people to stop by others' offices via video to simulate the analogous face-to-face activity. Unfortunately, this capability also allowed users accidently or intentionally to "spy" on someone. Some users kept their cameras turned off (or their lens caps on) most of the time to avoid the possibility of being spied on. This practice, of course, made the video less useful for legitimate purposes, for example, finding out if someone was in. People were concerned that someone might be watching them without their knowledge or permission. Several prototypes to address these concerns were developed (e.g., allowing only two-way video, a "who is watching?" command) or were considered for development (e.g., a "someone is watching" light, an "electronic door," or permitted-access lists). It is clear, however, that no purely technical feature of the system would have satisfied everyone's privacy concerns with the look-around option. Thus, users preferred multimedia calling for office-to-office interaction. The social protocol of a call was familiar to users, whereas the look-around protocol was not.

In all these modes of interaction, there are two ways to handle privacy (and other social protocol) concerns: (1) Develop software and hardware to enforce a view of privacy, or (2) maintain a relaxed set of logical protocols for privacy and allow social protocols that handle the situations to evolve. We believe that group size, composition, level of trust, and so on should influence the mix of these approaches. For example, with a small, highly cohesive group of professionals, there would be little need for a privacy protocol enforced by the system. However, in a larger organization where an adversarial relationship exists between various factions, protocols of some sort would probably have to be built into the system.

Document Sharing

The team's experience indicates that dispersed users need the ability to exchange, share, and manipulate documents. Electronic mail, facsimile, voice mail, network file access, paper mail, and print services were available to the TeleCollaboration user community and were heavily used. Multimedia calls provided the (optional) ability to include a real-time multiuser text and graphics environment, BBN's Slate[6] system (BBN Software Products Corp., 1989). The Slate software did not work particularly well in conjunction with other TeleCollaboration software and was therefore rarely used. Later a team member prototyped multiuser, real-time electronic manipulation of text, images, recorded audio, recorded gestures, and graphics. Although this work showed promise, it was not a generally available capability in the TeleCollaboration environment and so no data on its use can be related here.

Many users (primarily those with office stations) were assigned special telephone extensions for facsimile transmission. Fax messages sent to those numbers triggered a loudspeaker announcement (e.g., "Facsimile message arriving for Doug Corey") and also sent electronic mail to the recipient advising that a fax message had arrived. Using facsimile boards in a computer, the group also created a facsimile server.

In teleconferencing meetings, the ability to display visual material to dispersed colleagues was required. Whiteboards and projected overhead transparencies were sometimes difficult to read over the video link. When a talk involved overheads, users generally sent copies to the other site ahead of time (by either facsimile or electronic mail) so that everyone could follow the discussion from a personal copy.

Video Eye Contact

An important social cue in face-to-face interaction is eye contact or "gaze." Eye contact provides many of the nonverbal cues that control interaction (Krauss et al., 1977). Historically, video systems have not supported good eye contact because cameras and

---

[6]Slate is a trademark of BBN Software Products Corp.

monitors were physically separate; for example, cameras were mounted on top, next to, or under the video display. Thus, users appeared to be looking above, below, or to the side of remote counterparts. To solve the eye-contact problem, one member of the group used half-silvered mirrors (technically called "beam splitters") to display the image to be observed directly in front of a camera, thereby requiring users to look right into the camera to see the remote image. This system provides an approximation of eye contact that seems to work reasonably well for one-to-one interactions. It should be noted that other labs have independently developed the same idea; for example, see the description of the "video tunnel" in Newman and Smith (1989).

A larger question is, "How valuable is eye-contact support in videoconferencing?" Acker and Levitt (1987) studied this question: "...improved eye contact increases satisfaction with videoconferencing as a medium for negotiation." That is, the key uses of such a system are activities that resemble negotiation, the system should support eye-to-eye contact.

Remote Camera Control

In the TeleCollaboration environment, all stations included remotely controllable cameras. Controllable features included pan, tilt, zoom, and for selected cameras, focus. Because the camera was functioning as a remote participant's eyes, the team consciously decided to give default control of these controllable cameras to the remote participant. (Although remote control was the default in the system, by the push of a button, users were also able to obtain control of their local camera.) Users indicated that ubiquitous camera control was a very useful feature, especially in large meetings. They did not have to concern themselves with local camera placement or "trying to stay on camera." They did not have to interrupt meetings to request that the camera be moved; they could simply do it themselves.

Camera control did have some disadvantages. First, the actual pan, tilt, and zoom movements were controlled by electromechanical motors, which limited the speed with which users could move cameras to follow the conversation. In addition, adding camera control functionality to an interface adds complexity, for example, a large number of buttons, which makes any system interface that much more difficult to learn and to use. Finally, camera control interacts with several other potential features of video systems. For example, the design of an integrated station or video eye-contact system is made more difficult if the camera is not fixed.

CONCLUSIONS

The project team believes that multimedia technology will eventually be fully integrated. In other words, eventually one broadband multimedia network will supply the same capabilities as the project's multinetwork solution, and an integrated multimedia station will supply the capabilities that the TeleCollaboration project's multicomponent "station" does today.

Project results indicate that multimedia station vendors should consider issues like audio quality, document sharing, eye contact, and camera control in the development of integrated multimedia stations. In particular, any conferencing or multimedia collaboration environment that does not provide adequate audio quality is likely to fail. Also implementers will need to get the right people and locations on a multimedia collaboration system, provide convenient access (e.g., on the desktop or while traveling) for users, and make the systems easy and/or familiar to use.

A key finding of this work is the importance and usefulness of video, especially as it supports various types of office-to-office and informal interaction. It enabled us to maintain much of the day-to-day life of an organization with about a fifth of its members physically separated by 45 miles from the others. This result confirms the findings of the Xerox PARC Portland-Palo Alto experiment (Abel, 1990). Another key finding is that multimedia calling was greatly preferred over look around for remote office-to-office interaction. The familiarity of the telephone-call model, in particular the social protocols for privacy, made users much more comfortable than the look-around model, in which privacy was more problematic.

A number of these lessons are being incorporated into US West's broadband trials program. A thorough understanding of such issues will be critical to the successful deployment and utilization of broadband networks.

Section III

Task-Oriented Team Technology

In contrast to the preceding four chapters, the researchers in this section focus more on task-supported, workstation-based users of team technology, operating same time/same place. Picture these users as convening in a room large enough to accommodate them, seated with a computer or keypad, and participating in a structured meeting both through face-to-face interactions and by way of software programs that elicit their input (see Chapter 2 for a detailed discussion of an electronic face-to-face meeting). Although some of these systems incorporate communication support and are capable of supporting any-time/any-place meetings, the preponderance of the research to date has been with face-to-face groups.

We have chosen in our model to cluster these sites further based on their use of self-constructed technology, acquired technology, or a combination of the two. As we will discuss shortly, this factor is influenced by the orientation of the researchers and by the degree of funding available to them. However, there are a number of other dimensions on which these sites are analogous or dissimilar.

One factor that crosses dimensions in this section of our model is size and resource availability. Some sites have large programs (e.g., Arizona), and others have small ones (e.g., Hawaii). The sites also vary in their focus on small, self-managed groups (e.g., Minnesota and Michigan) versus larger, facilitated groups (e.g., Arizona). Another difference worth noting is the degree to which the site focuses on the physical context (room design, seating, and lighting) of the meeting room. Michigan bases its research on the premise that the physical environment plays a key role in the group outcomes and directs its research toward determining the ideal meeting milieu. Most of the other sites made early decisions on the meeting environment and then held that factor constant in their studies.

The final distinction to note among these ten chapters is that each one is attempting to mold its own set of resources into a research niche. Although the larger sites are able to research group processes across a broad domain, the smaller sites choose more narrowly defined focuses. For example, Queen's has targeted brainstorming, Hawaii has an international focus, Singapore is Macintosh-based, and Georgia is targeting facilitation.

Part A

Self-Constructed Technology

We now direct our attention to those sites that are using solely self-constructed software. These early entrants had no technology available. They were leading the way in the development of group support systems, so it was up to them to build the tools to meet their research needs. However, this process was expensive and only those universities with substantial funding were able to participate in this developmental stage. The early tools emerging from their research had a strict task focus and were initially designed to support planning or decision making. Arizona's entry was an outgrowth of research designed to elicit information from information system users in order to improve the systems development process. Minnesota's doorway was the synergy created there among a group of accomplished researchers by Gallupe's dissertation work with a small, simple group support system he built to run on the university's computer. The early tools of both of these sites later evolved into structures fashioned to support a variety of group tasks and processes.

The two chapters in this part of the book describe the development and use of the two most researched workstation-based same-time/same-place systems: GroupSystems (Chapter 8) and SAMM (Chapter 9). GroupSystems (GS) is also marketed by IBM under the name of TeamFocus (TF). Together they have over 70 commercial sites, and SAMM has about 5 commercial installations. Both have a number of academic-based installations. The large number of GS/TF commercial sites highlights the different focus taken by each group. Important major differences include the following:

Attribute	GroupSystems	SAMM
Team size	Medium to large	Small
Meeting management	Facilitator driven	Self-management (user driven)
Product focus	Commercial	Primarily research support, now extending into commercial domain

The two research groups have been driven by different theoretical perspectives and research strategies. The Arizona group has developed a process gain-and-loss framework to guide its efforts. Certain aspects of the meeting process can improve outcomes (process gains), whereas others impair outcomes (process losses). Technology can affect this balance of gains and losses in at least four ways: (1) process support, (2) process structure, (3) task structure, and (4) task support. Poole and DeSanctis of the Minnesota group have extended and applied adaptive structuration theory (AST) to groupware research. AST, like other sociotechnical theories, conceives technology use as a social practice that emerges over time. It suggests that meeting outcomes are not a direct result of structures introduced through the technology or facilitation. Rather, the outcomes reflect the manner in which groups appropriate and modify these structures, and thus the appropriation process becomes a critical aspect. Both of these perspectives provide useful conceptual maps to investigate and manage teamwork technology.

The strategy primarily followed at Minnesota has been laboratory research with recent extensions into the field, whereas the Arizona group has used a balance of laboratory and field studies. Both groups have carried out extensive research programs, the results of which are summarized and future research directions indicated.

There is one other distinction worth noting between these groups: the types of relationships they have formed to help carry out their work. The infrastructure required to support research and development in this area is extensive. As a result, a number of the research sites have forged alliances with a range of groups and individuals who have a stake in team technology (see Chapter 15 for a discussion of a research alliance model). Alliances provide expertise and resources. The Arizona approach has been primarily to develop partnerships, especially with vendors, and to spin off a commercial company linked to the university (Ventana Corp.). Chapter 8 describes the IBM-Arizona relationship. In contrast, the Minnesota group has relied primarily on research sponsors (e.g., NSF) and has only recently forged organizational partnerships (e.g., Texaco and IRS).

Chapter 8

GroupSystems

J. F. Nunamaker, Jr., *University of Arizona,*
A. R. Dennis, *University of Georgia,*
J. F. George, W. B. Martz, Jr., *University of Arizona,*
J. S. Valacich, *Indiana University,*
and D. R. Vogel, *University of Arizona*

INTRODUCTION

Groups have been meeting since the beginning of time. Specially designed meeting rooms for problem solving and decision making have a history almost as long. The Greeks and Romans had special-purpose facilities for planning and decision making. During World War II, Winston Churchill brought together his top advisers in a London decision room to plan the strategies that were to lead to an Allied victory. Decisions are made today in special meeting rooms in the U.S. Senate and the House of Representatives and other governing bodies and social institutions worldwide. It is widely recognized that group problem solving and decision making are critical parts of good management. However, meetings are often time-consuming and not always effective and efficient.

The University of Arizona has a long history in computer-augmented teamwork, including the development and operationalization of GroupSystems software intended to enhance meeting productivity through the application of information technology. Two operational facilities exist at the University of Arizona, with more in the planning phase. Further, GroupSystems software is currently installed at over 100 sites including 28 academic institutions and 35 sites at IBM.

The purpose of this chapter is to focus on the development, operationalization, and evolution of University of Arizona GroupSystems. Specific attention will be given to the origin of research interest, original purposes and goals, early problems, first version of the facility, current version of the facility, evaluation of use, continuing research, and future research plans.

ORIGIN OF RESEARCH INTEREST

The underlying concept for GroupSystems had its beginning in 1965 with the development of Problem Statement Language/Problem Statement Analyzer (PSL/PSA) as part of the ISDOS (Information System Design and Optimization System) project at Case Institute of Technology (Teichroew and Sayani, 1974). The PSL/PSA process started with the assumption that the requirements were known or that the individual or group responsible for the systems-building project was capable of stating the requirements. There was no emphasis on developing an organizational consensus on the "correct" set of requirements because at the time it was assumed that the systems analyst was in charge and would be able to define the systems requirements satisfactorily. Emphasis on involving the user in requirements analysis was not to develop for another ten years.

The collective wisdom of the ISDOS project members at that time was that the first priority should be to develop methods to reduce the time needed to build a system, starting with "the assumption of correct requirements" as a given. The rationale was that the correct requirements are not constant; they change with changes in the organization. The users themselves change with respect to what they think they need to do their job. The basic objective was to reduce the time from the initial statement of requirements until the target system was operational. Automation or computer support was envisioned for each task in the systems life cycle.

From this conceptual framework evolved a number of software tools for automating the systems-building process. This approach, utilizing computer support, resulted in PSL/PSA in 1965 (Teichroew, Hershey, and Yamamoto, 1982) and later in PLEXSYS (Konsynski and Nunamaker, 1982). PLEXSYS was derived from the word *plexus,* defined by Webster's as "an interwoven combination of parts or elements in a structure or system." The *sys* in *PLEXSYS* is short for "system." In 1965–1968, three activities shaped the development of PSL/PSA and eventually the development of PLEXSYS: (1) The first version of the problem statement language and problem statement analyzer was developed by Nunamaker (1976) as input to a computer-aided systems analysis and design software package called SODA (Systems Optimization and Design Algorithm); (2) the prototype for the problem statement language was developed by John Paul Tremblay; (3) the prototype for the problem statement analyzer was developed by Paul Stephan. These three developments led to the PSL/PSA version, which was used by well over 100 organizations for documenting and analyzing the set of requirements for an information system (Teichroew, Hershey, and Yamamoto, 1982).

A change in thinking took place during the process of using SODA/PSL, SODA/PSA, and ADS/PSA (Accurately Defined Systems), early prototypes of PSL/PSA, on a large project for the U.S. Navy (Nunamaker, Konsynski, and Singer, 1976). There were problems in depending on end users to utilize a formal language for requirements specifications. The end users at the Navy would not write their specifications in a PSL/PSA-like system, so an accounting firm was hired to sit with the end users and write the specifications in the language. Insights gained from the deficiencies in this solution led to the development of the GroupSystems concept. The idea was to develop a phase that came before the use of PSL/PSA, that is, to develop software to assist the users with the determination of requirements (Konsynski, 1976; Nunamaker, Applegate, and Konsynski, 1988). This phase would help developers determine what was needed in addition to the software in order to develop systems that would be used by the end users of the information system.

ORIGINAL GOALS

In many organizations, the user group is represented by a steering committee or task force consisting of 10 to 20 people. It became clear in 1979 that what was needed was a special meeting room for the task force to use, or a place for the user group to meet to address the information requirements of an organization. The function of the room would be to display the system flows, data structures, and information requirements on a large-screen projection system and permit each user seated at a workstation to interact with the set of requirements and the proposed design of the system.

The PLEXSYS-84 system (Konsynski et al., 1984), which was an extension of the PSL/PSA/ISDOS project, was a workbench/workstation environment for the systems development team. A collection of integrated tools, procedures, transformations, and models were available to the systems developer to analyze and design systems. It was expected that PLEXSYS would shorten the life cycle of development by facilitating a fast implementation of a prototype system. It was recognized that the design process could not be completely automated and that PLEXSYS would be a computer-aided support system with data bases, knowledge bases, model management, and inquiry facilities. This version of the first phase of PLEXSYS was the basis for the eventual development of the University of Arizona GroupSystems software.

EARLY PROBLEMS

The most persistent conceptual problem encountered during the early days of PLEXSYS was the use of a single terminology for all user environments. User groups were found to be reluctant to embrace the highly structured PSL/PSA syntax. Each user organization and factions within any organization wanted to use the terminology of their choice. This requirement led to the concept, illustrated in the GroupSystems Enterprise Analyzer, of independent definition of the terminology employed based on the characteristics of the user group. Emphasis is now placed on most effectively and efficiently capturing the information from the user group, with later translation, if necessary, to a more common structured terminology or language that crosses groups.

The most persistent practical problems in the early days were implementation-oriented. The systems used with early versions of PSL/PSA were based on mainframes with cumbersome interfaces and often poor response times. Worse yet, system programs were often relegated to tape, which further inhibited effective use and application. Early versions of PLEXSYS on networked microcomputers had significantly improved interfaces but still suffered in terms of response times. For example, the time required to obtain a new file during an Electronic Brainstorming session could be in excess of 20 seconds, far slower than the thinking rate of the participants. Over the years, this has been pared down to less than two seconds and is no longer deemed a problem. Anecdotal experience suggests that once file refresh rates exceed 4 seconds, users begin to feel slowed by the system.

FIRST VERSION OF THE FACILITY

Construction of the first computer-assisted group meeting facility at the University of Arizona began in 1984. The first facility, called the PlexCenter, houses a large U-shaped conference table with 16 computer workstations (Figure 8–1). Each workstation is recessed for line-of-sight considerations and to facilitate interaction among participants when appropriate. A BARCO large-screen (10-foot) projection system can display screens of individual PCs. In addition, a video switcher facilitates the movement of screen images from PC to PC or downloads the public screen (facilitator's) display to each workstation. The facility includes four breakout rooms, also equipped with PCs, for small-group discussion.

The facilitator's station provides access to and control over the group support tools. The role of the facilitator varies as a function of group and task characteristics. For large heterogeneous groups new to the facility, the facilitator helps the group get the most out of the process by both guiding the meeting and running the software. For more experienced homogeneous groups new to the facility, the facilitator acts more as a process consultant and is less actively involved during the meeting. For smaller groups with system experience, the facilitator station is typically inactive; that is the group is completely in charge of the process and running the software.

Software developed for use in the first facility consisted of an Electronic Brainstorming tool for idea generation, an Issue Analyzer tool for idea organization, a Voting tool to collect and display results, a Policy Formation tool to assist in the development of policies, and a single workstation version of Stakeholder Identification and Assumption Surfacing to help in evaluating the implication of plans or policies. (See Appendix 8–A.)

The facility, which opened in March 1985, was conceived as a meeting room for end users, systems analysts, systems designers, and project leaders to review and analyze system specifications and designs. During the first 18 months of the system's operation, however, we found that the software was valuable in planning efforts of all types and not just in information systems. In fact, the usage of the room shifted from requirements and design review to initial discussion of issues and problems. The participants in each session became the group responsible for decision making in regard to the organization's goals and objectives relative to the task under discussion. The system was built for one particular audience but was found to be useful in a broader context.

FIGURE 8-1.   University of Arizona's PlexCenter

CURRENT VERSION OF THE FACILITY

Based on the insights gained from the operation of PlexCenter, it was decided to build a second facility. The success of using Arizona GroupSystems in small and medium groups suggested that larger groups might benefit even more, so the second facility was designed to accommodate large groups. In addition, building a new facility provided an opportunity to improve the facility design, develop a new systems architecture, and take advantage of recent technological developments.

The second Arizona facility designed to support group meetings with information technology was opened in November 1987. The Collaborative Management Room was designed to accommodate 24 workstations with space for 2 people per workstation (Figure 8-2). In addition, gallery seating for 18 observers was included in the back of the room. The room has a distinct legislative feel to it, but it also facilitates talk across the room if appropriate. The 24 workstations house IBM PS/2 model 50s with high-resolution color monitors and individual microphones. In addition to the two large-screen displays, a high-resolution video projector with a remote control unit displays computer (analog

FIGURE 8-2.   University of Arizona's Collaborative Management Room

and TTL) and NTSC video signals. This system permits display of laser disks, transparencies, videotapes, 35mm slides and Videoshow 160, and a computer graphics presentation system with special effects.

A separate control room was built to house TV monitors, audio mixers, and video editing equipment for monitoring and processing session recordings. The capability exists to capture the computer inputs from all participants as well as audio and video recording of a session. Years later, one could reproduce a replay of a key corporate discussion or decision. This capability will provide tremendous insight for changes to corporate strategy, planning, and so on in the future as well as general research knowledge.

Participants interact with a variety of automated tools to support individual and group planning, deliberation, and problem solving. These broader tasks typically have subtasks involving aspects of idea generation, idea organization, voting, issue exploration, and knowledge accumulation and representation. These subtasks may or may not all be present in conjunction with the primary task, but they are related in that those that are present usually benefit from information developed from a previous subtask or external source and generate output for use in subsequent subtasks. The GroupSystems tools are designed as a loosely coupled tool set with the capability to pass information between tools in conjunction with the use of a knowledge base.

Over the past four years, Electronic Brainstorming, Issue Analysis, Voting, Policy Formation, and Stakeholder Identification and Assumption Surfacing tools have been significantly revised and enhanced to reflect what we have learned through extensive experience. In addition, new GroupSystems software tools have been developed to complement the earlier tools. (See Appendix 8–B.)

Infrastructure support for the GroupSystems facilities is provided by the Center for the Management of Information (CMI), which is housed in the University of Arizona MIS Department. CMI provides scheduling and facilitation support in addition to facility maintenance. Additional infrastructure and support are provided by faculty and graduate students within and external to the MIS Department with research interests in group support systems.

EDUCATIONAL USE OF GROUPSYSTEMS

University of Arizona GroupSystems has been used successfully in a variety of educational modes:

- Introducing MBAs to personal computing. MBAs need to use word processing, spreadsheet, data-base, and statistics software in conjunction with their course work. The Video Switcher is especially useful in helping an instructor provide individual as well as group interaction with students.
- Supporting case studies in the Arizona Executive Program. The Arizona Executive Program uses Harvard-style cases in conjunction with exploring the implications of management actions. GroupSystems allows executives to interact electronically and speed the process of case discussion. Simultaneously, the executives become familiar with the use of GroupSystems to help address their own organizational problems.
- Environmental scanning support. The marketing department at the University of Arizona has used GroupSystems to expose MBAs and executives to environment scanning techniques and methodologies in addition to the Wharton economic data base.
- Support for hearing-disabled groups. The University of Arizona and IBM have implemented GroupSystems at Galludet University in conjunction with education and communication support for hearing-disabled students.
- Executive support system analysis and design. GroupSystems software is used to provide classroom support for the analysis and design of prototype executive support systems as well as to familiarize students with key implementation issues.
- Education in group planning and decision making. The University of Arizona offers a course in group support systems. GroupSystems is used extensively during the course to familiarize students with system characteristics, issues in the application of such systems, and research opportunities.

- Survey and questionnaire administration. GroupSystems software has been used to administer questionnaires and summarize results as well as to give students an opportunity to provide anonymous feedback.

EVALUATION OF USE

The GroupSystems empirical research and system development program has included both laboratory and field research studies, as we believe that multiple methods are necessary to understand the impact of the technology; to identify the best fit for various system, task, group, and organizational configurations; and to identify opportunities to improve and (re)design tools to support group work. We will begin by examining the theoretical foundations of our work and then review laboratory research followed by the field and case research.

Theoretical Foundations

Prior research and theory with non-computer-supported groups provide a rich starting point. However, as information technology has the ability to affect profoundly the nature of group work, it becomes dangerous to generalize the outcomes or conclusions from research with noncomputerized groups to the computerized environment. A better approach is to examine underlying theory that explains why these events occur and consider how technology and various situational characteristics may affect the theory to produce different outcomes.

To understand these interactions, we need to examine group process at a lower level of detail. Certain aspects of the meeting process improve outcomes (process gains), whereas others impair outcomes (process losses) relative to the efforts of the same individuals working by themselves or those of groups that do not experience them (Hill, 1982; Steiner, 1972). Meeting outcomes are contingent on the balance of these process gains and losses. Situational characteristics (i.e., group, task, and context) establish an initial balance, which the group may alter by using GroupSystems.

There are many different process gains and losses. Table 8-1 lists several important ones, but this list is by no means exhaustive. Each of these gains and losses varies in strength (or may not exist at all), depending on the situation. For example, in a verbal meeting, losses due to air time, that is, the need to partition speaking time among members, depends on group size (Diehl and Stroebe, 1987; Jablin and Seibold, 1978; Lamm and Trommsdorff, 1973). Air time is a greater problem for larger groups, as the available time must be rationed among more people; if everyone in a 3-member group contributed equally in a 60-minute meeting, each person would speak for 20 minutes, whereas each member of a 15-member group would speak for 4 minutes.

There are at least four theoretical mechanisms by which GroupSystems can affect this balance of gains and losses: (1) process support, (2) process structure, (3) task structure, and (4) task support (Figure 8-3). Process support refers to the communication infrastructure (media; channels; and devices, electronic or otherwise) that facilitates communication among members, such as an electronic communication

TABLE 8-1   Important Sources of Group Process Gains and Losses

Common Process Gains

More information	A group as a whole has more information than any one member.
Synergy	A member uses information in a way that the original holder did not because that member has different information or skills.
More objective evaluation	Groups are better at catching errors than are the individuals who proposed ideas.
Stimulation	Working as part of a group may stimulate and encourage individuals to perform better.
Learning	Members may learn from and imitate more skilled members to improve performance.

Common process losses

Air time fragmentation	The group must partition available speaking time among members.
Attenuation blocking	This (and concentration blocking and attention blocking below) are subelements of production blocking. Attenuation blocking occurs when members who are prevented from contributing comments as they occur forget or suppress them later in the meeting because they seem less original relevant or important.
Concentration blocking	Fewer comments are made because members concentrate on remembering comments (rather than thinking of new ones) until they can contribute them.
Attention blocking	New comments are not generated because members must constantly listen to others speak and cannot pause to think.
Failure to remember	Members lack focus on communication, missing or forgetting the contributions of others.
Conformance pressure	Members are reluctant to criticize the comments of others because of politeness or fear of reprisals.
Evaluation apprehension	Fear of negative evaluation causes members to withhold ideas and comments.
Free riding	Members rely on others to accomplish goals because of cognitive loafing, the need to compete for air time, or perception that their input is not needed.
Cognitive inertia	Discussion moves along one train of thought without deviating because group members refrain from contributing comments that are not directly related to the current discussion.
Socializing	Nontask discussion reduces task performance, although some socializing is usually necessary for effective functioning.
Domination	Some group member(s) exercise undue influence or monopolize the group's time in an unproductive manner.
Information overload	Information is presented faster than it can be processed.
Coordination problems	Difficulty in integrating members' contributions because the group does not have an appropriate strategy can lead to dysfunctional cycling or incomplete discussions, resulting in premature decisions.
Incomplete use of information	Incomplete access to and use of information necessary for successful task completion.
Incomplete task analysis	The incomplete analysis and understanding of the task result in superficial discussions.

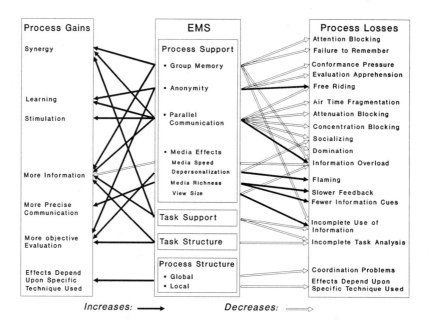

FIGURE 8-3.   Potential EMS Effects

channel or blackboard. Process structure refers to process techniques or rules that direct the pattern, timing, or content of this communication, such as an agenda or process methodology like Nominal Group Technique. Task support refers to the information and computation infrastructure for task-related activities, such as external data bases and pop-up calculators. Task structure refers to techniques, rules, or models for analyzing task-related information to gain new insight, such as those in computer models or decision support systems (DSS).

Task structure helps the group to understand and analyze task information and is one of the mechanisms by which DSS improve the performance of individual decision makers. Task structure may improve group performance by reducing losses due to incomplete task analysis or increasing process gains due to synergy, encouraging more information to be shared, promoting more objective evaluation, or catching errors (by highlighting information). Methods of providing task structure include problem modeling, multicriteria decision making, and so on. Although task structure is often numeric in nature, it is not necessarily so.

Task support may reduce process losses due to incomplete use of information and incomplete task analysis, and it may promote synergy and the use of more information by providing information and computation to the group (without providing additional structure). For example, groups may benefit from electronic access to information from previous meetings. Although members could make notes of potentially useful information before the meeting, a more effective approach may be to provide access to the complete sources during the meeting itself. Computation support could include calculators or spreadsheets.

Process structure has long been used by noncomputerized groups to reduce process losses. It may be global to the meeting, such as developing and following a strategy or agenda to perform the task, thereby reducing process losses due to coordination problems. GroupSystems can also provide process structure internal to a specific activity (local process structure) by determining who will talk next (e.g., talk queues) or by automating a formal methodology such as Nominal Group Technique. Different forms of local process structure will affect different process gains and losses. Process structure has been found to improve, impair, and have no effect on group performance; its effects depend on its fit with the situation, and thus little can be said in general.

GroupSystems can provide process support in at least three ways, either separately or jointly: (1) parallel communication, (2) group memory, and (3) anonymity. With parallel communication, each member has a workstation that is connected to all other workstations, thus providing an electronic channel that enables everyone to communicate simultaneously and in parallel. No one need wait for someone else to finish speaking. Process losses from air time, attenuation blocking, and concentration blocking should be significantly reduced. Free riding may be reduced because members no longer need to compete for air time. Domination may be reduced because it becomes difficult for one member to preclude others from contributing. Electronic communication may also dampen dysfunctional socializing. Parallel communication increases information overload (because every member can contribute simultaneously). Process gains may be enhanced by synergy and the use of more information. Increased interaction may also stimulate individuals and promote learning.

GroupSystems can provide a group memory by recording all electronic comments. Participants can de-couple themselves from the group to pause, think, and type comments and then rejoin the "discussion" without missing anything. This process should reduce failure to remember, attention blocking, and incomplete use of information and may promote synergy and more information. A group memory that enables members to queue and filter information may reduce information overload. A group memory is also useful if some members miss all or part of a meeting or if the group is subjected to interruptions that require temporary suspension of the meeting. GroupSystems may also provide other forms of group memory that do not capture all comments. An electronic blackboard, for example, may reduce failure to remember (by presenting a summary of key information) and dysfunctional socializing (by increasing task focus).

The electronic channel may provide some degree of anonymity. Anonymity may reduce the pressure to conform and evaluation apprehension, but it may also increase free riding because it is more difficult to determine when that is occurring. However, when the group meets at the same place and time, the lack of process anonymity—that is, members can see who is and is not contributing—as opposed to content anonymity—that is, members cannot easily attribute specific comments to individuals—may reduce free riding (Valacich, Dennis, and Nunamaker, in press). Anonymity may encourage members to challenge others, thereby increasing process gains by catching errors and a more objective evaluation. Anonymity may also provide a low-threat environment in which less skilled members can contribute and learn.

Arizona Laboratory Experiment Research

More than 20 laboratory experiments have been conducted at Arizona, so it is difficult to present their findings quickly. In this section, we focus only on three areas of our laboratory research: anonymity, group size, and group member proximity.

Anonymity is possible in the electronic component of GroupSystems meetings but not with their verbal component. Anonymity can affect use by reducing or eliminating evaluation apprehension and conformance pressure as well as social cues. The reduction of evaluation apprehension and conformance pressure may encourage a more open, honest, and freewheeling discussion of key issues. However, the reduction of social cues can lead individuals to behave in ways that are outside of the realms of socially prescribed behavior. Some evidence of the deindividuation associated with the reduction of social cues has been found in some forms of computer-mediated communication, the most extreme form of which is extremely inflammatory comments.

Changes in evaluation apprehension, conformance pressure, and social cues brought about through anonymous communication should have some effect on the meeting process, which should in turn affect the meeting's outcomes. The relaxation of social cues in anonymous electronic messaging systems (EMS) groups has been found in varying degrees in five laboratory experiments conducted at the University of Arizona. The use of anonymous EMS has been found to generate more critical comments than the use of EMS in which the author of each comment was identified (Connolly, Jessup, and Valaich, 1990; Jessup, Connolly, and Galegher, 1990; Valacich, Dennis, and Nunamaker, in press). Jessup and Tansik (1991) also found that anonymous, nonproximate groups generated the most critical comments. However, only one of five experiments found anonymous groups to have increased performance compared to nonanonymous groups (Connolly, Jessup, and Valaich, 1990); there were no performance differences in the other studies (George et al., 1990, Jessup, Connolly, and Galagher, 1990; Jessup and Tansik, 1991; Valacich, Dennis and Nunamaker, in press).

In all of these laboratory studies, anonymity was treated as a discrete variable; that is communication was either anonymous or it was not. However, the Valacich, Dennis, and Nunamaker (in press) study suggests that anonymity may be better thought of as a continuous variable—it may be more appropriate to think of degrees of anonymity. In this study, there were two independent variables, anonymity and group size. The small anonymous groups were more critical than the small identified groups, but there were no differences in the level of this factor among small and large anonymous groups and large identified groups. Because these groups had so many members, there was already a degree of anonymity built into their structure. This was not the case in the smaller groups, where the relative intimacy of the group reinforced existing social cues.

Group Size
In general, without computer support, process losses increase rapidly with group size (Steiner, 1972). Previous noncomputerized research has concluded that in general,

regardless of the task, context or group, the optimal group size is quite small, typically 3 to 5 members (Shaw, 1981), because process losses quickly overtake any process gains from increased size. Our research draws a different conclusion: The optimal group size depends on the situation and in some cases may be quite large.

One measure of process losses is participation because it is directly affected by air time, production blocking, free riding, and so on. Experiments in electronic meetings have found that per-person participation levels remain constant regardless of the size of the group (Dennis, Valacich, and Nunamaker, 1990; Valacich, 1989; Valacich, Dennis, and Nunamaker, in press), suggesting that process losses may remain relatively constant as size increases. Other experiments have found outcome measures such as effectiveness and member satisfaction to increase with size (Dennis, Valacich, and Nunamaker, 1990; Valacich et al., 1990). Another laboratory experiment built, tested, and confirmed a model of group performance that proposed process losses to be relatively constant across group size (Valacich et al., 1990).

Group Member Proximity

GroupSystems groups may be distributed with respect to both space and time, although the majority of our research to date has focused on groups interacting in a single room at the same time. Other researchers have also argued that advanced computer-assisted communication and decision technologies, such as an EMS, can be important for project-oriented work groups and temporary task forces that may be distributed geographically and temporally throughout an organization.

From a theoretical perspective, group process and performance for distributed groups may be substantially different from proximate groups. Social facilitation research has shown that the presence of others can improve a person's performance for easy tasks and hinder performance for more difficult tasks (Zajonc, 1965). Remoteness may also foster increased anonymity, which may have several effects on the group, ranging from reduced apprehension to increased social loafing and deindividuated behavior, as noted previously. Further, several small-group researchers have found that close group proximity may foster liking and fondness among group members (Zajonc, 1965), and in EMS environments, proximate groups have been as satisfied (Valacich, 1989) or more satisfied than distributed groups (Jessup and Tansik, 1991)

Our initial research in this area has built on our growing body of idea generation research (i.e., a problem of uncertainty, not equivocality), in which groups communicate only electronically. One laboratory experiment found no difference in the number of ideas generated between proximate and distributed groups but found proximate groups to be more satisfied (Jessup and Tansik, 1991). A second study using a similar research design found that distributed groups generated more ideas than proximate groups, with no satisfaction differences (Valacich, 1989).

During these experiments, proximate groups were interrupted more often by disruptive movements or by laughter prompted by a humorous electronic comment. Social facilitation research suggests that such reaction will generally be stronger when a person is proximate to other group members than when working alone in a distributed group (Zajonc, 1965). Thus we believe that the primary explanation for these performance effects in the laboratory was that distributed groups remained more task-focused than proximate groups.

However, the effects of the proximity manipulation may have been different if this research had been conducted in the field. Our groups worked without outside interruptions. Yet there are many potential interruptions for group members working alone in the privacy of their offices by events that cannot be helped (e.g., a call from the boss) or by purposely working on other tasks. As a result, distributed groups in the field may or may not be more task-focused than groups working together in the same room, and thus may find different effects.

Arizona Field and Case Research

Our field investigations of the effects of GroupSystems on organizational groups have a long history. Numerous groups, addressing various tasks, have used our facilities over the past four years. Because of space and time limitations, we will discuss only a few of these studies. Our objective will be to present a spectrum of groups and tasks in order to produce a more complete picture.

The field studies reported here are separated into two segments. First, a series of extended studies at several IBM corporate sites will be discussed in detail. Second, results from a series of studies conducted at the Arizona facilities with a variety of organizational groups will be compared to the IBM study results. The overall objective of these field studies was to evaluate the effects of EMS on effectiveness, efficiency, and user satisfaction. The emphasis was on realism in group characteristics and tasks to serve as a comparison to the rigorously controlled laboratory studies discussed previously. In most cases, tasks were much broader than those in the laboratory, usually moving from initial option generation to an agreement. Meetings typically began with option generation (using EMS) followed by option formulation and evaluation (using a variety of other tools).

IBM

Early in the GroupSystems project, IBM recognized the potential of the system to improve group meetings and organizational performance (Nunamaker et al., 1989). After visits by IBM corporate personnel to University of Arizona facilities, where they were given experience in the use of group support tools to address a major corporate planning problem, company representatives expressed satisfaction with the process and decided to install similar facilities within the corporation for operational use on a daily basis.

The site selected for the initial IBM installation was a manufacturing plant with approximately 6,000 employees, located in a rural setting in upstate New York. A room to house GroupSystems was remodeled according to the design of Arizona's PlexCenter. A U-shaped table was equipped with ten networked microcomputers. An additional microcomputer attached to a large-screen projection system was also on the network to permit display of work done at individual workstations or of aggregated information from the total group. An adjacent small room was designated for "backroom" functions such as printing session results.

The first phase of implementation began in the spring of 1987 with a site visit and was concluded in December of 1987 with a corporate evaluative report. Close communication and cooperation between IBM and the University of Arizona ensured that the implementation proceeded smoothly and established a strong foundation for extended facility use and evaluative efforts. The transfer of technology from an academic research environment to a corporate mainstream application was a new experience for the groups involved in this implementation at both the University of Arizona and IBM. Previous experience at the university had been based on six academic implementations. This cooperation at the initial site was so successful that it led to implementation of over 35 additional GroupSystems sites. Additional sites are now envisioned for the near future.

Problem-solving groups at every location were encouraged to use the facility. Groups most often heard about the facility through word of mouth from other groups. Group participants ranged from the plant manager and high-level executives to shop floor personnel. Representatives of several management levels were often included in the same group. Some groups were ongoing entities; others were newly established or even ad hoc. Group size ranged from four to ten members, with an average size of eight. Larger groups tended to be new ones, formed to carry out a particular task and representing a wide variety of functional areas. Group members typically had detailed knowledge of one aspect of the problem and general knowledge of the problem domain.

Tasks addressed by the groups were, for the most part, of a planning and problem-solving nature, for example, strategic planning problems, factors contributing to cost overruns, and functional data-processing needs. Some were cross-organizational, involving many functional areas; others represented several management and employee layers within a particular functional area. The groups participating in sessions brought with them myriad problem domains, for example, requirements analysis, strategic planning, and resource allocation. Most of the tasks were complex to the extent that they required creativity and had no known "right" answer, particularly those assigned to the larger groups. Groups also tended to address tasks that were oriented toward evaluating a set of issues. A preplanning meeting was typically held before each group session to align the tools with the task to be undertaken.

For purposes of this study, GroupSystems effectiveness was evaluated in two ways: quality of session process and quality of outcome. A measure of the former was the degree to which the participants took part in the process and contributed to its outcome. A measure of the latter was the degree to which the system provided the product that the session initiator wanted. A further indication of outcome quality came from follow-up results on how the results from the system were actually used.

Session process quality was measured by log files, through which it was possible to learn the distribution of participation among the participants, and from information gathered from participant postsession questionnaires and follow-up interview forms. Analysis of log file data revealed that compared to traditional group dynamics, GroupSystems tends to equalize participation. Results were independent of participants' typing skills and familiarity with microcomputer technology. The responses of participants in a postsession questionnaire indicated a strong agreement that the system did provide process effectiveness. Further, those who had used the automated system before consistently had a higher mean score on questions of process effectiveness (P <.0001). Managers who were participants consistently noted in the follow-up interviews that the session results were used, and useful. Follow-up in the form of feedback, additional meetings, and implementation of suggestions was commonplace, as were presentations to higher management levels. In some cases, ideas from a number of sessions involving a single group or groups from various corporate areas were combined to achieve a higher level of integration and comprehension. On the basis of these ideas, plans were developed and decisions made.

The efficiency of the system as revealed by this study is an indication of the relative costs and benefits to the organization in comparison to manual functions. It was not possible to run parallel sessions with control groups to measure efficiency directly. However, before using the facility (and without knowledge of automated support capabilities), each group leader was required to recommend and document a feasible project schedule for the accomplishment of his or her group's objectives, based on previous experience with similar projects. These schedules defined historical parameters for the projects and a baseline for comparison with the efficiency of the automated support systems. The plan was then translated into an outline to guide the use of the automated support tools. After completion of the project, the projected schedule was compared with the actual GroupSystems performance. Further, the output from the sessions was independently evaluated by a knowledgeable third party to measure what it would take to arrive at the same level of accomplishment with traditional manual processes.

Overall, there is reason to believe that the results gave at least a reasonable approximation of the estimated parameters, based on the years of experience of the various group initiators. Work hours were saved in every case recorded, with an average per-session saving of 51.15%. Percentages have been used to compensate for varying project lengths. A matched-pairs t-test was significant at a level (P <.0001).

High levels of performance in terms of work-hour savings were strongly correlated with the degree to which the group's task was stated clearly and concisely (P <.004). Larger groups (i.e., eight to ten members) tended to outperform smaller groups slightly, relative to expectations. Work-hour savings were independent of the individual knowledge of group members, the ongoing nature of the group, the degree to which cooperation was required, and the composition relative to the number of management levels or different departments represented. However, more formal, more recently established, and less cohesive groups tended to achieve higher levels of work-hour savings relative to expectations than similar groups that met without the benefit of automated support. These latter groups also tended to be larger.

User satisfaction was evaluated in three ways. First, records of utilization rates of GroupSystems were reviewed as an indication of general user acceptance and satisfaction. Second, a postsession questionnaire provided self-reports of user satisfaction. Finally, interviews with 17 users of the automated system provided a broad range of personal impressions.

Since it was opened in October 1987, the room has been fully utilized, and currently there is a three-week waiting period for its use. A further measure of the acceptance of the system by the organization has been the decision to install automated group rooms at additional company sites. Thus, user acceptance, which can be considered a measure of satisfaction, has been demonstrated.

Other Field Studies

Groups ranging in size from 8 to 32 members from more than 150 organizations have used the EMS facilities at the University of Arizona since the first one was opened in 1985 (Nunamaker, Applegate, and Konsynski, 1988; Valacich, et al., 1990). For example, eight community activists met with representatives from the Tucson Unified School District to generate options to improve public education. Fourteen representatives of key stakeholders in a diverse industry association spent four days generating options for and agreeing on a new mission statement, specific organizational objectives, and a plan to accomplish them. For the past two years, more than two dozen managers from all line and staff areas of Burr-Brown, a multinational electronics manufacturer, have spent several days generating options and evaluating plans for capital, staffing, and other resource allocations among eight corporate divisions (Dennis, Heminger, Nunamaker, and Vogel, 1990). More than two dozen managers from Greyhound Financial Corporation, a multinational financial organization with $1.6 billion in assets, spent one day generating options (and committing to their implementation) to improve competitive advantage. Fifteen elected representatives and senior appointed staff of a county government spent one day generating and prioritizing a list of key issues facing the county.

The experiences of these and other groups have been consistent with those in IBM. In virtually all cases, results from direct observation, postsession questionnaires, and follow-up interviews consistently indicate that option generation with EMS was perceived to be more effective, more efficient, and more satisfying than other approaches. These effects were noted for groups from both the public and private sectors, for groups that worked together regularly and groups that had not, for groups of varying sizes, and for groups in a variety of meeting contexts. Although EMS was in general preferred to non-EMS approaches, there is only weak support for two situations in which it was even more strongly preferred. First, larger groups (e.g., more than a dozen members) tended to report higher effectiveness, efficiency, and satisfaction with EMS than smaller groups. Second, groups working in more integrative, or "win-win," situations (e.g., Greyhound and Burr-Brown) tended to report higher effectiveness, efficiency, and satisfaction with EMS than groups in less positive settings (e.g., education activists or industry associations). However, more research is needed to verify these propositions fully.

To understand the impact of EMS use, Dennis, Tyran, Vogel, and Nunamaker (1990) conducted a survey of 17 groups that used these EMS facilities. Structured interviews were conducted with the leader of each group, after he or she had had the opportunity to use the session results and reflect on their usefulness (typically two to four months after the session), through an instrument developed and validated for evaluating systems to support strategic decision making (Venkatraman and Ramanujam, 1987). The group leader was chosen as the best person to evaluate success because the leader was the individual who would ultimately be held accountable for the quality of the group's performance. However, to determine if the leader's perceptions matched those of the other members of the groups, three items were placed on postsession questionnaires, which were completed by all participants of six groups. The correlation between the mean response of all members and that of their leaders was .80, indicating similar perceptions. Three of the items pertained to option generation, and EMS was reported to be more effective for generating options, identifying key problem areas, and fostering innovation than other non-computer-supported approaches. Furthermore, the overall EMS-supported process was reported to be more effective than non-computer-supported processes. Ten of the 17 leaders cited anonymity as an important, or the most important, feature of EMS.

FUTURE RESEARCH PLANS

The past years of research activity have continued to be productive through an iterative process of software engineering activities coupled with laboratory and field evaluations (Grohowski et al., 1990; Nunamaker, Dennis, Valacich, and Vogel, 1991; Nunamaker, Dennis, Valacich, Vogel, and George, 1991). However, many additional questions and unexplored areas remain. Three of these are particularly important. First, the studies have tended to focus on groups meeting for only a single session. Less attention has been given to the longitudinal use of GroupSystems across a number of integrated sessions. Second, the studies have tended to focus on only individual and group levels of analysis. Many questions remain concerning the implications of GroupSystems on project and organizational levels of analysis. Finally, the studies have focused primarily on the context of face-to-face meetings. Less attention has been given to the implications of GroupSystems in geographically and temporally distributed environments.

The University of Arizona Department of Management Information Systems is currently embarking on an integrated program of multimethodological research (with particular emphasis on software engineering coupled with laboratory and field studies) into the implications of group support system implementation and use on individual, group, project, and organizational levels of analysis. Research objectives reflect a continuation of the previous focus and extension to project and organizational levels of analysis with a longitudinal emphasis, that is, extension beyond meeting room environments to more geographically and temporally distributed domains involving multiple cultures and languages. The opportunity to use group support systems in a multilingual fashion is especially exciting.

The multimethodological and multidisciplinary research approach dealing with facility, hardware, software, and facilitation on multiple levels of analysis reflects a University of Arizona conviction that an integrative approach with a team of researchers is necessary to deal successfully with the complex network of interconnected questions associated with the implementation and use of GroupSystems. Failure to take an integrative approach tends to result only in a plethora of piecemeal studies, from which few, if any, meaningful, generalizable insights can be attained. Group support systems have the potential to influence the way we work. The challenge is to provide tools and direction based on sound empirical research to facilitate effective implementation and use. Through a combination of integrated software engineering, laboratory, and field studies with an iterative and longitudinal emphasis, we feel this challenge can be met.

CONCLUSION

The combined efforts of researchers investigating the potential of electronically supported group activities clearly indicate that these systems have a real future for many aspects of problem solving, decision making, and collaborative work in organizations. There is little doubt that the proliferation of information made possible by computers requires us to use computers not only to store and manipulate data but also as a medium for formulating and communicating ideas in the broader contexts of decision making and problem solving. We are in a pioneering phase in information technology, but initial GroupSystems results have been extremely encouraging and all indications point to an even brighter future.

APPENDIX 8–A: ORIGINAL TOOLS

Electronic Brainstorming supports idea generation by allowing group members to share comments on a specific question simultaneously and anonymously. Participants are encouraged to be creative or critical, depending on the nature of the question and group objectives.

Issue Analyzer helps group members identify and consolidate key items associated with previously generated text, for example, idea generation or previous familiarity with the topic. Support is also provided for integrating external information to support identified focus items.

Voting provides a variety of prioritizing methods including true-false, Likert scales, rank ordering, and multiple choice. All group members cast private ballots. Accumulated results are displayed in graphic and tabular formats appropriate for each method.

Policy Formation supports the group in developing a policy statement or mission through iteration and group consensus. Members contribute sample text, which is then edited through group discussion and returned to participants for further refinement. The process continues until consensus is reached.

A single workstation version of Stakeholder Identification and Assumption Surfacing helps to evaluate systematically the implications of a proposed policy or plan. Stakeholders and their assumptions are identified, scaled, and graphically presented to the group for discussion and analysis.

APPENDIX 8–B: RECENTLY ADDED TOOLS

Topic Commenter supports idea solicitation and provision of additional details in conjunction with a list of topics. Participants enter, exchange, and review information on self-selected topics. Each topic may be subdivided as required to solicit more focused comments.

Idea Organizer supports the Nominal Group Technique, in which group members have an opportunity to develop independently a list of issues, followed by round-robin sharing with other members, and culminating in discussion and prioritization. Idea Organizer also complements Electronic Brainstorming in helping to organize generated ideas.

GroupOutliner extends Topic Commenter capabilities by providing hierarchically organized topics. Participants enter, exchange, and review information on self-selected topics. The topic structure may be continually modified through group member input as the group's discussion progresses.

Alternative Evaluator provides multicriteria decision-making support. A set of alternatives can be examined under flexibly weighted criteria to evaluate decision scenarios and trade-offs. Results are displayed in a variety of graphic and tabular formats.

Group Matrix (GM) provides the capability for group members to define the relationship between cells, based on columns and rows of information objects, and then see the group consensus form as relationships change, based on group appreciation of alternative perspectives.

Group Writer provides full-group editing access to text created by group members or imported from other sources. Group members, who are updated as changes are made, can annotate as well as edit selected text. A history is kept of all revisions.

Questionnaire provides support for researchers, group leaders, and the facilitator in designing on-line questionnaires as well as summarizing the participants' responses. Questionnaires are dynamic in the sense that additional questions can be triggered by selected response values.

File Reader provides participants immediate read-only access to previously stored material at any point in a group session—even during the use of another tool. Users may browse through stored material and return to interactive participation at their own discretion.

Group Dictionary enables a group to define formally a word or phrase to focus their own thoughts or provide reference for future group work. The process is interactive and iterative, if appropriate, to encourage members to participate in arriving at consensus.

Enterprise Analyzer provides support for capturing characteristics of an organization, including data sets, information systems, and structure, to provide a foundation for impact analysis as well as general processes and the relationships between them.

Semantic Graphics Browser provides a graphic browsing system for reviewing related stored information, for example from the Enterprise Analyzer. Users can move through a "world space" and zoom in on specific areas of interest for more detail in graphic and text formats.

Chapter 9

An Overview of the GDSS Research Project and the SAMM System[1]

Gary W. Dickson
Marshall Scott Poole
Gerardine DeSanctis

University of Minnesota

INTRODUCTION

The purpose of the Minnesota GDSS project is to conduct theoretical and empirical research relating to the application of group decision support systems (GDSS). A comprehensive investigation of GDSS is being conducted by a team of researchers from the fields of information systems, speech communication, public policy studies, and computer science at the University of Minnesota.

The project has three major goals. First, it is building and testing a theory of how work teams use GDSS and other social technologies and of the effects of these technologies on group interaction and outcomes. Whereas simple (nonsocial) technologies are used by an individual, social technologies operate within an interpersonal context. Our focus is on adaptive structuration theory (AST), which offers a comprehensive explanation of how teams incorporate social technologies into their work (Poole and DeSanctis, 1990;

[1]This research is supported by the National Science Foundation, Grant No. SES-8715565 to Poole and DeSanctis, and by grants from the NCR Corporation and Texaco, Inc. At the University of Minnesota the project is supported by the MIS Research Center, the Carlson School of Management, the College of Liberal Arts, the Humphrey Institute of Public Affairs, and the Conflict and Change Project. The views expressed here are solely those of the authors and not of the research sponsors.

163

Poole, Siebold, and McPhee, 1985). In part, AST argues that social technologies gain meaning only as they are *used* in team interaction; teams form "interpretive structures" about the technology, and it is these structures, more than the technology itself, that have the greatest influence on team work. These interpretive structures evolve and change over time, and so GDSS impacts vary over time. The structures play a major role in the adaptation and reinvention of the GDSS as it is implemented. AST moves away from simple deterministic models of technological effects and assumes that the impact of technologies comes from how people use and adapt to them. It thus allows for both intended and unintended consequences of GDSS. The theory has implications for the design, implementation, and use of GDSS and related technologies for team meetings.

Second, the project is contributing to the current body of knowledge of GDSSs and other social technologies by exploring how their design combines with contextual factors to affect the process and outcomes of organizational meetings. Our studies are attempting to sort out rigorously competing explanations for GDSS effects. They also define a set of basic dimensions underlying GDSS design that can serve as a unifying analytical scheme for this and other research. GDSS design variables in our research include the system's sophistication, the degree of user control over the technology, and whether the system provides decision structuring (Level 2) or communication support (Level 1) only. Contextual factors of interest include the size of the team, the configuration of individuals within the group (their personalities and status within the group), the nature of the team's task, and whether meetings occur in a face-to-face or dispersed mode.

Third, in the long term this work will contribute to the development of a general theory of group and organizational structuring. AST implies a general theory of how groups and organizations function in the context of GDSS and other social technologies. In this way we can understand how organizations are shaped by social technologies and how these technologies, in turn, are shaped by the actions of organizational members.

The project involves a multiyear, systematic program of interlocking studies that combines a strategy of experimental and field studies devoted to user-driven systems for small (3 to 16 persons) team meetings. A fundamental activity of the Minnesota GDSS project is the construction of an environment to support our research. As a result, and founded on the research questions we wish to pursue, we have constructed a decision room that houses a specific group decision support system.

The purpose of this chapter is to describe the genesis of the Minnesota GDSS project, describe the GDSS we have implemented, articulate problems and opportunities we have faced in building our system, briefly describe our research studies, and indicate the future directions of our project.

ORIGINS OF MINNESOTA GDSS RESEARCH

Late in 1983, Brent Gallupe was searching for a dissertation topic in order to complete his Ph.D. degree at the University of Minnesota's Carlson School of Management. His thesis advisors were Gerardine DeSanctis and Gary Dickson. A meeting held to discuss possible research topics for a paper competition sponsored by the ACM Special Interest Group on Business Data Processing (SIGBDP) resulted in a number of potential ideas for the dissertation. The idea that had the most appeal was to investigate the support of group or team decision making with information technology.

Gallupe took the suggestion seriously and began planning a group decision support study, searching for existing GDSS technologies to facilitate the research. Among the systems available at that time was the Mindsight system developed by Dr. Gerald Wagner and his associates at Execucom Systems in Austin, Texas. For his research, Gallupe was returning to the institution at which he had previously taught, Lakehead University in Thunder Bay, Ontario. Because of this fact and the technical resources that would be available to him, Gallupe determined that implementing Mindsight would be logistically difficult; he decided to program his own small GDSS system in BASIC and run it on his university's VAX computer.

Gallupe tested his GDSS in a problem-finding environment (Gallupe, DeSanctis, and Dickson, 1988). He had three user terminals and a monitor serving as a public screen. This system was a prototype for the GDSS later developed at the University of Minnesota. Gallupe's GDSS had three simple features: idea input and display, ranking, and voting.

At this time, DeSanctis and Dickson were active members of a research group concerned with the managerial use of computer-generated graphics, a program of research under the title of the Minnesota Managerial Graphics Project (DeSanctis, 1984; Dickson, DeSanctis, and McBride, 1988; Vogel, 1986). At the time, the project was winding down and its energy began flowing into what was to become the GDSS project. A commitment was made to a new program of research that would merge the graphics work into a GDSS line of inquiry. A study of graphics in small-group decision making by McBride (1988) helped to bridge our research in graphics to the study of group decision support.

In addition to his thesis research, Gallupe began to work with DeSanctis on a series of "foundation" papers that spelled out what GDSS was about, and they developed a research agenda that would be addressed in programmatic fashion (DeSanctis and Gallupe, 1985, 1987). By late 1985, a group of researchers had come together to move from the Gallupe prototype GDSS to a full-fledged GDSS that could provide the basis for a research program. In other words, the research team set out to build a GDSS that would be based on group research, would focus on solving problems that were known from the literature to cause trouble in task performance, and would support research on GDSS design and impact.

The initial design team consisted of two faculty members, DeSanctis and Scott Poole from the Department of Speech Communication at the University of Minnesota, and two doctoral students in management information systems (MIS), Richard Watson and Ilze Zigurs. Gary Dickson served as a design reviewer, and Mike Beck, a professional systems analyst, was engaged to program a number of screen layouts (again, using the BASIC language). The intent of this design phase was to create the look and feel of a GDSS on a personal computer without a massive programming effort.

The system moved from this design stage to programming when Richard Watson began developing the actual GDSS. After some investigation and consideration of the availability of computing resources, Watson began to implement the GDSS on an IBM

PC/AT, using the C programming language running under the Xenix operating system. The PC/AT was selected because at low cost it could run four workstations simultaneously. Xenix was chosen because its "messaging" feature could be used to communicate data stored from workstation screens to a public screen without the complication of programming a network. It should be recalled that in 1985 and early 1986, the local-area network (LAN) technology was less well developed and available than it is today, and a system based on a host computer was considerably less expensive (and likely to be more reliable).

A VERSION 1.0 GDSS: CAM

Richard Watson taught himself the C programming language and set out to build a GDSS to support his doctoral research. This system was to become the initial platform for the Minnesota GDSS activity. Watson named the prototype CAM, which stood for Computer-Aided Meeting. He developed CAM by the fall of 1986. Meanwhile, DeSanctis and Poole had been successful at tapping a variety of sources for relatively small amounts of funds to support building a GDSS facility.

Enough money had accumulated from these sources to purchase a 24-inch monitor to serve as the system's public screen, a reasonably large conference table and four chairs for users, and four side tables to hold workstations. Computer equipment was acquired through a grant from IBM to the school's MIS area (for the host PC/AT) and through Dickson's project with the American Assembly of Collegiate Schools of Business (AACSB) (responsible for training business faculty to teach the subject of MIS). Three IBM PCs from the AACSB project were connected to the host PC/AT.

Space for the GDSS system was obtained in the back half of a long and narrow room located in the Carlson School of Management at the University of Minnesota. It was in this facility that the first Minnesota GDSS experiments were conducted during the fall of 1986 and winter of 1987 (Poole and DeSanctis, 1987; Watson, DeSanctis, and Poole, 1988; Zigurs, Poole, and DeSanctis, 1988). The CAM system had nine features: (1) problem definition, (2) input of alternatives, (3) input of decision criteria, (4) rating, (5) ranking, (6) voting, (7) public messaging, (8) public spreadsheet, and (9) solution definition. These features were intended to reduce process losses in groups and to support communication needs, particularly in problem-solving tasks. CAM was, in effect, a Level 1 GDSS.

A VERSION 2.0 GDSS: SAMM

While Watson was experimentally testing the CAM system, the project team was successful in obtaining resources to support the expansion of the GDSS project and in undertaking a major redesign of the CAM system to develop an architecture that would facilitate a flexible migration pattern as the GDSS system evolved.

Resource Acquisition

Richard Watson headed an effort to improve the equipment environment for the Minnesota GDSS system. The IBM system was limited to four user workstations, and the project and its programming were ahead of Xenix in many ways. It was felt that the project needed to move into a full UNIX environment supported by much more powerful hardware. We were pleased with the UNIX architecture, which involved a host computer and the C language.

Kathleen Klaas, from the local office of NCR, was familiar with NCR's university relations policies, and she worked with the Minnesota GDSS project team to structure a proposal for a supermicrocomputer to support the further development of the GDSS system. NCR made an equipment grant to the University of Minnesota of a Tower 32 computer with six workstations, delivered during the Christmas vacation of 1986. Watson had the equipment installed and was running the CAM system in a matter of hours after delivery. The speed with which the UNIX and C-based software were transferred to the NCR environment reinforced the decision of the team to work with these technologies.

Meanwhile, another faculty researcher, John Bryson, had become involved in the project from the university's Hubert H. Humphrey Institute of Public Affairs. Bryson played a key role in obtaining something from the institute that was not available from the Carlson School of Management—high-quality space in which to locate a GDSS facility. The institute, which is adjacent to the Business School, made a room available to the project that was attractively furnished and located in a building less than two years old.

About a year later, two project members, Poole and DeSanctis, were successful in obtaining a large three-year grant from the National Science Foundation (NSF) (see Poole and DeSanctis, 1987). This grant made it possible for the group to design and have built special furniture for our GDSS facility. In addition, three more workstations were purchased (making a total of nine connected to the system). The large (and unattractive) monitor for the public screen was replaced by a very large screen on which system output was displayed by an overhead projector and LCD display. Finally, and perhaps most important, the NSF grant made it possible for the group to hire a computer science student as a half-time programmer dedicated to the GDSS project.

In summary, by mid-1988, the Minnesota GDSS environment was much enhanced, expanded, and substantially more attractive than in the early days of the CAM system. The room as it currently appears is shown in Figure 9-1. Equally important, we had an expanded GDSS software package in operation and were poised for additional system development.

System Redesign and Development: SAMM

During 1987, the Minnesota GDSS team of faculty and Ph.D. students spent a considerable amount of time and effort in redesigning the CAM system. The architecture selected was based on a setup module and a set of operations modules. The notion was that the researcher or meeting manager would select a set of options in the setup module that would then constitute a particular GDSS implementation for a specific meeting or research session (see Dickson et al., 1988).

The architecture of the operations module was such that various general functions of the GDSS would be separated but linked together. Figure 9-2 is a hierarchy chart the

FIGURE 9-1. Current Minnesota GDSS Decision Room

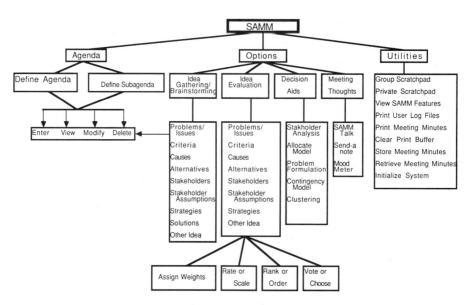

FIGURE 9-2. Structure of the SAMM Program Provided to Each Team Member

complete set of features as of this writing, in the Minnesota GDSS system (all of which are in the operations module). Note that the current version of our GDSS includes both Level 1 and Level 2 features. The latter are contained in the Decision Aids modules. Whereas the other options support exchange of ideas and opinions, the Decision Aids provide systematic modeling techniques and the ability to conduct "what-if" analyses on group data.

By mid-1987, the Minnesota GDSS team began to realize that the system that had been developed needed a better name than CAM (which also referred to computer-aided manufacturing). In addition, enough creativity and effort had gone into the system to make the research team feel that some legal protection was in order. Thus, it was decided to choose a new name and to work with the university's legal department or copyright protection.

To complete the copyright process, the product name had to be unique in the domain of software. The team spent quite a bit of effort creating names and acronyms for our GDSS product. (Of course, we used the system to generate and evaluate possible names.) The outcome of this process was the name Software-Aided Meeting Management (SAMM). We had some logic in selecting a humanlike name. SAMM differs from most GDSS in that it incorporates behavioral features oriented toward "friendly" and "fun" technology and directed at human behaviors that exist in non-GDSS-supported meeting environments. Thus choosing a name like SAMM was one small step in this direction. The name also suggested a relationship to the previous CAM.

It may be useful for the reader to understand basically how SAMM is used and to appreciate some of the underlying philosophy. One thing that separates SAMM from most other GDSS is that it can be user-driven; that is, the entire power of the system resides in the hands of each user (at each workstation), in contrast to those GDSS that must be facilitated or operated by a chauffeur (SAMM can be run in these ways as well). SAMM is designed on the principle of empowering the team to create its own structure from a set of tools and techniques. Furthermore, members can work at their own pace and use the modules of their choice; it is not necessary for everyone to use the same modules simultaneously.

The user-driven design implies that team members can share, or rotate, responsibility for such actions as recording minutes, noting comments, sending group information to the large viewing screen, or printing data displays. Although this responsibility could be taken over by a technician or meeting facilitator, such specialized support is not required. Each group member has the capability to perform these functions at any point in the meeting. Another important philosophical choice was to include the support of the socioemotional needs of groups along with the more rational decision-making needs. SAMM has a special module called Meeting Thoughts, which allows members to express their elation, frustration, and fear and helps the team to assess its morale level.

Overview of System Use

The SAMM architecture consists of two programs: a public screen program, which sends output to a large monitor or large-screen projector, and a private terminal program, which drives the private workstation assigned to each team member. The two programs use the message exchange facility within the UNIX operating system for communication with each other. Figure 9–3 illustrates this concept.

Each member of the team uses the private terminal program during a meeting; the public program operates automatically. Team members typically enter some inputs at their respective terminals and view all the team's inputs on the public screen. Teams normally follow an agenda of system features; however, the sequence in which they use the various features may vary across meetings.

In a SAMM-supported meeting, team members typically begin by individually entering agenda items, problems, decision alternatives, or the like at their individual workstations. Next, someone in the team displays all the individual items together on the large screen in front of the team (the public screen). Anyone can put up all the individual items on the public screen at any time. What is displayed there is the state of the list of items at the time a team member decides to view them ("view" means to display to the public screen). Normal group procedure is to examine the list of items generated by the team and to delete any duplicates, restate items, or reorder them. During this process, considerable discussion normally takes place among the members of the team. SAMM tends to generate relatively short periods of input (ideas, problems, etc.) and longer periods of group discussion and rework of the items entered.

SAMM has a rich set of weighting, ranking, rating, and voting tools for evaluating the list of items that the team has entered. In a working SAMM session, it is a common practice for the team to move on to the evaluation stage once a list of some sort (problems, decision criteria, alternatives, etc.) has been agreed on by the team. After

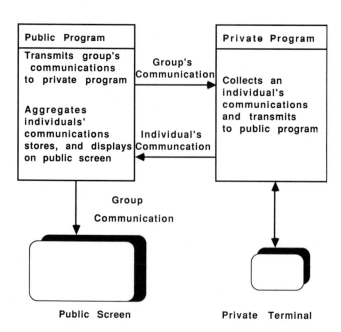

FIGURE 9-3.   Relationship Between Public and Private Programs in SAMM

evaluation, a team may go back and revise the content or the description of the original list of items. As a team is doing so, members are sometimes entering text on their terminals, engaging in group discussion, and/or selecting someone to serve a secretarial function and clean up the entries or restate them. Other times the members are using the evaluation feature to express opinions. The public display of the outcome of the evaluation frequently leads to considerable group discussion and iteration back to previous steps.

SAMM is quite easy to learn and use. The addition of a facilitator (e.g., for strategic planning in a one-time meeting) requires about ten minutes of user training, and then the computer-supported meeting can begin. Groups making repeat use of SAMM (such as quality teams) frequently use the technology without a facilitator in the user-driven mode. For these groups, it takes less than an hour to learn the basic SAMM features. We have found that most user-driven teams become proficient after about two uses, on the average. Of course, the more practice a team has in using the software, the more proficient and comfortable members become with the system. (See the appendix at the end of this chapter for a more detailed description of SAMM.)

CURRENT SAMM STATUS

SAMM presently is implemented in approximately 35,000 lines of code in the C programming language and is running under the AIX (UNIX) operating system. The IBM RISC System/6000 is the most common hardware used. User workstations are some mix of character-oriented terminals, personal computers, and X-terminals. The latter two workstations support color display at the workstation and on the public screen.

In the summer of 1991, NCR donated its newly developed 486 server system and six 386-based workstations to facilitate operation of SAMM in an OS/2 Windows environment. Plans are underway to use NCR's Cooperation software to link SAMM running in a UNIX environment to Windows-based applications. This equipment is located in a new laboratory at the University of Minnesota.

Installations include a variety of university and commercial sites, for example, the Internal Revenue Service, Texaco, IBM, Washington University in St. Louis, Marquette University, and Stanford University. A distributed version of SAMM is being used in research at Marquette University. It runs on a Northern Telecom Meridian computer, which is a unique UNIX environment. This machine integrates speakerphones into the terminals and has a two-position switch on the display. The switch allows users to display either their private screen or the public screen at their private workstation. SAMM has also been reengineered for operation on Macintosh equipment by the National University of Singapore. (The Macintosh version is called SAGE. See Chapter 12.)

SAMM DEVELOPMENT

SAMM development is currently taking two directions: (1) design enhancements for the present system and (2) more advanced technical environments that will allow considerably expanded capabilities. Enhancements all involve the addition of more features in the

Decision Aids area. One such aid is a module designed by Poole that will deal with conflict and negotiation tasks; initial programming of this module is now underway. Also under development is a group memory manager and a design for distributed group support. The technology directions include moving into a full X-Windows interface (which can involve sessions with other host software such as executive information systems or data base query) to the NCR 486 environment and to an IBM mainframe. These steps all involve state-of-the-art technology, which will allow enhancement of SAMM's capabilities.

As of this writing, another development is the movement to make SAMM commercially available. A Minnesota corporation has been established to further development and to market and support the software. Currently this enterprise is engaged in changing the SAMM technical architecture to support future development and to take advantage of X-technology interface capability. A marketing and support organization is also being developed. This corporation has become an IBM Business Partner and is working with the Twin Cities marketing office of IBM to offer SAMM-facilitated meetings and to sell SAMM to commercial customers.

BARRIERS TO GDSS DEVELOPMENT

Our project exists in a university environment, and most of SAMM's features are based on a research need. That is, the characteristics of SAMM have been designed to meet specific research questions. The Decision Aids module, in particular, has features that allow the research team to investigate such questions as the degree of decision structure embedded in GDSS software (in contrast to only supporting communication among team members). The important point is that SAMM was not designed to be a commercial product and the developers and designers are not in the business of creating market-driven software. The university environment is "resource poor" in contrast to that of most commercial developers. Faculty members, for example, have teaching and service duties that take them away from GDSS activity. Money to support development must be raised, and there is not always a free choice of hardware and software. Frequently university personnel must use what is available to them. Finally, we work with a development staff (students) that turns over on the average of once every two years. This staff is part time and has priorities other than GDSS work. With this background in mind, we present some specific barriers that we have encountered in the Minnesota GDSS project. Most are resource-related.

Technological Limitations

SAMM has been criticized by some as having a "1960s interface." The project team has only recently acquired color graphics, mouse capability, object-oriented data-base software, and so on. Until recently, the UNIX environment available to us (through the good will of NCR) was limited to monochrome character-oriented output and keyboard input. To this point, we would argue that this limitation was more apparent than real for three reasons. First, we were able to learn a lot with the technology we had, and more fully featured capability may have distracted us from some of our initially required fundamental activities. Second, there is some research evidence to suggest that GDSS performance differences are much more related to the structure of the GDSS and the social processes it creates than to interface characteristics (see DeSanctis, et al., 1989; Watson, DeSanctis, and Poole, 1988). Third, a number of field users have commented that the simplicity of the text and menu-based system greatly enhances rapid learning. At least for beginning users and for users not accustomed to graphic interfaces, the menu and text interface may actually be advantageous.

Staff Limitations

Because our project team members have skills and experience in systems development, we think the project is strong in its ability to use state-of-the-art software design methods and to manage the software development and quality assurance process. The software development resource we are managing is one half-time computer science graduate student. The good news is that we have a relatively simple situation in terms of communication and control; additionally, the software is consistent and well understood since there is only one developer. The bad news is obvious in that we could accomplish much more if we had more programming resources.

Given that SAMM is now 35,000 lines of executable code, managing the change and testing process is becoming difficult. Every time we correct a known problem or introduce a new feature, the amount of testing that is required increases. Given the limited staff, this has become a challenge for the project.

Another issue worth raising is the testing time needed to check the operation of new system features. It is testing not only what happens when users hit the proper keys that is the problem, but also what happens when the user does something wrong. With GDSS, it is very important that a robust system exist when being used by real groups.

Laboratory Space

Obtaining an adequate room in which to locate the GDSS facility has been a major problem. Not only does the project require a fair amount of space for the decision room and the computer and staff work area, but also we want the facility to be attractive. An attractive facility is, we believe, highly related to favorable attitudes on the part of users (especially managers from outside the university). Our project has been fortunate to find a home provided by the research partnership with the Hubert Humphrey Institute of Public Affairs. However, we are constantly worried about losing our laboratory space; space for research laboratories comes at a premium in most universities, and the University of Minnesota is no exception.

Institutional Support

To develop something as complex and resource-intensive as a GDSS requires a support-ive institutional environment, particularly in a university setting. It helps greatly when the institutional unit in which the development is taking place views the GDSS activity as a strong priority, for example, if the leaders of the unit (deans, department deans, and university administrators) view the GDSS facility as a showcase. In this case, one can expect resource support from those with resources available.

The Minnesota GDSS project has been given reasonable support by its institution. Nevertheless, the members of the project team have been on their own in obtaining project resources. Developing a reliable source of funding for a project as resource-intensive as GDSS development requires the staff to spend a great deal of time in seeking resources from both within and outside the sponsoring institution. This need can take away valuable time from building the GDSS and doing research around it.

Site Visits

Interest in computer-augmented teamwork is very high at the current time, representing both an opportunity and a problem to projects such as ours. On the one hand, outside parties bring new perspectives to our work when they visit our facilities. On the other hand, demonstrating SAMM to visitors takes an enormous amount of staff time. Given our limited staff and budget, we cannot host all of the visits that are requested.

Nonproblems

It may be worthwhile to identify briefly some areas that have not been problems for our project.

- System design: We have many more good ideas than we could possibly implement in several years. Our team has a formal design process and one for priority setting as well.
- Reliability: One strong attribute of the central, host-based configuration and UNIX is that it is reliable. We have had literally thousands of hours of SAMM operation with virtually no hardware or software failures.
- Room design: We designed our furniture and had it specially built. At very reasonable cost, it supports a room environment (with an overhead projector and LCD display or SONY color projector) that meets our quality standards.
- Programming quality: We have been fortunate to have two extremely competent programmer/analysts, each of whom worked with the project for about two years. Each is articulate and can interact well with both the system design team and with users and managers.[2]
- System interface: Given our restricted interface environment, we have worked very hard (with a lot of testing) to design a consistent and easy-to-use user interface.
- Simplicity: SAMM is very easy to learn and to use. This aspect is very important when research is being conducted and time is in short supply.
- Obtrusiveness: We have considerable evidence that teams do not find the SAMM system obtrusive in meetings. Users tend to forget that the meeting room contains technology, and problems with keyboarding rarely arise. Team members are able to interact verbally with one another, as they normally do, at the same time incorporating SAMM into the meeting.

[2]We acknowledge the contributions of Aditya Gurajada and Surya Prasad to the development of SAMM.

SAMM IN TEACHING AND RESEARCH

SAMM has been used to illustrate the GDSS concept to our classes. Meetings have been conducted by student teams as part of their coursework in undergraduate, master's, and extension programs at the University of Minnesota. In some cases, students have used the GDSS facility for all of their team meetings throughout an academic course. Recently a fourth Minnesota faculty member, Les Wanninger, joined our project team and has worked extensively on incorporating SAMM into MBA and other graduate curricula.

Our GDSS research utilizes two primary methods, laboratory experimentation and field studies, briefly summarized, below. For details on the procedures and the findings of these studies, see the original references.

Laboratory Experiments

A variety of comparison studies have been conducted to date, including more than 1,200 meeting participants:

- GDSS vs. unsupported groups pursuing a problem-finding task (Gallupe, DeSanctis, and Dickson, 1988).
- GDSS vs. manually supported (paper and pencil) and unsupported groups for making a consensus decision (Watson, DeSanctis, and Poole, 1988).
- GDSS vs. manually supported (paper and pencil) and unsupported groups for a multiattribute forecasting problem (Zigurs, Poole, and DeSanctis, 1988).
- Communication support vs. structured decision support for a strategic planning problem (Sambamurthy, 1989).
- User perceptions of alternative GDSS interfaces (DeSanctis et al., 1992).
- Conflict management in GDSS vs. manually supported and unsupported groups (Poole et al., in press; Sambamurthy and Poole, 1991).
- Three methods of system introduction to GDSS and their impacts on group consensus (DeSanctis et al., 1989).
- One-time vs. repeated use of GDSS for strategic planning meetings (Billingsley, 1989).
- User attitudes during early adoption and later use of GDSS (Zigurs et al., 1989).
- User-driven vs. chauffeured vs. facilitated operation of GDSS (Dickson et al., 1989).
- Group-process vs. argument-based problem formulation in groups (Niederman, 1990).

Field Studies

The first field study was initiated in January 1989. The Manhattan District of the Internal Revenue Service (IRS) has replicated Minnesota's GDSS facility in its New York office. (DeSanctis, Poole, Desharnais, and Lewis, in press). Computer-supported meetings are part of a large-scale quality-improvement program at the IRS, in which teams of workers address specific problems confronting management. GDSS-supported teams are being compared with unsupported teams in a longitudinal study that consists of interview, survey, and recorded (audio- and videotaped) meeting data. More than 1,000 IRS employees have used the SAMM system over the past two years.

A second field study was initiated at Texaco, in Houston, in March 1990 (DeSanctis et al., 1991). Texaco initially duplicated the Minnesota facility but recently completed construction of an executive-style facility for SAMM use. It has installed SAMM on a mainframe-based system that allows remote use, including videoconferencing. Like the IRS, Texaco initially applied SAMM in a quality-improvement context and now is moving to other areas of application, for example, system design teams. Again, as with the IRS, Texaco is jointly gathering research data with the Minnesota group.

FUTURE DIRECTIONS

In our experiments and field studies we are examining SAMM across various work group and task settings. Our hope is that by comparing alternative configurations of the technology in a variety of contexts, we will gain some understanding of when GDSS is most effectively used by teams and when it is less effective. Our studies to date have already provided some insights in this regard. For example, we know that (1) the electronic communication channel provides a new means for team members to influence one another during meetings (Zigurs, Poole, and DeSanctis, 1988); that conflict is more openly expressed when groups use GDSS technology but not necessarily better managed once it is aired (Poole et al., in press; Watson, DeSanctis, and Poole, 1988); (2) groups using GDSSs with decision aids and process structure handle conflict more effectively than groups using GDSSs without these features (Sambamurthy and Poole, 1991); (3) mental models, or different ways of training groups in the use of the technology, can make substantial differences in effectiveness (DeSanctis et al., 1989); (4) the benefits of GDSS are more detectable for relatively difficult tasks (Gallupe, DeSanctis, and Dickson, 1988); (5) chauffeuring can ease user acceptance and lead to higher group consensus than operation of the system entirely by users (Dickson et al., 1989); and (6) significant performance benefits accrue from using a Level 2 rather than a Level 1 system (Sambamurthy, 1989).

Most of our studies have compared GDSS-supported groups with groups receiving manual support structures (such as agenda setting and flip charts to record ideas and preferences) and with groups left to their own devices when conducting their meetings. In this way we can sort out the effects due to the GDSS from effects due to the manual structure alone. In general, our results suggest that the benefits of GDSS lie largely in the structure the system provides rather than in the electronic communication channel per se. That is, groups with poor meeting procedures stand to gain more from GDSS than those who already have good manual procedures in place. The greatest benefit of GDSS may lie in Level 2 systems and above, because they contain meeting procedures that are difficult to implement manually.

A key finding in our research, along with other studies of group decision making and GDSS, is that groups vary widely in how they adopt this type of technology. For example, some groups approach SAMM as a tool to be applied to specific tasks as they arise, whereas others view SAMM as a person, rather like an electronic leader or facilitator

(DeSanctis et al., 1989; Poole and DeSanctis, 1989); some groups are positive about the system from the start and embrace it quickly and with enthusiasm, whereas others are more pessimistic and adopt it only grudgingly (Zigurs et al., 1989). We believe that adaptive structuration theory can be useful in explaining these interesting variances; moreover, in the long run, we hope that AST will provide the ability to predict the outcomes of groups' use of GDSS and other social technologies, based on careful observation of team discussion and other forms of interaction (e.g., electronic communication and nonverbal behavior) (see Poole et al., in press). The Minnesota GDSS project will continue to study AST within the GDSS context. We believe that this theoretical framework, in conjunction with our empirical studies, will enable us to contribute to researchers' understanding of how social technologies can be designed and implemented most effectively to improve team work.

APPENDIX

As shown in Figure 9-2, there are three divisions at the first level: (1) agenda, (2) options, and (3) utilities. We will describe each of these but focus on the options section, which is the heart of the system.

AGENDA

There are two choices at the next level of agenda: Define Agenda and Define Subagenda. For each topic entered as an agenda item, members can define a subagenda comprising steps the team wishes to follow to address that agenda item. Frequently, in practice, the agenda is set ahead of the meeting by the meeting manager or a researcher.

OPTIONS

Idea Gathering/Brainstorming

Once teams have established their agenda, they are supported in generating and displaying problems or issues for discussion, criteria to be applied to alternatives, causes of problems, alternatives for consideration, identification of stakeholders, assumptions that might be held by these stakeholders, and other types of ideas. Ideas, which can be entered, viewed, modified, or deleted, are privately listed by team members at their workstations and then displayed at the public screen for discussion. Information entered in this option can be used later in the Idea Evaluation and Decision Aids options.

Idea Evaluation

This option provides a choice of weighting, rating, ranking, and voting techniques to team members for evaluation of information entered in Idea Gathering. In each of these techniques, members input their individual assessments; then they can view the team assessments in the form of group averages and ranges on the public screen. Assign weights allows each member to distribute a total of 100 points across the list of ideas. Members then have the option to indicate their degree of commitment to the weights they apply. Commitment can be designated as low, medium, or high. Rate or scale allows each member to enter a preference for each idea on a scale from low (1 point) to high (10 points). Again, members have the option to indicate their degree of commitment to the weights they apply. Rank or order allows each member to enter a number corresponding to a rank preference for each alternative. Ideas are ranked from most preferred to least preferred. Again, members have the option to indicate their degree of commitment to the weights they apply. In the Voting option members can (1) vote for one item from the list, (2) vote yes or no on each item on a list, (3) distribute votes across all items, or (4) use multivoting. Multivoting is a very powerful tool for paring down a long list of items to a relative few that are most important through several rounds of voting. The team sets a cutoff number of votes an item must receive to make the list for the subsequent round.

Decision Aids

A set of structured decision techniques is available. More are under development because this is the area in which most of our design and programming efforts are being devoted. A team typically uses only one of these techniques in a given meeting. The menus in each module are followed in a sequential manner. Once a structured technique is selected, the team should complete each step within each menu of the module as instructed by the SAMM system.

1. Stakeholder Analysis is a strategic planning technique in which members identify key stakeholders for an organizational plan and then define and evaluate their assumptions. Important stakeholder assumptions are then used by the team to determine an organizational strategy or action plan.
2. Allocate Model is used to allocate a number of points or dollars to a set of options (e.g., departments, projects, and expense items) through a multicriteria model. The model represents a fixed sequence of steps, which includes identifying decision criteria, weighting the criteria, identifying decision alternatives, scoring each alternative on each criterion, and calculating a total score for each alternative. This decision aid allows what-if analysis based on average or individual weights and ratings.
3. Problem Formulation is designed to generate various perspectives on a troublesome situation or issue along three lines of reasoning: by case, by category, and by cause. Items can be rated, ranked, or voted on for each line of reasoning. The goal is to formulate a team problem definition to structure the problem.
4. Contingency Model is a decision aid for rating items on two or three dimensions. Items and appropriate dimensions can be identified and rated by each member of the team. As in Stakeholder Analysis, SAMM presents a graph of the ratings, which allows the group to focus on items rated high on all dimensions.
5. Clustering is an electronic representation of multiple manual flip charts. A list that results from brainstorming can be ordered into clusters that are identified by the team. Anonymous voting by team members is used to form clusters and to place items within clusters.

Meeting Thoughts

Meeting thoughts facilitates the exchange of opinions about the progress of the meeting. Additionally, members of the team can use this feature to exchange comments or relieve tension through quips or jokes. The module consists of SAMM Talk, which sends any one of a number of present messages to the public screen, for example, "Right on!" "Yawn..." and "Let's take a break." Send-a-Note allows any member of the team to construct a free-form message to the public screen and also permits messages to be sent to the system administrator. The Mood Meter provides two ways of polling the team during the meeting. First, members' attitudes toward the progress of the meeting can be recorded on a 1 to 5 rating scale by selecting Enter Meeting Progress. Second, any team member can enter a yes-no question for the team to consider. Each team member can then Enter Quick Poll Yes/No Vote to respond to the question.

UTILITIES

The utilities include a Group Scratchpad that records team notes for display on the public screen; a Private Scratchpad that records an individual's notes for later printing or private viewing; and View SAMM Features for a listing of all features in the SAMM system. Meeting Minutes prints a record of all outputs of the public screen, typically at the end of the meeting. User Logfiles will print the private meeting minutes of each team, including private scratchpad notes. The team can save its SAMM work through Save Meeting Minutes and later bring it into SAMM from disk by using Retrieve Meeting Minutes. Stored meeting minutes constitute a team history, or memory.

Another feature that is available to researchers is the logging of all inputs and uses of SAMM. This capability allows the analysis of all keystrokes and uses of the SAMM system in a meeting session.

Part B

Self-Constructed and Acquired Technology

The researchers' decision to acquire technology rather than to develop it is based on two important considerations. First, they may lack the resources or expertise required to construct a system. Second, they may prefer to concentrate their time and other resources on studying implementation and application rather than on development. However, some prefer to straddle the construct/acquire divide, and the researchers in this section exemplify this choice.

Development efforts are almost always driven by a need to support research activities. The products created often extend or fill a void in acquired technology, which is often used as either a prototype or source of ideas for new technology. For example, the National University of Singapore (NUS) (Chapter 12) used SAMM as a model for the development of the Macintosh-based SAGE system.

The Indiana researchers (Chapter 11) have used their extensive experience with various products to produce an any-time/any-place system called COMMENTS. The Calgary group (Chapter 13) have focused on developing functioning prototypes that use graphic interfaces and the MS Windows environment to support both synchronous and asynchronous work. Its chapter also describes what is involved in software development research. Although Michigan (Chapter 10) has done some software development, especially for microlevel processes (e.g., shared editing), the key contribution of its chapter is the discussion of its physical facilities. The development of a flexible, functional, workstation-based furniture unit (named ELMER) is of particular interest. The goal of this work is to provide collaborators with a high level of flexibility in configuring the work environment.

The chapters in this part of the book add additional conceptual maps for exploring teamwork technology. The Singapore group presents an overall research framework that integrates the cultural differences model developed by Hofstede. This framework guides NUS's cross-cultural studies. The Calgary group outlines an overall model that drives its research. Its model depicts three fundamental aspects of teamwork technology under investigation: development, introduction, and actual use. Its chapter discusses current and planned research activities in each of these areas. The Calgary chapter also discusses the approach it is developing to study methodological and measurement issues involved in teamwork technology research. The Indiana chapter introduces two new conceptual maps. It discusses how Weick's self-organizing information-processing model might apply to GSS research and management. It also introduces the concept of electronic-supported communities as an extension to the team technology time and place model introduced in Chapter 1.

The major research themes for Singapore and Calgary were discussed in the previous paragraph. Indiana's research has focused heavily on the social aspects, including team development, gender issues, and facilitation. Its focus has been on face-to-face environments, but it is now extending these research themes into different-time/different-place settings. The Michigan group also discusses its extensions to physical facilities to support distributed meetings and its research efforts in this area.

The chapters also highlight and discuss a variety of research relationships that the groups have formed to help accomplish their work. Michigan, Indiana, and Calgary all have strong industrial relationships. Indiana has developed an interesting cross-college partnership, and Singapore has a strong cross-continental relationship to support its cross-cultural research. Both Indiana and Singapore represent examples of the strong collaboration that exists among different research programs and universities. Indiana and Calgary are good examples of how research alliances can be developed and strengthened by hiring faculty from other research programs.

Chapter 10

Flexible Facilities
for Electronic Meetings[1]

Gary M. Olson
Judith S. Olson
Lola Killey

University of Michigan

Lisbeth A. Mack

Andersen Consulting, Inc.

Paul Cornell

Steelcase, Inc.

Robert Luchetti

Robert Luchetti Associates, Inc.

In most work on technology-supported collaboration, primary attention is given to the activity of the collaborators involved and to the technology—usually either computers or video—used to support the work. Less often, attention is given to the physical environment in which the work occurs (see Mantei, 1988). It is our belief that the environment, including the arrangement of the players as well as the immediate workspace that houses their tools, does more than provide a setting for collaboration to occur. We believe it can play a central role in the success of the enterprise.

Several studies indicate that the design of the physical environment is important to

[1] A number of people have contributed materially to the work described in this chapter. First and foremost, Jacque Passino of Andersen Consulting played a major role in getting this whole enterprise off the ground and has been instrumental in arranging funds for the support of the Michigan facility. Carl Luckenbach of Luckenbach and Associates has been involved in the design of the Michigan facility almost from the very beginning and has taken a personal interest in the project far beyond what would be expected of an architect for a modest renovation. Finally, we thank the following people for assisting us in using or learning about various facilities: Mark Stefik, Deborah Tatar, and Greg Foster for the Colab; Gail Rein for the Nick Lab; Marilyn Mantei, Ashby Woolf, Mary Elwart-Keyes, and Joyce Massey for the Capture Lab; Robin Seward for the ICL Pod; and Jay Nunamaker and Doug Vogel for the Arizona facilities.

group work (see reviews in Cornell and Luchetti, 1989; McGrath, 1984; Shaw, 1981). Hall (1966) describes proxemics as an area of study that focuses on the spatial location and orientation of people when they encounter one another. Much subsequent work has related this research to the workplace. Steele (1981) describes how our sense of space, our reaction to our experience with a place, is a mixture of physical as well as social and personal factors. Stone (1988) and Allen and Gerstberger (1973) describe how the environment can facilitate the number of contacts between groups as well as the quality of that communication. Sundstrom and Altman (1989) discuss how the environment can be used to reinforce the character and mission of the group. DeMarco and Lister (1985) have found that qualities of the physical environment are significantly related to the productivity of software developers.

Much is known about how to make the workplace for an individual both comfortable and ergonomic. This body of research is substantial enough to serve as the basis for standards such as the ANSI (1988) guidelines. But these standards are unlikely to help us with figuring out how to support the workplace for collaboration. Their focus is the dedicated, task-intensive computer user, working in isolation. To be sure, many important aspects of collaborative work occur through a person working alone in an office. But collaboration also involves interaction with collaborators, often in face-to-face settings. These may be either quite structured, as in a formal meeting, or quite informal, as when several people huddle together to discuss a point. The use of technology in these interactive cases will be of mixed intensity, with the users often more focused on one another than on the technology. There should be as much attention to social and group process in the design of the work area as to the use of the technology in supporting the work. Thus, we need to expand on the existing guidelines to incorporate requirements for work areas for group use of technology.

In the spring of 1988 several of us at the Cognitive Science and Machine Intelligence Laboratory (CSMIL) at the University of Michigan entered into a partnership with the Center for Strategic Technology Research (CSTaR) at Andersen Consulting in Chicago and its parent organization, Arthur Andersen & Co. The purpose of this relationship was to deepen our understanding of how information technology might play a role in the support of collaborative enterprises, such as the design of software systems in Andersen Consulting practice. We discussed an ambitious program of work and agreed to seek other partners in supporting the pursuit of our joint goals. One of our earliest additional partners in this work was Steelcase, Inc. Much of the work described in this chapter is the outcome of our three-way collaboration.[2]

One key component of our joint undertaking was to design advanced facilities for holding computer-supported meetings, one to be built at Michigan and one at Andersen. In the summer of 1988, we embarked on a joint design project to develop plans for these facilities. We agreed to pursue this task from two angles. First, we began to develop a set of design goals that reflected what we would like to achieve, based initially on our own ideas about the uses we envisioned for these facilities. Second, we decided to learn as

---

[2] We have subsequently acquired funding from the National Science Foundation (Grant No. IRI-8902930) for joint projects involving CSMIL, CSTaR, and Microelectronics and Computer Technology Corporation (MCC); from Apple Computer for the development of the CSMIL facility; and from Ameritech to develop the extensions to the Michigan facility for support of distributed meetings.

much as we could from those who had gone before us. We learned more about a representative sample of existing facilities through relevant articles, first-hand visits, and talks with the developers and users.

At both CSMIL and CSTaR, our primary focus was on supporting team software development and team problem solving. But we also wanted facilities flexible enough to support a variety of groups doing a variety of tasks, from formal presentations to policy making and strategic development and intense, detailed planning and design of large software projects. We sought to design a space that would accommodate up to 12 users, each of whom would have his or her own computer with a monitor, keyboard, and mouse. The workstations would be networked and linked to a large public display of shared information. Both off-the-shelf applications and special groupware would be available. It is interesting that many of these goals overlap with those of a similar facility at Hohenheim University in Stuttgart, Germany (Ferwanger et al., 1989).

DESIGN SPECIFICATIONS

Several sets of considerations framed our overall approach to the design of our facilities. Perhaps most important was the principal focus of our research, the support of relatively short-term, goal-driven collaborations that characterize task forces or ad hoc work groups (McGrath, 1984; Peters and Waterman, 1982). A representative work group has fewer than ten members and works on its task for a period of weeks or months. Many work groups last only as long as their task takes to complete. We chose this focus for several reasons. First, although such groups constitute a natural form of group activity, their study is methodologically tractable (McGrath, 1984), making in situ research feasible. Second, their members are often organizationally and geographically dispersed and represent several disciplines, meaning that problems of coordination, representation, and communication are central— problems that new collaboration technology might help solve. Third, they are organizationally interesting as well as important. Their effective use has been pointed to as a characteristic of organizations that work exceptionally well (Peters and Waterman, 1982). They constitute a key aspect of what have been referred to as "adhocracies" (Bennis and Slater, 1968; Toffler, 1980), a more flexible form of organization that is contrasted with bureaucracies.

In addition, we chose the early stages of system design and specification as our domain of focus, for several reasons. First, much software is designed collaboratively, and at least since Brooks (1975), it has been widely recognized that there are large coordination costs in software design by teams. This seemed to be a rich prospect for the investigation of collaboration technology. Second, there are currently very few tools to assist this stage of software development and none for groups, even though it is widely recognized as both a difficult and an extremely important stage in the software life cycle. Third, our collaborative research team had extensive experience in either the study of software engineering as a human activity or the actual doing of it.

As a result, we envisioned our facilities being used for a broad range of small-group meetings, both formal and informal. We set an upper bound of 12 users for full-information technology support. Although the rooms might hold more people for special purposes, we wanted to offer up to this number of people full-computing support of the kind we were going to design.

Two factors led to a stress on flexibility in the space we were developing. First, we surveyed a number of existing facilities and were uncertain if any one design for a meeting space was ideal. We visited, used, or interviewed the developers of the Colab (Stefik et al., 1987), MCC's Project Nick (Begeman et al., 1986; Jarvenpaa, Rao, and Huber, 1988; Rein and Ellis, 1989), the Capture Lab (Mantei, 1988; Elwart-Keyes, et al., 1990), ICL's Pod (Seward, 1988), and the Arizona Group Decision Lab (Nunamaker, Applegate, and Konsynski, 1987). We felt that the best thought-out design from a physical standpoint was the Capture Lab, although it is a very rigid facility, with a fixed arrangement of machines and seating positions. Second, the kind of project groups that are the focus of our research are less likely to use a meeting space exclusively for formal business meetings and more likely to hold a variety of informal, highly interactive sessions, with varying numbers of participants. We decided to explore the feasibility of designing space and furniture that would allow a highly flexible layout, all under the control of the end users. This was to be a major design feature in our work, and it is perhaps the most important feature that differentiates us from other recent designs for meeting facilities (e.g., Ferwanger et al., 1989).

Part of our vision of how such facilities might be used in the future is that they would be an integral part of the everyday computing and workspace infrastructure of the users. Thus, we required both facilities to be designed into the work environments of their respective organizations, meaning that they had to be networked to support the easy transfer of electronic information between local offices and the meeting room. Although we realized that both facilities would be used by people from off-site, we wanted to make the rooms as integrated as possible into the regular working environment of those in the area.

We also wanted to allow our facilities to incorporate a wide variety of computing. We wanted to be able to take advantage of interesting groupware no matter what the computing platform. Further, we wanted to be flexible about what kinds of computing environments we might want to explore in detail in the future. Thus, in the design of the furniture modules in particular, we did not want to preclude using any reasonable contemporary personal computer or workstation. Further, we wanted to be able to use large display screens if our work and that of others showed screen size to be an important consideration for collaborators.

It was important that each facility be equipped for observational work. A key part of our research is to observe groups working under a variety of circumstances. We usually do so by making videotapes of work sessions and later analyzing them according to a variety of schemes (Olson and Olson, 1991; Olson et al., in press). An asymmetric need for this feature led to more elaborate requirements for observation at Michigan than at Andersen Consulting.

It was also important for the two facilities to have a professional look and feel so that they would be taken seriously by our constituents. At Michigan, the facility was built in the School of Business Administration, where in addition to its role in our research, it is a showcase for students, faculty, visiting scholars, and a high volume of corporate visitors. For instance, the facility was built adjacent to the Executive Education program, where annually 7,000 executives take special courses. At Andersen Consulting, the facility was built where a wide range of internal Andersen users and outside clients would be exposed to it.

Based on both our initial design ideas and on our survey of existing facilities, we came up with a list of design specifications that governed the detailed designs of our facilities (see Table 10-1). To achieve flexibility in the use of the meeting room space, we planned to house each person's computing unit in a small furniture module that could be arranged in many different groupings. This vision drove our design of the meeting room and of the individual furniture units.

THE FACILITIES: ANDERSEN'S GROUP LAB AND MICHIGAN'S COLLABORATION TECHNOLOGY SUITE

We implemented our functional specifications in the space we had with additional constraints in mind. We envisioned a meeting room of some particular size, in a more or less regular shape.[3] The exact layout of this space depended on studies of alternative ways of configuring the flexible furniture. Fairly early on we established an approximate footprint for the flexible furniture, based on ergonomic and proxemic considerations. Then we studied the different ways in which these modules could be arranged. We wanted to be able to use a variety of physical arrangements to support a wide range of different kinds of meetings. We envisioned both formal clusters, in the shape of traditional conference or classroom setups, and informal clusters that could support breakout

TABLE 10-1   Primary Design Considerations for Michigan and Andersen Facilities

Full support for up to 12 people

Support mix of formal and informal meetings

Computer for each fully supported person

Available but not intrusive computers (monitors out of the way of social interaction)

Reasonable distances between people in various setups to avoid excessive formality

Minimized glare on screens but reasonable lighting

Networked computing into general environment

Separate module for each computer

Easily reconfigured modules (without special tools in a few minutes)

Large rear-projection screen

Large conventional whiteboards

Observational area with one-way mirror, able to accommodate at least six observers

Video facilities for making tapes of meetings

Easily accessible storage adjacent to meeting room

A place for computer system units outside of the meeting room

Professional look and feel to the meeting room

Accommodation for any current standard computing (i.e., not dedicated to only one vendor)

---

[3]We considered, but decided not to pursue, some highly imaginative ideas of Bob Luchettis for how to make the space more irregular and flexible. In part these ideas were constrained by the space we had available. We were also not sure that such a radical change of environment was the best next step when we were concerned about our users' acceptance of the new environments we were offering.

sessions or other small groups. We wanted room for people to be able to move about comfortably regardless of the layout of the furniture. Thus we determined that the ideal size for our meeting room would be 21 by 33 feet. Our actual rooms, constrained a bit by the nature of the space we were given, are quite close to this size.

We also needed additional space for various kinds of support functions:

Rear projection. We wanted large rear-projection surfaces for displaying computer output, video output, or anything else we might want to project. This feature required a space at one end of the room since we wanted a display area that could provide a single focus of attention for participants and that would be in a familiar location. Several critical issues affect the choice of rear vs. front projection: the amount of space available (rear projection takes more room), how well the participants can be isolated from the noise and heat of the projection devices, the quality of the projected image, and interference from other ceiling fixtures.

Computer system units. We wanted to keep the system units of the machines in a separate room to minimize noise and heat in the meeting room itself. Thus space had to be made for racks and cabling in an area convenient to technical support staff, and a raised floor had to be installed in the meeting room.

Storage. Since not all of the flexible furniture modules would be in use at the same time and since their design included a number of add-on parts that would be used in different configurations, we needed readily accessible space adjacent to the meeting room for the storage of unused units.

Observation. Because both the Michigan and Andersen facilities were designed for research, we wanted an observational area where observers could watch or videotape the activities in the meeting room. Since the facility at Michigan would house a wider variety of research uses, its design included a more ambitious observational area than in the Andersen suite. Both facilities have one-way mirrors that look into the meeting room but are out of the line of site of meeting participants. The Michigan facility has space for video recording and editing.

At both Michigan and Andersen, final designs were developed through an iterative process from these general goals. Figures 10-1 and 10-2 are photographs of the two facilities. The Andersen Group Lab was finished during the summer of 1989, and the Michigan Collaboration Technology Suite was finished in the spring of 1990.

FLEXIBLE FURNITURE MODULES: ELMERs

Based on our review of existing facilities, ergonomic principles of design, and our desire for flexible facilities, we generated a set of design requirements for the workstation units:

1. Environmental flexibility to support a variety of group sizes and working styles, including furniture arrangements wildly different from standard meeting rooms
2. Technical flexibility so that various computer monitors, CPUs, and input/output devices could be housed
3. Technical design for the power, cooling, and cabling necessary for reliable performance of the rearrangable units

FIGURE 10-1. Photograph of the Collaboration Technology Suite

FIGURE 10-2. Photograph of the Group Lab

4. Good ergonomics for the individual vs. some requirements concerning a group's occasional need for a single focus (e.g., a common screen) and proxemic requirements concerning the line of sight, angle of interaction, and overall distance from the other group members
5. Familiar ambience in both color and texture as well as a sense of normative arrangement and style; no feeling of intimidating technology; possible support for meeting without technology as well

The first three requirements prescribe a group technology "table" made up of parts that can house a variety of different equipment safely (i.e., without pinched cables and with proper ventilation and stability). Each part must be reconfigurable, ideally without special tools or expertise. The fourth requirement dictates the use of ANSI guidelines, with a minimally obstructed field of view and minimized distances between group members. We sought a good-sized, level work surface for papers, materials, and personal effects; the surface materials and colors would be consistent with the rest of the facility, with a familiar ambience. Of course, the ANSI guidelines are for a single person using a single VDT device. We were also very concerned with the proxemics of our units, especially the distance between group members who would be using our units in various arrangements. We wanted to keep the distance between people as minimal as possible, and in our prototypes we literally worried about shaving inches off the depth of our units so we could follow this principle.

Perhaps the major design constraint was wanting to keep our options open about the kinds of computing and display monitors the modules could hold. The most serious was the desire to hold to a 19-inch display monitor (later actually enlarged to a 21-inch monitor). Right now, to present a user with this much screen space at a practical cost requires putting a very large object (the monitor) into the module. Although we knew that display technology would evolve to eliminate this problem, we were eager to pursue our research now. Thus as an interim measure we would need to design furniture modules that would accommodate a very clumsy display technology, while providing comfortable viewing angles and ample leg room for users.

We proceeded through a series of design stages, beginning with drawings of wildly different concepts, such as overhead monitors with projections onto teleprompters and embedding controls in the chairs. For a variety of feasibility and cost considerations, we settled on three initial designs and built foamcore mock-ups of them. Using similar mock-ups of computer displays, we tried them out under realistic work scenarios. Adjustments to these mock-ups were made in situ: The heights and surfaces were literally cut down or boosted with little extra pieces of foamcore while we sat at them. Next, four units were built out of wood to serve as working prototypes that could house real technology. These four units were installed at Michigan and outfitted at various times with Macintoshes and Suns, with both 13- and 19-inch monitors. They were networked, allowing them to be used in a meeting with shared software, such as Timbuktu (Farallon Computing, 1991) or MMConf (Crowley and Forsdick, 1989), to allow joint access to electronic workspaces. On occasion a simple overhead projector with a liquid crystal display was used for the large shared screen. This setup was used for a large number of meetings over a period of several months.

These experiences led to the design of our current unit, named ELMER (from *Electronic Meeting Room*). The tabletop itself is removable from the core monitor housing, allowing a variety of shapes in various configurations. The core of ELMER is a pedestal that houses the monitor, covered with a glass top. The monitor itself is in an adjustable box, shaped somewhat like a breadbox. This box, and thus the monitor, can be tilted from 0 to 90 degrees under the control of a foot switch. To minimize the height of the fully raised monitor, we designed a special mechanism that lowers the bottom edge of the monitor as the angle becomes steeper. The back of the breadbox is covered with a perforated material to promote cooling airflow, and the cables are hung so that no pinching would occur as the monitor is raised and lowered. The cables can come out as a bundle from any of the three sides of the pedestal to support connections to power and networking. The units hook together tightly through a series of spool and O-ring connectors vaguely analogous to hook-and-eye closures on clothing. When ganged together in a regular arrangement, the effect is that of a continuous, fixed, stable conference table whose surface is made up of sections of wood and glass. Each site has eight ELMERs (see Figures 10-1 through 10-3).

SOFTWARE

We have been quite opportunistic in our use of software in these facilities, using off-the-shelf commercial software, research prototypes from other laboratories, and some prototypes of our own (see Mack, 1989; Olson et al., 1990).

Some of the most useful commercial software are those systems like Timbuktu and Carbon Copy that allow a group of users on a network to share access to a running application.

FIGURE 10-3.   ELMERs in use

We have found that Timbuktu, often in conjunction with a projector that allows a large image, is an easy and useful way to exploit off-the-shelf software for collaboration. We have used outlining tools, project management tools, spreadsheets, word processors, and drawing tools in this mode to good effect. More recently, the Michigan site has made extensive use of Aspects (Group Technologies, 1990), a new groupware system for the Macintosh that allows fully concurrent editing of text, images, and drawings.

At Michigan we have used some prototype software from other laboratories. As part of a partnership with MCC, we have installed the GROVE system (Ellis, Gibbs, and Rein, 1991), which runs on SUN workstations, and when needed we have set up a small cluster of ELMERs with SUNS in them. With the flexibility of the physical space and the ELMERs, we have been able to have a cluster of Macintoshes at one end of the meeting room and a cluster of SUNS at the other, supporting the running of two different experiments in the space at the same time.

We have also been developing our own software. One of our first projects was a group editor called ShrEdit (for *Shared Editor*), which allows all members of a group to access a shared work object. In our first prototype, the shared object is text. We think of ShrEdit as an electronic version of a scratchpad or whiteboard in which all members of a group can make their comments and edit the emerging object. Our immediate goal in this project is to develop an experimental platform to investigate the kinds of coordination support groups need in order to use tools like this successfully and how to present the functionality in the interface (see Olson et al., 1990, for a more detailed discussion of these issues). Although Aspects has capabilities that overlap with and extend those in ShrEdit, the latter allows us to collect a time- stamped log of all user events, necessary in our research on group processes. We have also found HyperCard a useful way to mock-up various functions, and we have built such items as brainstorming and voting tools to explore the support of other functions.

Following our extensive investigations of group work with ShrEdit, many questions about such systems have arisen. Should the tool allow parallel work, and if so, how should it be supported? How do we support the process by which people, having finished parallel work, show or explain their contributions to one another? What kinds of public, shareable displays should there be? What information do participants need or want about the activities of other participants in the electronic workspace? What kinds of private or personal workspaces need to be provided? These and a host of other issues are now the object of intensive research that will help us design further prototypes for our flexible collaboration environments.

TYPICAL USES OF THESE FACILITIES

Both facilities have been in use for some time, and we have gained considerable experience with a wide range of groups. We will briefly describe some representative uses here.

At CSTaR, the Group Lab has been used by groups from within CSTaR as well as outside groups from other parts of Andersen. The meetings are often chauffeured; that is, one person at one computer (whose screen is displayed on the large projector) takes notes and leads a discussion or gives a presentation or computer-based demonstration. The chauffeur's ELMER is usually positioned at one end of the room. The other ELMERs are normally arranged, with the monitor units horizontal, forming a contiguous table surface for all the other participants. The CSTaR lab is also used by teams working together, using either commercially available screen-sharing software (Timbuktu or Carbon Copy) or internally developed groupware applications. Since this software is very new and experimental, it is most often used by teams that include the developers. However, on a few occasions when other groups have tried these special systems, they have been favorably impressed by the unique combination of room, furniture, and software.

Because of its flexibility the lab is also useful for individuals who want a quiet, comfortable place to work, especially since the machines are networked to all computing in the office. Often several people will be working in the room at the same time but on separate tasks. The ELMERs can be positioned at some distance to support this type of work; usually they are positioned almost vertically. This single-user use means that the facility is used much more often than if it were a dedicated meeting environment. This is an unanticipated benefit of flexibility.

At Michigan, the Collaboration Technology Suite (CTS) has been used most extensively by the research group itself. All project meetings are held in the CTS, and often presentations are under software control (e.g., with MORE 3.0). In working meetings, shared software is used for note taking so everyone can help develop a record of the session, although in reality it is usually a single scribe who takes most of the notes. We have found the facility to be especially useful for highly interactive working discussions about such items as research design, theoretical models, and schemes for data analysis. An individual or a subgroup can create a proposal outside of a larger meeting and bring in a live document that is both an agenda and a work object, undergoing continuous revision during the session. One important constraint on the usefulness of the CTS is the response speed of applications. We often use MORE 3.0 (Symantec, 1990) for chauffeured meetings, but we find that when people link to it via Timbuktu, the response speed of the software slows down so much that the meeting is disrupted. Responsive software is essential in group settings.

The CTS has been mainly used for research studies. Small groups come into the laboratory to do work under a variety of conditions. The flexibility of the lab means we can run control groups, who do not use computer tools, in the same space since the CTS, with the computers recessed into the flat tabletop position, is an excellent traditional meeting room as well. The software used most often in our studies is ShrEdit, in part because it includes automatic data logging that creates a file of all system interactions by all participants in a session. This feature, combined with a videotape of the session, gives us a rich log of activity that can be used to study the group process. Most of our recent studies have focused on groups of three doing a design task, though we have also had other kinds of groups doing a variety of other tasks.

The CTS has been used from time to time for the work of university committees and task forces. As the only facility of its kind on campus, it is an attractive option for many groups. So far there has been very limited use of the CTS by groups outside the university, mainly because we have tried to save time in the facility for our research needs. But we have had groups of six to eight doing tasks like strategic planning and project coordination. These outside groups do not experience the full advantage of CTS because it is not integrated with their everyday work environment.

The CTS has not been used for teaching except for an occasional meeting of a graduate seminar in which software is demonstrated on the projection screen or a shared editor is used to structure and record discussions. There is nothing other than limited availability to prevent its use for instruction. It would be an ideal facility for small classes, especially with the extensions described below that connect it with the rest of campus through high-speed networks and video.

At both labs, the monitors are constantly adjusted from person to person, from task to task, and from individual to group work. We have found situations in which the adjustability supports various meeting styles, as described by Mantei (1988) and Elwart-Keyes et al (1990). When a group task is being chauffeured by one person, that person's monitor is usually raised to nearly the full height, allowing easy readability for the person most in need of it. Others in the meeting keep the monitor at about a 20-degree angle, sufficiently raised to make it readable but not high enough to interfere with the eye contact necessary for easy group processes. When all members are nearly equally active in controlling the shared display, the monitors are set at about 45 degrees, and almost all are uniform. Almost all users speak very favorably of the adjustability of the monitors.

A persistent technical problem is lighting. At both labs we have experimented with recessed lighting, adjustable lighting, and spot lighting, but we continue to have difficulties with glare on the computer screens and glass panels of the ELMERs. Turning the lights way down or off is unacceptable since it creates an unusual environment for face-to-face meetings.

Rearranging the ELMER units has proven to be much more difficult than expected. It usually takes a half day or longer to make big changes in the configuration. The primary obstacle is the cabling for network, power, and projection hookups, which requires a knowledgeable technical support person. Of course, wireless networking and self-contained notebook computers will make rearrangement much simpler. But the flexibility we do have at present has been ideal for research and development. For instance, at Michigan the CTS is often set up to support several different experiments, and we can mix Macintosh and Sun platforms as our needs vary. We typically leave it set up in a particular configuration for several months as a specific study is run.

In general, both facilities require some degree of technical support. At Michigan we have a half-time person whose sole responsibility is keeping the CTS functioning. This job is especially critical when subjects are being run, for the CTS may be busy 12 hours a day, 6 or 7 days a week. Such steady support is needed partly because of the large amounts of data that are collected and need to be managed and partly to keep the computing environment functional and to keep the ELMERs working.

SUPPORT FOR DISTRIBUTED MEETINGS: EXTENSIONS TO THE MICHIGAN COLLABORATION TECHNOLOGY SUITE

Recently, a new line of work was begun at CTS. Based on pilot work initially carried out at Rank Xerox EuroPARC by Judy and Gary Olson while they were on sabbatical leave, we have become interested in using software like ShrEdit or Aspects to create shared workspa-

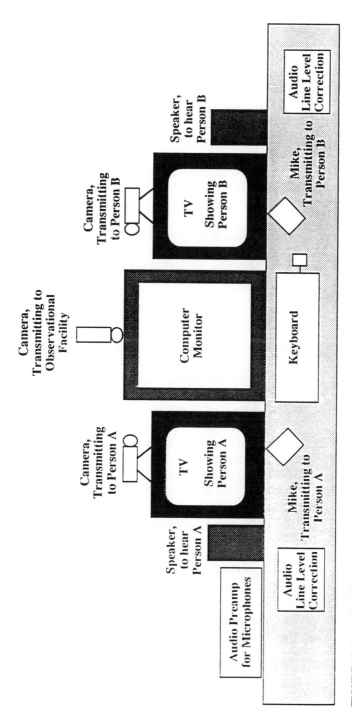

FIGURE 10-4. Subject Station for CTS-Distributed Workspace

195

ces for groups whose members are physically distributed. With support from Ameritech, we have created within the same space as the CTS an arrangement in which three collaborators can work on a task by using shared software and are linked by audio or video for purposes of communication (see Figure 10–4). There is a computer monitor for shared work and two video monitors, one for viewing each collaborator. A camera provides a directionally sensitive image to each of the other collaborators, and a third camera is set at midline for data recording. There are three such setups, all in small, private rooms. The observational room of the CTS contains an experimenter's station where data are captured and where the experimenter can interact with the subjects to give instructions or handle problems. In our experiments we are comparing work under these distributed conditions with that under face-to-face conditions. The video links are at present analog, but in the near future we will be migrating to digital video, where a number of interesting options present themselves.

We also have video links into and out of the main meeting room of the CTS, which make video conferencing with remote sites possible. We have already conducted such remote meetings between the CTS and the Engineering College at Michigan, which is on a separate campus about 3 miles away. Work is shared over high-speed network connections, and video goes over the campus broadband network. We will shortly have a similar arrangement with Ameritech's laboratory in Chicago.

CONCLUSIONS

Most CSCW research has focused on developing new kinds of flexible software and new social or organizational procedures for facilitating group work. But as we outlined earlier, the physical environment is also an important component of group work. Our goal is to give collaborators some of the flexibility in configuring their work environment that is also achieved through groupware. We recognize that as technology develops (e.g., flat panel displays, true laptops, and new forms of I/O), providing physical flexibility for collaborators will be even easier. But we have come a long way already, using today's technology, toward creating a research platform that will allow us to study and improve on flexible environments for collaborators.

We of course have not gone as far as we could have in providing flexibility. Both the CSMIL and CSTaR labs are fairly conventional, rectangular conference rooms, finished with a professional look and feel that make them blend into their office and work environments. More radical environments, with considerable flexibility in the nature, arrangement, and style of the walls, ceilings, and floors, would have been possible and, indeed, are being explored in other settings. We must reassess the norms that apply to the group work spaces that we now know. The introduction of new technology into otherwise familiar group work settings may sell short the impact and potential of a new set of assumptions, contexts, and devices.

The addition of remote collaboration capabilities to the Michigan CTS adds a new dimension to this facility. We will investigate in considerable detail the implications for new conditions of work (computer-supported and remote or distributed participants) on both the quality of the work and the effectiveness and enjoyableness of the group process itself.

Chapter 11

Support for Organizational Work Groups: An Applied Research Program of Theory Building and Field Testing

Bayard E. Wynne, *Indiana University*
Robert Anson, *Boise State University*
Alan R. Heminger, Joseph S. Valacich, *Indiana University*

INTRODUCTION

Just imagine that you are a manager of a human services research and training institute that provides assistance and consultation to a large number of human service agencies throughout the state of Indiana. Your employees are responsible for communicating among themselves and with other professionals on a wide variety of issues, all of which are likely to have an important impact on the client population. Within this framework, you are faced with the task of uncovering and capturing user requirements for a comprehensive information system to link electronically local disability agencies across the state.

In 1983, this exact problem confronted the Institute for Study of the Developmental Disabilities (ISDD), a federally funded organization affiliated with Indiana University. During the early 1980s Henry Schroeder, director of ISDD, and a multidisciplinary advisory board responded to this challenge by initiating a program to apply computer technology to support group collaboration. Since its inception, the Indiana University group support system (GSS) research program has moved through five major phases. In this chapter we describe those evolutionary phases, from the inception of our first facility in 1983 to our present research program. We also discuss some of our key observations from this experience and present several of our future research objectives.

PHASE I: CHAUFFEURED SUPPORT
FOR GROUPS

Initially, a single PC running a spreadsheet application was used to accept interview responses during group discussions with local community agency clients. During the first two years of early development, 1983–1984, the system operated in a chauffeured mode (i.e., one person entered the group information into the computer). The chauffeur recorded members' ideas and votes by using a round-robin technique. Initial success with this crude prototype was exciting and led to the following realizations. First, it became clear that computer technology could be used as a substitute for easels, charts, and blackboards. Second, this enhanced technology could greatly influence group processes and outcomes. Both of these realizations laid the foundations for much of our subsequent work.

PHASE II: AN EVOLVING GROUP
SUPPORT ENVIRONMENT

Phase II involved many changes. The first was the development of a set of group support tools during 1985–1987 by David Dibble, a School of Business doctoral student. This software was explicitly designed to provide process support for brainstorming and evaluating ideas. The designs for these tools were greatly influenced by the large body of research related to the support for group processes. To use the newly designed software most effectively, the laboratory evolved into a multiuser system of eight portable personal computers and a local area network. The system's architecture included a file server to manage the group information. The Phase II laboratory allowed groups to enter information in parallel; thus members no longer had to wait their turn to make a suggestion. We observed that this parallel processing reduced the tendency of any one individual to dominate the group process.

A second change was the addition of a public overhead screen. This display provided a central focus for all group members as a shared work space for the group to edit ideas jointly and make comparative evaluations. This anonymous viewing of ideas was used as a means to gain unbiased feedback and evaluation.

One meaningful result of the move from Phase I to Phase II was that the Phase I chauffeur became the Phase II facilitator. Not yet clearly realized at this stage was that facilitation encompasses both technical and social process support, each of which is distinct from providing content expertise to the group. (We will discuss these important differences, and how they influenced our subsequent research later in the chapter.)

Crude as it was by today's standards, the Phase II facility truly represented the advent of *groupware* at ISDD's developing GSS laboratory. Much of the effort at this early time was expended in designing and testing new and different configurations. Three dissertations were conducted in the facility during this phase, all laboratory experiments. One focused on GSS (Beauclair, 1987), and the other two explored different end-user training applications (Olfman, 1987; Sein, 1987).

A major advantage of using portable computers in the Phase II design was the ability to transport the laboratory to the client location for either demonstrations or actual sessions.

This portable GSS served our purpose very well: traveling throughout the state of Indiana to aid human service agency clients on a variety of managerial tasks. In this process, we developed our own expertise in applying the technology to a wide variety of groups and situations. This experience served to set the stage for major changes during Phase III.

PHASE III: FROM DECISION LAB
TO COLLABORATIVE WORK SUPPORT

Phase III is marked by the transition from the locally produced software to the University of Arizona GSS software in August 1987 under the direction of Bob Bostrom. This software, developed at Arizona under the direction of Jay Nunamaker, was then called PLEXSYS (Dennis et al., 1988). However, henceforth we will refer to the software as GroupSystems, its current and commercial name. (We feel that it is important to note that Indiana served as the first contributing beta test site for GroupSystems in an academic setting. Much of our initial effort was in fitting this software to a different environment and providing troubleshooting and enhancement feedback to Arizona.)

The new software immediately changed our perspective on group technology. The lab designation was changed from decision lab to CWSS (collaborative work support system) lab to symbolize its broader potential. We intended to take advantage of the expanded scope of the new software, providing a wider spectrum of support environments and tools. No longer was our focus to be primarily on decision making. In fact, we found that our early work with organizational client groups had little to do with making decisions as such. It involved such areas as academic curriculum planning, eliciting knowledge from experts, and developing an individualized education plan for a disabled child. Thus, although decisions flowed from the work done in the facility, the sessions covered a wide variety of group tasks.

As was our earlier software, GroupSystems is a file-based, multiuser system operating across a network. In addition to multiple user workstations, it also has both a facilitator's workstation and a file server. The tools in GroupSystems can be linked together in a few specific sequences to support different task agendas. We will return later to the issue of premeeting process design, which is implied by the idea of tailoring a system to a particular session. At this stage, none of us realized the extent to which the world of GSS had been opened up by an array of tools that could be tailored to specific group needs.

PHASE IV: AN EVOLVING PROGRAM
OF RESEARCH

Bye Wynne served from 1986 through 1990 as the initial director of IRMIS (the Indiana University Business School's Institute for Research on the Management of Information Systems). In late 1987, he, Bob Bostrom, Rob Anson, and others had been using the Phase IV laboratory for about four months for a variety of groups and purposes. Over this time, it became clear that more and better workstations as well as other upgrades were required to realize many of their shared research goals.

IRMIS had thus far limited itself to providing research workers, faculty and graduate students, in support of ISDD's CWSS operation. The ISDD and IRMIS directors decided to upgrade the CWSS laboratory hardware at the same time as a major new release of the GroupSystems was installed. This upgrade included faster computers and color displays. Additionally, a much improved color public screen was installed. We also updated our network software, installed new electrical systems and communications cabling, and bought new furniture. Indiana's lab had now become a professional electronic conferencing facility.

With a quality facility and improved software, the lab entered a period of rapid activity. During the next three years, we conducted over 200 sessions in the CWSS laboratory. These sessions were about equally divided among demonstrations, actual electronic meetings, and pedagogic applications in an electronic classroom frame (*ISDD Lab Vita,* 1991). We also occasionally traveled with the lab so that organizational groups could work at their site (Hoffer et al., 1990). Our participant groups were drawn from many sectors: human services, business, government, university administration, and students. The work they came to accomplish was equally diverse: strategic planning, curriculum development, systems development, conference planning, case analysis, team building, budgeting, problem solving, qualitative data analysis, to name a few. The only real themes to these diverse applications were the marriage of computer technology with group collaboration and our own "learning by doing."

In January 1989, Alan Heminger joined the faculty of the Indiana School of Business and replaced Bob Bostrom (who moved to the University of Georgia) as the director of the GSS facility at ISDD. Vicki Pappas of ISDD took over from Heminger in 1990. A strong cooperative environment continues between ISDD and the Business School's MIS faculty. This is exemplified by the degree to which the Indiana MIS Ph.D. program has focused on GSS related issues, using the ISDD facility as the primary GSS research site.

A lesson learned through all this experimentation is that the technology is essentially a set of tools, the successful use of which depends on the appropriateness and skill in using the tools as well as on the quality of the tools themselves. Thus, two clear ways to enhance our group support environment would be to enhance our set of tools and our set of skills. We enhanced our tool kit by developing or purchasing various utility programs to permit new, more *flexible software linkages* between GroupSystems tool outputs and to perform other useful tasks.

We enhanced our skills by increasing our understanding of the *role of the facilitator.* As we gained experience with the application of GSS to a group's needs, we identified a clearly delineated role for the facilitator, which contributed to the success of a GSS session. The role involves the responsibility for the implementation of each group's chosen *process.* We differentiate the process from the session's *content,* which is the responsibility of the participants. By making this clear distinction between process and content we were able to develop further the role of the facilitator in the GSS session to focus on this responsibility. Thus, our second lesson involved establishing what a given's group process was to be, then adapting the system and using facilitative techniques to implement that process in the session.

Before a GSS session, the facilitator routinely meets with the group's organizer, or other responsible person, for a preplanning session. In this meeting, the goals and objectives of the upcoming session are identified and a process for achieving them is outlined. This outline is then mapped to the particular tools and capabilities of the GSS, including the expected roles of the participants and the facilitator. From this step comes an agenda for the meeting, which is made available to all participants and which forms the basis for the facilitator's efforts during the session. This preplanning process helps both us and the participants to have a clear idea of what to expect both during the session and afterward. It also helps to clarify to the group members what they can expect from the system and what must be provided by them. This knowledge can be particularly important for first-time users, who may have quite unrealistic ideas about what a computerized system will do for them.

During the session itself, the facilitator helps the group to implement its agenda, which includes the process issues of tasks to be accomplished as well as the technical assistance with the system software. Facilitation also involves assisting the group with its interpersonal processes, such as promoting useful verbal discussions, clarifying messages, and keeping the group on track. Often, the facilitator helps the group to modify the agenda based on what occurs, so that the value of the meeting is enhanced. Recent experiments by Anson (1990) and Anson and Heminger (1991) have demonstrated that the role of the facilitator is perceived by the group to be a valuable aspect of a GSS session.

A third lesson concerns what might be loosely called group personality. Beyond the ever-present idiosyncratic component, other factors such as group size, history, and gender composition appear to influence how effectively different groups interact. Controlled experiments, conducted as dissertation research, examined these factors. Fellers (1989) compared various computerized and manual techniques for groups of five and ten members. He found that computer support helped overcome many of the problems that plague larger groups. Chidambaram (1989) compared computer- and non-computer-supported groups over four sessions. He found that computer support over repeated use actually improved cohesion and the ability to manage conflict. Herschel (1991) studied intact groups of varying gender compositions. He concluded that GSS can serve as an intervention, moderating some of the effects of gender as seen in non-GSS-supported groups.

Joint investment in upgrading the facilities and the associated research lessons just cited marked a significant advance in the degree of cross-college partnership in the applied GSS research program at Indiana University. It had become clear that ISDD's clientele was admirably served by the marriage of the GSS facilities and the expertise of the researchers from the Business School. In addition, the Business School researchers were gaining an international reputation for the breadth and depth of field and laboratory research being done through the ISDD facilities. From the university's standpoint, a wide variety of its constituents and stakeholders were benefitting from the activities of the Indiana GSS research team (*ISDD Lab Vita*, 1991).

PHASE V: MOVING FROM THE PRESENT TO FUTURE TENSE

GSS researchers have evolved an informal worldwide consortium. Many of the research sites and programs outlined in this book are active in at least some aspect of the consortium. Most of these sites are universities, and each typically has several types of group support technologies. Knowledge generated through research is often rapidly shared through the exchange of research designs, results, working papers, and personnel (e.g., a doctoral student trained under one GSS paradigm often becomes a faculty member at a program pursuing another).

We ended the decade of the 1980s with a GSS laboratory on the threshold of expansion into an advanced research facility. This evolution has been stimulated by further development and investment in facilities, technology, and people. In this section we will discuss these critical elements and how they influenced our evolution to a facility capable of supporting investigation into, and the application of, a wide variety of GSS groups and tasks.

The laboratory is also now used by several ongoing working groups, especially groups from the ISDD, who have easy access. What has been most heartening is to see groups finding that they can routinely create jointly owned work products more readily through GSS than by their past practices. On several occasions we have used GSS to support electronic classroom activities. The versatility of this concept was recently underscored by classes of fourth- and sixth-graders. They used the technology to support their discussion of how they could help other children with disabilities. The result was commitment to work with a class of learning-disabled students in their school. There are numerous exciting pedagogical applications of GSS technologies to be made and distributed as productive innovations (Bostrom and Anson, 1988b). (As a matter of policy, every graduating MBA from Indiana takes part in at least one working GSS session, which may be for business case development, for example, or for any number of other integrative experiences.)

Updated versions of GroupSystems software are regularly installed as they become available. In addition, Indiana has developed a set of software utilities to augment the basic GroupSystems environment. For example, utilities to direct outputs from one GroupSystems tool as inputs to other tools in ways not originally contemplated by or included in the GroupSystems software have been developed. These utilities have greatly enhanced our ability to fit the technology to diverse groups and tasks and have been made available to other research universities in the GSS research consortium.

To date, the bulk of the Indiana GSS research has been conducted through GroupSystems, a system designed to support groups working at the same time and place. However, recent research interests have led us to develop a new system that can support groups distributed in both time and place. This system, called COMMENTS, is specifically designed to operationalize the anytime-anyplace concepts of GSS (Heminger and Valacich, 1991). COMMENTS is built on a networked data-base system and supports multiple concurrent meetings and groups, with appropriate security features in order to use and study the technology within organizational settings.

We have also acquired, installed, and appraised GSS technologies from a variety of other sources. Office Express, a semi-intelligent or at least self-organizing E-mail system (Brookes, 1985), was provided by the University of New South Wales. Although we have discontinued the use of that software, it is not the fault of Office Express. Rather our user group cannot support a third E-mail system, however good. Other GSS-related products such as COMPETE!, OptionFinder, Expert Choice, Cope, Negotiator, COORDINATOR, SAMM, and Prefcalc have been appraised or acquired and applied. We have also installed VisionQuest from Collaborative Technologies Corporation of Austin, Texas. Thus, a wide assortment of GSS products is expected to become available during the 1990s, and we regard this process of exposing ourselves to the spectrum of environments as vital to our evolving research program. We are currently also looking at how the concept of workflow automation can be extended and applied to coordinating distributed group meetings and activities.

A second developmental activity is that of a new, more modern GSS facility under construction within the Business School. Separate and apart from electronic classrooms, this second Indiana University GSS research facility is based on more advanced technology and will support groups of up to 16 members. The facility is outfitted with custom furniture for maximum flexibility and thus supports many different space, time, channel, and process configurations to facilitate variant designs for both applied and experimental research. The facility has numerous breakout rooms that will aid in the controlled investigation of dispersed group work. This additional facility will greatly enhance our research agenda (see Figure 11-1).

Personnel flow is another way to trace the development of the GSS field. For example, Bob Bostrom (an author in this book) moved from Indiana to Georgia to add GSS direction and expertise to its existing research team. This move not only made the Indiana experience available as an additional base for the Georgia developments but also was the

FIGURE 11-1.   Indiana University's Newest GSS Research Facility

catalyst for the joint research program of the two universities. We, in turn, brought into the Indiana School of Business two new faculty members to work in the GSS research program, Alan Heminger and Joe Valacich. Both are products of the University of Arizona Ph.D. program in MIS. Indiana has also placed several GSS-oriented researchers in other consortium universities, including Claremont Graduate School, Florida International University, University of Nebraska, University of Hawaii, and Boise State University. This flow of personnel among and beyond the GSS consortium schools contributes to a healthy cauldron of research cooperation and competition. In the same vain, Wynne served as visiting senior research scientist for CSCW at FAW, the Institute for the Application of Knowledge-Based Systems, of Ulm, Germany.

Historically, a large percentage of the GSS research has evolved from doctoral dissertations led by Bye Wynne, Bob Bostrom, Jeff Hoffer and Bill Perkins as well as Tawfik Jelassi (who is no longer at Indiana). Abby Foroughi (1990) and Beth Jones (1988) each worked on negotiation applications of GSS, Foroughi coupling individual DSS to the shared GSS environment. Bostrom and Wynne, with their student Jack Fellers, extended the use of GSS into the extraction of knowledge from groups of practicing knowledge engineers (Fellers and Wynne, 1988). Rob Anson (1990) highlighted the potential major role to be played by the GSS facilitator. Laku Chidambaram (1989) studied GSS group development over a sequence of meetings. Several students have extended these works to a focus on intact groups, with Rick Herschel (1991) studying the effects of group gender composition and Tim Noel examining issues of justice and anonymity. Brian Mennecke is exploring GSS as a means for team development as an objective in itself (Mennecke, Hoffer, and Wynne, 1992). Lai Lai Tung is studying nonconsensus group processes in a GSS setting. Wynne's most recent thrust in research is focused on fostering organizational innovativeness through the use of GSS as a generic project management environment that spans time and space. Additionally, Heminger and Valacich are leading several field studies on the application of GSS in distributed team environments. Valacich is also looking at how GSS technology can be used to support group decision making under time pressure.

A strong interdisciplinary research program has been developed at Indiana. Pat Andrews and Joe Scudder, from Indiana's Speech Communications Department, have joined with the Department of Decision and Information Systems faculty in this research program. Faculty from the Department of Management routinely serve as active members on dissertation committees. Researcher Vicki Pappas, current manager of the ISDD GSS laboratory, brings her expertise in the naturalistic inquiry approach to some of the Indiana GSS research.

BROADENING OUR UNDERSTANDING OF THE FIELD

All sound research is grounded on one or more theoretical bases. Other chapters in this book have put forth positions, with which we agree and do not repeat here, advocating specific seminal work for this field. Certainly McGrath (1984) summarized and portrayed well an integrated picture of group interaction and performance. Poole and

DeSanctis (1989) espouse adaptive structuration theory as a means of viewing how groups adopt and adapt from their environments. Huber (1990) proposed a theory of how advanced decision and communication technologies will affect organizational design, intelligence, and decision making. We concur in and endorse these works as key anchors for GSS research. However, the diversity of phenomena affected by the rapidly evolving group technologies requires additional conceptual tools if we are to grasp and comprehend the essence of what occurs in group operation.

Consider one example of our evolving frame for the GSS work here at Indiana. A major realization for us has been that contrary to common wisdom, a huge proportion of group work does not involve decision making. Much more frequently, groups serve to develop and expose "permissive consensus." That is, groups engage in some combination of acts that are geared to create a common, shared vision of the problems and solution sets available. These acts include finding facts, testing logic, surfacing issues, identifying and creating alternatives, assessing risks, testing consensus, suggesting direction, comparing options, and so on. Throughout these processes, the key outcome is for group members to develop a common understanding, statement, and acceptance of the issues involved, when the group process must generate sufficient commitment and direction for members to implement group conceptions effectively.

Thus, in our view, when a group develops a consensus, two things are happening: First, a sense of ownership of the group's output is created in the individuals; and second, the jointly owned consensus is best viewed as a statement of the latitude that the group grants to a leader or implementation team. This latitude delimits the arena within which the leader is free to determine a solution path or action course, which the group will behaviorally endorse after the fact. Conversely, and certainly more positively, the granting of latitude on a consensus basis is really empowering the leader of the group. Thus, an important outcome for GSS research is in building *collaborative consensus* rather than solely generating quality decisions.

Another major theoretical touchstone in Indiana GSS research is Weick's (1979) *organizing model.* Weick proposed that organizing consists of processing information in order to resolve equivocality in an environment by means of a set of interlocked behaviors embedded in conditionally related processes. Weick pictures an organization as being in a constant state of change, consisting of individuals who process information in concert with one another. This view envisions an individual at the boundary of an organization as being in an enactment role. Such a person interacts for the organization with some part of the environment and creates an instance of experience. This experience becomes a filtered picture that is subsequently shared with some other organizational member in a selection (or information-receiver) role.

This selection person accepts or rejects an information packet as being relevant or not, based on current executive direction (i.e., does this new information reduce equivocality?). If information packets are relevant, they are sent to a person in an organizational retention role. The retention process acts to organize the packet of significant information so that it fits consistently into the retained memory of the organization. A further reduction of equivocality of the information occurs at this point as far as the given organization is concerned. These sequential steps of enactment, selection, and retention take place at a myriad of locations in an organization, and through this collective, perhaps bureaucratic, process the organization's collective memory has been revised. These changes reflect themselves as possibilities and choices to entrepreneurial management.

So how do we see the Weick self-organizing model as applied to GSS research and utilization? Our suggestion is that both the many individuals and the team using a GSS are information-processing entities in the sense of Weick's model. In the GSS context, enactment, selection, and retention take place in an organizationally supportive environment. The inherent organizing and focusing capabilities of GSS appear to have significant impacts on how and what groups learn and understand about themselves and their issues. If we take that fact as given, many of our experimental results may be explainable in this new context. Some of our strange or seemingly conflicting results may thus be rendered quite natural. Most productively of all, Weick frame on GSS should generate a host of provocative hypotheses for investigation. We have hopes that this viewpoint may shed light on the use of GSS for conflict resolution.

THE CONCEPT OF ELECTRONICALLY
SUPPORTED COMMUNITIES

GSS research is exploding, as a casual examination of the growing share of the proceedings from the annual HICSS Conference (Hawaii International Conference of System Sciences) from 1987 through 1992 would show. A similar tracking of the number of universities with GSS installations reflects the same exciting growth. The number of researchers trained or operating in the GSS field also shows a drastic increase.

A problem with our current and previous work is that there is no commonly shared guiding theory to help integrate prior and guide future research. In an area as dynamic as GSS, such a lack of apparent direction could be a problem. Consider the fact that the GroupSystems software developed out of a program whose goal was to enable more effective documentation of systems design and programming efforts. Now reflect on the fact that the IBM installations of GroupSystems proliferated within IBM at an unprecedented rate over the past few years. Then consider that GroupSystems is only one of what will soon be many commercially available GSS environments. We propose the concept of ESC (electronically supported communities) (Wynne and Heminger, 1990) as the device or framework for metaintegration across this burgeoning research arena. The concept of ESC, as the name implies, is defined as the building, maintenance, and proliferation of existing and evolving social communities through the evolution, application, and adoption of collaborative technologies by individuals, organizations, and societies.

The primary focus of the ESC concept, whether from an individual, organizational, or societal standpoint, is on the community networks that are created and how they influence processing, structures, and outcomes. They are created and justified on one basis (goal-oriented work) but will quickly be utilized for more exciting and ostensibly more productive (socially oriented) activities. The resulting informality and directness of the issue-oriented communication that develops appears to improve the effectiveness of the organization. Thus, we expect to see an explosive impact of ESC on organizations.

Peter Keen (1988) has documented the wholesale impact of one minor harbinger of these community networks or ESC systems, COORDINATOR. Keen installed COOR-DINATOR in his own organization, ICIT, the International Center for Information Technology. The result was as suggested above: A flatter and more rapidly acting firm that could (after Weick) "enact, select and retain" much more entrepreneurially. The future may hold many more organizations of the sort Drucker (1988) has described. These "new organizations" are more fluid, are made up largely of temporary teams, and are outcome-focused. Such organizations will rely heavily on social networks, and thus such community networks, whether the same or different in both time and place, should become a much stronger basis of our organizational lives.

We believe that ESC will be characterized by greater efficiency, broader participation, increased flexibility, and automation of many routine information-processing chores. ESC will be further characterized by the provision and contingent application of elec-tronically applied group process-structuring techniques on a routine basis. It will also incorporate and facilitate enhanced group or social memory (as well as factual data bases) with tools to maintain and grow these memory organisms. Expert Systems will be an integral part of these electronic social networks through which we develop our ESC. However, the real application of artificial intelligence in ESC will be that the networks will develop into self-organizing, interactive, participative, person-machine, knowledge-based application armories. Bostrom and Anson (see Chapter 2) created an outline of some of the potential ESC benefits, which we can see now as probable outcomes of using GSS support mechanisms.

Applications and evolution of GSS technologies are much easier to comprehend and evaluate within the 2 by 2 framework presented in Chapter 1 by Johansen. We feel, however, that this framework is insufficient to categorize some existing and emerging GSS-related technologies. Consider two examples: FREENET is the forerunner of the very broadly based community electronic bulletin board serving an entire metropolitan area (and anyone else who wishes to dial in to the service). Swift (1989) studied the "Audience activity in computer-mediated communication," as evidenced by the users of Cleveland's FREENET, which combined aspects of all corners of this topology except that of same time/same place. What he found was a vast *social* network with subsets devoted to particular interests or to particular modes of (electronic) behavior.

The second example of a system difficult to fit in Johanson's topology is TEIES, the tailorable electronic information exchange system (see Chapter 4), *a true prototype ESC.* It was explicitly designed to allow, with appropriate tailoring, support for a wide range of applications in the areas of GSS. It was also designed to allow complete integration of communication and information services for users and groups. TEIES has been im-plemented in several machine-software environments. We think of it as a specialized and friendly operating system. In this analogy, the GSS applications that it hosts are best thought of as application programs—not an inappropriate labeling.

Both FREENET and VC/TEIES are examples of ESC that are not readily character-ized in the time and place topology of computerized support for groups. Figure 11-2 (adopted from Wynne and Heminger, 1990) is presented here simply to suggest the breadth and diversity of ESC applications that exist today, although it may not encompass

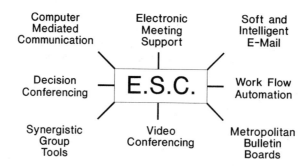

FIGURE 11-2.   Classes of Electronically Supported Communities

all possible support environments because we view this to be an evolving concept. Consider the extensions possible with, say, video conferencing. Fiber optics is having a major impact on the continuing development of and expansion to new dimensions of ESC capability and application (Drunkel, 1989). Bell Communications Research (Bellcore) has in routine operation for its own employees, and sells to others, a fiber-optic-based product called Video Window. This product provides real-time interactive imaging and voice communication between and among conference rooms. The picture-window-like images are in full color, are life size, and provide a very good semblance of virtual presence. This product works between continents as well as it does between adjacent offices. Bellcore is developing a desktop prototype of VideoWindow, Cruiser, to enable fiber-connected workstations to provide the comparable facility among pairs of employees at their desks. (A similar system is in use at US West; see Chapter 7).

SUMMARY AND CONCLUSION

This chapter has provided a short tour of the Indiana University GSS research program. We want to stress that we cannot make specific claims to the future direction of our research, as we learn more with each group and each study. However, our major emphases in the immediate future will attempt to build on our existing strengths in light of the GSS technologies available and to continue the evolution of the ESC concept.

Another near-term research focus relates to facilitation, an existing strength of our GSS facilities. Although studies have shown that facilitation provides valuable benefits in the GSS context (Anson and Heminger, 1991), there is much to learn about what should be included in this role and how it can or should be delivered. Much of what we have experienced and observed so far has led to a host of additional questions. What are the boundaries between individual and group, between leader and participants, between task and group maintenance, and between content and process that affect the need for facilitation? How do they affect the type of facilitation that should be used? To what extent are these boundaries fluid or malleable, and how might that affect the impact of facilitation? Finally, how can technology itself be brought to bear on what we learn?

An example of this last issue appears in the opportunity, and perhaps the need, to relate expert systems to the issues of facilitation. Our work on facilitation will extend far beyond its current boundaries. Can we automate to a large degree the preplanning of GSS sessions? How do aspects of the group and task affect this process. Can Expert Systems be employed effectively to manage computer support as technical facilitators during the actual work sessions for groups? Can this be done for groups who also function without a group dynamics or social process facilitator?

A wealth of opportunity exists in identifying more effective ways to operate, and to support the operation of, groups that collaborate without the luxury of being face to face. We intend to be at the forefront of that segment of GSS research. We expect to use the adapted Weick model of self-organizing information systems as a guide in designing our research as we move beyond the realm of face-to-face GSS group research.

We also intend to continue to enhance our understanding of how technology can be used to support groups that are distributed by time or space. This work will be both empirical and developmental. Our empirical work will focus primarily on issues of technology adoption and diffusion and the subsequent effects on organizational design, intelligence, and decision making. Our developmental work will investigate how our current processes and structures for support group activities can be enhanced and extended.

Our last area of continuing research will be related to the evolution of the ESC concept. We will continue to probe the as yet very ill-defined boundaries of where GSS can be most useful for organization teams. This work will involve iteration among theory development, laboratory experimentation, and field demonstration. We believe that based on the resulting applications, ESC will increasingly play a central role in changing our society's organizations.

ACKNOWLEDGEMENT

We wish to acknowledge the contributions of both Patricia Harvey-Anson and Carol Pierce to this chapter.

Chapter 12

The GDSS Research Project

K. S. Raman and K. K. Wei
The National University of Singapore

INTRODUCTION

Groups are pervasive and nearly universal in organizations around the world. However, groups are often perceived to be inefficient and ineffective (Schein, 1970). Frequently, they fail to utilize the full resources of their members because of process losses. (The main sources of process losses are listed in Chapter 8.) Despite these shortcomings, groups remain the major decision makers in organizations, and there is a need for developing and implementing new approaches for making meetings more effective and efficient. The National University of Singapore (NUS) is exploring the application of computer and communication technologies, that is, group decision support systems (GDSS), to address this need.

A review of literature on groups (Hill, 1981) and GDSS technology (Dennis et al., 1988; Pinsonneault and Kraemer, 1989) shows that most group research up to 1981 and all GDSS research up to 1988 had been carried out in the US with American subjects. Research has shown that cultural differences among nations have important implications for group and organizational behavior. Theories in psychology, sociology, group behavior, organizational behavior, and related disciplines that deal with people and organizations are ethnocentric and culturally specific; a theory that applies to one culture need not necessarily apply to another (Boyacigiller and Adler, 1991; Hofstede, 1980, 1984, 1985). Because GDSS technology has a direct impact on the behavior patterns and communication processes of people in groups, the applicability of the body of American-based GDSS research findings to other cultures is unknown.

An important assumption in present GDSS theory and design practice is that addition of an anonymous electronic medium to verbal information exchange in a group will lead to a more balanced involvement among the group members and better group decision outcomes. It is frequently argued that a GDSS enables members of a group to express their views anonymously, and hence encourages those members who may be reticent about communicating their views verbally. Consequently, the resources of a group are better extracted in a group discussion (DeSanctis and Gallupe, 1987).

This theory makes three implicit assumptions that may be specific to American culture. First, the theory assumes that it is important for each group member to have an equal opportunity, regardless of status, to express an opinion in a group, and that each group member derives satisfaction from an equal opportunity to influence or present information to the group. Second, the theory assumes that each group member prefers open and direct communication to indirect communication to resolve conflict or disagreement in a group discussion. This assumption is reflected in some of the existing GDSS designs, which impose a meeting structure that encourages group members to state their views more clearly and have more open communication. Third, the theory assumes that group discussions and decisions should maximize organizational objectives rather than preserve group harmony. This view is reflected in some of the existing GDSS designs in which task-oriented considerations have precedence over social-oriented considerations.

Whereas these assumptions may be valid in American culture, they may not be in many of the Asia-Pacific cultures. For example, in Singapore, "belongingness" may rank above ego needs such as self-actualization and self-esteem, disagreement may be more effectively expressed in indirect ways rather than in a direct and open confrontation, and preserving group harmony may be more important than maximizing organizational objectives (Hofstede 1980).

PROJECT GOALS

This brief introduction has identified the need for research on the applicability of existing theories and designs of GDSS to different cultures. To address this need, the main goals of the NUS GDSS research project are

1. To study the effect of GDSS on group performance in conjunction with group size, group proximity, task type, and culture.
2. To use the results of these studies to review existing GDSS theories and designs and contribute to their improvement.
3. To develop a GDSS suitable for different cultures, especially the Singaporean culture.
4. To collaborate and cooperate with GDSS researchers in other countries on all aspects of this research.

As can be seen from these goals, the project consists of two complimentary parts. The first part focuses on the behavioral aspects covering group dynamics, group processes, and group outcomes, with particular attention to cultural factors. The second part concerns the design and development of GDSS software that incorporates the findings of the first part.

CONCEPTUAL FOUNDATIONS OF THE RESEARCH

The conceptual foundations of this research are the theory of small-group dynamics, the theory of GDSS, and observed differences of work-related values and decision environments between cultures. McGrath's (1984) framework for the study of groups provides the foundation for the study of group dynamics. The theory of GDSS proposed by DeSanctis and Gallupe (1987) has identified three dimensions and several dependent variables to be studied in GDSS research. The seminal work of Hofstede (1980, 1984, 1985) on cultural differences and literature on decision making in Asia-Pacific countries provides the foundation for the study of culture as the fourth dimension of GDSS research.

Research Model and Research Problem

The conceptual model of this research (shown in Figure 12-1) involves a group, a group support, a group task, and group performance. These entities are tightly coupled and interacting in an environment. The research problem is this: Given a group with certain group properties, a task with certain task properties, and a GDSS with certain support

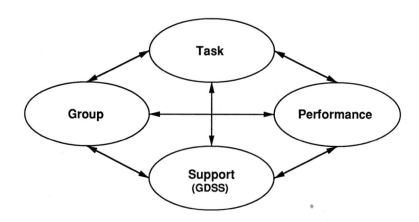

Environment
- Organization Culture
- Decision Environment
- Physical Environment

FIGURE 12-1.   Research Model

features in an environment with certain environmental properties, determine the influence of group support on group process and outcome. The converse problem is as follows: Given a group with certain group properties and a task with certain task properties in an environment with certain environmental properties, determine the type and features of group support that will result in the most desirable performance of the group.

McGrath's (1984) framework offers a suitable conceptual basis for studying the effects of GDSS on group performance. According to this framework, the central feature of a group lies in the interaction of its members. There are four sets of properties that influence the interaction of group members:

1. The biological, social, and psychological properties of individuals
2. The physical, sociocultural, and technological properties of the environments
3. The patterned relationships among group members prior to the meeting
4. The characteristics of the group task

The effects of these four sets of properties, singly and in combination, are the forces that shape the group interaction process, which is itself both the result of these forces and the source of some additional forces. The interaction process and outcomes represent forces that potentially lead to changes in input variables. In other words, the input variables and the group interaction process and outcome variables interact with one another. The bidirectional arrows in Figure 12–1 represent this two-way relationship.

The properties or variables associated with the four nodes in the research model have been discussed in the literature on groups and group decision-support systems. For example, McGrath's (1984) framework and group task circumplex provide the basis for generating a comprehensive list of variables associated with the group, task, environment, and performance nodes. The multidimensional taxonomy proposed by DeSanctis and Gallupe (1987) offers a comprehensive list of group support technology variables.

The Cultural Dimension in Group Decision Making

Cultural differences between nations have been extensively researched by Hofstede (1980, 1984, 1985). In a major piece of cross-national research, Hofstede identified four attributes of national culture on the basis of a statistical analysis of 116,000 questionnaires completed by members of a large U.S.-based multinational corporation with operating units in 40 countries around the world. Hofstede matched employees in terms of jobs, age, and sex and argued that national culture can be identified as an independent variable. The four major cultural attributes identified by Hofstede are as follows:

1. Individualism (IDV) stands for a preference for a loosely knit social framework in which individuals are supposed to take care of themselves and their immediate families only, as opposed to Collectivism, which stands for a preference for a tightly knit social framework in which individuals can expect their relatives, clan, and other in-groups to look after them, in exchange for unquestioning loyalty.

2. Power distance (PDI) is the extent to which a society accepts the fact that power in institutions and organizations is distributed unequally.
3. Uncertainty avoidance (UAI) is the degree to which a society feels threatened by uncertain and ambiguous situations, which leads them to support beliefs promising certainty and to maintain institutions protecting conformity.
4. Masculinity (MAS) stands for a preference for achievement, heroism, assertiveness, and material success as opposed to Femininity, which stands for a preference for relationships, modesty, caring for the weak, and the quality of life.

Cross-Cultural Differences

Sociotechnical research findings in one country may be generalizable to another country with the same scores for the cultural attributes but not across culture with widely different scores. Instances have been cited by Hofstede (1980, 1984, 1985) to illustrate the various problems that could arise from applying the management philosophy of one culture to a different culture. The US and Singapore belong to different cultural groups. The American culture is characterized by high IDV and low PDI, whereas the Singaporean culture is characterized by low IDV and high PDI.

Differences in Decision Environments

Huber (1981) suggests that the type of decision environment will determine the nature of data, dialogue, and models (decision aids) required in a decision support system (DSS). National and organizational cultures influence decision environments, which in turn determine the nature of the support required from a GDSS. For example, the decision environment in Singapore today is strongly influenced by the collectivistic Chinese culture, British government and legal systems, and Western and Japanese management philosophies and decision-making process. A brief review of decision environments in Japan, Taiwan, and Singapore will reinforce this point.

Japan

The Japanese society and its decision environment is known to be different from Western societies and their environments. Hatvany and Pucik (1981) describe the Japanese decision-making process as follows:

> The usual procedure for management decision making is that a proposal is initiated by a middle manager, most often under the directive of top management. This middle manager will engage in informal discussion and consultation with peers and supervisors (*Nemavasi*). When all are familiar with the proposal, a request for a decision is made formally and, because of earlier discussions, it is almost inevitably ratified, often in a ceremonial group meeting (*Ringi*)....This kind of decision making is not participative in the American sense of the word. Nor is it bottom-up...rather, it is a top down interactive consultative process, especially when long-term planning and strategy are concerned.

Taiwan

Farn and Sung (1987) suggest that the process of making collective decisions in a Chinese society is highly influenced by the way the Chinese civil service has operated for the past several centuries. In this tradition, the first step is to identify who has the authority and responsibility for the problems and issues at hand. The head of the organizational unit that has the responsibility for the final decision will coordinate the decision-making process and any interpretation of the rules and regulations. When an issue spans several functional units, the responsibilities of each unit are identified, and each will contribute to the decision-making process from its position, bounded by its authority. There are two types of meetings, *Huai* and *Yi*. A *Yi* is a meeting in which all interested parties participate and the final decision is made. Before the *Yi*, the alternate proposals are discussed and almost settled through a series of *Huai*, which are coordination meetings among the staff members of the units involved. No new alternative will be considered in the *Yi*. If any differences arise in the *Yi*, the meeting is suspended and more coordinating *Huai* meetings will be held to include the interests of all the parties.

There are three important differences between the Chinese and American decision environments. First, a group member in a Chinese environment is passive and will not offer an opinion unless it is elicited or unless the issue is related to his or her area of responsibility. Second, a manager in a Chinese environment seeks an alternative that minimizes internal conflict rather than maximizes organizational objectives. Third, Chinese organizations may behave illogically from a rational viewpoint in order to preserve internal harmony.

Singapore

Singapore was a British colony. After independence it retained the British government, business, and legal systems. In recent years, Japanese corporations have set up manufacturing plants and operational headquarters in Singapore, which has resulted in an infusion of Japanese management philosophy and decision-making processes. Raman and Rao (1988) indicate a collaborative and consensus-building decision environment for Singapore. The collaborative aspect is similar to that in the Chinese environment. It aims to include the interest of every member and to achieve harmony among group members through a series of coordination meetings in which various views and alternatives are discussed before the final decision is made. In the consensus-building aspect, leaders in high positions rally support for what they perceive to be good policies and programs through a series of meetings covering all affected parties.

Implications for GDSS Design

Differences in cultural attributes and decision environments have important implications in the design of GDSS for different cultures. In collectivistic cultures, group members may prefer indirect ways to open and direct communication to resolve conflict and disagreement. Therefore the features of a GDSS that encourage open communication may not be appropriate. The anonymity feature of a GDSS may have both positive and negative consequences in collectivistic cultures. On the one hand, it may encourage more even member participation. On the other hand, dominant members may use it to express openly negative opinions about other members' contributions, a behavior that is normally unacceptable in the culture. Dominant members may also take advantage of the anonymity feature to gain influence without open and direct confrontation. Moreover, in collectivistic cultures, preserving group harmony may be more important than achieving short-term organizational objectives, and social-oriented considerations may take precedence over task-oriented considerations. As a GDSS tends to reduce social-oriented communications, it may introduce some unintended consequences into the group interaction process.

Different decision environments may require different types and levels of communication support. In Japan and Taiwan, a series of coordination meetings are held before the decision is made at formal *Ringi* and *Yi* meetings. Therefore, a GDSS for Japan or Taiwan would be required to support the coordination phase of group decision making. This feature may necessitate a different-time/different-place system that supports dispersed asynchronous communication. In a Chinese society, a GDSS with a mechanism to expose hidden assumptions would result in more effective decision making. The anonymity feature is essential to encourage group members to contribute new ideas. This feature will not only preserve group harmony but also improve group interaction. The voting feature of a GDSS may not be useful in Japanese and Chinese cultures because voting is virtually nonexistent in the final *Ringi* and *Yi* meetings. A GDSS for the Singaporean culture will have to combine and modify the features of a GDSS for the American, Japanese, and Chinese cultures. For Singapore, a GDSS that provides more structure may be more appropriate because workflow and procedures are not codified and prescribed to the same extent as in Japan.

GDSS RESEARCH AT NUS

Teaching and research in information systems at NUS is carried out in the Department of Information Systems and Computer Science (DISCS), in the Faculty of Science. This department in its present form was constituted in 1982. The first class of students graduated with a bachelor's degree in computer and information sciences in 1986, and the first class of students with postgraduate degrees graduated in 1987. Research in information systems started in 1987.

Location of the GDSS Research Facility

GDSS research in NUS is carried out in DISCS, which has several laboratories with facilities to support undergraduate and postgraduate teaching and research. Of particular interest are two information systems laboratories with IBM-compatible personal computers, Macintosh PCs, and audiovisual facilities that include BARCO projectors. These laboratories are designed and equipped to support teaching and research in information systems in general and can be converted to GDSS research laboratories by rearranging the furniture and PCs (Figure 12–2).

The GDSS Hardware and Software

SAMM System
Early GDSS research at NUS used the UNIX-based Software Aided Meeting Management (SAMM) system developed at the University of Minnesota (DeSanctis, Sambamurthy, and Watson, 1987). IBM-compatible PCs in the information systems

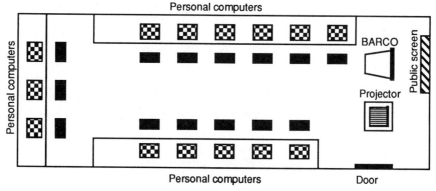

(a) Information Systems Laboratory

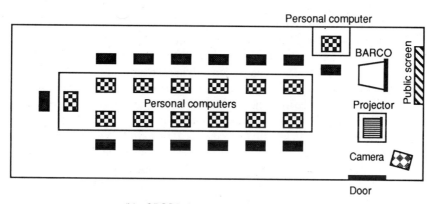

(b) GDSS Laboratory for Large Groups

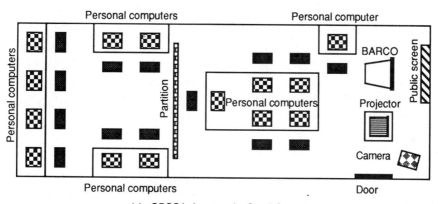

(c) GDSS Laboratory for Small Groups

FIGURE 12-2.

laboratories were converted to GDSS workstations by connecting them to an AT&T computer with UNIX operating system. (SAMM is described in Chapter 9.)

SAGE System

Current GDSS research in NUS uses the HyperCard-based Software Aided Group Environment (SAGE) system developed in DISCS as part of the NUS GDSS research effort (Wei, Tan, and Raman, 1992). SAGE is implemented on a network of Macintosh PCs using HyperCard and AppleTalk. It is adapted from SAMM under licence from the University of Minnesota.

SAGE consists of a public and a private program. In a group meeting, each group member is served by a copy of the private program running at his or her private terminal (Macintosh PC). The group as a whole is served by a copy of the public program running at a public terminal (Macintosh PC). The public terminal also contains the shared data base. The functions of SAGE are organized into hierarchies of menus in both the public and private programs. The current version of SAGE (Version 2.0) supports face-to-face meetings and offers limited support to synchronous dispersed meetings. In the face-to-face mode, SAGE displays all public information on a shared public screen. In the dispersed mode, group members view the public screen in a separate window on their private terminals. The concepts underlying the structure and design of SAGE and the characteristics of the user interface are discussed in Wei, Tan, and Raman (1992).

A considerable part of the NUS GDSS research efforts has been devoted to developing and testing SAGE. It has been tested in Singapore in several research experiments involving more than 500 student subjects. It is also currently undergoing thorough testing at a field site in Singapore and two academic sites in the US. Feedback on SAGE, both from experimental student groups and organizational groups, has been very encouraging. Users find SAGE easy to learn, easy to relearn, and easy to use. SAGE is also easy to install. It can be set up in an office with Macintosh PCs in about 30 minutes.

RESEARCH EFFORTS TO DATE

The NUS GDSS research efforts to date have addressed both the behavioral and technical aspects of the research. The behavioral research in the three-year period from 1988 to 1990 investigated the effects of support level, culture, leadership, task type, and communication mode on group decisions by using experimental research methodology. The technical research focused on improving SAMM for use in Singapore and on developing SAGE. These research efforts are summarized here.

Culture and Support Level (Outcome Study)

A study of the effects of culture and support level on the decision outcome of groups solving a preference task compared the results of Watson's (1987) study with those of an NUS study. The independent variables were culture (Singaporean or American) and support level (baseline, manual, or GDSS). The dependent variables were postmeeting consensus and equality of influence. The GDSS used was SAMM (Version 1.3). The findings are reported in Ho, Raman, and Watson (1989).

Leadership and Support Level (Outcome Study)

A study of the effects of leadership and support level on the decision outcome of groups solving a preference task used the independent variables leadership (yes or no) and support level (baseline, manual, GDSS). The dependent variables were postmeeting consensus, equality of influence, and influence of leader (for groups with leaders). The covariate was premeeting consensus. The GDSS used was SAMM (Version 1.3). For a discussion of the results see Ho and Raman (1991).

Leadership and Support Level (Process Study)

A study of the effects of leadership and support level on the decision process of groups solving a preference task used the independent variables leadership (yes or no) and support level (manual or GDSS). The dependent variables were amount of influence behavior, influence imbalance, and dominance significance. The GDSS used was SAMM (Version 1.3). See Lim, Raman, and Wei, (1990) for more information.

Task Type and Support Level (Outcome Study)

A study of the effects of task type and support level on group decision outcome used the independent variables task type (intellective or preference) and support level (baseline, manual, or GDSS). The dependent variables were consensus change, equality of influence, decision satisfaction, and decision scheme satisfaction. The GDSS used was SAMM (Version 1.4). The findings are discussed in Tan, Wei, and Raman, (1991).

Task Type and Communication Mode (Outcome Study)

The study of the effects of task type and communication mode on group decision outcome used the independent variables task type (intellective or preference) and communication mode (face to face with public screen, face to face without public screen, or dispersed). The dependent variables were consensus change, equality of influence, decision satisfaction, decision scheme satisfaction, actual decision quality (for intellective task groups), and perceived decision quality (for preference task groups). The GDSS used was SAGE (Version 1.2). Refer to Raman, Tan, and Wei, (1991) for further discussion.

Evaluation of GDSS

The GDSS facility at NUS DISCS has been used by more than 1,500 students and a few groups from industry. Comments have ranged from "a great idea and concept, but it needs a lot of further development" to "I do not see the need for such a sophisticated and expensive tool to support small groups solving simple problems." Groups from industry have been very excited about GDSS, especially SAGE. One organizational group used the paired comparison and allocate model in SAGE to identify 5 of the most critical issues from a list of 20. The group achieved high levels of postmeeting consensus, equality of influence, and decision satisfaction.

A senior public policymaker who studies sociopolitical problems in Singapore thinks that GDSS technology could be very useful in arriving at consensus in some of the large groups of grass-root leaders, of which he is chair. But he pauses and ponders: "Is GDSS a solution in search of a problem, or can it really improve member participation, consensus, and satisfaction with the decisions in some of my meetings?"

CONTINUING RESEARCH

In comparison with the GDSS research projects in universities in the United States, the NUS GDSS research project is modest in size and scope. Two faculty members and three students work part time on this project. Over the next few years, the NUS DISCS research efforts will be divided equally between the behavioral and technical aspects of GDSS research.

The behavioral part of the research will continue to focus on the effect of GDSS in different national cultures and organizational types. Experimental research with student groups and field studies in organizational settings will continue to be conducted in Singapore and other countries, which are likely to include Malaysia, Taiwan, People's Republic of China, and some European countries. In the long term, the NUS GDSS research team hopes to contribute to the development of a comprehensive theory of GDSS that includes the cultural dimension.

The technical aspect of the research will focus on improving SAGE by providing more decision aids and developing it into an international GDSS. Currently, the team is working on developing a notepad interface for SAGE and a Chinese-language version. Performance in the synchronous dispersed mode needs to be improved, and the asynchronous dispersed mode needs to be included so that SAGE can effectively support the premeeting phase of group decision making in some Asia-Pacific countries. In the long term, a version of SAGE based on the IBM/PC Windows platform will be developed.

Because of shortage of office space, the NUS GDSS research project does not have a dedicated GDSS laboratory at present. When more office space becomes available in the future, a GDSS and behavioral research laboratory facility will be set up in DISCS.

MEMBERS OF THE NUS GDSS RESEARCH TEAM

Raman, Krishnamurthy Sundara (Dr.), principal investigator
Wei, Kwok-Kee (Dr.), principal collaborator
Ho, Teck-Hua, M.Sc. student; presently a Ph.D. candidate at the University of Pennsylvania
Lim, Lai-Huat, M.Sc. student; presently a Ph.D. candidate at the University of British Columbia
Tan, Bernard Cheng-Yian, M.Sc. student; presently a Ph.D. candidate at the National University of Singapore

Chapter 13

GSS Above the Snow Line

Abhijit Gopal
Stephen Hayne
Paul Licker
Carol Pollard
Wynne Chin

The University of Calgary

INTRODUCTION

Research in the group support systems (GSS) domain occupies a central position at the University of Calgary's Faculty of Management. Here, GSS symbolizes the rapid modernization of management practices and methods and reflects the growing organizational focus on task groups. Indeed, GSS use is high, both for administration and for research. Administrative uses include network planning sessions, strategic planning meetings of the Management of Technology Committee, area meetings for several disciplinary areas represented at the Faculty of Management, and feedback and evaluation sessions for students. The research initiative has a multidisciplinary flavor. Researchers in marketing, human resources management, operations management, accounting, and management information systems are actively investigating the impact and implications of GSS in their disciplines and are involved in cross-functional research with the information systems area.

The pervasive use of GSS is the result of a carefully planned initiative, which is consistent with a broader program in the management of technology that was initiated at the faculty in 1989. Several advantages of this planned approach have been realized. First, physical facilities to accommodate the hardware, software, and network infrastructure were identified and developed before the installation of the first GSS, thereby facilitating the subsequent processes of learning and adoption. Second, new faculty members involved in GSS and related research at prominent North American universities were brought on board. These faculty members provided the technical knowhow that helped to activate the GSS initiative effectively, and they brought with them multiple perspectives on GSS research. Third, once the infrastructure for GSS had been established, a unique approach was taken to its management. An interdisciplinary committee was formed to direct the GSS initiative and to formulate a long-range plan for GSS use. Once the long-range plan was formalized, the committee was charged with the responsibility of managing the GSS facility on an ongoing basis and facilitating multidisciplinary research projects.

A consequence of bringing in new faculty members with diverse perspectives on GSS research, and of kindling interest in GSS research among a diverse set of disciplines, is the channeling of a wide variety of skills and viewpoints and the consequent enrichment of the GSS research effort. The main result of this synergy is expanded opportunity. First, faculty researchers have the opportunity to study the systems themselves in a wider variety of settings, including functional areas, management levels, and research settings (laboratory and field). Second, researchers within functional areas have the opportunity to extend their investigations of phenomena of interest to them to domains that had been previously restricted to researchers in the information technologies.

GSS proves valuable in another way that is consistent with the faculty's strategic objectives. In keeping with its policy of maintaining a synergistic relationship with Calgary business by helping companies stay abreast of the latest trends in management thinking and techniques, the faculty encourages the extensive use of its GSS facilities by members of the business community. Two important benefits are realized through this arrangement. First, the faculty's image among local businesses continues to be enhanced, resulting in the expansion of cooperative ventures between the two sides. Second, this arrangement results in the increasing availability of research subjects and sites from the corporate world and the opportunity to conduct GSS field research to complement that being conducted in university laboratories.

The remainder of this chapter describes the GSS facilities at the University of Calgary and how they are currently used, outlines the research agenda of GSS researchers in the information systems area, identifies the issues associated with GSS research and use, and describes specific research projects.

INFRASTRUCTURE AND USE

GSS is installed and used in several different modes. Each mode represents a different physical configuration capable of supporting one or more of the several different forms of GSS. Some of these are commercial products, and others are research systems being developed. This section describes the systems in use, the modes in which they are used, and current usage patterns. Table 13-1 shows how different GSS settings are used to support the available systems.

TABLE 13-1   Systems and Modes of Use

	System				
Mode of Use	GroupSystems	VisionQuest	OptionFinder	Experimental	Planned
GSS Meeting Room	✓	✓	✓	✓	✓
Class/Conference Rooms			✓		✓
Faculty Network	✓	✓		✓	✓
Multiple Meeting Rooms	✓	✓	✓		✓
Medium-sized Room (planned)	✓	✓	✓	✓	✓
External Access (planned)	✓	✓		✓	✓

Systems in Current Use

The first commercial GSS, GroupSystems, was installed in August 1990. A second GSS that has recently been introduced commercially, VisionQuest, was installed in December 1990, while it was undergoing beta testing at several North American universities. A third commercial GSS, OptionFinder, was acquired in December 1990. In addition, several experimental systems, described in a later section, have been installed since 1990. Many of them have been developed in the Microsoft Windows 386 environment and utilize the extensive graphic capabilities of that platform.

In addition to the commercial and experimental systems in current use, the installation of at least one other product that facilitates group work is planned in the immediate future. This system, Confer II (Quarterman, 1990), operates in a mainframe environment. Although Confer II is currently implemented in a VAX/VMS environment at the University of Michigan, its use in a UNIX environment at the University of Calgary is being investigated.

Physical Settings

The most commonly used physical setting is a dedicated meeting room configured with 34 IBM PS/2 Model 55SX computers (Figure 13-1). The computers are connected by a 16 megabit/second IBM Token Ring network, which runs Novell's Netware 386 network operating system. Each computer is configured with a VGA monitor, 60 megabytes of hard disk storage, one 3.5-inch and one 5.25-inch floppy disk drive, and 2 megabytes of RAM. The network server, an IBM PS/2 Model 80 computer, has 25 megabytes of RAM and 2 gigabytes of hard disk storage. One computer is connected to an Electrohome Video Beam projector, which makes the screen contents of that computer available for public viewing. This computer is frequently used by a meeting facilitator or coordinator. The meeting room supports all the forms of GSS available. The most frequently used GSS in this environment is GroupSystems.

A second physical setting for GSS use is the classroom. Most faculty classrooms are equipped with video presentation equipment, which can be conveniently connected to external devices. Minimally, the video presentation equipment consists of retractable

FIGURE 13-1.   GSS Meeting Room

screens and connections for projection equipment. Several classrooms are actually equipped with projection devices similar to the Electrohome Video Beam projector, and a few classrooms have projection rooms attached that contain slide projection equipment and video cameras. Currently, all classrooms support the use of OptionFinder and demonstration versions of the other GSS. There are plans to utilize emerging telecommunications technologies, such as local area networks using radio communications in conjunction with portable computers, to allow the expanded use of GSS in classrooms. The faculty's conference rooms are used in a manner similar to classrooms for GSS use and will also see expanded GSS use as new technologies are brought on board.

A third physical setting for GSS is faculty offices. An IBM Token Ring network operating at 16 megabits per second has recently been installed and currently connects approximately 20% of the faculty offices. It is expected that all offices will be connected by the summer of 1992. The network uses Novell's Netware 386 network operating system and is connected to the network that links the student microcomputer laboratories and the main GSS room. The network supports all the GSS products other than OptionFinder. The primary GSS used in this environment is VisionQuest because of its any-time/any-place architecture. The use of GroupSystems in a distributed mode is currently being explored.

The fourth GSS setting is actually a combination of previously described settings, in that it involves accessing a GSS simultaneously from two meeting rooms. The characteristic of this environment that sets it apart from the others is that it uses same-time/same-place systems in that mode, while simultaneously using them in a same-time/different-place mode. Experiments have been conducted that successfully accessed GroupSystems from the primary GSS room as well as from a student laboratory containing 30 computers. The combined session utilized 60 user stations. An experiment, described in a later section, involves the use of OptionFinder simultaneously by two groups of users in two cities.

Two other environments for GSS are scheduled for implementation in the near future. The first of these settings is a medium-sized meeting room containing the same facilities and connectivity as the current GSS room but only six personal computers. The objective of such an environment is to investigate GSS use by small groups. The technology in the current meeting room often proves to be overwhelming for small groups, as a result of which the GSS technology rather than the content of the meeting becomes the primary focus. GroupSystems and VisionQuest will be the primary GSS supported in this environment, along with the experimental systems being developed.

The second planned mode involves access to the faculty's network from outside the university. This access will be implemented in two ways: through dial-up lines and by accessing the campus ethernet network to enter the LAN at the Faculty of Management. The primary advantage of this environment will be to allow GSS access to local business partners, thereby providing a unique research opportunity in distributed GSS use. The primary GSS supported in this environment will be VisionQuest and some of the experimental systems currently under development.

Support Infrastructure

The existing systems are supported by people who fill three roles. The first role is administrative and includes functions such as scheduling and liaison with business and academic users. One full-time person is responsible for overall administration of the GSS facility and for liaison activity. Another person conducts scheduling activity on a part-time basis. The second role is related to conducting meetings. One person, a faculty instructor, is responsible for the meeting process, in the form of presession planning, meeting facilitation, and follow-up activities. The third role is that of technical support. The information technology support group fills this role, with the network administration personnel taking on the primary responsibility.

Current Use

GSS represents a revolutionary approach to group process to the faculty's researchers and to the Calgary business community. Consequently, much of the use in the first year was of an exploratory nature. This method has allowed the people involved to ponder the implications of this new technology for their own situations and to plan their levels of involvement in its future use.

Lately, the patterns of usage have shown subtle but significant changes. Whereas early use involved relatively low levels of commitment to the technology, in the form of demonstration sessions and faculty area meetings, current patterns show greater commitment, both from faculty and business users. Faculty users are now exploring ways of using the new technology in research projects and as a vehicle for the improvement of current management practices, for example, for quality-of-work-life surveys and advertising campaign planning. Business users, including university administrators, are increasingly using GSS for corporate planning sessions and other processes that are clearly in need of improvement. Another sign of increasing commitment among business users is the willingness of busy senior executives to visit the university for up to a whole day at a time to use the GSS facilities. Moreover, many of these executives have returned for follow-up sessions, and several more such sessions have been scheduled.

Business users have also demonstrated an increasing commitment to facilitating GSS research. Although all users have willingly completed questionnaires administered at the time of their use of GSS, several companies have indicated their willingness to have university researchers visit their premises to learn more about the potential for continued GSS use.

GSS is also used to support teaching activities, which fall into two primary categories. The first involves GSS as a teaching tool, for example, demonstration of GSS in joint application development and team-based development in classes on information systems development. The second category involves classroom evaluation. The existing systems have been used to elicit background information about students in early classes, to allow students to provide ongoing feedback during courses, and to conduct teaching evaluations at the end of an academic term.

RESEARCH AGENDA

The rich variety of perspectives on GSS research that has been assembled gives the researchers in the information systems area the opportunity to study several facets of group support systems, ranging from their development to their use. Accordingly, the research team has developed a model that outlines the research agenda (see Figure 13-2). The model depicts the three fundamental aspects of GSS that are being investigated: its development, its introduction into organizational settings, and its actual use by organizational members—that is, its life cycle: The systems are first developed, then introduced into (or implemented in) the organizational setting, and finally are actively used within the organization.

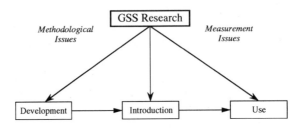

FIGURE 13-2.   Research Agenda

Two important research issues pervade all three areas, both of which are being addressed through the faculty's research. The first issue is measurement. As GSS is a relatively new domain, little work has been done to develop valid measurements of the constructs used in GSS research. The measurement issue is certainly facilitated by the use of constructs borrowed from reference disciplines, but it is confounded by the fact that these constructs often have to be redefined in the GSS domain. An important GSS research objective at Calgary is to develop and validate measures of these constructs. The second issue concerns methods. Although there are several methodological concerns in GSS research, one of the most pressing is that of achieving the appropriate balance between field and laboratory research. This is a primary concern and is actively addressed in the research program.

Methods and Measurement Issues

Our data-gathering approaches recognize the trade-off between what Mason (1989) terms the *richness of worldly realism* and the *tightness of control*. This trade-off is particularly applicable to the GSS domain. Consequently, studies need to vary from controlled laboratory experiments to quasi-experimental studies and ethnomethodological studies. There is also a need for measurement techniques that are applicable to the special requirements of the GSS domain. There are several data-gathering and statistical analysis techniques that have rarely been utilized in GSS research but can be invaluable in helping to address the complexities associated with GSS development, introduction, and use.

This explicit recognition of the methodological and measurement issues has resulted in an attempt to combine field studies and laboratory experiments with second-generation multivariate techniques and other psychometric techniques in ways that provide the greatest insights. Four factors affect these combinations: the particular stage of the research model being considered (development, introduction, or use), the level of substantive knowledge regarding the specific research question, the degree of relative emphasis on objective and subjective measures, and the complexity of the phenomenon in question.

The stage of research has a significant influence on the choice of method. Although laboratory experiments tend to lend themselves reasonably well to development projects, it is felt that quasi-experimental studies and field-based surveys should be used more extensively for introduction and use research. It is believed that this approach helps progress from greater control to greater realism in a logical and ordered manner, in which technology is developed in a controlled environment and is tested in a realistic setting.

The level of current knowledge regarding the effects of GSS during group meetings is another consideration. Enough studies have been conducted to allow the preparation of both qualitative (Dennis et al., 1988; Pinsonneault & Kraemer, 1989) and quantitative (McLeod, 1991) reviews, which have identified appropriate variables for consideration (e.g., task performance, task and interpersonal process, and members' attitudes toward their task and processes). However, we still lack the theoretical models and empirical evidence to generalize current findings to a wide variety of GSS use. Furthermore, knowledge about conditions under which GSS is successfully introduced and infused into organizations are still tentative (Pollard, 1991) and in need of further exploration.

The level of substantive knowledge about the GSS domain is, therefore, quite low. Consequently, there is a need to apply and test new theories such as adaptive structuration theory (Poole and DeSanctis, 1990), to identify the criteria by which GSS are evaluated by potential users, and to identify and investigate the causal linkages between components of GSS and its environment. These considerations call for the use of data-gathering and analysis techniques that lend themselves to research containing an exploratory component, for example, second-generation multivariate techniques like partial least squares Lohmöller, 1989; Wold, 1982); and other psychometric techniques such as multidimensional scaling and conjoint analysis.

Another consideration in the choice of appropriate methods and measurements relates to the selection of objective and subjective measures. Although objective measures provide greater accuracy, the constructs of interests are often measurable only through subjective measures. A measurement issue associated with this constraint is the need to develop group-level scores rather than individual-level scores. The practice of aggregating individual scores to yield group scores is not a convincing method of obtaining such scores when subject measures are used (Gopal, Bostrom, and Chin, 1992). Consequently, there is a need for statistical analysis techniques that account for the existence of the group entity while using individual-level data to represent the group.

Finally, the study of group use of information technology is considerably more complex than the study of individual use. Many of the second-generation multivariate techniques explicitly address this complexity. Also, because we understand group use to a smaller extent than individual use, there is a further need for data analysis techniques that facilitate exploratory research, the result of which is improved understanding of GSS and its use. Toward this end, techniques such as multidimensional scaling and conjoint analysis impose the fewest constraints on the tentative models that are developed and might result in a better understanding of the complexities associated with GSS.

In general, the approach that is being developed is to recognize the factors that influence the methodological and measurement issues and to use a wide range of methods and techniques to address them. The results are a better understanding of the appropriate methods and measurements and greater insights into GSS development, introduction, and use.

Research in Development

The first branch of the research agenda is that of GSS development (see Figure 13–2). Olson (1987) defines this research methodology as a combination of the disciplines of software engineering (application development) and social sciences (assessing the ways in which people use applications). Nunamaker and Chen (1989) describe five steps in the process: Construct a conceptual framework, develop a system architecture, analyze and design the system, build the system, and observe and evaluate the system. The process feeds back on itself at any step to take advantage of learning through creation.

Extensive prototyping is used to investigate the potential capabilities of a platform, the initial functionality of a system, and the use of the system by its intended audience.

The object-oriented development paradigm supports the easy reuse of functions. Prototyping also allows the gathering of technical performance measures and is an excellent method for generating and evaluating alternative implementations.

Observation (experimental and field) is employed during the final step to validate the system. Formal and informal feedback is gathered and analyzed to determine the effectiveness of the system and to specify enhancements. The current set of research projects satisfies the requirements of two initiatives: the exploration of the role of graphics as applied to GSS and the determination of the requirements for supporting dispersed groups.

We will now turn to projects involving systems that allow synchronous or asynchronous group work. All the systems described are functioning prototypes, and their common technology platform is any local-area network that supports NetBIOS and any microcomputer that runs Microsoft Windows.

Group Issue Analyzer (GIA)

The gains in efficiency and effectiveness that occurs when groups share text electronically may be realized more effectively by groups sharing graphic symbols and text, such as issues and related comments. The output may also reflect the group's thoughts more accurately when the group follows a process model consisting of three steps: Create the issues and comments, share them with others in real time, and resolve simple naming conflicts.

Group Issue Analyzer (GIA) presents the user with what appears to be a blank sheet of paper. The mouse is used to select objects; to place the various objects on the screen; and to perform diagram management, such as zooming and suppression of displayed objects. View slaving and gesturing are supported. Issues must be created before they can be commented on, but any issue can be commented on no matter who created it. When a new issue is to be entered, the user types in its name in a small, pop-up dialogue box. This issue is drawn on the screen as a blue square. If the diagram has been zoomed large enough so that text can be read, it is labeled. Users type comments in a larger pop-up edit dialogue box. When finished with a comment, the user must choose which issue(s) it is related to from a dialogue box containing a list of issues created. As each issue is selected, the user must designate whether the comment is *for, against,* or *indifferent* to the issue. Lines are drawn from the comment to the related issues in green, red, and black, respectively. The comment is placed beside the first issue chosen. As more comments are added, they are made to overlap one another like fanned cards around the issues.

GIA discussions can be arranged in a network by "drilling down" through issues to new diagrams. In this way, issues can be consolidated or exploded. Using the multitasking capabilities in Microsoft Windows, users can participate in multiple discussions as well as in multiple views of the same discussion. The final output of GIA is a text file, with the comments following each issue. GIA is currently being used by Shell Canada to investigate petroleum production problems.

Group View Modeling System (GVMS)

When requirements for a data base are being captured, many user views are modeled. To build the global conceptual schema, these views must be integrated. Attempts have been made to build expert systems that detect similarities among views and assist in their integration. However, integration has proven to be a difficult practical and theoretical problem. The research team takes a different approach to the problem. It is believed that by gathering the different users (or their representatives) to participate simultaneously in modeling their views through an appropriate GSS, the task of integration will become considerably easier.

Group View Modeling System (GVMS), an extended entity-relationship modeling tool, supports this data-base design process (Hayne, 1990). The underlying model is the Semantic Data Model (SDM), including extensions for transactions and distribution information (Hayne and Ram, 1990). Groups of users interact to create a "community" view of the data base being designed. Symbols representing classes, attributes, relationships, and transactions are used to create this view. Again, the mouse is used to select objects, to place the various objects on the screen, and to perform diagram management. View slaving and gesturing are supported. An experiment conducted to test this tool found that small groups took less time and made more complete designs than individuals working separately (Hayne, 1990).

Group ScratchPad

Often during a spontaneous meeting, group members wish merely to sketch out an idea or rough drawing to illustrate a point or to initiate a design document. The ScratchPad allows groups to draw (and erase) on a common work surface. With eight colors, the drawing can be built in layers, thereby supporting a what-if capability. When all members are satisfied with an addition to the diagram (in a different color) it can be merged into the main drawing. If group members are not satisfied with the modifications in that color, they can be completely erased without affecting the other drawings. Group ScratchPad is currently being evaluated empirically by undergraduate students in computer science.

Folder

After the divergent process often followed by groups, there always remains the arduous tasks of weaning out redundant ideas (consolidation) and grouping like alternatives (clustering). Typically, these tasks are performed serially and have received minimal computer support. The Folder tool was developed to address this problem. The tool accepts output from any brainstorming tool. Each user creates folders for grouping like items (dragged and dropped with the mouse). When all users are finished, two specific algorithms (Coxon, 1979) are used to aggregate the sortings. One provides the group average measure of similarities among the set of ideas. The other algorithm produces a measure of how similar each user's sortings were to one another. The interitem and intersubject measures are then used in multidimensional scaling and cluster analysis routines. The results obtained are both graphic and numerical representations of the more parsimonious set of underlying concepts that the original set of ideas represents along with the group's level of consensus. These concepts become discussion topics and are labeled. It is believed that this process allows increased group input and will help groups reach consensus more swiftly. The use of Folder has been studied in a few medium-sized groups; the initial results indicate that it may well help to decrease the time and energy expended on idea consolidation.

MeetingChair

The tools described above function quite adequately for spontaneous group work or for planned sessions in which only one tool is used. However, as can be seen by the usage patterns of GroupSystems and VisionQuest, an agenda is often followed that invokes a progression of tools to enforce a particular process model. A meeting coordinator must be able to define who attends, start and stop tools, communicate with the group, direct the group's attention to items of importance, and be aware of individual activities. The MeetingChair was designed to provide this functionality in a graphic mode. A script can be created before the meeting that consists of the meeting participants, the tools to invoke, and their proposed elapsed times of execution (to prompt the coordinator). Text can be entered that appears at each user station (and vice versa). Items can be "gestured" at through control of the cursor, and the control can be passed to others if requested. MeetingChair can retrieve "snapshots" of each member's screen if an indication of participant activities is needed. The functionality of this tool is continually evolving as the differences between the requirements for text- and graphics-based group facilitation are better understood.

Future Software Development

Much of the future development activity in the GSS domain will focus on the continued refinement of the current systems. In addition, other development areas, such as the incorporation of sound in group activity, will be actively investigated. Sound, in the form of audio signals indicating the level of group activity and the annotation of agendas in the any-time/any-place environment (see Chapter 1), is already being studied for its impact on group work. Technologies such as still-motion video windows are also being explored. Finally, techniques such as decision trees and information flows are also being investigated for their potential use in the graphic group support system environment.

Research in Introduction

The second primary research thrust is in the introduction of GSS technologies into organizations. Introduction is an especially challenging field of inquiry because it calls for organizational change of considerable magnitude and consequently, a high level of organizational commitment to the GSS concept. Although GSS introduction is inextricably linked to GSS use, we describe the faculty's involvement in the latter in a later section. The two areas are divided because of the several differences that give each one a unique scope. However, it should be recognized that aspects of many of the research projects being conducted investigate factors in both areas.

The research on GSS introduction is informed by several theoretical approaches that have been used in related academic disciplines such as social psychology and consumer behavior. The two primary approaches are drawn from the diffusion of innovations theory (Rogers, 1983) and the theory of reasoned action (Ajzen and Fishbein, 1980; Fishbein and Ajzen, 1975). Both theoretical approaches have been employed in research concerning other information technologies (Alexander, 1989; Moore, 1989) and are easily adapted for research in GSS.

Both field and laboratory research are being used to study GSS introduction, with an emphasis on the field. A series of field studies in various stages of planning and execution is expected to answer several questions concerning the issues of adoption, diffusion, and implementation of the different types of GSS technology. The studies will articulate the process by which the different types of GSS are being introduced into organizations and the critical incidents that need to occur at each phase of the process to ensure its successful implementation.

The first study in this series employs an in-depth case study methodology to investigate the process of organizational adoption, diffusion, and implementation of OptionFinder in multiple business units in a large Fortune 500 company (Pollard, 1991). The study seeks to answer questions about the organizational adoption, diffusion, and implementation of keypad GSS. The questions concern why GSS is considered for adoption, how GSS is diffused in organizations, how GSS is used in organizations, and the contextual factors that influence adoption. As an extension of this project, a joint research project of the universities of Georgia and South Florida is examining the introduction of keypad-based GSS technology in organizations throughout North America, Europe, and Asia (Watson et al., 1991).

Another current avenue of research relates to the impact of GSS technology on the meeting cycle itself (Oppenheim, 1987). In a combination of interview and survey methodologies, GSS users are being questioned about computer-supported meeting preparation, meeting processes, and postmeeting follow-up. Although this research overlaps the GSS use area, it is described here because of its value in providing insights into the introduction of GSS.

Follow-up studies will examine attitudes of nonadopters and explore GSS user attitudes concerning the value of different types of technology. The overall purpose of our research on introduction and use is to develop strategies that will aid in diffusing different types of GSS technology within the business community and examine and report the extent of implementation and user acceptance.

One study being formulated uses both field and experimental research to investigate the specific user attitudes toward different types of GSS that result in their adoption or rejection as an organizational technology. Of specific interest are questions concerning the attitudes that best predict outcomes, the attitudes that influence adoption, and the effects of different forms of GSS technology on attitudes. This project searches for its answers in the controlled environment of the laboratory as well as in the generalizable environment of the real world. It is expected that the results, besides providing information on the questions of interest, will go a long way toward improving understanding on the relationship between field and laboratory data.

Research in Use

The third branch of GSS research at the University of Calgary involves actual GSS use, which to date has been focused on meetings, or the same-time/same-place environment. In many ways, this is the most fundamental form of GSS research and has been the primary mode of research at most centers. Consequently, it tends to step beyond the exploratory, drawing on the work of other GSS researchers and programs. However, an exploratory component persists, as the research team has begun to examine GSS in a distributed environment. The research is conducted both in the laboratory and in the field, with the former tending to be the predominant setting. Several themes related to use have been studied through laboratory experiments.

One set of experiments extends work begun at the University of Georgia in technology comparison (Gopal, 1991). This project examines the conditions under which the outcomes of GSS use differ and how these outcomes differ from those resulting from other forms of group interaction. Specifically, the project examines VisionQuest, GroupSystems, OptionFinder, and manual modes of group work on the basis of their applicability to different tasks and other contextual conditions.

Another set of experiments is designed to explore the effects of anonymity and related constructs in a manner that moves beyond the scope of previous work on the subject. Rather than treating anonymity as a dichotomous construct, this study begins by defining the multiple dimensions of anonymity and investigates the effects of GSS on these different dimensions.

One ongoing study uses both experimental and field research strategies to explore the value of GSS in common value bidding. The impetus for the study is of a practical nature, in that oil companies are often faced with the negative consequences of the "winner's curse" in bidding for oil leases, wherein the high bidder in an auction overestimates the value of an object, given some initial cue concerning its value. The study investigates the possibility of using GSS to improve estimates made by bidders.

Several studies are being planned on the use of GSS technologies in different management disciplines. These studies, which include the quality of work life and advertising campaign planning, are typically conducted in conjunction with researchers in the relevant disciplines. Although these studies are effective in expanding the knowledge base concerning GSS in different settings, they provide new and often exciting avenues of research for investigators in the other areas and show promise as a means of expanding the use of GSS.

Another aspect that interests researchers is facilitation and session management. These factors are being studied on an ongoing basis as well as through specially designed studies. The ongoing investigation is based on GSS sessions conducted by a specialty team of facilitators for members of the Calgary business community. Studies investigating phenomena related to facilitation are also being planned.

All these projects involve research that is closely related to research themes at other universities and research centers; however, two research projects have been initiated that investigate GSS use in distributed environments. One project explores several aspects of GSS in an any-time/any-place mode. Issues of interest include the group processes involved, the coordination required, the outcomes of working in this manner, and the technical requirements of these forms of GSS. As this area of research is extremely new, it is being conducted in conjunction with research on development and introduction. A second project, described in an earlier section, looks at GSS in a different-place/same-time context. This project is being carried out jointly by the universities of Calgary and

Georgia. The study involves two groups of up to 30 people at each university using OptionFinder simultaneously; group output is displayed in both environments, showing consolidated outcomes as well as comparing the outcomes of the two groups.

CONCLUSION

The GSS project at the University of Calgary is among the youngest in North America. Several factors, however, compensate for the lack of a cumulative tradition. The most critical factor is commitment by top management. The GSS initiative was spearheaded by the dean of the faculty in 1990. Today, the dean assumes the position of executive sponsor and encourages active participation in the GSS project by the entire faculty. A consequence of this commitment from the top is continued financial support for the project. It is hoped that this support will help propel the fledgling project into a leadership position in GSS research. Several other advantages enjoyed by the GSS research team are a result of this continuing commitment. One is the breadth of the available GSS facilities. As already described, GSS is installed and studied in a variety of settings, all of which receive strong technical support. The main GSS room alone is one of the largest facilities of its kind in North America, and enables research that would be difficult at best at other locations.

The suite of systems available for research is another important advantage. Whereas many research centers are restricted to a single GSS, the faculty currently uses three commercial systems and several experimental systems. Plans are also in place to install other systems, including at least one system in a mainframe environment.

Another advantage is geographic location. The proximity to a forward-looking business community is already making the GSS installation a success through its continued use and support. Also, as the only university GSS installation in western Canada, it attracts several other western Canadian universities as well as several businesses in the region. Finally, the size and width of perspectives of the core research team are expected to sustain and expand the program. These factors also allow the team to research GSS in a comprehensive manner, from development through introduction to use, while addressing the entire range of methodological issues.

The vision at Calgary is of integration: an integration of perspectives on GSS and of the disciplinary areas involved in its research. Most important, the vision sees the integration of GSS into the office of the future.

Part C

Acquired Technology

The researchers in this section can be considered technology evolvers. Acquirers become beta test sites for the technology—extensions of the developers. Evolution of the technology benefits from this separation of development and testing. The acquirers typically use, evaluate, and compare a number of available systems. Because they lack the inventor's emotional investment in any one system, they are therefore in the position to be more objective about the advantages and disadvantages of each system.

There is a need for more comparative research since most computer-supported teamwork research has concentrated on comparing a particular technology to a noncomputer approach. Comparative research within and between technology classes would enable the strengths and weaknesses of each to be determined, leading to integrated technologies or further development of existing technologies. One focus could be on how groups appropriate and use different team technologies. A related research issue is the development of task technology "fit" models, which outline the most appropriate technologies for different team tasks. With their emphasis on effective use of technology, the research groups in this part of the book provide the best sources of this type of research. Georgia (Chapter 15), Queen's (Chapter 16), and Hawaii (Chapter 17) all have research efforts related to these issues.

The modes of human facilitation to support the different teamwork technologies described in this book vary widely and are perhaps the best source of variation among, and within, the applications of the technologies. Facilitation is not a major issue in the technologies that primarily support communication in a distributed and asynchronous mode (see Section II). As these technologies become more supportive of team tasks, facilitation will become critical. However, in the decision conferencing approaches described in Section IV, the facilitator is preeminent. These approaches are facilitator-driven and consequently facilitator-dependent. The approaches in Section III use technology as an additional source of facilitation. Computer software is used to implement and manage the meeting process. However, researchers throughout this book agree that human support for the facilitator role is critical to the successful application of teamwork technologies. The disagreement may be more over the appropriate mix or balance between human and computer facilitation in particular contexts. This is only one of many important facilitation-related research issues. The researchers at the University of Georgia describe its extensive research program is this area, as do those at Queen's University and the University of Hawaii. All chapters in this part discuss how technology is used to facilitate classroom training.

The authors in this part also provide some useful conceptual maps for exploring teamwork technology. Chapter 15 describes the research alliance model used at Georgia to guide its research project and develop research relationships with project sponsors, partners, and clients. This model would be particularly useful to any group wanting to start a research project in this area. Chapter 16 presents the research framework at Queen's, which includes a discussion of how team technology affects decision making. It also discusses in more depth the benefits and obstacles framework presented in Chapter 2.

The research themes discussed in the various chapters are diverse. The need for longitudinal research has been stressed by researchers in this area; little currently exists, although longitudinal projects at Claremont, Queen's, and Hawaii are being developed. The research program at Queen's is intended to explain why electronic brainstorming is such a productive and satisfying technique for idea generation and at the same time to discover ways to improve it. This program also represents one of the few efforts to tackle micro-level analysis, that is, the effects of one technique or technology tool. Hawaii uses its unique geographical location to focus on cross-cultural research, and

Georgia has built alliances with foreign universities (e.g., National University of Singapore) to investigate this area. Claremont has focused on one cross-cultural task, international business negotiation. Claremont is also investigating crisis management and team technology interface design. All groups have an interest in getting more involved in studying any-time/any-place computer-supported team interactions, expanding on their previous focus on face-to-face interactions.

Chapter 14

The Decision Laboratory

Paul Gray

Claremont Graduate School

HISTORY

The Claremont Graduate School Decision Room was established in 1986 under grants from the IBM University Grant Program for the Management of Information Systems (MoIS), from the Hewlett Packard Foundation, and from AT&T. The facility is a direct outgrowth of the Decision Room established in 1980-1981 at Southern Methodist University (SMU). That room, which was built at the same time as the Planning Laboratory at Execucom Systems Corporation, was established under a grant from the ARCO Foundation and with equipment from the Xerox Corporation. The SMU facility, which included two rooms in separate buildings connected by video, was built around the Xerox Star, the first mouse and icon technology available. The SMU facility is described briefly below.

Origins

The concept of the Decision Room dates back to the early 1970s. At that time, as a faculty member at the University of Southern California (USC) and a member of the Center for Futures Research at USC, I wrote a concept paper pointing out that interactive computer technology, which was generally available in the offices of firms, disappeared as soon as one went into a conference room. I therefore suggested that we build a facility that brings terminals into the conference room and uses a large projection display to make information available to everyone. Although well received, the concept paper did not lead to any enthusiastic response or to funding.

SMU Facility

In 1980, about a year after I had moved to SMU, the dean of the Business School, Alan Coleman, found out that the ARCO Foundation gave large grants to private universities in cities where they had headquarters and that they had a headquarter in Dallas. I proposed the decision room concept and he backed it enthusiastically. A proposal was written jointly with the School of Engineering and accepted. A research team was formed including Julius Aronofsky, Nancy Berry, Gerald Kane, Thomas Perkins, and myself. Aronofsky was a senior professor who had led the Mobil Oil Operations Research group in its heyday and provided great wisdom. Berry, from the School of Fine Arts, offered the interior design skills. Kane was the computer scientist with the technical skills, and Perkins added software knowhow. The system was built around a Prime minicomputer and a network of six Xerox Star workstations. The Stars were connected through a file server and a communication server on an Ethernet network. Unfortunately, Dean Coleman moved on to another assignment at SMU and a new dean was hired in the fall of 1982. I left SMU in 1983 to found the Programs in Information Science at Claremont, and the room was dismantled shortly after I left. The SMU project is described in P. Gray (1983).

Claremont Facility

As part of the founding of the Programs in Information Science, the Claremont Graduate School decided to build a new two-story building, the Academic Computing Building, which would house its computing facilities on the first floor and the programs on the second floor. A Decision Laboratory was included in the initial design of the second floor. The concept was that the laboratory would provide a research focus for information science.

The Academic Computing Building was completed and occupied in 1985. While the building was under construction, IBM announced its university grant program for the management of information systems. These grants consisted of $1 million in cash and $1 million in equipment. Some 217 schools applied for the grants, of whom 13 were selected, among them the Claremont Graduate School. The Decision Laboratory was a centerpiece of the Claremont grant application, and a portion of the grant, particularly equipment, was dedicated to the laboratory.

Since the award of the IBM grant was by no means certain, the Graduate School also wrote a backup grant proposal to the Hewlett-Packard (H-P) Foundation for equipment. While the Claremont team was in New York accepting the IBM grant, we were notified that H-P had awarded us a grant of an HP-3000 and a network of HP-150 touch screen

PCs. Somewhat later, we received an additional grant from AT&T of a number of UNIX-based 7300 PCs and some 3B-2s.

Motivation

A major motivation in creating the Decision Laboratory at Claremont was to provide a facility around which a stream of Ph.D. dissertation research could be performed. As a small institution with a small faculty, we are not able to provide guidance to doctoral dissertations across the whole spectrum of information systems issues. The concept, therefore, was to select a leading-edge research area and build a facility around it. The facility, together with research seminars and research support, provides a natural direction for many (but not necessarily all) doctoral students. It was felt that, as a new program, we needed research focus for which we would become known.

INITIAL DESIGN

The initial layout consisted of a Decision Laboratory supported by a Practicum Room, an Observation Area, and a Printer Room.

The Practicum Room

Our M.S. program in information science requires a practicum, that is, a real project for a real client against a time deadline. The Practicum Room, with a network of PC/ATs, gives students a place to work on their projects. Because the Practicum Room is next to the Decision Laboratory, it also serves as a staging area where people can work on preparations for experiments in the laboratory, particularly software projects.

The Observation Area

The Observation Area is the technical control room for the Decision Laboratory and also serves as a place where people can observe the experiment while it is in progress. One-way glass separates the Observation Area from the Decision Laboratory. Thus, people in the Observation Area can observe what is going on in the Decision Laboratory without being seen. This arrangement is a natural outgrowth of the structure of management laboratories used in many business schools. It was also used in the Execucom Planning Laboratory and the SMU Decision Room.

The Printer Room

The Printer Room, which is the anteroom to the observation area, houses an IBM laser printer. Since printers are noisy and used infrequently, it was decided to put the printer in a separate, nearby location.

THE TWO-ROOM APPROACH

When the Academic Computing Building was finished, it became clear that the space allocated to the Decision Laboratory was quite large, in fact, much larger than we really needed or wanted. At the suggestion of Paul Albrecht, then the executive dean of the Graduate School, we divided the room into two parts by building a floor-to-ceiling divider. This divider is of the type used in hotels to convert large ballrooms into smaller meeting rooms. When closed, it serves as a soundproof wall between two separate rooms. When open, it creates a single, large room.

The two-room concept has proven to be advantageous. First, it permits us to have two facilities, one of which may be in use for one project and the other for another project. Second, with the video equipment that was added in 1991, we will be able to simulate and hence study the effects of videoconferences on group decision support situations. The initial facility consisted of a larger room with a U-shaped configuration and a smaller room with a single table. We will refer to these two rooms as the Large Room and the Small Room hereafter.

ROOM DESIGN FEATURES

The basic concept in the room design was to create a highly flexible facility. We knew that we would learn as we progressed and that different experimental conditions might call for different room configurations. This flexibility principle is reflected, for example, in the modularity of the floor and table designs. A second principle was to create as elegant a design as we could with the budget available. We wanted this room to have an executive feel, to be a place that people would consider "special." We also tried to pay attention to human factors as much as possible so that the room would be comfortable for the participants; we knew that for new people coming in, the use of electronics in conferencing would be distraction enough. In particular, we have tried to hide as much of the wiring as possible.

Floor

Because the facility uses microcomputers, it was not necessary to create a fully raised floor of the type used in mainframe facilities. Rather we built an artificial floor, using 2-×-4 beams covered with plywood, which in turn was covered with carpet squares. The result is a neat-looking floor with great flexibility. The plywood is set up in 4-×-4-inch squares. Thus, it is easy to open a section of the floor and get underneath when necessary. Several conduit openings in the floor allow cable to be routed to the observation area. The floor also contains a large number of plugs for power.

Lighting

The lighting in the Large Room was specially designed for varying levels during meetings. During discussions, we would want normal light levels, whereas when the computers were being used, we would want lower light levels to reduce glare. A U-shaped fluorescent setup was devised in which the fluorescents point up, so that the light is reflected off the ceiling and walls, and the light levels are adjustable. The design has worked quite well.

Walls and Curtains

A neutral color was selected for the walls and for the divider. Blackout curtains, which match the wall colors, are provided for the windows. The walls have been deliberately left bare because our interior design staff advised us that putting artwork on the wall tends to distract the participants.

Tables

We believed it imperative that the computer screens not interfere with lines of sight so that people could talk to one another as well as use the equipment. However, we did not want to spend a small fortune on customized tables. One of our M.S. students, Peter Garst, a human factors engineer at Aerojet General Corporation, undertook the desk design as his practicum project. He created a design and then drew a series of three-dimensional views using CAD/CAM equipment to make sure that the lines of sight were correct. The results are shown in Figure 14–1. We started with standard 60-inch computer tables, which allow two people to share a single PC and have space on the desktop for papers. Next we cut a hole in the table at one end for the screen.

A small sheet metal assembly allows variation of the angle of the wood base on which the screen sits. The arrangement is suitable for those whose height is between the fifth and ninety-fifth percentile in the population. A metal bracket was put under the tops of the table to hold the disk drives for the HP-150s or other equipment that required access by participants. The keyboard is also located under the desktop and slides out when needed. A power strip was put under the table so that all power could come to a single point and thereby assure the neatness of the wiring. By using individual tables we are better able to change the configuration of the room when desired.

Cabinet

A large cabinet at the front of the room serves as the location of the public screens and as a storage cabinet, where software and hardware supplies can be kept out of sight. The cabinet has a 10-foot diagonal screen for the Panasonic projector (see below) and four rectangular spaces for additional screens. Thus, the cabinet serves as the basis for a video wall on which multiple images can be displayed. From a philosophical point of view, we believe that information does not just come in the 25-line, 80-character format of PC screens and that people can, and do, deal with multiple information sources.

HARDWARE

Large Room

The Large Room (see Figure 14-2) presently is built around PS/2 Model 70s connected in a 16-MHz token ring network. The room contains 8 user stations, each with 60 Mb of

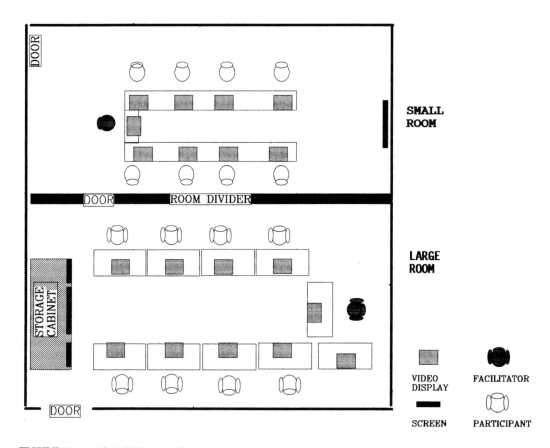

FIGURE 14-1.   The Initial Layout of Claremont's Decision Laboratory

hard disk storage and a VGA color monitor. A PS/2 Model 70 with 121 MB hard disk, also on the network, is used as a file server and as the chauffeur station. The image on the chauffeur's station can also be shown on a Panasonic three-gun color projection video display. The Panasonic is a variable scan device that permits showing all display formats, including VGA.

The video wall at the front of the room currently has two CONRAC color 19-inch displays. We anticipate adding two 30-inch color displays. We have not yet found good switching equipment or software that allows sharing what is on individual screens with the screens on the electronic wall. Therefore, as an interim measure we are using PS/2 Model 30/286s to drive these screens. These additional screens are controlled from the chauffeur's station.

When the Academic Computing Building was built, a Sytek local-area network was wired into the walls. Therefore, we have used the Sytek network as a means of connecting the PS/2s with the VAX/11-785 that serves the Graduate School and the

FIGURE 14-2.   Claremont's Large Decision Room

AT&T 3B2s (see below). In this way, the Decision Laboratory has access to minicomputer power.

An IBM 8514 laser printer is connected to the network through the server. Any station can send material directly to the printer. Other capabilities include an optical scanner and the ability to integrate video pictures on the chauffeur's (and hence the public) screen by using IBM's multimedia hardware.

Small Room

Two networks are available for the Small Room. One network consists of HP-150 Touchscreen PCs on an Ethernet. Each PC is a two-disk system. The server has a 20-Mb hard disk. The second network consists of AT&T 7300s connected to one of our 3B2s. We have two Model 400s and one model 320. This arrangement is basically a STARLAN network, with the PCs communicating with one another through the minicomputer. The 7300s each have 20-Mb hard disks and run UNIX. Although neither the HP-150s or the 7300s are state-of-the-art machines as far as speed is concerned, they have special properties that make them interesting for research. The touchscreens allow experimenting with situations in which users can work almost without keyboards. The 7300s are the only UNIX capability at the Graduate School and are also compatible with the Minnesota SAMM software. Both networks use monochrome displays.

Therefore, a 6-foot (diagonal) Limelight projector connected to the server is used as the public screen.

SOFTWARE

The principal software packages available are as follows:

1. GroupSystems, developed at the University of Arizona
2. VisionQuest from Collaborative Technologies Corporation
3. The Claremont GDSS Support Environment (usually referred to as the CGS Environment), developed by M. Mandviwalla at Claremont; this Windows-based environment allows users to do private work during a session. The CGS Environment is described in more detail later in this chapter under software development. A fuller report can be found in Gray et. al. (1993)
4. Pilot, the Executive Information System from Pilot Executive Software
5. An early version of SAMM from the University of Minnesota
6. Co-op, developed by Tung Bui of the Naval Postgraduate School and rewritten at Claremont
7. The Interactive Financial Planning System (IFPS) from Comshare (previously Executive Systems Corporation)
8. A touchscreen-based voting system developed at Claremont for the HP-150s
9. SUCCESS (Strategic Business Unit Comprehensive Computer Based Expert Support System), developed at Claremont for business unit strategy analysis by Eli Segev and Paul Gray, with programming by Victoria Goodrich
10. A geographic information system being used in sessions devoted to land use planning

In addition, standard commercial packages such as Windows, Storyboard, Expert Choice, Guide, Hyperpad, Word, and various CAD/CAM graphics and computer languages are available at individual stations. GroupSystems, VisionQuest, Pilot, SAMM, and Co-op were kindly made available to Claremont by their developers.

INFRASTRUCTURE

The Decision Laboratory is administered under the Information Science Applications Center, the research arm of the Programs in Information Science at Claremont. One adjunct faculty member and I jointly supervise the Decision Laboratory. Typically one or two student research assistants are assigned to maintain the equipment and software and assist in setting up the facility for a particular use. Masters of science and Ph.D. candidates in the management of information systems perform the needed development as part of their degree programs. Several students each year choose to undertake a software development or a design project in the Decision Laboratory as their practicum project. For example, the unique table design and the planning of the videoconferencing capabilities were carried out as practicum projects. Doctoral dissertations in the Decision Laboratory are supervised by both Lorne Olfman and myself.

COMPARISON WITH OTHER FACILITIES

In many respects the main Claremont facility is similar to that at other universities. We have a medium number of stations (eight plus a chauffeur), a large projection device, a network, and connection to the mainframe. Several features distinguish Claremont's setup from others. One, of course, is the availability of two adjacent rooms, which allows experimentation with video conferencing as an adjunct to meetings. Since the rooms have a movable divider, they can be combined into one large facility if so desired. Another feature is the availability of multiple software packages, including large commercial packages such as Pilot as well as packages and data sets that the participants brought with them. These packages are interconnected through the CGS environment. A third distinguishing feature is the unique design of the computer tables. This ergonomic design facilitates verbal communications among participants during sessions by maintaining unobstructed lines of sight. A fourth feature is the modular design of the floor to allow rapid reconfiguration of the facility.

USE OF THE FACILITY

The facility has been used for research, for teaching about GDSS, and for live groups involved in planning. The following are representative of the groups that have used the facility for planning exercises:

1. The staff of IDSC (the Information and Decision Support Center) of the Ministry of Cabinet Affairs of the government of Egypt, headed by Dr. Hisham El Sherif, came to Claremont to explore the appropriate design for a planned crisis management center to be built in Egypt. As a result of their two-day session, they concluded that a decision facility similar to, but larger than, the Claremont facility was appropriate to their situation. Since that session, they have been implementing the facility in a new building adjacent to the cabinet building in Cairo.

2. An IBM branch office management group, whose head had used GroupSystems at an IBM facility, undertook a major planning exercise. The members reported that they had accomplished more in one day at our computer-assisted facility than they normally do in a highly facilitated two-day manual session.

3. The faculty of the Humanities Center at the Claremont Graduate School spent a day using GroupSystems to plan their future. The center had just been established as a way of combining the efforts of a number of small humanities departments (including English, history, philosophy, religion, and music) and a director had been appointed. The director brought ten faculty members to the session. For most of this group, computer literacy extended to word processing only, but they were able to use the system and accomplish their task.

4. The GDSS group members of the ISDP (Information Systems and Decision Processes) study used the facility for the main portion of their work. ISDP is a large study program undertaken by six working groups, with over 50 senior people in decision support systems (DSS) and related fields examining the research agenda needed to move DSS forward intellectually. It was appropriate for the eight members

of the GDSS group to use a GDSS facility for their deliberations. To speed matters, we defined the domains of interest and asked each participant to seed the meeting with ideas he or she believed were appropriate. We then used the Electronic Brainstorming of GroupSystems to expand on the list of ideas and the Topic Commentor to obtain detailed input on specific topics. The results of this session formed the basis for the draft report. A second session, held at the large University of Arizona facility, involving all the people in the ISDP study, provided additional input that led to the final report.

5. MISTIC, the association of the schools who received grants from IBM for the management of information systems, held their 1989 meeting at Claremont. As part of that meeting, we used our existing facility plus a second, lashup facility consisting of 8 PS/2 Model 50s supplied by IBM. The GroupSystems software was used for several brainstorming sessions.

Two dissertations have been completed. The first (Park 1990) focused on the use of GDSS facilities for international business negotiation. Specifically, the scenario considered a bilateral negotiation between a Korean and U.S. firm for distributing Korean-made goods in the United States. Software provided the ability to switch between Korean and English character sets; a trade dictionary; and information about the two cultures, prepared in hypertext format. The conclusion reached was that the system improved the quality of the negotiation. A second dissertation (Satzinger 1991) examined interface consistency. If a group uses several software packages during the course of its deliberations, to what extend does software consistency (or inconsistency) help (or hinder) the quality of the output?

In most of the sessions we have run, we have provided a chauffeur and two or three advanced graduate students familiar with the equipment. The graduate students are available for individuals who need assistance in operating the software. On occasion, a graduate student has served as a typist for a nontyping participant.

SOFTWARE DEVELOPMENT

Claremont is a small, graduate-only institution, most of whose information science students work full time. As a result, not many students are available for software development tasks. Although we are not in the software development business, we have undertaken a few software projects.

1. A voting system using the HP-150 touchscreen computers (Gray and Olfman 1989) has most of the capabilities available for voting in GroupSystems. However, rather than requiring cursor movements, users simply touch their preferences. For example, in the case of rank order, the user first touches the item he or she wants to move and then touches the desired location. The system performs the interchange.

2. Porting Co-op was developed by Tung Bui of the Naval postgraduate school and SAMM was developed by the University of Minnesota to our IBM and AT&T setups, respectively.

3. Creating an environment in which multiple applications can be run simultaneously at a workstation, this project began by using Matrix Layout (from Matrix Software Technology Corporation) to develop two prototype systems (named NUCLEUS and PIPELINE) to aid work on the interface consistency dissertation. Then, using Bridge (from Softbridge) and Windows (from Microsoft), we created a multiapplication environment. Thus, for example, a user working in GroupSystems can put that software in a window and turn to, say, an Excel or an IFPS spreadsheet or an Expert Choice hierarchy and work in that environment until ready to return to GroupSystems. The software also allows group members to send short messages and files to one another. That is, group members can communicate with one another privately. This windowing arrangement forms a metasystem that sits on top of individual applications and hence permits group participants to do private work in a richer environment than that provided by individual software packages.

TEACHING USE

The Decision Laboratory, as its name implies, is primarily a research facility, although it is used from time to time to support specific courses such as Decision Support Systems, Computer Languages, Expert Systems, Expert Systems for Managers, and Executive Information Systems. The first three are offered in the Programs in Information Science and the last two in the Executive Management Program in the Drucker Management Center. Occasionaly, a summer course called Decision Support Laboratory is run. Most teaching use, except for the Decision Support Laboratory course, involves demonstrations of software, presentations by students, and occasional hands-on experience. Practicum projects, which involve individuals or small groups, of course are also considered to be teaching use.

FUTURE DIRECTIONS

The third software development just described is representative of the way in which Claremont plans to support the Decision Laboratory in the future. It is our intention to work with existing packages wherever possible and to provide ways of integrating the different software packages.

Hardware

Our short-range plans for hardware include

- Installing the video hardware we have purchased, which will allow us to simulate video conferencing
- Completing the video wall
- Adding multimedia to the system (already obtaining IBM's multimedia offerings that provide on-screen artificial speech and video)
- Upgrading the hardware in the Small Room to obtain better response and added software capability

Research

In terms of research, the principal role of the Decision Room is to support Ph.D. dissertations. Several projects currently in their beginning stages are expected to lead to dissertations. The following two are representative:

1. Working with the Lincoln Land Institute, a nonprofit organization in Cambridge, Massachusetts, interested in land use planning, we are bringing in several land use planning groups from Southern California to the Decision room. To extend our capabilities, we have obtained georeference software that allows retrieval of information about land use by location. The purpose of the study is twofold: (a) to study the effects of GDSS on ongoing groups of mature decision makers involved in live problems and (b) to determine whether the enhanced data retrieval and visual presentation capabilities provided by GDSS can enhance land use planning.
2. The Decision Laboratory can be configured as a crisis management center. To explore how GDSS can be used in crisis management, we are working with EPIC, a Pasadena-based consulting firm specializing in crisis response for the food industry. With recalls, natural disasters, and hostile attacks on grocery items (such as the Tylenol incident), the food industry is particularly vulnerable. As a first step in this direction, we have built a knowledge base for crisis managers. At a more basic research level, we are studying the possibilities of using the GDSS facility as a means of reducing both individual and group stress in crises.

In addition to these specific projects, we are particularly interested in the use of

- hypertext and document retrieval in GDSS
- modeling in GDSS
- GDSS for visual decision making such as packaging decisions in marketing or land use decisions in the public sector

CONCLUSION

The Decision Laboratory is meeting the goals set for it. It gives us a viable stream of research. It allows outreach to the community by providing a facility for business and government groups. It is the centerpiece for the Programs in Information Science at Claremont.

Chapter 15

The Computer-Augmented Teamwork Project

Robert P. Bostrom
Richard T. Watson
David Van Over

University of Georgia

INTRODUCTION

Effective teams require skilled communication to coalesce quickly members into collaborative teams (those that utilize the expertise of each individual member). Academicians and practitioners are exploring new techniques and technologies to build and support collaborative teams and improve meetings. A computer-based technology aimed at improving meetings and team functioning has gained recent prominence. This technology is referred to by many names, but we will use the general terms, *team technology* and *group support systems* (GSS). By whatever name, the common focus is to provide a set of electronic tools to support teams and meeting activities (e.g., generate information) in the same sense as word processing or spreadsheet packages are tools to support individual work activities.

Electronic meeting environments have social (individuals and team structure) and technical (task and technology) dimensions. As researchers, we need to pay attention to both dimensions and their interactions because the introduction of a new technology can affect both technical (team efficiency and effectiveness) and social (attitudes, team cohesion, and job satisfaction) aspects. This chapter is an overview of our program of research, which takes this sociotechnical perspective. In the introduction we will discuss the program's overall research outcomes, present a brief history of the program, and introduce our research alliance model. This model is the guiding vision of our research program and provides the framework for the remainder of the chapter.

Overall Research Outcomes

Our overall research outcome is to improve organizational meeting systems through the use of information technology. An individual meeting is a component in a meeting cycle (preparation → meeting → follow-up) (Oppenheim 1987), which may be part of a larger meeting system (many cycles that have a meta-purpose, e.g., the ongoing activities of a project team). Our initial focus has been on the meeting stage of face-to-face meetings, that is, same-time and same-place environments. We are expanding our focus to include meeting systems and different environments, especially different-time/different-place meetings.

The major ways to improve meeting systems with technology are through good design and effective diffusion and use. These means define our two major research areas:

1. Research on team technology design: What are the most effective technology configurations for different team and meeting environments? How do we create an effective match between different team and meeting tasks (decision making, planning, etc.) and computer-based technology? How can computer technologies be used to create new working patterns in teams?
2. Research on team technology adoption, use, and impact: How and why do organizations adopt GSS technology? What factors are related to successful or unsuccessful adoption and use? What are the learning and training needs of teams when new computer technologies are introduced? What theoretical models meaningfully explain the effects of computing on team productivity and quality of work life?

Brief History of GSS at the University of Georgia

The team technology research program began in the Department of Management at the University of Georgia in the summer of 1985 with funding from an IBM grant for the management of information systems. This funding was used to construct the facilities described in the next section. The initial exploration of team technology took place in 1987 when the PLEXSYS (now named GroupSystems) software was obtained from the University of Arizona by Hugh Watson. Thus, the 1987–1988 academic year was the beginning of our research program. It was a year characterized by Ph.D. students becoming familiar with the software, classroom demonstrations, and classroom projects.

Two faculty members who had strong interests in team technology joined the program in the fall of 1988. Bob Bostrom was hired specifically to develop and head this area; David Van Over had done his dissertation work in this field. The major accomplishments during the second year of our program were (1) the development of the infrastructure (people, technology, and other resources) to support the research program; (2) the generation of income through electronic meetings, rental of facilities and so on; and (3) the development of a research agenda for the area. A number of projects that Bob

Bostrom had started at Indiana University were completed, and several new projects were started.

The research agenda was part of a larger research program entitled Executive 2000 (Watson et al., 1990) which involves research in three distinct, yet related areas. The Department of Management has a history of research in executive information systems (EIS), a project headed by Hugh Watson), and executive presentation systems (EPS), and we wanted to combine this expertise with team technology to study the conference room of the future. The focus of this program has been on EIS and GSS. (This integrated research program is discussed in more detail later.)

The major problems encountered during these first two years were software bugs, problems running team software in LAN environments, lack of technical knowledge, limited view of GSS technology as an extension of DSS technology, lack of knowledge of general group research literature, and generating money to support and upgrade facilities. Only the last two remain ongoing problems, which we are trying to solve through the development of research partnerships.

We have pursued a policy of creating research alliances within and outside the university to broaden the range of accessible expertise. Some of these alliances have been developed and strengthened by hiring new faculty. For example, Rick Watson joined us in the fall of 1989, bringing his experience from the University of Minnesota project. Our faculty has served on dissertation committees at Indiana and Georgia State University, and our studies have entailed researchers from other universities and departments. Research alliances have been forged with groups such as the Center for Creative Leadership and Georgia's Institute of Community and Area Development. In 1991, recently minted Ph.D.s Alan Dennis (Arizona) and John Satzinger (Claremont) joined the group (and David Van Over left the project). The result is a project faculty (Bostrom, Watson, Dennis, and Satzinger) that is a highly fertile amalgam of investigative skills initially nurtured at major GSS research sites.

We are in the midst of executing the research agenda discussed above and outlined in this chapter. Our energies continue to focus on developing and maintaining partnerships to help us better influence the direction of team technology and sustain and develop our research program. This focus is captured in our research alliance model.

The Research Alliance Model

The GSS research program at the University of Georgia is centered on the forging of alliances and relationships with a range of groups and individuals who have a stake in team technology. The key components of the alliance model, which is graphically depicted in Figure 15-1, are inputs, allies, and outputs. The University of Georgia research team provides inputs in the form of general research themes, team technology application domains, research strategies, and facilities. This combination of inputs can support several mutually beneficial alliances. Allies provide inputs to the research process in the form of field sites, hardware, software, expertise, personnel, or money. In return, three major outputs are produced: academic research, knowledge to further the development of team technology, and services and facilities to groups using team technology for various organizational purposes.

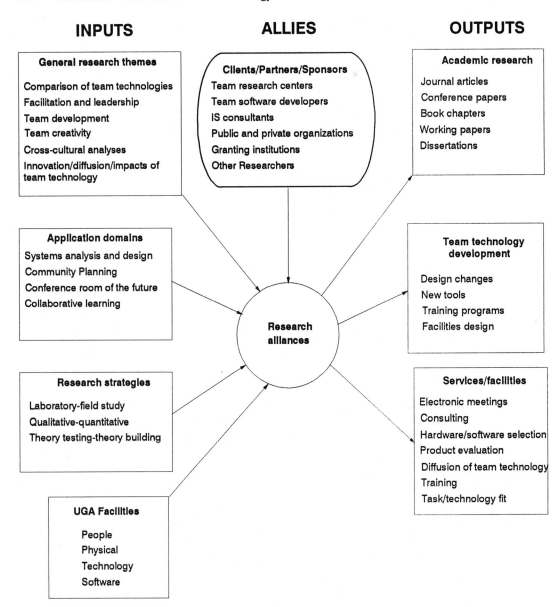

FIGURE 15-1.   Research Alliance Model

Research alliances provide the support to carry out our program of research. Our skills in shaping partnerships determine the success of the overall plan. Because research alliances are critical to our goals, the model depicted in Figure 15-1 provides the organization for this chapter. The focus is on our research projects and the alliances we are forming to help accomplish our research goals.

UNIVERSITY OF GEORGIA FACILITIES

Physical Facilities

Physical support for the computer-augmented teamwork technology is located at the Department of Management's conference room of the future, the Smart Office (Figure 15-2), and at its companion facility, the PC Research Laboratory. The Smart Office is a state-of-the-art conference room with a high degree of built-in modularity. In one of its many configurations, the Smart Office is set up as a decision room (Dennis et al., 1988; DeSanctis and Gallupe, 1987), as depicted in Figure 15-3 In this configuration, the room is typically used to support groups of 10 to 30 members engaged in activities that rely on face-to-face communication.

The Smart Office offers extensive computer-based meeting and presentation support. Hardware support includes several high-speed microcomputers and an advanced projection system. A video camera and videocassette recorder are linked to the projection system, allowing groups instantaneous access to multiple media. Fluorescent and incandescent lighting controls allow effective customization of the room's ambience. The sound system incorporates most of the major technology in current use, including

FIGURE 15-2.   Smart Office—Conference Room of the Future

FIGURE 15-3.   Smart Office Set Up as a Decision Room for a Small Group

compact disk. An electronic podium acts as the room's nerve center, with controls for the lighting, sound, video, and computer graphics equipment.

Groups of up to 40 members are accommodated at 20 workstations in the PC Research Laboratory. Typically, this laboratory is used for generate tasks in which face-to-face discussion is not vital. Unless the group is small, the room design is not conducive to verbal interaction. The laboratory is equipped with a bank of microcomputers and projection facilities similar to those in the Smart Office.

All microcomputers in the two facilities are connected by an IBM Token Ring network, supported by a versatile network operating system. The network also connects all of the department's faculty offices and research sites and is itself connected by a gateway to the department's IBM 4381 mainframe computer as well as to the other computing resources available at the University of Georgia.

Teamwork Technology

Teams that utilize the computer-augmented teamwork facilities at the Department of Management can expect a highly customized meeting environment, made possible by incorporating several different types of team support technology. This variety is a result of the department's multisystem approach to team research, which in turn is based on the assumption that variations in the nature and composition of teams and planned meeting outcomes call for variations in technological support configurations.

The University of Georgia facilities incorporate all three basic configurations that have emerged in the marketplace. These configurations can be viewed as three points on a continuum of the extent of information technology (IT) support provided to the group and to the group's leader or facilitator (see Figure 15-4). Any team meeting may utilize one or a combination of these technologies.

Workstation-based support is provided through GroupSystems (see Chapter 8), SAMM and SAGE (see Chapters 9 and 12), and VisionQuest. Each of these systems provides a comprehensive toolbox of team support. Each team member has the use of a microcomputer workstation that is linked to other workstations through a network. This type of environment gives full support to all major team information-processing tasks— generate, organize, evaluate, and select information—and provides an additional electronic channel for communication. GroupSystems and SAGE were developed primarily to support same-time/same-place environments. The SAGE system is typically run on portable Macintoshes (which allow a high level of portability) so that meetings can be held literally anywhere. Given appropriate network connections, the computers can be used in a same-time/different-place mode. A recent version of GroupSystems provides an asynchronous mode to support any-time/any-place environments. VisionQuest was designed to support any-time/any-place meetings.

The second technology environment provides keypad-based support to all meeting

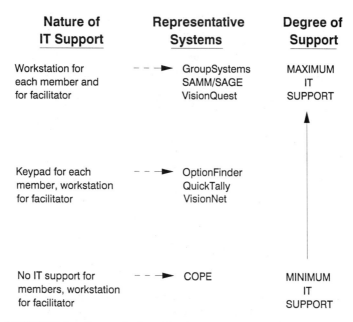

Nature of IT Support	Representative Systems	Degree of Support
Workstation for each member and for facilitator	GroupSystems SAMM/SAGE VisionQuest	MAXIMUM IT SUPPORT
Keypad for each member, workstation for facilitator	OptionFinder QuickTally VisionNet	
No IT support for members, workstation for facilitator	COPE	MINIMUM IT SUPPORT

FIGURE 15-4.   Support Configurations for Computer-Augmented Meetings

participants. We use OptionFinder, a portable evaluation tool developed by Option Technologies. Each group member has the use of a keypad that is connected to other keypads and to an interface box at the facilitator's workstation.

The third technological environment, usually referred to as a chauffeured environment, is designed to provide information technology support only to a group's facilitator. It is the facilitator's responsibility to structure the meeting process, interact with the team, and use the system to develop appropriate representations of the team's problems. Any software for a single workstation can be used in this mode. Our focus is on decision support system (DSS) tools that help team members build good cognitive representations of their situations. For example, COPE (see Chapter 19) is an excellent cognitive mapping tool that is particularly useful in planning. Computer-aided software engineering (CASE) tools provide specific modeling tools for systems design. We are interested in integrating these stand-alone modeling tools with interactive team tools.

Some of these team support technologies have been developed commercially, whereas others have evolved in academic environments. A common objective of most developers is the desire to test their products in live settings, such as that provided by users of our computer-augmented meeting resources. Our objective is to understand more fully what roles these different products play in the variety of team tasks that are carried out in the real world. The goals of these two groups—commercial and academic—are effectively met in this rich research environment. These joint efforts generate information for the effective use of current technology and guidance for future developments.

Human Resources

Our focus in team technology research is not on the technology per se but rather its effective application and integration in team settings. Therefore, we have developed a three-level research team: technical infrastructure, core MIS researchers, and researchers from other disciplines. Our technical infrastructure is maintained by one full-time technician/manager and several part-time graduate and undergraduate students. They provide hardware and software maintenance, test new versions of software packages, keep the networks running, and schedule laboratory use. Some of the students have been trained to be process and/or technical facilitators for team sessions.

The second level of our team is the core group of four MIS researchers, who have a diverse set of experiences and research interests. The common theme of the group is the use of group technology in both applied and theoretical research. With a focus on the application of technology, the group has established links with a number of researchers in other departments and universities. Thus, many of our research projects are cross-disciplinary and involve researchers from other universities.

ALLIES: CLIENTS, PARTNERS, SPONSORS

Research is a product and must be marketed. The execution of a research plan needs a selling phase, during which the team finds the resources to underwrite the research. The classification of allies helps us to develop a marketing plan. We have segmented the market and developed separate strategies for each class of ally. Based on their relationship with the research team, we can identify three categories of allies: clients, partners, and sponsors.

Clients

Clients are organizations who pay a fee for the use of the services and facilities. For example, our Veterinary School used our facilities and the services of a researcher, in the role of facilitator, to develop a strategic plan. Our goal is to use our facilities and services to apply what we have learned. We use the revenues generated from this applied work to enhance the facilities and support ongoing research. Although this is primarily a revenue-generating activity, we are able to capture some data concerning task, client satisfaction, and facilitator reactions.

Partners

Partners are individuals or organizations who become actively involved in a research project by supplying funds, expertise, personnel, and/or field sites. For instance, we will work with a partner to identify a research project of mutual benefit and then proceed to meet the objectives of the project, for example, our partnership with the Center for Creative Leadership to study creativity in electronic environments. Partnerships offer the greatest potential for fruitful research because of the additional expertise that a partner can bring to a project. We are seeking partners for each of the application domains and many of the themes in the research alliance model. Our marketing strategy is to approach a small number of clearly identified potential partners with a carefully tailored proposal.

Sponsors

Sponsors are organizations who agree to provide funds for research but are not actively involved in the research process. Sponsors are passive in that they do not provide expertise or personnel. Potential sponsors are primarily public and private research foundations. We primarily seek funds from sponsors to pursue the project's research themes, the more fundamental and less applied part of the program. For example, we obtained a grant from the 3M Meeting Management Institute to study the diffusion and use of keypad technology (Watson et al., 1991).

OUTPUTS

A successful research program founded on alliances will produce a variety of outputs that should satisfy the multiple objectives of those who have a stake in the research (see Figure 15-1). Meeting these objectives is the key to our success. Our primary goals are to have a positive impact on the development and use of team technology and to build excellent business and academic alliances. The publication of the research results in top-tier academic and practitioner journals can certainly contribute to the achievement of these goals. Other outlets for academic research such as conference papers, book chapters, working papers, and presentations are also pursued. Because Ph.D. students will be actively involved in the project, another important output will be doctoral dissertations.

Another group of stakeholders, mainly those with whom we form partnerships, are more concerned with the practical implications of the research findings. This group wants information that will enhance team technology systems, effective programs for training adopters of the technology, and guidelines for designing decision rooms. Some examples of out outputs in this area are the active involvement of team members in the development of the software products discussed previously, the design and development of a facilitators' training program for electronic meetings, and support for corporations developing electronic conference rooms.

Clients are the third major class of stakeholders. The outputs that clients require include productive meetings, advice on selecting and implementing team technology, and support for the implementation. For example, in the 1988–1989 academic year (our start-up year) we ran a total of 320 hours of electronic meetings for a variety of university, private, and public organizational teams. Meetings ranged in duration from two hours to three days.

RESEARCH

Overview

The research framework used in most GSS studies is adapted from the work of McGrath (1984). The framework views a meeting from an input → process → output perspective. The major classes of input variables are individual, group, facilitation, task, and environmental/technology. Output variable classes include task, relational/group, individual, and technology. The process is viewed as a sociotechnical interaction resulting in the planned meeting outputs. However, a shared framework is not enough; good theory is needed to guide research.

Many theories are applicable to GSS research, depending on the specific phenomenon being investigated. However, given our sociotechnical perspective, adaptive structuration theory (AST), as described by Poole and DeSanctis (1989, 1990), provides a useful overall perspective on how teams develop after the introduction of a new technology. AST holds that a primary goal of group action is *adaptation* to the situation. Exogenous variables, such as task and technology, form a context in which a group develops. Group outcomes are not directly affected by exogenous variables but rather by how these variables are appropriated and used by the group. AST focuses on group interaction processes as the key to *what* structures are appropriated and reproduced from the group's context and *how* the structures are adaptively applied to meet the group's outcomes.

Thus, in investigating the effects of GSS, it is the structures the technology promotes in the team that are important, not the features of the technology per se. Any intervention into the team process includes both a set of structures to improve team functioning and a means of faithfully implementing those structures. In addition to technology, the other major structural sources are the facilitator or leader; the task; cultural, organizational and physical environments; and group members. Our research themes focus on the effects of these structural sources, individually and jointly, on team functioning. AST provides the general framework, with more specific theories and frameworks used to supplement detailed investigation. For example, the substitutes for leadership theories (e.g., Howell, Dorfman, and Kess, 1986) provide concepts that may be useful in exploring and describing potential interactive effects between GSS and people-structural sources.

Each research center has developed its own research agenda, that is, its own niche. Given our facilities and expertise, we have translated our research agenda into a number of research themes and application domains. (see Figure 15-1).

Research Themes

Research themes focus on issues that are applicable to a variety of team tasks and contexts. The following research themes are included in our research agenda.

Comparison of Technologies

Several researchers have suggested that differences in group support technology have been partially responsible for inconsistent results concerning the efficacy of computer-based technology in improving team performance (Dennis et al., 1988; Poole and DeSanctis, 1989). However, most studies in the area have focused on a single technology at a time, primarily because research centers have concentrated on a single technology.

At the University of Georgia, however, the focus is on the wide range of technologies that are used to support work teams. One of our primary streams of research compares outcomes from teams using different types of technologies, both within types and between types (see Figure 15-4). Sometimes these comparisons use a prototyped or simulated GSS rather than an actual system, allowing us to experiment with a variety of design and/or training options. An additional outcome is to develop models or typologies that describe differences in technology.

This research program goes beyond the basic comparison of technologies to investigate the relationship between task and technology. The intent is to find the best way to match team technologies to team tasks. The research outcome is a task-technology model that will help teams identify the technology that best suits their needs. For example, one experiment (Gopal, 1991; Gopal, Bostrom, and Chin, 1992) used a within-groups repeated measures design to assess the effect of two forms of team technology (workstation and keypad) across two task types. This study also provided an experimental test of AST. Data analysis is currently being carried out on a second study in this area: small-group (dyads) decision making varying the medium (communication richness) and task type (Kinney and Watson, 1992). The media used were face-to-face, telephone, and electronic mail media. The study was a direct test of information richness theory.

Facilitation and Leadership

The current focus of another research theme is the role of facilitation in effectively utilizing computer support for teams. Facilitation is viewed as a set of functions or activities carried out before, during, and after a meeting to help a team achieve its own outcomes. Facilitative activities may be accomplished by group members or leaders, by external facilitation specialists, or by GSS. The critical importance of facilitation has been stressed by a number of researchers, and the human facilitator has been viewed as a critical factor in the relative success of field or real teams using GSS (Bostrom, Anson, and Clawson, 1993). Our initial research supports these claims. However, except for a few exploratory studies, facilitation has not been examined in any depth in the lab or field.

Our first experiment (Anson, 1990; Anson, Bostrom, and Wynne, 1991), a 2 by 2 full factorial design, addressed this basic question: What is the *combined* and *comparative* effectiveness of computerized (GSS) and personal facilitation (PF) mechanisms for improving team process and outcomes? The dichotomous independent variables were computer support and PF. Follow-up experiments will focus on team development over time and the importance of facilitation in different technological and task environments, especially different-time/different-place environments.

In conjunction with the Anson experiment, we have developed a training program for process facilitators in electronic and nonelectronic environments (Bostrom, Clawson, and Anson 1991). The development of this program included a comprehensive literature review on facilitation to identify key skills. We continue to investigate key facilitator skills through the development of profiles of excellent facilitators. Systemic research in this area can help improve the weak literature on team facilitation.

Our initial field and laboratory research fully supports the importance of facilitation in electronic meeting environments. However, the agenda is large and challenging because of the scarcity of research in this area. We have outlined an agenda for studying facilitation in GSS environments that highlights critical research questions and issues (Bostrom, Anson, and Clawson, 1993).

Team/Group Development

Electronic meeting environments influence not only task-related meeting outcomes but individual- and group-related outcomes as well. Specifically, the investigation of whether the technology assists or inhibits group development is important. The development of a team spirit is in itself often the prime goal of some meetings, especially for implementation of a decision. Indeed, for teams with a future, team development is a crucial issue.

Well-developed teams have a high degree of cohesiveness and manage conflict productively (Chidambaram, Bostrom, and Wynne, 1991). These two aspects of team development have been linked to a number of positive team outcomes, for example, better decisions, greater creativity, and enhanced motivation. Our general hypothesis is that GSS facilitates the appropriation and reproduction of structural features that lead to the development of mature teams.

The GSS literature has generally ignored the issue of team development, possibly because of the prevalent use of single-session experiments of field studies to investigate GSS effects. Group development theories, models, and research clearly document the need to study groups over multiple sessions. (See Chidambaram and Bostrom, 1989, for a summary and implications of group development theories.)

Our fieldwork with real teams, even in a single session, has consistently indicated that GSS could be used in this area (Bostrom and Anson, 1989). Through a combination of facilitation and GSS, we were able to enhance the team development process. Our laboratory studies have grown out of our observations from running real teams. Our first laboratory study was an attempt to explore this area in a more controlled setting (e.g., control for facilitation) to isolate GSS effects (Chidambaram et al. 1990). The results supported our fieldwork because they indicate that both cohesiveness and productive conflict management are initially higher for control groups, but this pattern reverses itself in the last two sessions (four sessions total), in which GSS groups scored significantly higher.

This first study suggested a number of factors and theories that might explain the differences in development profiles between GSS and manual groups. The focus of the first laboratory study was on outcomes from a simple input-output model. Future studies will adopt an input-process-output model, which incorporates adaptive structuration concepts and a focus on processes that lead to particular outcomes. Our second laboratory study (Miranda, 1991) had this focus, while replicating and extending the Chiadambaram et al. (1990) study. Additional studies will focus on added effects of facilitation and the impact of the technology on such issues as group development in non-face-to-face GSS environments.

Field studies have also demonstrated that team technology will change the current thinking on another important group variable, team size (Bostrom and Anson, 1989; Dennis et al., 1988). The research literature argues that the optimum group size is five (see Fellers, 1989, for a summary), but electronic meetings have been run with much larger numbers without negative effects. In fact, the ability to tap additional resources (additional members) was found to be a real advantage. The Fellers (1989) laboratory experiment was our first attempt to look at size in a controlled environment. The experiment involved five- and ten-person groups, with each group participating in two idea-generation sessions, one with computer support and one without. Results showed that groups generated significantly more ideas, different ideas, ideas of higher total quality, and more good ideas (as rated by expert judges) and were more satisfied with the group idea-generation process when given computer support. Computer support also allowed groups of ten to perform at the same per-person level as groups of five for performance variables (quantity and quality of ideas) as well as to maintain the same level of satisfaction. Future studies will explore the relationships between team size and development and between size and other important context variables.

Team Creativity

Creativity (the development of original and useful ideas in products, systems, etc.) and innovation (the successful implementation of creative ideas in an organization) are major concerns of U.S. business organizations as they compete in turbulent global markets. In addition, there has been a tremendous growth in the use of business teams for making organizational decisions. These two facts make the use of technology to stimulate creativity and innovation in teams a very rich research area. Our experience from running electronic meetings and our results from pilot experiments indicate that GSS can, in fact, stimulate both individual and team creativity.

We want to develop a major research program in this area. In psychology and management, there is a large body of knowledge on creativity and innovation. For example, there are a number of creative problem-solving techniques for different phases of the decision-making process. (Few of these have found their way into GSS tools.) We are currently establishing partnerships with investigators in these areas to help us formulate a shared research agenda. Research will include the development of computer-based creative problem-solving tools and methodologies, laboratory and field experiments, and field surveys.

Cross-Cultural Analyses

Many theories in psychology, sociology and organizational behavior concerning humans and organizations are culturally specific, but a theory that applies in one culture does not necessarily apply in another (Boyacigiller and Adler, 1991; Hofstede, 1980). Because team technology has a direct influence on an important cultural variable, communication within a group, a theory of team technology will almost certainly need to incorporate a cultural dimension. Reviews of team technology research (Dennis et al. 1988; Pinsonneault and Kraemer, 1989, 1990) indicate that nearly all existing empirical research has been conducted in North America with local subjects. The applicability of this body of findings in another culture is relatively unexplored.

To investigate the cross-cultural impact of team technology, our research agenda includes a continuation of the present partnership with the National University of Singapore. Initial outcomes from this partnership (Ho, Raman, and Watson, 1989) suggest that cultural factors are very important and will play a key role in the design and implementation of team technology. The University of Oulu, Finland, has recently joined the cross-cultural research program. Thus, we now cover the three major industrialized regions: east Asia, Europe, and North America. Our plan is to replicate experiments in each of three sites. Thus, we vary culture and hold constant all other variables, including the GSS. We also plan to have matching field studies where opportunities permit. Cross-cultural analysis of team technology promises to provide elucidating glimpses into both design and implementation and to facilitate a better understanding of the effects of culture and other environmental factors on group processes.

Adoption and Diffusion Impacts of Team Technology

Team technology offers an opportunity to track the introduction of a new technology with wide organizational impacts. Although field research will be the primary approach to the adoption and diffusion impacts of team technology, laboratory experiments are still useful in certain areas, especially in training. Motivating teams through training to use GSS effectively is critical to successful adoption.

Our first lab experiment (Robichaux, 1990) investigated a team's initial exposure to GSS. The introduction of a new technology often involves learning aids such as conceptual models and training. What effects do learning aids have on user understanding and motivation? Group members' mental models and attitudes toward the technology help to determine their understanding and motivation as well. Conceptual models and presentation methods were manipulated to investigate their impact on mental models, attitudes, understanding, and motivation to use the technology.

Field and lab research will be used to investigate the adoption and diffusion impacts of team technology. The first field study under this theme examined the introduction of keypad-based technology (Watson and Bostrom, 1991; Watson et al., 1991). Besides providing an extensive picture of the diffusion and use of keypad technology, several conceptual models, both macro and micro in scope, were identified that assist in understanding how GSS successfully supports groups. These models were integrated to develop a dynamic model of a keypad-supported meeting (Watson and Bostrom, 1991). Data analysis is currently being carried out on our first lab dissertation in this area. Doran (1991) investigated the effect of GSS on the decision-making and decision-implementation process and on stress experienced by the participants. The study included the comparison of three treatments over multiple sessions: baseline (no support), manual (structured support), and GSS.

Application Domains

There are two major approaches in developing team technology, generic or application-specific. Generic technology can be used for a variety of tasks. Huber (1984a) argues for this form because he believes there are so many different types of tasks that an application-specific team technology would be underutilized. However, because some highly specialized tasks are frequently performed, an application-specific technology would be useful. There are other cases in which the sheer importance of the task may warrant an application-specific technology and supporting mechanisms to facilitate infrequent use of the technology.

We have identified four application domains that may warrant special-purpose team technology. First, we have extensive practical experience in systems development and believe that this knowledge could be used to integrate team technology with other technology (e.g., CASE) to support project teams. Second, we believe there are excellent research and funding prospects for developing technology for community planning, and we see this as a niche we can pursue. Third, as part of the Executive 2000 project, we have created the conference room of the future, which integrates team technology with other relevant technology. Finally, as educators, we see opportunities to use team technology to enrich collaborative learning. Each of these four application domains is now discussed in more depth.

System Analysis and Design

One of the most promising applications of group technology is systems analysis and design, the original focus of University of Arizona's GroupSystems; however, until recently little research has been conducted in this area. Team technology has two major applications in supporting the social system surrounding systems analysis and design. The first application is support for information gathering by users. The more promising areas are joint application development, stakeholder analysis, screen and report design, structured walk-throughs, and postimplementation audits. The second application is support for analysts and designers who could use the technology to brainstorm, for example, for generating program specifications, data flow diagrams, data dictionaries, and so on.

Ultimately, a general-purpose team technology could be integrated with CASE tools to create a complete design environment. The CASE tools could extract information gathered by the team tools and generate system representations in the form of data flow diagrams, data dictionaries, and so on. One of our current interests is to investigate the merging of CASE and team technologies. Bostrom and Anson (1988a) outline in depth how this integration could take place.

We are currently developing a research agenda in this area and looking for partners to help us carry it out. Research will include software development, field experiments, classroom studies, and longitudinal research. Our first field experiments will investigate the application of team technology to support the joint application development process. We feel that longitudinal case studies that include comparisons between teams using different types of technology will be very useful. A case study was recently conducted that investigated the application of GSS to the "multiple expert" problem in developing expert systems (the problem is getting multiple experts to collaborate effectively in a development project) (Lipp, FORTHCOMING). The research data gathered in this study are currently being analyzed.

Community Planning

The University of Georgia's Institute for Community and Area Development (ICAD) has a long-established program for assisting economic planning and dispute resolution in rural communities. Recently, ICAD received a grant to purchase GSS technology. In conjunction with ICAD, we will investigate the application of the acquired GSS technology to community problems, thus studying its impact on groups who generally have had less exposure to information technology. As a variety of GSS technologies will be used, we will also focus on the match between task and technology. In addition, we will evaluate the long-term effect of GSS technology on the outcomes of meetings.

Conference Room of the Future

The University of Georgia has, as part of the Executive 2000 project, a history of research in executive information systems (EIS) (e.g., Houdeshel and Watson, 1987) and executive presentation systems (EPS) (e.g., Huseman and Miles, 1988), and we intend to combine this expertise with team technology to study the conference room of the future. Executive 2000 involves research in these three distinct yet related areas. EIS gives team members access to timely and concisely presented information that adds both efficiency and effectiveness to the process. With the help of EPS, information can be presented in a clear, paperless form. Our first integrated research projects will explore the potential interactions between EIS and team technology. We will also continue to upgrade the conference room of the future (see Figures 15–2 and 15–3) to reflect the current state of the art of these three technologies.

Collaborative Learning

One of the more exciting uses of team technology is in the classroom. Case discussions seem especially promising. Currently, three members of our team are investigating this area with strategic and MIS management cases. Data collection was recently completed for a study comparing case analysis with and without GSS (Watson and Dowling, 1991).

All of the advantages of electronic meetings (broader, more active participation; more efficient processing of information; reduced individual inhibitions to participate; etc.) apply to an electronic classroom. Very little research has been done on the application of team technology to classroom teams.

CONCLUSION

In closing this chapter on teams and technology, this quote from Joseph Campbell, the eminent scholar who spent a lifetime studying mythology, seems appropriate: "It's what Goethe said in Faust but which Lucas has dressed in modern idiom—the message that technology is not going to save us. Our computers, our tools, our machines are not enough. We have to rely on our intuitions, our true being" (Flowers, 1988, p. xiv).

Our computers are certainly not enough, although they can be useful vehicles for developing teams and unlocking human potential. But it will also take the development of the social and human component to realize fully the potential of this technology. The quotation reflects the sociotechnical theme stressed throughout this chapter. Team technology will have a major impact on organizations only if the technical (task and technology) and social (individual and group) dimensions are jointly optimized. By accomplishing our research agenda, we will help organizations realize the incredible potential of this technology.

The other major theme of this chapter is alliances. Research in team technology is costly and complex. Clients, partners, and sponsors are needed to nurture and support research efforts. By continuing to develop positive alliances, the research community can influence the impact of team technology.

Chapter 16

The Executive Decision Centre

R. Brent Gallupe

Queen's University

INTRODUCTION

In 1986, the School of Business at Queen's University in Kingston, Ontario, set up a program of research to investigate computer support for organizational meetings (using computer-based group decision support systems, or GDSS). The GDSS Research Program is currently in its seventh year and is growing in research funds awarded, experimental sessions conducted, and actual computer-supported meetings held. This chapter outlines the history of the GDSS Research Program at Queen's, describes the group facilities that have been developed, and provides on overview of the teaching activities and support for external groups that this program has helped nurture.

The Research Focus

The focus of the GDSS Research Program at Queen's is to investigate in a controlled and rigorous way (primarily through laboratory experiments), the effects on face-to-face meetings when information technology supports the meeting process. The program is based primarily in a social sciences experimental framework. The basic paradigm is to compare the outcomes and processes of groups using a control treatment (no group computer support) and those using the experimental treatment (with group computer support) for the same task. This program assumes that the group task is a major factor in meeting processes and outcomes. Of special interest is the match between group task and the specific group computer support tool.

The intent of the program is twofold: The first is to build and test theory related to information technology in face-to-face meetings (discussed in greater detail in the research section). The second purpose is to use the research findings from the program to improve the teaching of small groups and the functioning of administrative and external, or real, groups that use the facilities at Queen's. Research, teaching, and administration are considered the cornerstones of scholarly work in the School of Business (see Figure 16-1). The group support facilities at Queen's, although mainly research facilities, are intended to support all three areas.

A Brief History of GDSS at Queen's University

The research into computer-supported meetings began in 1986 when Brent Gallupe became a member of the faculty of the School of Business. He had completed his Ph.D. dissertation on a group decision support system (GDSS) at the University of Minnesota in 1985, and his main purpose in coming to Queen's was to continue this research and build a program that would accumulate knowledge about computer support for groups.

The first year of the Queen's program was spent developing GDSS software and attempting to acquire hardware resources and a permanent room that could be used as a GDSS lab. The original GDSS, written in BASIC on a DEC VAX computer for Gallupe's dissertation, was not compatible with the IBM mainframe environment at Queen's. An

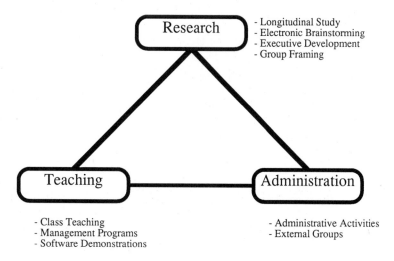

FIGURE 16-1.   Activities Supported by the Decision Centre

attempt was made to convert the software to run on the IBM system but was quickly abandoned when the conversion problems became too great. It was decided that a better, more manageable GDSS environment was a network of microcomputers (in this case, MS-DOS machines). The software was then redesigned, and with some design suggestions from the University of Minnesota, enhanced into a multifaceted GDSS research tool called DECAID1. (A brief description of DECAID1 is found in the section on software resources.)

The hardware resources and a room to conduct GDSS research were difficult to acquire. The first experimental GDSS session conducted at Queen's used 32 four- to five-person groups of senior business students. The data gathering took place in a regular classroom, on weekends, because no permanent space was available. The hardware, the wiring, the projection equipment, and the audio and video equipment had to be set up and taken down three consecutive weekends for that experimental session to be completed. The lesson learned was that a temporary group facility would not support an ongoing program of GDSS research at Queen's.

After that first experimental effort, grants totaling $100,000 over three years became available to set up a group decision support lab with appropriate hardware and software. Along with this grant money came the allocation of a room to be used as a GDSS lab.

The first version of the Decision Lab, as it was called, was set up in June 1987 in a small seminar room. Standard tables, with microcomputers, were placed in a U-shape. The first major purchase was a Compaq 286-40 MB drive microcomputer, which became the file server on the Novell ArcNet network that was installed. Six PC/XT compatible microcomputers served as workstations. The initial public screen projection device was an LCD display on an overhead transparency projector. The initial software was DECAID1, with the following basic features: (1) problem definition, (2) alternatives generation, and (3) voting support. In addition, Lotus 1-2-3 was used in a decision conferencing mode, with only the group facilitator having access to the public screen and software tools.

The limitations of the original facility in space, hardware, and software were quite severe, and an upgraded version of the Decision Lab was completed in June 1988. This version consisted of the same file server as in the first version, but the workstations were changed to PC/AT compatible machines. The projector was a Sony three-gun device that could project CGA graphics. The major piece of software that was added in the fall of 1987 was the PLEXSYS software developed by Jay Nunamaker and his associates at the University of Arizona.

With this new equipment and software, the GDSS research program at Queen's became productive. From 1988 to 1990, over 800 group sessions (both experimental and field studies) were conducted in the Decision Lab. In 1991, a joint study agreement was signed with IBM to improve further the equipment and software. (The section on facilities and software outlines the current state of the Decision Lab at Queen's.) The GDSS research team at Queen's has also grown since 1986. The team now consists of one director and five associate research faculty (two from MIS and one each from organization behavior, marketing, and production).

QUEEN'S FACILITIES: QUEEN'S EXECUTIVE DECISION CENTRE

Physical Facilities

The current version of the computer-supported group facility is called the Queen's Executive Decision Centre. It consists of the main computer-supported Decision Room, or Decision Lab, and four small, traditional meeting rooms (called breakout rooms). The Decision Room is a permanent facility capable of handling groups of up to 12 persons at 6 group stations (see Figure 16-2). The network file server is an IBM PS/2 model 80, and the facilitator's station is an IBM PS/2 model 70. A high-resolution VGA Sony Wide-Screen Color projector is now connected to the network. The network is an upgraded Novell system, and the group stations are IBM PS/2 model 55s. The U-shaped table is modular (can be reconfigured to meet group needs) and was custom-built to fit the room and hide the computers and wiring beneath the top of the table. The color monitors are sunk into the top of each desk so that group members can easily see one another around the table. The room is carpeted, and special incandescent lighting was installed to provide better illumination for the public screen and reduce glare on group station screens. The feeling of the room is one of comfortable task-orientation.

Software Resources

The group software currently running in the centre is of two types. The first type is multiuser software, to which each group member has access. Examples of this type of software are GroupSystems, VisionQuest, and DECAID1. The second type is single-user software. With this software, one user controls the use of the tool at any one time. Examples are Lotus 1-2-3 and Expert Choice.

The first piece of multiuser group software to be used in the centre was DECAID1. A research tool for laboratory experiments, DECIAD1 is a system that allows individuals to use any tool at any time, as opposed to GDSS systems, which allow use of a tool only when a facilitator triggers it. DECAID1 is written in dBase III+, which facilitates easy program changes and uses the dBase file structure to store ideas, votes, and discussion. The current version of DECIAD1 has a number of features including (1) agenda setting, (2) problem definition, (3) alternatives generation, (4) voting support, and (5) group discussion support. DECIAD1 is used in experiments to modify the group technology to determine the impacts of such changes on group outcomes. For example, a brainstorming experiment was conducted with DECAID1 in which the software was changed so that a ten-second delay was implemented in allowing individuals to enter their ideas into the system.

GroupSystems, a multiuser system developed at the University of Arizona (see Chapter 8) has been used extensively at the Queen's Centre. GroupSystems (under the name PLEXSYS) was installed in September 1987. It has been used for approximately 15 different experiments and over 30 real group sessions. The third multiuser technology that has been installed in the centre is VisionQuest by Collaborative Technologies Corporation (Wagner, 1990). This software was just recently installed and is being investigated for its most appropriate use.

FIGURE 16-2. Queen University's Executive Decision Center

A number of single-user software packages support group work in the decision conferencing mode. These packages include Lotus 1-2-3, Expert Choice (a multicriteria modeling package), Harvard Graphics, Statgraphics, and PROPS (an operations research tool). The network software called CloseUp/LAN has been added to the Novell network to enable this single-user software to become multiuser. For example, if a budget model developed in Lotus 1-2-3 is to be discussed by a team of accountants, CloseUp/LAN enables each workstation to see the budget model (shown also on the public screen) and each team member to change that spreadsheet at his or her own terminal. In effect, CloseUp/LAN allows individual team members to control the modeling without interacting with a facilitator.

Human Resources

The Decision Support Centre team is divided into two subgroups. The first is the technical group, which consists of one part-time technician/manager who divides her time between the centre and the other computing facilities in the School of Business, and a number of part-time graduate and undergraduate research assistants. These assistants help maintain the hardware and software in the centre. They have also been trained to use and to facilitate meetings with all the software in the Centre.

The second group is the team of faculty researchers: a director, two MIS researchers, and three faculty members from other disciplines including organizational behavior, marketing, production, and policy. The mix of disciplines emphasizes the cross-disciplinary nature of the research that has been conducted in the Centre.

RESEARCH WORK

Overview

The social sciences provide the research framework for the work done at Queen's. It is assumed that the group support technologies are "social technologies," designed to shape group behavior in ways that ensure effective adaptation to the group task. Any adequate theory of its effects must specify (1) key contextual variables requiring group adaptation, (2) key configurations of the group technology that might respond to situational demands, (3) an account of how group technology would shape or influence group interaction, (4) important group composition variables that moderate group interaction, and (5) outcome variables. These elements cover the whole input → process → output sequence that McGrath and Altman (1966) and Hackman and Morris (1975) advocate as an organizing paradigm for group theory and research. These relationships are illustrated in the model shown in Figure 16-3.

The model depicts the following explanatory scheme, which forms the basis for the research work at the centre: Members of groups perceive a need for adaptation to situational demands in order to accomplish their goals (quality and quantity of ideas, satisfaction and confidence in the process, etc.). They alter their interaction in response to contextual variables. For example, members might respond to an idea-generation task

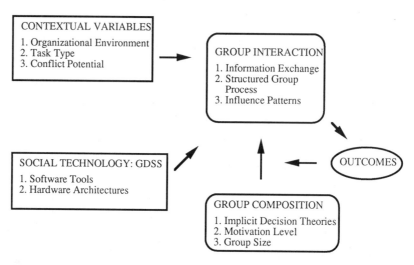

FIGURE 16-3.   The Research Model

by attempting to generate as many unique ideas as possible in the shortest amount of time. Members will use whatever resources are at their disposal when adapting to contextual variables, such as an expert or, in this case, computer-based technology. Thus group technology is a tool for adaption to perceived environmental contingencies. The system will, therefore, affect both group interaction and group outcomes. But members are not totally aware of the consequences of drawing on social technologies. The technology will constrain and influence their behavior, and outcomes are a product of the interaction between contextual variables and the group support tool itself. Each of the components of the explanatory model will now be briefly discussed, and then a summary of three research programs will be outlined.

Contextual Variables
A large number of contextual variables are relevant to the study of group technologies, including task, group cohesiveness, power relationships, urgency, and so on. Research at the centre focuses on specific task types because it has been shown that the task exerts particularly powerful effects on group behavior and outcomes (Hackman and Morris, 1975; McGrath, 1984).

GDSS Technology
GDSSs are defined as interactive, computer-based systems that assist groups in a variety of tasks such as generating ideas, formulating problems, analyzing information, and building consensus. Group support technology in the centre has been described previously.

GDSS Effects on Group Interactions
Decision making is accomplished through group interaction. Its effectiveness depends on the quality of the interaction and of the reasoning carried by it (Gouran and Hirokawa,

1986; Hoffman, 1965; Janis, 1972). To determine how a social technology such as GDSS can affect decision outcomes, it is necessary to determine how the system affects interaction. In principle, a GDSS can influence decision-making interaction in four ways:

1. *The GDSS alters the information-handling capacity of the group.* GDSS has the potential to increase greatly the amount of information a group can consider and the speed with which that information can be arrayed and analyzed. This feature will affect the type and quality of reasoning in the group. It should affect several process and outcome variables, including decision quality, speed of decision, members' understanding of the problem, and members' confidence in the group decision.
2. *The GDSS is a medium for group interaction.* For a face-to-face group, GDSS is a complement to and sometimes a substitute for direct interaction (as when the group ranks preferences on the computer). For a computer teleconference it can be the sole medium of interaction. Numerous studies suggest that machine-mediated interaction differs from free interaction (Johansen, Vallee, and Spangler, 1979). Use of GDSS should affect process variables, such as participation patterns, conflict management behavior, and methods of evaluating solutions. It should also affect outcome variables, including decision quality and members' acceptance.
3. *The GDSS imposes process structures on groups.* A particular formula for making decisions, such as the Nominal Group Technique or Delphi (Gustafson et al., 1973; Van de Ven and Delbecq, 1971) may be built into GDSS and imposed on the group. This feature should affect process variables, such as how thoroughly the group defines problems and explores disagreements, as well as outcome variables, such as decision quality, perceived influence in the decision, and members' confidence in the decision.
4. *The GDSS provides a resource for influencing the group.* A member with control over a particular skill can use it to influence the group. This capacity is heightened by the possibility that computers and computer-based data may be accorded great credibility by some decision makers (Turkle, 1984). This feature should affect leader behavior, the exercise of influence in the discussion, conflict management behavior, and members' commitment to the decision, among other things.

Group Composition
The set of individual styles, attitudes, and knowledge inherent in the group is a moderator of GDSS effects. The group's composition influences interaction and may prevent the group from using the technology effectively. In particular, a member's need's and motives in working in a group and leadership and conflict management styles affect how a group will interact.

Outcomes or Dependent Variables
To assess adequately the impact of the group technologies, both process and outcome variables are measured. The outcome variables that are assessed include outcome quality, members' acceptance of the outcome, confidence in the outcome, speed of outcome, each member's understanding of other's positions, perceptions of who influenced the outcome, attitudes toward GDSS, and attraction to the group.

Process variables are measured with interaction coding systems that depend on behavioral observation. For example, task behavior, including problem analysis, solution development, and orientation behavior, is coded with a coding scheme adapted by Poole (1986) from those of Bales (1950) and Fisher (1970). Participation patterns and computer use are also recorded. Experimental sessions are videotaped to allow multiple codings.

Research Programs

A Longitudinal Study Into the Use of GDSS

The first major research program at the Centre, entitled Longitudinal Study Into the Use of GDSS, began in 1987 and finished in 1990. This research was funded by a grant from the Social Sciences and Humanities Research Council of Canada and by the Associates Program in the School of Business.

The intent of the study was to determine (in a rigorous way) the effects of repeated use of GDSS on group performance. This was an experimental study that compared groups that used the computer support versus those that did not. Groups were randomly assigned to treatments. Some groups used the technology for all their tasks, other groups used no technology, and the remaining groups used the technology for half the tasks and no technology for the other half.

In this study, 200 senior undergraduates in groups of 4 and 5 were tracked over two years while they used GroupSystems and DECAID1 for a variety of different tasks. The 40 groups remained intact for the duration of the study. The tasks were business cases in the required courses of the third and fourth years of their undergraduate program. Six formal experimental sessions were conducted with these groups over the two years, resulting in 240 group sessions. Multiple measures of decision quality, satisfaction, use of GDSS features, amount of assistance from a facilitator and many more were taken. All technology sessions were videotaped, and nontechnology sessions were either videotaped or audiotaped.

This study has generated a large amount of data, which is still being coded and analyzed. Preliminary results have been presented at IFORS, TIMS/ORSA, and ASAC Conferences. The results indicate that as groups become more experienced with GDSS technology, they adapt the computer support tools to their group process and not vice versa. Satisfaction with the process for the technology groups increases with repeated use and remains constant for nontechnology groups. There appears to be a direct relationship between the amount of facilitator intervention (measured by the numbers of comments the facilitator made) and the satisfaction of the group. The most popular and widely used GDSS tools are those that are the most flexible in supporting the particular group task (such as Topic Commenter and Voting Support in GroupSystems). The least popular tools are those that require an enforced sequence of steps or are difficult to use (such as Idea Organizer in GroupSystems).

A Research Program Into Electronic Brainstorming

The second program at the centre is the electronic brainstorming research, which began in 1989 and is still in progress. Seven different studies involving over 800 graduate and undergraduate subjects have been conducted in this program in the last three years. Electronic brainstorming is implemented with the Electronic Brainstorming tool in

GroupSystems. The intent of this program is to explain why electronic brainstorming is such a productive and satisfying idea-generation technique and at the same time determine if the technique can be improved.

The traditional, verbal brainstorming technique is not very effective for generating ideas. A review of the literature (Diehl and Stroebe, 1987) indicates that over 20 studies have been conducted during the last 25 years and *none* have found that real, interacting groups using the brainstorming technique were more effective than nominal groups (individuals generating ideas alone that are then pooled together).

A number of theories have been proposed to explain why group brainstorming is not more effective. One theory argues that an interacting group blocks the production of ideas by not letting individual group members get their ideas out when they have them. This production blocking theory (Lamm and Trommsdorff, 1973) states that individuals generate more ideas because they can get ideas out as soon as they are thought. Another theory, the evaluation apprehension theory (Collaros and Anderson, 1969), states that brainstorming is not as effective because individuals in the interacting group feel that their ideas may be ridiculed or criticized by other members of the group, thereby inhibiting idea generation. A third theory, the social loafing theory, argues that brainstorming is not effective because individuals working in groups have a tendency to "free ride" on the efforts of others (Latane, Williams, and Harkins, 1979). This program of research has attempted to test these theories by comparing electronic brainstorming with traditional brainstorming in groups.

The first two studies in the program sought to determine if electronic brainstorming was more productive than traditional and nominal brainstorming (Gallupe, Bastiannuti, and Cooper, 1991). Two hundred subjects in groups of four were used in the two studies. Groups were randomly assigned to conditions: technology (either electronic or traditional brainstorming) and group type (interacting or nominal). The main dependent measure was the number of unique ideas generated by the group. Other measures of perceived satisfaction and quality were also taken. The results showed that electronic brainstorming was not only the most productive technique in the number of unique ideas generated but also the most satisfying.

The third study[1] was designed to determine if the lack of production blocking was the major cause of the superior performance of electronic brainstorming. The same design was used as in the first two studies, but the technology was modified so that a delay was built into the system; that is, individual group members could not enter their ideas immediately but had to wait five to six seconds. The intent was to simulate production blocking. The delay reduced the number of unique ideas generated compared to normal electronic brainstorming, but the results were not statistically significant. This result led to the conclusion that either the delay did not induce real production blocking or that there is more going on than production blocking.

The next study also examined production blocking, but instead of using the technology to enforce a blocking process, it controlled the manual procedure of generating ideas in the group. In traditional brainstorming groups, the protocol is to wait until another group member has expressed his or her idea before you express yours. This protocol was enforced in

---

[1] The findings of studies three through six have not been published.

the electronic brainstorming treatment. A group member had to wait until another member had finished typing in his or her idea before the second member could proceed. The results of this study are dramatic. Electronic brainstorming is significantly less productive than traditional brainstorming with this procedure. The conclusion is that production blocking is a major factor in the productivity of electronic brainstorming and that electronic brainstorming overcomes the speed disadvantage of typing compared to speaking ideas.

The evaluation apprehension explanation was examined in the fifth study. Does anonymity of idea generation make a difference? In this study, we varied the controversiality of the idea-generation topic to determine if the anonymity of electronic brainstorming helped groups generate ideas on controversial topics. Two tasks were tested. The controversial task was "How can AIDS be reduced?" The noncontroversial task was "How can tourism be improved in Kingston?" The major result of this study was that for both tasks, electronic brainstorming groups generated more unique ideas and were more satisfied than traditional brainstorming groups. One conclusion is that anonymity does help but is not as powerful a factor as production blocking. Another conclusion is that electronic brainstorming can be a productive idea-generation technique when the topic is controversial for the group members.

The sixth study attempted to address the social loafing explanation by comparing normal electronic brainstorming groups whose members could see and hear one another typing in ideas (and see the ideas on their screen) with electronic brainstorming groups whose members could not (although they could see the ideas on their screens). The results of this study did not support the social loafing explanation. The group members who could not see or hear other groups generated as many unique ideas as normal groups. The groups whose members could not see or hear one another, however, were significantly less satisfied than normal groups.

The final study in this program only peripherally examined the competing explanations for electronic brainstorming productivity. A joint study with the University of Arizona examined the impact of group size on electronic brainstorming (Gallupe et al., in press). Queen's University studied groups of 2, 4, and 6 members, and Arizona looked at groups of 6 and 12 members. Electronic brainstorming and traditional groups were compared on the quantity and quality of the unique ideas generated. The results show that electronic brainstorming is not a useful technique for groups of 2, but as group size increases, it becomes a very productive and satisfying technique.

This research program has demonstrated the effectiveness of the electronic brainstorming (EBS) technique (see Table 16-1). Production blocking appears to be the major reason why the technique is so of effective. Anonymity appears to be important but only when the topic brings out various views from group members. The social loafing explanation seems to be of minimal importance for productivity but is important for the satisfaction of group members.

Executive Development with GDSS
The third research program is the study of teams of executives in the executive development programs at Queen's, especially the impact of group technologies for team building. The theoretical basis is similar to the brainstorming studies. The use of group technologies through simultaneity of inputs, anonymity, and group modeling supports

TABLE 16–1   A Research Program Into Electronic Brainstorming

Study	Main Independent Variable	Results
1	EBS vs. traditional vs. nominal	EBS more productive EBS more satisfying
2	EBS vs. traditional vs. nominal	EBS more productive EBS more satisfying
3	Production blocking—electronic delay	Delay groups generated fewer ideas than traditional
4	Production blocking—procedural delay	Delay groups generated fewer ideas than traditional
5	Evaluation apprehension—anonymity	Anonymity helps but not significantly
6	Social loafing	EBS productivity not affected by absence of social cues
7	Group size	Productivity of EBS increases with group size

active participation by all group members. It is hypothesized that this feature should facilitate the development of cohesive and productive teams.

Each summer, the Queen's School of Business conducts executive development programs for public and private sector executives. For each of the last four years, 240 executives have participated in these programs. Groups, or syndicates, of six members are formed to analyze cases and develop class presentations. Each summer, 14 of these groups use the centre for their tasks. Self-report measures of quality, satisfaction, cohesiveness of the team, and other measures have been taken. Data collection started in the summer of 1988, and four years of data have been gathered so far. The data will be analyzed for the four-year period to determine whether group technologies supports or inhibits team development. Our subjective observations indicate that these technologies are an effective tool for building rapport among team members and stimulating team creativity.

Group Framing

The fourth research program which is just beginning, is the "group framing" study. One of the fundamental notions of cognitive psychology is that individual decision makers establish cognitive frames of reference to solve problems and make decisions (Minsky, 1968). A frame is affected by the way a problem is described, by the education and experience of the decision maker, and so on. Individuals enter into a group decision with their own frames about the decision to be made. A pilot study has been conducted to investigate the impact of GDSS (GroupSystems) on individual and group frames. The hypothesis being tested is that a GSS intervention will reframe individuals and change the "risky shift" or "choice shift" that is commonly associated with group decision making.

TEACHING SUPPORT

Class Teaching

The centre has become an integral component of teaching in the School of Business and is used for such activities as seminars, hands-on tutorials, Ph.D. classes, and group case analyses. For example, the first-year required MBA course Computers and Information Systems for Managers uses the centre to demonstrate the concepts of decision support systems. As part of the course, students are given hands-on experience with different types of modeling packages, data-base software, and user interfaces.

In the undergraduate and graduate courses in systems analysis and design, the centre uses CASE packages such as EXCELERATOR and EasyCASE to teach automated systems development tools. An assignment in the course is a simulated joint application development (JAD) session. Each student group is asked to play the role of a systems design team. Students are required to hand in a description of the JAD process, outlining its advantages and disadvantages.

The centre is the site for the MIS Ph.D. seminar. Typically, no more than six students take this course at one time, so the centre is an ideal size for the seminar. GroupSystems software is used during the seminar to stimulate discussion and record research ideas. The centre's facilities support hands-on presentations of a variety of MIS topics, from information systems to executive information systems.

A major part of senior production and marketing courses at Queen's are small-group presentations on some major issue in the field. For the last three years, students have used the audio, video, and computer facilities in the centre to make these presentations. The instructor or evaluator uses the GroupSystems software to record notes from the presentations.

Finally, student study groups are allowed access to the centre for group case analysis (Gallupe, 1988). To use the centre, one member of the group is trained in the use of the facilities and is responsible for the group's sessions. These case groups tend to use GroupSystems almost exclusively. The Electronic Brainstorming, Voting Support, and Topic Commenter tools are the most popular. If discussion questions are given with the case, each window in Topic Commenter represents one question. If no discussion questions are given, Electronic Brainstorming is used to generate problems and issues in the case. Voting Support helps the group reach consensus on alternatives, and Topic Commenter develops action plans.

Management Programs

The centre supports the activities of the two major executive development programs at Queen's. As part of the program, executive "syndicates" or teams use the centre's facilities to analyze cases that cover such topics as evaluating the viability of new product introductions, planning the strategic use of information systems, and solving labor relations problems. Discussion questions are part of each case. GroupSystems is the primary tool in supporting the deliberations of these syndicates. The general process is for individual syndicate members to enter their ideas on a particular question and then use the public screen and group discussion to refine and prioritize those ideas. Group Outliner, Topic Commenter, and Voting Support are the best tools for the process, whereas Electronic Brainstorming, Idea Organization, and Policy Formation are less effective.

Another management program supported by the centre is the Canadian Urban Transit Association Marketing Program. Offered to senior managers, the focus of the program is on the acquisition of applied marketing knowledge and the development of marketing plans. The centre is used by small groups of participants to assist in the development of transit marketing plans. GroupSystems is again the system of choice. Participants find Electronic Brainstorming most effective for generating and sharing ideas because of the diverse situations they come from. With Topic Commenter, the windows represent components of the plan (such as ridership, government support, etc.).

Software Demonstrations

The centre is used as the main site for software demonstrations. For example, a package called PROPS (using Lotus 1-2-3 as the base) was developed at Queen's by the management science faculty to support courses in quantitative methods. The addition of CloseUp/LAN enables participants to acquire hands-on experience with the package.

The Small Business Consulting Program at Queen's is funded by the Ontario provincial government to provide small businesses with consulting advice from senior undergraduate and graduate business students. Typically, clients of the program are invited to the centre to see a demonstration of an accounting system that has been set up by the consultants. In another case, the client and the consultants use the centre's facilities, such as Lotus 1-2-3 and CloseUp/LAN, to develop a business plan interactively.

In summary, the centre has become an important teaching site in the school. It supports all the teaching activities in the school, particularly those involving small-group work.

ADMINISTRATIVE AND EXTERNAL GROUPS

The third and final use of the centre is as support for administrative committees in the school and university and support for groups from outside the university.

Administrative Activities

Administrative committees that use the centre are the Computer Committee, Research Committee, MBA Society, MIS Discipline Group, and Employment Equity Task Force. For example, the Computer Committee of the School of Business is responsible for all computing activities in the school including adequate mainframe support, the Computer Resource Centre, the Electronic Classroom, microcomputer support for individual faculty members, and office automation support. This committee consists of six faculty members and a student representative. Its primary purpose is to develop plans for computing resources in the school. Planning meetings are held on a regular basis (about four meetings a year), and GroupSystems is used to organize the planning issues for discussion. The Alternative Evaluator tool is also used to evaluate new hardware and software acquisitions, for example, when the committee was considering which laptop computers to acquire for the Electronic Classroom. Four vendors had submitted proposals to supply 35 laptops. The committee used Alternative Evaluator to rate the proposals on a variety of criteria, including initial cost, maintenance support, and vendor reputation. Before Alternative Evaluator was used, one vendor was considered by the Committee to be in the leading position. However, as a result of this process, other issues came to light about the various vendors and the Committee decided on a different vendor.

External Groups

The centre has also been used by a variety of management groups and task forces from outside the university. These groups use the centre with the understanding that data will be collected on how the team used the group support tools and their perceptions of the computer-supported meeting.

Two examples provide some insight on how the centre and its facilities are used to support real meetings. The first is a meeting of a senior management team from Revenue Canada-Taxation, a department of the Canadian federal government located in Ottawa. The assistant deputy minister requested a meeting of his senior staff to generate ideas and an action plan to foster excellence in the Department of Revenue-Taxation. He had held traditional, in-house brainstorming sessions before but decided to use the facilities at the centre to try out this new approach.

A premeeting planning session was held in Ottawa two weeks before the meeting was scheduled. This session was attended by the assistant deputy minister (ADM), his assistant, and the meeting facilitator. An agenda was set, with most of the items addressing the topic of developing a first-class organization. The objective that was set for the meeting was an agreed-on list of items that individual team members would take away and attempt to implement. Electronic tools were discussed in general terms, but agenda items were not assigned to the electronic tools.

The team arrived in Kingston the evening before the meeting to become familiar with the centre and its facilities. The meeting started at 9:00 A.M. with the electronic brainstorming tool. Individual team members quickly learned how to use the system, and a large number of ideas were generated in about 30 minutes. The next phase of idea organization proved to be more difficult for team members. It was at this point that the facilitator adjusted the process to focus on categories for ideas that the team had agreed to verbally. This approach worked well, and the team selected a set of the best ideas in each category and agreed on a rank ordering. After lunch, a similar process was used to generate and consolidate ideas for two other brainstorming tasks. The final task of the day was to combine the best ideas from the sessions into action items that individual team members could pursue.

The data from the postsession questionnaires provided by the ADM and the team members were uniformly positive, although some members stressed the importance of the facilitator, particularly when the process became too cumbersome. The general feeling of the group was that to accomplish what was done by the team in a traditional meeting would probably have taken two or three days. The ADM saw a subsidiary benefit to the facilitated electronic meeting besides the formal objectives. He felt the experience was a very good team-building exercise.

A meeting of the Kingston Literacy Foundation was held in the summer of 1991. The size of the foundation had tripled in two years in terms of staff, funds received, and clients served, and the current resources were being severely strained. A meeting was scheduled of the senior staff to develop a strategic plan for the next three years.

A premeeting planning session was held with three senior staff members. Because of the size of the complete team, 16 members, it was decided to divide the team into two groups. The first group would use the Decision Room in the morning while the second group used one of the traditional meeting rooms. The locations were reversed for the afternoon. Agendas were established for both groups and meeting deliverables were defined. For the Decision Room meetings, one deliverable was to generate a prioritized list of fund-raising activities that the group would undertake in the next three years. A second deliverable was a prioritized list of items and activities that would be needed to support Kingston Literacy staff. This list would be used for fund-raising activities.

GroupSystems software was used for this meeting. Electronic Brainstorming was used to generate ideas for fund-raising activities and items to support the staff. Topic Commenter was used to organize the ideas into categories, and Rank Order Voting was used to prioritize the refined ideas. Finally Alternative Evaluator was used to evaluate the refined ideas according to three criteria: cost, impact on staff, and feasibility.

The data from the postsession questionnaires provided by the 16 team members were again positive. All team members liked the Electronic Brainstorming tool but found Alternative Evaluation tool difficult to use. All members stated they would return for another meeting in the centre. A follow-up meeting with the three senior staff members who were responsible for the meeting in the centre showed that the outputs from the meeting were incorporated into the strategic plan with very few changes.

CONCLUSION

Our experience with the centre at Queen's has provided us with a number of insights into the use of real-time computer support for managerial meetings. These insights might be categorized as benefits and guidelines. One of the benefits is the increased task-orientation of meetings. This finding has been confirmed from data collected from all of the groups that used the centre. The technology helps structure the meeting and focus the group on the task at hand. By using a GDSS such as GroupSystems, the team is able to concentrate its activities to the task and minimize the diversions that characterize group meetings.

A second benefit is the anonymity of input that the technology allows. Ideas are separated from personalities, which allows participants to voice unpopular or negative views. Anonymous input from group members also reduces domination by individuals whose contribution to the meeting may be substantially less than others.

A third benefit is the simultaneity of input during the meeting. The technology allows group members to input ideas at the same time and yet still see others' ideas. All team members are able to rank-order a list at the same time, which speeds up the information-gathering process.

A fourth benefit is the ability to manipulate quickly the information presented during the actual meeting. The use of such tools as LOTUS 1-2-3 and Expert Choice in conjunction with the group support facilities of DECAID1 and GroupSystems helps to model what would occur if someone's suggestion or idea were implemented. This process of moving from group support to decision conferencing and back has proven to be very efficient. Questions brought up during discussion could be answered immediately instead of having to be put off until the next meeting.

In terms of guidelines, probably the most important lesson is that some sort of human support or leadership is always needed during a meeting when group technology is used. This support may be a specially trained facilitator or a member of the group who has been trained to use the system. Our work with experimental groups and real teams points to the appropriate facilitation as an important factor for success.

Another guideline is ensuring that the group software used during the meeting are tailored to the task at hand. Our experience has indicated that the inappropriate choice of tools can lead to frustration and decreased group productivity. Careful planning in selecting the appropriate software tool is important if the meeting is to be productive.

A third guideline is the idea that group support technologies are not useful for all tasks. Our experience has indicated that there are meetings in which equal participation by all groups members (supported by the technology) is inappropriate, for example, a group task that requires the special expertise of one group member. This member's views must dominate the group, and the use of the group voting technology, if not properly handled, can minimize his or her influence.

In summary, the Queen's Executive Decision Centre has developed from a temporary facility in 1986 into a permanent, state-of-the-art facility in 1991. The centre is now an important ongoing research, teaching, and administrative component of the School of Business at Queen's University. The centre's research team of ten faculty members and research assistants provides support for an active GDSS research program. The centre has become an integral part of the teaching activities of the school. Support for administrative groups and external teams has enhanced the reputation of the centre as a productive meeting environment. A number of ongoing challenges must still be met, such as acquiring a bigger Decision Room and improved hardware. However, if past trends are any indication, the centre will be around for many years to come.

Chapter 17

The Electronic Meeting Room With An International View

Laku Chidambaram

University of Hawaii

INTRODUCTION

The Electronic Meeting Room (EMR) was established at the University of Hawaii to examine the impact of computer support on multicultural communication. The primary objective of the EMR is to develop a paradigm for understanding computer-mediated group performance and behavior in international environments. Research has shown that basic modes of communication and decision making differ among people from different national and cultural backgrounds (Blackman, 1983; Carbaugh, 1984). The differences are apparent in such areas as the locus of decision making, initiation and coordination mechanisms, temporal orientation, mode of reaching decision, decision criterion, and communication style. These differences often tend to hinder effective communication among groups from different cultural backgrounds.

The long-term outcome of the EMR is to reduce these barriers to multicultural communication and to increase intercultural understanding. Studies at the EMR facility involve various behavioral dimensions of intercultural communication and group decision making such as intercultural conflict management, group cohesiveness, group performance, and intergroup communication patterns. These issues are currently being studied in our EMR lab, and eventually, the results will be verified in field settings. The overall position of the College of Business Administration (CBA), in terms of both its geographic location and its strategic thrusts, provides an excellent platform for our investigation of computer-supported, multicultural communication. Despite the importance of multicultural communication in today's global economy, very few studies have examined the impact of cultural differences on computer-supported communication.

Our research program seeks to examine the impact of computer support on multicultural communication and develop a paradigm for understanding computer-mediated communication in international environments. A related objective is understanding how computer support affects the behavior and performance of multilingual groups engaged in international business. Specifically, our plan includes the analysis of how groups from different cultures appropriate group decision support systems (GDSS) and the examination of computer support on group decision making, the management of conflict, and the formulation of negotiation strategies in cross-cultural settings. The uniqueness of this program lies in its cross-cultural aspect. This research aims to build a foundation for the use of GDSS to support group meetings in a global environment. This chapter describes the growth and evolution of the EMR, its primary uses, and its future plans.

HISTORY

The EMR project was initiated in 1989 with the hiring of two faculty members from Indiana University, Laku Chidambaram and Jack Fellers, both of whom had pursued their doctoral research in GDSS. Two key events made the idea of an EMR a reality. First, the CBA funded a proposal coauthored by Chidambaram and Fellers for establishing the EMR. Second, a grant was given by the Hawaii Information Systems Roundtable (HISR), a consortium of chief information officers from the local business community, to develop the EMR further. Receipt of the grant from HISR was made possible by the efforts of Ralph Sprague, an ardent advocate of the EMR. These two developments enabled us to plan for a small start-up room. The current facility was established in 1990 and is a comparatively new and modest one, comprising six workstations and a facilitator terminal. The relatively low capital outlay of our EMR is evidence that this technology is within reach of even small businesses and universities with tight budgets.

Toward the end of 1990, we hired and trained a full-time meeting facilitator. She has a communications degree, is fluent in Chinese, and her professional background fits well with the multicultural focus of the EMR. Her duties include room scheduling, preplanning meetings, session facilitation, postsession debriefing, groupware demonstrations, facilitator training, technical liaison, and supervising the facility's graduate assistant. Policy decisions about use of the facility are made by the director of the Center for Business Education and Research (CIBER) with input from the EMR Faculty Advisory Committee, a group of tenure-track faculty members in the CBA.

SPONSORS

The mission of the CBA at the University of Hawaii at Manoa is to provide students with a broad view of the world's cultures and business systems, as well as to provide the tools necessary to ensure competency in the management of technology both at home and abroad. The two main strategic thrusts of the college are international business and information technology. The EMR, with its focus on applying emerging technologies in an international environment, forms a natural bridge in linking these two thrusts. Hence, the CBA—through its various programs, like PRIISM—has been the primary sponsor of the EMR.

In the fall of 1988, the CBA established CIBER, a federally funded program sponsored by the U.S. Department of Education. The CBA was one of the first five colleges nationwide to establish such a center, and there are now 15. The objective of this initiative by the Department of Education is to further international business research and education in American universities. The EMR's goals are in line with this objective. Hence, CIBER has helped fund the position of a full-time facilitator and that of a graduate assistant for the EMR.

PHYSICAL FACILITIES

The EMR funtions as part of the CBA's local-area network. Plans are underway to develop a separate local-area network for the EMR, which will then be linked to the CBA's existing network. Currently the CBA has a Novell (2.15C SFT) network using thick/thin ethernet as the transport media. A major network upgrade (Novell 3.0) is expected by the end of 1991. The network, called the CBANET, is connected to the campus (ProNet 80) network by a Proteon router. The CBANET has SMTP gateways that gives users electronic-mail (E-mail) access to Internet/Bitnet. Resources on the network include a wide variety of IBM-PCs and compatibles, Macintoshes, an Oracle server, laser printers, and the EMR. Remote dial-in capabilities are available through Novell NAS, and remote printing is established with Lanports and LanSpool software. A wide variety of application software—word processing, spreadsheets, data base, statistics, graphics, scheduling, programming, and E-mail—is also available on the CBANET, primarily for faculty and staff.

The EMR's hardware setup consists of six IBM 386-SXs with 1 MB of RAM and a facilitator workstation (also a 386-SX) connected to the CBANET file server (see Figure 17-1). Eventually, an independent server is expected to be installed. At present, the groupware in use is GroupSystems, developed at the University of Arizona and marketed by Ventana Corporation, and Collaborative Technologies' groupware product, Vision-Quest. Several other groupware products—Optionfinder, Lotus Notes, and Coordinator—are also being evaluated for possible future use. Possibilities for developing our own in-house groupware products are also being examined.

PRIMARY USES OF THE EMR

The primary uses of the EMR are faculty research; teaching; and administrative, corporate, community, and doctoral dissertation activities. These activities are discussed in detail below.

FIGURE 17-1.   University of Hawaii's Electronic Meeting Room

Conducting Controlled Lab Experiments
with an International Focus

Three research projects examining various aspects of GDSS are currently underway. Results from these studies could have important implications for doing business in today's global economy.

Project 1: Studying Geographically Dispersed Meetings

This research is aimed at comparing the decision-making performance of computer-supported groups in remote and face-to-face settings. Although several researchers have pointed out the need for examining this important issue, very little empirical research has been undertaken. A pilot study was carried out last summer with GDSS (Chidambaram and Jones, 1991). Two factors were manipulated: communication medium (face to face vs. telephone) and decision support (GDSS vs. no GDSS). All GDSS groups that participated in the study used the University of Arizona's Group Systems software; half the groups used it in a face-to-face setting and the other half in a remote setting. All other factors—other than geographic dispersion and communication medium—were held constant.

The variables examined included perceptions of communication media, group attitudes, and group performance. The results of this study support the idea that communication mode plays an important role in group decision making, with groups from different cultures. In addition, this study also helped identify some of the variables that affect group performance and attitudes. Overall, the dispersed GDSS groups performed better than the dispersed groups without the technology. However, they also perceived some significant drawbacks of using an impersonal medium for communicating. These results have important ramifications for global managers exploring feasible alternatives to the costly choice of international travel. Although geographically dispersed decision making with collaborative technology has not become as established as once predicted, many organizations are examining this option seriously. With the pioneering research undertaken at the EMR and elsewhere (Hiltz, 1988; Kinney and VanOver, 1989), dispersed meetings may become commonplace in the near future.

Project 2: Examining Group Development
in Multinational Groups

Research is underway into an important aspect of group behavior in multinational groups: longitudinal studies of group behavior and content analysis of group processes. Most of the studies in GDSS have examined the effect of computer support on group decision making during the first (and in fact, the only) meeting of ad hoc groups. The importance of longitudinal research designs in examining information systems in general has been emphasized (e.g., Vitalari, 1985). Recent studies in GDSS have also recommended that researchers use repeated measures designs in studying collaborative technology (Watson, 1987; Zigurs et al., 1988) because the full impact of a GDSS on group decision making would not be evident until groups used the system repeatedly.

One of the first longitudinal examinations of group behavior and performance in a controlled lab setting was conducted at Indiana University (Chidambaram, Bostrom, and Wynne, 1991). This study showed that the one-time performance of ad hoc experimental groups is really not indicative of the longer-term performance of well-established groups in general. Group performance and behavior changed over time for GDSS and non-GDSS (manual) groups. Moreover, in manual groups, performance fluctuated more and exhibited a declining trend over time, with groups gradually becoming less cohesive. However, with GDSS support, performance steadily improved over time and groups tended to become more cohesive.

Results suggest that there was a gestation period in which the technology took effect. Subjects had initial difficulty in incorporating the technology into group processes, followed by awareness of the system's potential, and finally by acceptance and productive utilization. Hence, the full impact of the system was not felt until the third meeting. The findings from this study indicate that use of GDSS improves group performance only when the group has appropriated the technology into group processes and is completely comfortable with it. Hence, GDSS technology, like all other types of technology, takes time to understand and master. Current research examines this issue in greater detail with multinational groups.

Project 3: Studying Technology Appropriation
in Multicultural Groups

Another related stream of research examines the efficacy of the adaptive structuration theory (AST) as described by Poole and DeSanctis (1990). AST provides valuable insight into how groups appropriate technology. GDSS provides a set of specific structures in the form of linked software tools as well as global structures such as anonymity, simultaneity, process structuring support, electronic recording and display, and enhanced information-processing capabilities. GDSS makes these structures available for potential appropriation by the group. However, group factors like history and degree of cohesiveness, individual factors like cultural and ethnic background and learning style, and contextual factors like the type of task and the nature of the problem affect the way in which a group appropriates the structures offered by the GDSS. Current research examines how multicultural groups appropriate the technology into group processes by using content analysis.

Learning and Training in Multicultural Environments

Today's global economy requires increasing interdependence among peoples of different nations and cultures. Such interdependence implies growing intercultural interaction and multinational communication. GDSS can help facilitate this process. Plans are underway to test the effectiveness of the EMR in developing training programs for multinational corporations. Lab studies will be conducted to develop programs for managers from various cultural and national backgrounds. Various analogical and abstract learning devices will also be tested to determine their efficacy in a multinational setting. This program will help firms reduce the money spent on training and educating foreign managers and increase the effectiveness of such programs.

GDSS can also be used as powerful teaching and training tools, especially in multicultural environments. The CBA, with its numerous international programs, will serve as a source for experimental subjects. The results of research conducted in the EMR will help faculty develop effective programs for teaching and training students with various cultural and national backgrounds. Already a number of classes in the CBA have visited the EMR as part of their regular coursework. Discussions are underway with several business faculty to use the EMR for case analysis by project teams in such courses as business policy, international business management, and marketing management. Ultimately, the objective is to integrate GDSS into the business curricula. Seminars will be given and instructional materials, including working papers, handouts, and videotapes, will be distributed to interested faculty members. Such integration will give the faculty a flexible tool for teaching and students a powerful tool for learning in a multicultural environment. The GDSS facility will also strengthen the efforts of the university and the college to deal innovatively with the cultural and ethnic diversity of its student body.

Other Uses

The EMR has also hosted a number of administrative, corporate, and community activities. Several CBA departments and affiliated programs like the Real Estate Center and PAMI have used the EMR for conducting strategic planning, team development, problem solving, and other meetings. Demonstrations of the EMR have been given to several other units in the university including the School of Social Work, Program on Conflict Resolution, School of Travel Industry Management, and Peace Institute. The local chapter of the Financial Executives Institute; the PRIISM Consortium of International Universities from China, Singapore, South Korea, Australia, Hong Kong, the United Kingdom, and the United States; the Kentucky Real Estate Commissioners; and HISR are a few of the outside groups that have used the EMR. In addition, some doctoral students in our Communication and Information Sciences (CIS) Program are currently working on their proposals to explore various aspects of computer-supported cross-cultural communication.

Members of HISR—representing a cross section of Hawaii businesses—have also used the EMR to hold strategy formulation, planning, and performance evaluation meetings at various levels. Use by community groups has also increased. For instance, in the summer of 1991 the facility was used by Kamehameha Komputer Kamp, a group of elementary school students of Hawaiian and part-Hawaiian ancestry. A training program for prospective facilitators is also in place. Several doctoral students and graduate research assistants have been trained as process and technical facilitators. The rising requests for demonstrations and increasing use by various entities reflect the growing interest among the local community and businesses in computer-supported communication.

FUTURE EMR PROGRAMS

Three new programs with a global emphasis will be undertaken in the near future, and preliminary work has already started.

Facilitating Computer-Supported Japanese-American Communication

The basic modes of communication and decision making differ between American and Japanese managers. The differences are apparent in such areas as the locus of decision making, initiation and coordination mechanisms, temporal orientation, mode of reaching decision, decision criterion, and communication style. These differences may hinder effective communication between Japanese and American managers. The GDSS facility will be used to support and enhance communication between American and Japanese managers and increase intercultural understanding. A tentative three-year plan is outlined in Table 17-1.

A related objective is to facilitate Japanese-American negotiation. Increasingly, international trade negotiations are becoming commonplace in today's global economy. The multilateral GATT (General Agreement on Tariffs and Trade) talks are a good example. The EMR will probably help to reduce the cognitive overload that decision makers have in such complex, cross-cultural, and often political situations. Moreover, initial research in two-person settings has already established the advantages of such negotiation support systems (Jones and Hill, 1990).

TABLE 17-1   Three Year Plan to Foster Japanese-American Communication using the EMR

Year 1

Conduct background research*
Set up six-terminal pilot facility*
Extensive pilot testing to remove glitches in software*
Develop experimental procedures, tasks, and instruments*
Train facilitators in bilingual facilitation
Demos to local business community and Japanese executives; students and faculty*
Use of facility by Hawaii Information Systems Roundtable (HISR)*
Faculty research projects examining Japanese-American interaction
Publish preliminary results in academic and practitioner journals
Actual use of system by Japanese-American executives from:
    the East-West Center (EWC);
    the Pacific-Asian Management Institute (PAMI);
    the Japan-American Institute of Management Science (JAIMS);
    the University of Hawaii Special Programs.*

Year 2

Recruit full-time facilities manager and process facilitator*
Doctoral student dissertations using group room facility
Extensive bi-lingual group software development
Extend facility to a twelve-terminal group system
Put in observation deck and video/audio equipment
Acquire and install translation facilities
Renovate/refurbish room to accommodate new extensions
Install dedicated server for GROUPNET; offload from CBANET
Invite Japanese-American groups to actively use facilities
Continue research examining Japanese-American communication
Publish results of on-going research projects in journals
Establish state-of-the-art groupware development facilities:
    Visual scanners and OCRs;
    Voice input interfaces; and,
    Multi-media equipment.

Year 3

Recruit full-time technical facilitator and translator
Continue doctoral dissertation work
Expand software development efforts to include new facilities
Invite Japanese and American executives to use the group room
Explore non-face-to-face, asynchronous electronic communication
Examine computer-supported negotiation in bi-lingual settings
Develop course materials for classroom instruction purposes
Prepare videotapes for sharing information with Japanese firms
Use facilities for actual Japanese-American meetings
Invite Japanese academics to tour facility
Embark on joint research projects with Japanese colleagues
Field trip to visit Japanese research institutions
Publish research results in Japanese and American journals.

*completed

292

Understanding International Experiences with Collaborative Technologies

The specific goals of this project are as follows:

1. To identify what are the important issues in managing and implementing collaborative technologies globally and to determine what differences, if any, exist between the approaches utilized by U.S. institutions and those from other countries.
2. To bridge the two main thrusts of the CBA—international business and information technology—from a curriculum development perspective, that is, to develop a new course entitled An International Survey of Collaborative Technologies.

GDSS facilities have now been established in Mexico, the Netherlands, England, Singapore, and Australia. Data gathered from studies at the EMR can now be compared with the data collected at these other, international sites. Such comparisons will help us increase our understanding of the impact of technology on group processes and performance in an international context.

Since previous research in this area is currently lacking, a survey is being developed to provide an initial assessment of the approaches used by U.S.-based and foreign multinational corporation and universities to implement and manage GDSS. This survey will solicit organizational experiences in the implementation and use of GDSS, what cultural factors are critical to its use and success, what issues are important in effectively managing it, what issues are perceived to be of increasing importance in the future, and what additional challenges are presented in utilizing GDSS in a multinational environment.

Developing Multilingual Groupware

Software development for GDSS is in it's early stages. GDSS products are currently being developed and tested at universities and corporate research labs. However, very few institutions—academic or corporate—have ventured into the area of multilingual groupware development. Our primary research focus—computer-supported multicultural communication—will serve as a natural testbed for developing and testing multilingual GDSS. Moreover, the University of Hawaii, with over 40 languages taught in its various programs, is a world leader in multilingual education. This supportive environment at the university should prove conducive for developing multilingual GDSS.

A related issue deals with designing user interface. Although user-interface design for individual decision makers has gained a lot of attention in the literature, very little consideration has been given to its design for groups. In a multicultural context, this design needs particular attention because of the difficulty that many people from different cultures have in dealing with purely command-driven interfaces. The use of menus, icons, voice input, and touch screens as interfaces needs to be investigated more closely in a multicultural setting.

An objective of this program is to develop multilingual GDSS to support groups involved in transacting global business. Strategic links with the university's Software

Engineering Research Lab will enable us to achieve this goal. The end result is to help groups from all over the world communicate better by reducing imprecise signals and enhancing overall understanding. Multilingual GDSS software will also be tested in non-face-to-face settings on a local-area network. This work will be followed by extensive testing in other geographically dispersed environments involving multiple decision makers from several countries.

RESEARCH METHODOLOGIES

When precision and control are important, laboratory studies will be the primary method of data collection. Ongoing laboratory experiments continue to allow us to build a cumulative base of knowledge about the effects of specific factors (e.g., decision task and physical proximity) on the multicultural group interaction process. In the past, these studies were undertaken with undergraduate students as subjects. However, we expect increasingly to utilize graduate students as subjects in future studies. There are a number of graduate and executive programs at the CBA. In addition to providing valuable data about the effectiveness of GDSS, these studies will provide excellent hands-on training for our students in using emerging technologies.

In the near future, field studies will provide an opportunity to assess the impact of GDSS for real-world groups addressing actual problems. The location of Hawaii as a gateway to the Pacific makes the CBA's EMR an ideal locale for conducting cross-cultural field studies. The various executive programs at the CBA provide a rich source of real-world groups operating in a multicultural setting. During the summer sessions, managers from multinational corporations with different cultural, national, linguistic, and ethnic backgrounds enroll in the international programs sponsored by the CBA. These managers will also have an unique opportunity to participate in the activities of the EMR. Moreover, we also expect to invite Japanese managers enrolled in the Japan-American Institute of Management Science (JAIMS)—an educational institution sponsored by Fujitsu Corporation—to participate in the research projects.

CONCLUSION

The key aspect that sets apart research and teaching activities being conducted at the University of Hawaii's EMR is its international focus. The strategic thrusts of the CBA—international business and information technology—and the geographic location of Hawaii as a gateway to the Pacific region enable us to maintain this focus. Although the EMR is only a year old and relatively modest in comparison to other mainland facilities, it has garnered a lot of attention from local businesses, government agencies, international scholars, and global corporations. In the future, we expect to expand the programs carefully, with a view to forming strategic links with national and international partners. In keeping pace with the rapid global changes, we hope to build and sustain an EMR that is truly responsive to the changing needs of the world's people and cultures.

Section IV

Decision Conferencing

The final chapters describe decision conferencing, a face-to-face meeting skillfully managed by facilitators supported by modeling software. The facilitators—usually there are several for a decision conference—drive the meeting. Software plays a less intrusive role than in the settings described previously. Its purpose is to assist in the creation of models that provoke discussion and considered examination of the information presented in the meeting.

In contrast to the settings discussed in previous chapters, meeting participants do not directly enter data into a computer. Participants' ideas are captured through manual techniques such as writing on index cards. Often these data, with the assistance of facilitators, are further processed by the group to create clusters of higher-level concepts.

These concepts are then entered into a computer program by a facilitator. Modeling techniques embedded in the software are then used to analyze the relationships between concepts. The facilitators guide the participants through an explicit consideration of the key assumptions and contentious issues highlighted by the model.

Decision conferencing software stresses data analysis. As a result, the output of a decision conference is frequently a shared mental model of the organization. In comparison, other team technologies spotlight data capture and evaluation of issues and tend to leave the group with a shared understanding of organizational priorities. The advantage of going to the extra stage, to a shared mental model, is that, as demonstrated by Eden and Ackermann (Chapter 19), it provides a very effective benchmark for evaluating strategic initiatives. It can also be used as a foundation for an executive information system that monitors decision making. In the future, we expect to see some vertical integration of team technology software, with modeling tools being added to participants' workstation systems and decision conferencing systems adding user workstations to capture input directly.

We suggest that you read this section's chapters in the order presented. The first chapter provides a broad introduction to decision conferencing, and the second gives in-depth coverage of the application of the methodology in an organization.

Decision conferencing researchers are solidly positioned in the action research or demonstration experiment sector. Their investigations are based on working with live groups attempting to solve complex and messy problems. They assert that there is no other way to study such problems. Consequently, it is difficult to validate empirically the successes claimed. However, this is not really an issue. A group problem-solving system that can stand the test of the market and generate repeat business is certainly doing something to improve the quality of group work. The real research issue is to find out why decision conferencing works, which of its phases are more critical to its success, and how modeling software can be changed to improve group performance further. In this regard, other researchers may be interested in examining the decision conferencing process and identifying research opportunities for tackling these questions.

Rohrbaugh's chapter (Chapter 18) highlights the elusiveness of assessing the effectiveness of group processes and identifies four competing perspectives (rational, political, consensual, and empirical) that might be used to judge the effectiveness of group processes. For example, the rational perspective emphasizes task completion, whereas the political viewpoint seeks flexibility and creativity. Thus, he argues that evaluation of group processes must be assessed by multiple criteria. In many respects, Rohrbaugh's notion of competing values assessment (CVA) echoes Hannan and Freeman's (1977) assertion that the measurement of organizational effectiveness is evasive because organizations typically have multiple and conflicting goals. This parallel is not surprising because groups microcosmically mirror organizations.

CVA also resonates with the work of those interested in assessing the influence of culture on GSS-supported teams (see chapters 12 and 15). A group's culture can be conceived as its typical reaction when it has to make a trade-off between competing values. For example, a U.S. group might side with individualism and a Singaporean team favor collectivism. Thus, CVA not only offers a framework for evaluating group processes but also supports thinking about how different cultures might use GSS. For example, a culture that emphasizes the rational perspective might be inclined to use primarily a team technology's modeling tools, whereas a group that accentuates the consensual perspective might use information exchange tools to enhance meeting participation.

The decision conferencing chapters demonstrate the power of team technology to improve the quality of group work. However, more important, they underscore how the successful application of team technology is critically dependent on a skillful facilitator. On reading these chapters it soon becomes apparent that the authors are very experienced, competent facilitators and know how to ply their skills. Another strength of these chapters is that they provide an excellent finale to this book because they illustrate the final stage of a progression of group outcomes—shared opinions, a shared understanding, and a shared mental model. Although a shared mental model is not the target of all group problem solving, many important tasks, such as strategic planning, do seek this goal. The communication research of Section II focuses on systems that support opinion sharing; Section III describes team technologies that are often used to develop a shared understanding; and this section, Section IV, completes the trip by showing how a shared mental model can be created.

Chapter 18

Cognitive Challenges and Collective Accomplishments

John Rohrbaugh

The State University of New York at Albany

INTRODUCTION

The apothegm "two heads are better than one" carries an explicit warning to any individual with the hubris to take on a cognitive challenge independently. In fact, considerable empirical evidence about group performance has accumulated during this century to establish the added value of collective effort on a wide variety of intellectual tasks (McGrath, 1984; Shaw, 1973, 1981). Unfortunately, we also know that "too many cooks spoil the broth," a testament to the extraordinary difficulty of achieving synergism with even a small number of collaborators. When the best of mental activities are demanded in response to important cognitive challenges, collective accomplishments are often a grave disappointment.

For the past 15 years, The University at Albany has hosted a sizable and diverse research program on cognitive challenges and collective accomplishments. The unifying purpose of the studies during this period has been to understand the limitations of individual and group responses to cognitive challenges in order to design improved methods for enhancing their performance. The research program has run the gamut of intellectual tasks, incorporating sustained focus on perhaps more types of cognitive challenges than are investigated at any other site. The variety of cognitive challenges include all of the following:

- Reactive responses to problems and proactive initiatives for opportunities
- Problem finding/diagnosis, problem solving, action planning/implementation, and evaluation
- Estimation and forecasting
- "Intelligence" tasks (collecting information) and "design" tasks (integrating information)
- Assessments of "what could be" and preferences for "what should be"
- Identification and organization of alternatives (i.e., options), criteria (i.e., costs and benefits), and scenarios (i.e., futures)
- Single-party resource allocations and multiparty negotiations
- Judgment making and choice making

The Albany work of the last decade has been supported in part by at least ten different grants from the National Science Foundation. It encompasses the efforts of eight faculty members and more than twice as many doctoral students in three academic departments (marketing, psychology, and public administration) and three research centers (Center for Policy Research, Center for Applied Psychological Research, and Institute for Decision Systems). The variety of work at the University of Albany has considerable pertinence to the development of computer-augmented teamwork. Since it is impossible to represent adequately the full scope of research within the limits of this chapter, special attention is given to five focal areas: expert estimation and forecasting, conflict management and analytical mediation, simulation and system dynamics, modeling of judgment and choice, and small-group interaction processes. Following this discussion, attention is turned to the description of a ten-year demonstration experiment supported by Albany's Decision Techtronics Group, in which the effectiveness of one form of computer-augmented teamwork, decision conferencing, was introduced to and appropriated by a large number of organizations. The experiment is of particular interest because it built directly and formally on all five focal areas of research described below.

FIVE FOCAL AREAS OF RESEARCH: AN OVERVIEW

Expert Estimation and Forecasting

Organizations rely on expertise to guide virtually all aspects of nonroutine work, yet relatively little has been established about the cognitive skills that experts use. This lacuna has profound implications for the design of computer-augmented teamwork in which experts are involved since so much remains to be learned about techniques that might enhance the unique strengths and overcome the particular weaknesses of expert groups. Research at the University at Albany has identified seven distinct components of cognitive skill that define expertise in estimation and forecasting tasks. In isolating each skill component, it is now possible not only to determine the ways in which experts can narrow the gap between potential and actual achievement (or accuracy) but also to create improved mechanisms for expert teams to perform more effectively.

One particularly important line of research has investigated the relation between the amount and quality of information made available to experts and the accuracy of their subsequent forecasts. Findings have indicated, for example, that as the amount of information is increased, experts' ability to process information, as well as their agreement, decreases. The advantage of a group average forecast over the forecasts of individual experts increases as the amount of information is increased. This research investigates under what conditions the amount and complexity of information made available to experts widens or narrows the gap between their potential and actual achievement and increases or decreases disagreement among experts. See Appendix 18-A for references to the five focal areas discussed in this section.

Conflict Management and Analytical Mediation

Although much work has been devoted to specifying motivational and behavioral elements of conflict between parties, little attention has been paid to the definition of negotiation as a cognitive challenge. How does the complexity of a bargaining task reduce the potential of disputing parties to find a mutually advantageous solution? A series of Albany studies has demonstrated that the bargaining positions of two or more parties (with the implicit trade-offs between issues that each contains) can define a "settlement space" that may expedite or virtually cripple a negotiation process. By examining how negotiators move toward an agreed settlement over time under differing settlement space conditions, researchers are finding practical ways to facilitate agreements that are in the mutual best interest of all parties involved.

One technique being advanced by this line of research is termed *analytical mediation* in which all parties agree to the definition of unsettled issues and the differences that remain on each. Working independently with a mediator, each party agrees on a bargaining position expressed graphically as a set of utility functions associated with all of the disputed issues. The specification of utility functions allows the mediator to define analytically the settlement space as a multidimensional coordinate system and to scan mathematically all possible solutions for a small subset that appears both efficient and equitable. Investigation of analytical mediation suggests that this alternative approach to conflict management may help the negotiating parties identify and agree to settlements that do not leave joint gains on the table.

Simulation and System Dynamics

Individuals and groups face extreme cognitive challenges when thinking about problems in complex systems that change over time. The dynamic complexities of social, managerial, economic, and environmental systems often defy individual analysis and group consensus. Complex interrelationships make it difficult to know all the ramifying effects of a policy initiative, well-understood pieces combine to create misunderstood wholes, circular causality and loops of information feedback turn short-run policy improvements into long-run policy mistakes, and dynamic problems foster ever-changing problem definitions. Nevertheless, little attention currently is being paid in the design of electronic meeting support to the development of techniques for problem definition and policy analysis in complex dynamic systems.

In contrast, the University at Albany in the past 15 years has become one of the foremost research centers in the development of system dynamics models, especially for computer-augmented teamwork. Systematic work has progressed to facilitate model building by managerial groups and expert teams, to create "microworlds" for learning laboratories as mechanisms for advancing systems thinking, and to enhance collaborative decision making by better integrating simulation models into the intervention process. In addition, linkages are being explored between the use of system dynamics models (that help decision makers examine "what would be" and "what could be" questions) and preference models of judgment and choice (that help decision makers examine "what should be" questions). Simulation allows the testing of proposed programs and policies in a model that remembers all the complexity built into it by the decision-making team and infallibly deduces all the dynamic implications of the group's assumptions.

Modeling of Judgment and Choice

Although much effort has been devoted in other academic fields to explicating cognitive processes such as the making of judgments and choices, the value of modeling in computer-augmented teamwork remains largely unexploited. Modeling enhances interaction by providing a common language that participants can use regardless of their substantive backgrounds. Explicit representation of others' priorities, preferences, and trade-offs facilitates interpersonal understanding. Furthermore, extended thinking about the strengths and weaknesses of a model structure can build insight not only about the manner in which the problem is being formally represented but also and more important, about the nature of the problem itself. Since well-constructed models of preference structure and behavioral intent are quite predictive of subsequent actions, many of the uncertainties that are associated with implementation of decisions can be reduced.

Modeling work at the University of Albany builds primarily on three complementary theoretical paradigms in social psychology: social judgment theory, information integration theory, and the theory of reasoned action. Research in a variety of problem areas has focused on comparing and refining idiothetic approaches to describe individual judgment or choice. For example, because the importance attached to attributes is a fundamental and critical element of most models, considerable attention has been given to determining the strengths and weaknesses of alternative assessment techniques. Modeling is also studied as a useful mechanism for revealing errors and inconsistencies in judgment and choice processes that, if avoided, might lead to improvement in individual as well as collective accomplishments.

Small-Group Interaction Processes

There is no doubt that the study of small-group interaction processes has great pertinence to the development of computer-augmented teamwork. Research in this focal area takes the group, rather than the individual, as the basic unit of analysis. Why are some groups highly effective, whereas others fail to meet even minimal performance standards? What should minimal performance standards be? Given the variety of cognitive challenges faced in organizations, even the question of whether to assign a particular type of task to a group or to an individual is often a critical issue, especially when meetings take valuable time away from other commitments.

Extensive laboratory research on the Albany campus addressing small-group interaction processes has been conducted in three academic departments; marketing, psychology, and public administration. Groups have ranged in size from dyads to seven members, and special facilities have been constructed to permit unobtrusive documentation of meetings by observers and videotape equipment. Significant empirical findings and less formal insights gained as a result of the wealth of experience with laboratory groups have been instrumental in the design of the ten-year demonstration experiment described below. Furthermore, the development of an assessment method for evaluating group decision process effectiveness, detailed at the end of the chapter, has also been supported in large part by ongoing research in this focal area.

A DEMONSTRATION EXPERIMENT
BY THE DECISION TECHTRONICS GROUP

Research concerning cognitive challenges and collective accomplishments in field settings may take several forms. The most common, nonexperimental form of research in field settings is the field study (or fieldwork project). In a field study, decision makers are unobtrusively observed at work in their typical routine. It is the hallmark of a field study that no intervention in the regular decision-making process is planned. When a field study includes only one organizational unit at a single research site, it is known as a case study.

In contrast, field experiments are designed to intervene directly in the decision-making process with the use of treatment (i.e., experimental) and baseline (i.e., control) conditions and the careful control of nuisance variables. Such "true experiments" are uniquely characterized by the random assignment of multiple participants (or multiple groups of participants) to the experimental and control conditions. Because the opportunity for complete randomization is rarely available in field settings, research projects are more commonly designed as quasi-experiments with the use of pretest-posttest designs (i.e., designs that require before and after measures).

Perhaps the least understood and least appreciated experimental method available for field settings is the demonstration experiment (Williamson et al., 1982). Unlike a field study, a demonstration experiment provides for the introduction of an experimental treatment to individual participants or groups of participants. Typically, it includes several interventions of the same type, providing multiple units of analysis, rather than being merely a one-shot case study. Unlike a "true experiment," there are no comparison conditions, no nuisance controls, and no random assignments. A demonstration experiment may make use of before and after measures as in a quasi-experiment, but such a design is not essential. Milgram's (1963) study of authority and obedience represents an outstanding example of the power of the demonstration experiment to produce dramatic findings and valuable insights.

This section describes a ten-year project at the University at Albany that has focused on one type of organization intervention, the decision conference. The research design was developed as a demonstration experiment in a field setting. Findings from the project have led to many important insights about the sources of variation in the level of collective accomplishments observed.

Decision Conferencing for Collective Accomplishment

A decision conference is an intensive, computer-supported meeting, typically scheduled for a two-day period at a site away from the regular workplace to avoid its usual interruptions and distractions. Conference participants, most often 6 to 18 managers or executives, are included in the group because they share a substantial stake in reacting to a pressing organizational problem or in responding proactively to an attractive opportunity. Cognitive challenges at a decision conference span the full range of decision-making activities (Simon, 1960). Participants engage in the highly divergent thinking and parallel processing that are well matched to intelligence tasks (i.e., eliciting information) in problem solving or design work and in the highly convergent thinking and sequential processing that are well matched to choice tasks (i.e., evaluating options). As groups move toward more convergent thinking in decision conferences (in developing a shared understanding of their problem and in achieving consensus on a clear plan of action), they commonly feel an increasing need for greater social and cognitive process support. Decision conferencing especially gives a group greater social and cognitive process support in two ways: through decision modeling and through group facilitation, as shown in Figure 18-1.

The central feature of decision conferencing is the on-the-spot construction of a computer-based model. This model is developed by the participants to incorporate their differing perspectives and priorities and to allow interactive analysis of options and assumptions. Johansen (1988) depicted decision conferencing as broadly synonymous with GDSS; Kraemer and King (1988, p. 123) were more explicit: "What distinguishes the decision conference from the other GDSSs is its explicit focus on improving decision making by groups and its emphasis on the use of structured decision processes...." DeSanctis and Gallupe (1987) described decision conferencing as a Level 2 GDSS because of the extensive use of computer-based models. Each decision conference is designed around the use of one or more software packages to support decision modeling, for example, HIVIEW for multiattribute utility models, ALLOCATE for resource allocation models, POLICY PC for judgment analysis models, STELLA for system dynamic models, SMLTREE for decision trees, and LINDO for mathematical programming (as shown in Figure 18-2). All software is commercially available (see the Product Index).

A second distinguishing feature of decision conferencing is the extensive group support provided by a team of three or more conference facilitators. The primary facilitator, a specialist in the techniques of group dynamics and decision modeling, works directly with the conference participants and takes responsibility for the interaction process by focusing discussion, managing conflict, and enhancing the pattern of communication. By systematically integrating the various aspects of group discussion into a decision model that takes shape on available whiteboards, the facilitator helps the group

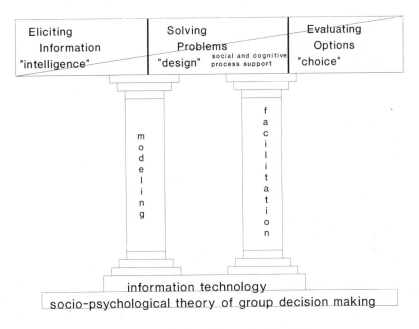

FIGURE 18-1.   Sociopsychological Theory of Group Decision Making

achieve a shared understanding of the pertinent issues. A second facilitator serves as a decision analyst, transferring the decision model from the whiteboards to a microcomputer as the discussion unfolds, periodically providing feedback from the analysis with large-screen computer projection, and updating the model as changes in group understanding or judgment occur. A third facilitator works as a correspondent to monitor this entire process, electronically recording the important details of the group's discussion so that thorough documentation of the deliberation is available at any time during the meeting and as a printed report by conference end.

The information technology employed to support the facilitation team and the model-building activity is a highly portable, chauffeur-driven electronic meeting system. Conference participants are seated in comfortable, executive-style chairs with casters, typically set in a semicircle, to permit a completely connected pattern of face-to-face communication (see Figure 18-3). The arrangement includes several whiteboards and a large projection screen to provide ample workspace (both traditional and electronic) for organizing the many aspects of the problem and for building the decision model. A portion of the room (often to one side or to the back of the group) is set aside for conference support, including at least one microcomputer connected to an LCD panel for large-screen projection and another microcomputer dedicated to maintaining a record of the key aspects of the group's deliberations. Customizing the arrangement of the meeting room for the size and composition of each unique group is essential to enhance interpersonal interaction and creative thinking in decision conferences. Square spaces are more suitable than long, rectangular areas.

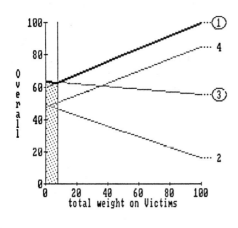

HIVIEW

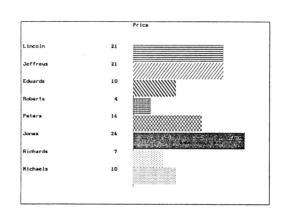

POLICY PC

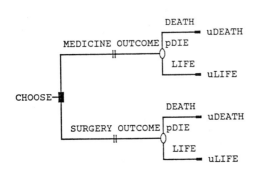

SMLTREE

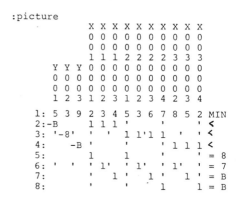

LINDO

FIGURE 18-2.   HIVIEW, POLICY PC, SMILTREE, LINDO, STELLA, ALLOCATE

As participants initially develop their decision model in the first morning of a decision conference, a representation of the group's collective thinking about the problem begins to emerge. Knowledge of the key issues is integrated into the model from available data as well as subjective judgment. Typically, the process of structuring the problem takes much of the first conference day. When the initial version of the model is complete, the computer is used to project its implications for decision making on the large screen so all

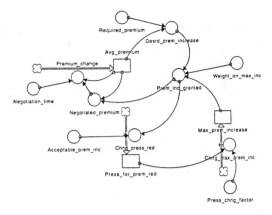

STELLA

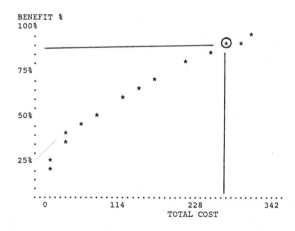

ALLOCATE

FIGURE 18-2.   *(con't)*

participants can give them careful review. Group members can be expected to challenge these initial results since the analysis is frequently at considerable odds with intuition. A good portion of time on the second day of a decision conference is used to collect suggested modifications to the model and to test conflicting judgments, thereby ruling out ineffective strategies and focusing quickly on primary issues of major impact. These sensitivity analyses continue until the group is satisfied that the model captures their best

FIGURE 18-3.   The Decision Conferencing Room at SUNY at Albany

thinking about the problem and consensus is achieved. The model then provides the basis for the wording of a detailed action plan of "next steps that must be taken," backed by a printed summary of the session produced by the correspondent.

Decision conferencing is perhaps the most widely applied type of Level 2 GDSS (Adelman, 1984; Carper and Bresnick, 1989; Phillips, 1984a, 1984b, 1985, 1986, 1988a, 1988b, 1990; Ring, 1980; Weiss and Zwahlen, 1982; Wooler, 1986; Wooler and Barclay, 1988). Fifteen organizations around the world provide decision conferencing as an integrative method for combining information technology, decision modeling, and group facilitation; the total number of decision conferences conducted is estimated to approach 500. Among the more common foci of decision conferences are these:

- Defining organizational goals and priorities
- Making budget allocations
- Establishing five-year strategic plans
- Redesigning service delivery systems
- Developing new methods for performance appraisal
- Evaluating alternative reorganization plans
- Clarifying staffing assignments and priorities
- Predicting long-term effects of financing options
- Determining and allocating office space needs
- Selecting sites
- Identifying new products and markets
- Planning information systems

The History of the Decision Techtronics Group

The Decision Techtronics Group (DTG) at the Rockefeller Institute of Government, University at Albany, is one of the more active centers of decision conferencing. Since its inception, DTG has hosted over 80 decision conferences for private and public sector organizations in the United States and Europe. A majority of these conferences have been conducted for agencies of the State of New York. For this reason, DTG has been recognized for its innovative work in decision support for senior executive teams in government, as well as for the application of a variety of structure and preference technologies (P. Gray, 1987; Kraemer and King, 1988; Meyer and Boone, 1987; Steinbach, 1990; White, 1991).

DTG is an outgrowth of the research on cognitive challenges and collective accomplishments at Albany. In the mid-1970s, the university began a faculty hiring initiative in the Department of Public Administration and Policy to strengthen research and development support to New York State government. The new faculty, brought to Albany to contribute to the university's public service mission, began to create and undertake projects that would better link campus research and development efforts to public management and policy-making.

Most projects initiated by the early 1980s were arranged to provide substantive expertise to meet the needs of a specific state agency. Faculty were to investigate thoroughly a problem and recommend a course of action. However, one small group of faculty explored an alternative consulting model. They conceived of a form of process consultation whereby their expertise in decision modeling, group facilitation, and information technology might support a wide variety of problem-solving efforts by executives and policymakers in any state agency. Whether the policy issue were to be acid rain, AIDS, or solid waste, or the management issue were to be reorganization, training, or paperwork reduction, this faculty group believed that their collective expertise in group decision processes would enable teams of managers and policymakers to solve their own problems more efficiently and effectively. Whereas traditional faculty projects would take 12 to 18 months, their goal was to achieve results in two days.

The design of decision conferencing developed slowly but steadily in this small faculty group. Robert Quinn, a specialist in organizational development, began to offer his services to facilitate executive retreats. John Rohrbaugh, a cognitive social psychologist, began to extend the mathematical representation of individual judgment and decision processes to managerial work groups. David Andersen, a management and systems scientist, began to develop workshops for public policymakers to understand the inherent problems of dynamic systems. Their collaboration in planning and supporting two- and three-day meetings led to a unique blending of group process expertise, including the skills of team building (Quinn), judgment analysis (Rohrbaugh), and computer simulation (Andersen).

The faculty group was aware that a Washington-based consulting firm, Decisions and Designs, Inc., had developed a procedure for bringing computer-supported decision analysis to group meetings. In 1981 Suny at Albany entered into a $50,000 contractual agreement to incorporate Decisions and Designs software and meeting management techniques into its New York State decision support project. The university allocated an additional $20,000 to lease, equip, and publicize a computer-supported meeting room called the Decision Technology Laboratory; its location was in a small, on-campus conference facility. A large, round table capable of seating 16 conference participants was custom-manufactured for the room. Two large, double-sided whiteboards were purchased (the first whiteboards on the campus). Two dedicated telephone lines were installed to provide a connection via modem from a Terak terminal to both on-campus and off-campus mainframes. Large-screen computer projection was provided by a Kalart Tele-Beam projector obtained at no cost from another state university campus.

In February 1982, to indicate his full commitment to the project, Vincent O'Leary, the president of Suny at Albany, inaugurated the facility by convening a computer-supported meeting of all of the campus vice presidents to set their fiscal year 1982–1983 budget. The Albany County Association for Retarded Children was the second organization to use the new decision conferencing approach. Since the computer-supported process was still viewed as experimental and success could not be assured, the association was not charged. During the decision conference the association staff constructed a resource allocation model that led to major shifts in program priorities, with substantial funds directed to new projects. The participants were so delighted with their success that they spontaneously bought a bottle of champagne to celebrate. This was a momentous event for everyone involved.

By the end of the year, the group had conducted four more decision conferences. No longer an experimental process, New York State agencies paid for conferences under a fixed-price arrangement. The New York State Division of the Budget recognized the group as the sole-source provider of a unique service, thus eliminating the need for a lengthy bidding process for contracts with state agencies, and created a special account to handle the group's funds. The formalization of accounts and active conferencing work demanded that the group give itself a permanent name. After considerable deliberation, the name Decision Techtronics Group was chosen to describe the innovation: techtronics—the application of technical methods and electronic equipment to address social and economic problems. The subsequent evolution of DTG is best described in four phases: (1) building credibility, (2) adapting new technology, (3) developing a portable base, and (4) maturing and expanding.

Phase 1: Building Credibility (1982–1983)

After completing the joint work with Decisions and Designs, DTG occupied its on-campus meeting room, which was to be used exclusively for all decision conferencing activity. DTG was chiefly concerned with establishing its legitimacy with state executives. Numerous senior executive teams were invited to the facility to participate in demonstrations and learn about decision conferencing. Data-gathering activities were strictly prohibited to minimize any threat to credibility from a negative impression that participants were the subjects of laboratory-like manipulations. During this period DTG hosted 14 decision conferences for 5 New York State agencies. In addition, 2 decision conferences were conducted for state governments in Rhode Island and Texas.

Phase 2: Adapting New Technology (1984–1985)

Having acquired the first model of the IBM PC, DTG translated its decision modeling software and made the transition to microcomputer technology. Microcomputers allowed DTG to reduce substantially reliance on mainframe and minicomputers with their incumbent problems of unreliable telephone connections, high time-sharing costs, and large size. Additional decision models were added to DTG's repertoire to diversify the range of problems that could be addressed. During this period DTG hosted 13 decision conferences for 8 New York State agencies, and it began to respond to a growing number of requests for computer-supported meetings from not-for-profit and private sector organizations as well.

Phase 3: Developing a Portable Base (1986–1987)

Demand for decision conferencing services at other locations, as well as the availability and reliability of laptop computers and lightweight projection systems, led to the development of portable decision conferencing in 1986 and termination of the leasing arrangement with the on-campus facility. Additional faculty members became involved in DTG, bringing to bear their own facilitation methods and modeling expertise. A base of agency clients was established, resulting in repeated use and word-of-mouth referrals. Research efforts for the first time were coordinated in conjunction with DTG's work to modify and improve the decision conferencing process. DTG conducted 13 decision conferences for 9 state agencies during this period. With the new flexibility allowed, each agency selected a different conference facility for its meetings.

Phase 4: Maturing and Expanding (1988–1991)

Having established a good and consistent record of consultancy performance, DTG sought to strengthen its relationship to state agencies by moving organizationally from the university at Albany to the Rockefeller Institute of Government, the public policy research and government service arm of the university at Albany. Technology transfer projects were undertaken with several organizations that wished to acquire decision conferencing capacity, and a special initiative was begun to explore the applicability of decision conferencing in legislative settings. During this period over 20 different organizations contracted with DTG for one or more decision conferences in 5 states, and demonstration conferences were hosted in Hungary, Chile, and Russia.

Day-to-day operations of DTG are managed currently by an executive director who reports to the deputy director of the Rockefeller Institute. Oversight and guidance for DTG are provided by a Faculty Advisory Committee, consisting of 4 faculty members of the Department of Public Administration and Policy, University at Albany. There are now 11 associates of DTG, including the members of the Faculty Advisory Committee, who provide professional services on a project-specific basis through payroll compensation or per-diem consulting fees. These associates are faculty, staff, and advanced doctoral students of the Department of Public Administration and Policy. Another 5 individuals, earlier associates of DTG but now located at other institutions, also are invited on occasion to support certain decision conferences as special needs require. Administrative support is provided by the Rockefeller Institute.

In 1989 the Rockefeller Institute made available a pool of approximately $40,000 to underwrite decision conferencing for New York State agencies; altogether the total investment of the state university in DTG since 1981 is under $400,000. Currently DTG has no continuity of funding from New York State, and the operating costs for decision conferences are borne entirely by the organizations that schedule them. Fees are approximately $8,000 to $12,000 for a typical two-day decision conference, in addition to facility and travel expenses. Some conferences are conducted for reduced fees when public and not-for-profit agencies cannot afford to pay the full cost (and DTG has accumulated funds that are available to offset expenses).

DTG Applications of Decision Conferencing

The problems tackled by DTG through decision conferencing have been diverse. In Georgia, a decision conference for 30 community leaders was convened to develop a $100 million, 10-year strategic plan for their city. A national professional organization based in Washington, DC, used a decision conference to support the work of a 10-member task force charged with the review of alternative revisions in its dues structure. Three AT&T executives in New Jersey arranged a small decision conference to plan the consolidation of regional offices. A Texas decision conference of 15 child-welfare experts prioritized the urgency of response to individual abuse cases. A state regulatory agency in New York scheduled 2 decision conferences for senior executives to identify their common data-base needs across divisions in preparation for their first integrated information system. In Michigan, a private foundation gathered 35 influential leaders in environmental policy from the private and public sectors statewide to prioritize and endorse a set of funding initiatives for legislative action. A strategy to respond to increases in Vermont's medicaid costs was advanced by a multiagency team developing a system dynamics model of the problem.

As a result of two decision conferences, the New York State Division of Alcoholism and Alcohol Abuse was able to draw on the experience and knowledge of service providers, policymakers, and insurance representatives to refine policy regarding the levels of care required for various treatment programs, to reorganize the delivery system, and to develop a five-year plan for meeting alcoholism treatment needs across the state. The new system is described in the division's report to the governor's office: "Five-Year Comprehensive Plan for Alcoholism Services in New York State 1984–1989" (1987 update). The Governor's Office of Employee Relations, in conjunction with the Public Employees Federation, used decision conferencing to design education curricula for the $3.6 million Public Service Training Program. Both the curricula product and the union and management team development process were recognized as a national model and described at length to the readership of the Public Administration Review (Faerman, Quinn, and Thompson, 1987). The New York Insurance Department arranged a series of decision conferences for developing and evaluating policy options to deal with the medical malpractice insurance crisis. Based on the foundation of their work during three separate meetings, the department issued its report to the New York State Legislature: "A Balanced Prescription for Change: Report of the New York State Insurance Department on Medical Malpractice." This application won an excellence award in the Second International Competition for Outstanding DSS Applications and Achievements from the Institute of Management Sciences.

Beginning in 1985, DTG has taken an interest in advancing group decision support in legislative settings. The first DTG initiative was to assist the Temporary State Commission on Returnable Beverage Containers, constituted by the New York State Legislature to recommend changes in the so-called "Bottle Bill." More recently, DTG facilitated the New York State Assembly Conference on the Future of Fire Protection, with over 70 representatives of 17 different organizations, including professional associations, unions, industry associations, local government associations, and state agencies as well as members of the Assembly. Since 1988, DTG has worked in collaboration with the University at Albany Center for Legislative Development (CLD) to advance parliamentary adoption of group decision support in other countries. For example, a demonstration conference in Valparaiso, Chile, was conducted for consideration as a consensus-building method in the newly forming Chilean Parliament. Two decision conferences have also been hosted by DTG and CLD in Budapest for the new Hungarian Parliament, the first for prioritizing information system needs, the second for agreeing on research emphases to support the preparation of the national budget.

DTG also has demonstrated that other organizations can successfully establish their own decision conferencing service. The first technology transfer project was undertaken by DTG with the Institute for Community and Area Development at the University of Georgia. The institute hired one of DTG's founding associates who had facilitated some of the early decision conferences in Albany. In 1987, DTG helped to train additional facilitators in Georgia, provided essential software, and jointly conducted several decision conferences with the institute. Now decision conferencing is one of the major services that the institute offers the state government and local governments in Georgia. Its recent work with the Georgia Growth Planning Commission, featured in the June 1991 issue of *Governing*, provides clear evidence of the success of this initiative. Technology transfer of decision conferencing has also been offered to the private sector. In 1988, managers in AT&T Bell Laboratories expressed interest to DTG in developing a decision conferencing capacity to expand the management support services provided by the Kelley Training and Education Center. Five decision conferences within AT&T were jointly conducted by DTG and Kelley staff over a two-year period, leading to a decision conferencing capacity in Bell Laboratories that is now fully self-sufficient and in continuing demand (Cassidy, 1988; Cassidy, Conway, and Rodriguez, 1988).

DTG was included in an evaluation study of computer-augmented teamwork conducted by N. Dean Meyer and Associates, Inc., an independent consulting firm specializing in strategic use of information technologies. The reported results (Meyer and Boone, 1987, pp. 246–259) estimated one-year returns on investment between 400% to 2,800% to DTG clients using decision conferencing and concluded that "...we expect to see the rise of 'decision centers' with the right tools and trained support staffs, such as the DTG at SUNY Albany." The highest honor that DTG has received, however, came in 1990 from the National Committee on Innovations in State and Local Government, an awards program of the Ford Foundation and Harvard University. DTG was selected as a finalist program (from over 1,500 nominated programs nationally) for its innovative work in government decision support. Former Michigan Governor William Milliken, chair of the National Committee, observed, "The 1990 Innovations finalists exemplify the best in American government today. Each demonstrates that resourceful leadership is alive and well in states and localities throughout the nation."

THE EVALUATION OF GROUP DECISION PROCESSES

Despite the positive responses to the work of DTG, rigorous evaluation of the effectiveness of group process interventions such as decision conferencing is problematic. Most often a single decision process is assessed by case study, noting the outcomes that occur following the decision itself. This use of outcome-oriented evaluation flows from the belief that good outcomes are produced by good decisions and bad outcomes are produced by bad decisions. In fact, there is little doubt that the value of a decision depends on the confluence of subsequent events: A revenue forecast is accurate only if actual revenues match the projection; the worth of an investment depends wholly on the return it produces. Such widely accepted tautologies (i.e., that good decisions are good or that bad decisions are bad) beg the much more fundamental and important question of whether ineffective decision processes sometimes result in good outcomes. It is quite possible that a most unreasonable group process will be linked over time with a windfall, whereas in another instance a most reasonable approach to collective choice will fall far wide of the mark.

The decision process of a group, unlike the decision itself (made as a result of such a process), cannot be evaluated readily on the basis of observed outcomes except in the most carefully controlled social experiments. Such research designs (i.e., those that assess the effectiveness of a particular form of decision process based on outcome data) must be able to rule out not only the possibility that alternative group interventions at work in the same environment could produce equally satisfactory outcomes but also the possibility that alternative decisions could do as well or better than the actual choice made by the group.

Linking the "goodness" of outcomes to particular decision processes is extraordinarily difficult, especially if the intention is to identify a set of interventions that will improve the effectiveness of a variety of managerial groups or executive teams. The research design at a minimum would need to involve multiple teams working on multiple tasks in multiple ways and producing multiple decision rules (not just one preferred rule) that could be tested over multiple periods of time. Even if such a research program were to provide empirical support (on the basis of outcomes) for the relative superiority of a particular decision process in a specific organizational setting, the preferred use of the same decision process could not be reasonably generalized to other circumstances. Therefore, any assessment of the effectiveness of a group decision process requires directing primary attention to the process itself, not to subsequent outcomes. Yet when group research took a process focus in the 1950s and 1960s (as in interaction process analysis, for example), virtually all investigation was descriptive rather than evaluative, with primary attention given to individual behavior rather than to collective performance (Zander, 1979). Such study typically depends on some method of content coding the remarks of each participant (Bales and Cohen, 1979; Sillars, Coletti, and Rogers, 1982;

Sims and Manz, 1984); rarely, however, are these data used to draw conclusions about the performance of the whole membership as a single unit of analysis, that is, to assess the effectiveness of the group decision process.

Steiner (1972) reintroduced an evaluative dimension to the study of group work when he clarified the relation among task demands, group structure (e.g., size and composition), and group productivity. Steiner's reemphasis on groups as task-performing systems once again directed the attention of the field to the need for assessment measurement, but his focus on the group as the unit of analysis was, as in the 1930s and 1940s, much less on process than on the outcome of task-related work: quantity of ideas, proportion of correct solutions, number of games won, or accuracy of prediction. McGrath (1984) continued to stress the need for task-based theories of group performance, but despite more inclusive treatment of the "acting group" (i.e., group interaction processes), he relied almost as exclusively as Steiner on outcome measures to infer regularities of collective performance, a very singular approach to an improved understanding of group decision process effectiveness. What is required is a larger conceptual framework with multiple criteria by which to judge the effectiveness of group interaction in decision making. The competing values approach (CVA) provides such a framework.

The Competing Values Approach

The conceptual framework used to investigate small-group decision processes is based on CVA (Lewin and Minton, 1986; Quinn, 1988; Quinn and Rohrbaugh, 1981, 1983). The earliest work in developing the CVA was a multidimensional scaling project that identified 3 axes undergirding judgments about the similarity of 16 commonly used criteria for assessing collective performance effectiveness (Quinn and Rohrbaugh, 1981); the same 3 dimensional space was found again as the result of a larger replication study of organizational researchers and theorists (Quinn and Rohrbaugh, 1983).

Figure 18-4 graphically illustrates the coordinates of the 16 assessment criteria provided by the replication study. The first dimension (the horizontal or x-axis) was interpreted as reflecting differing collective preferences for *focus* by representing the contrast between an internal, person-oriented emphasis (toward the left) and an external, environmentally oriented emphasis (toward the right). The second dimension (the vertical or y-axis) was interpreted as reflecting differing collective preferences for *structure* by representing the contrast between an interest in flexibility and change (toward the top) and stability and control (toward the bottom). The third dimension (a depth or distality axis) was interpreted as reflecting the degree of closeness to desired collective outcomes, or a *means-ends* continuum, by representing the contrast between a concern for ends (nearer and larger) and a concern for means (farther away and smaller).

Research on the CVA has demonstrated that the criteria commonly used to assess collective performance effectiveness reflect alternative priorities for any group or organization. The need for *flexibility* competes with the need for operational *control*; attention to *internal* organizational issues competes with attention to conditions *external* to the organization; and an emphasis on process and procedures (as *means*) competes with an emphasis on outcomes or objectives (as *ends*). Of course, these dimensions are

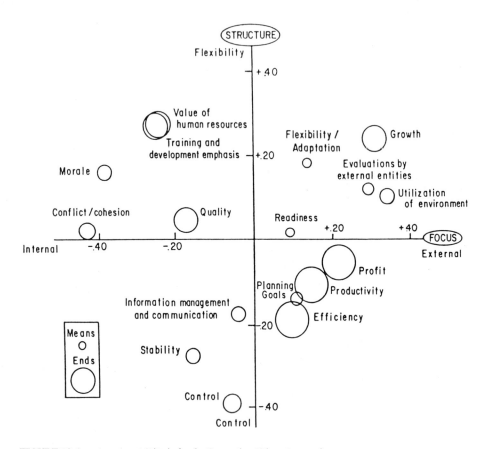

FIGURE 18-4.   Assesment Criteria for the Competing Values Approach

not unique to the CVA since they define three sets of competing values that have been long recognized in the study of collective performance. For example, Lawrence and Lorsch (1967) identified these dimensions as *structure, interpersonal orientation,* and *time,* and they used them to explore and explain differences that were observed in the way that managers think and work.

The unique contribution of the CVA, however, lies in the connection drawn between the three value dimensions of organizational analysis and Parsons's theory of functional prerequisites for any system of action (Hare, 1976; Parsons, 1959). As shown in Figure 18-5 the orthogonal representation of the first two dimensions of competing values (i.e., focus and structure) yields four distinct models of organizational analysis in quadrants that parallel Parson's specification of functional prerequisites:

- *Rational goal model* (where the primary function is goal attainment)
- *Open systems model* (where the primary function is adaptation)

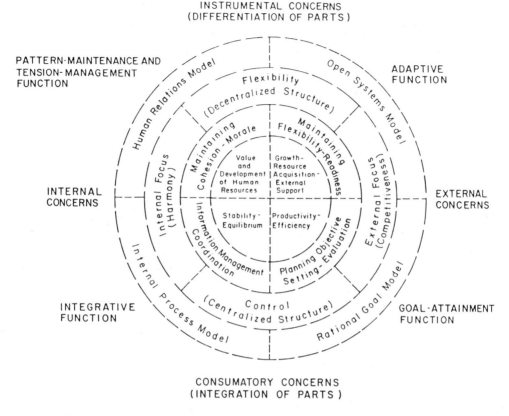

FIGURE 18-5.   The Orthogonal Representation of the Competing Values Approach

- *Human relations model* (where the primary function is pattern maintenance and tension management)
- *Internal process model* (where the primary function is integration)

The third value dimension, the means-ends continuum, is reflected in each model since each model is concerned with both process and outcome effectiveness. For example, from the perspective of the rational goal model, better planning is the means by which greater efficiency is achieved; the effectiveness of a group or organization would be assessed with attention to both its planning processes and its efficiency outcomes.

Competing Values in Group Decision Process Effectiveness

Similar competing values also appear to undergird the evaluation of group decision process effectiveness. Four distinct perspectives concerning effective decision making have been identified in extending the CVA framework to a group setting:

- *Rational perspective* (corresponding to the rational goal model)
- *Political perspective* (corresponding to the open systems model)
- *Consensual perspective* (corresponding to the human relations model)
- *Empirical perspective* (corresponding to the internal process model)

The four perspectives reflect competing values because they emphasize what often appear as conflicting demands on any decision-making process. The values most salient to the political perspective (instrumental, external concerns) differ strikingly from those most salient to the empirical perspective (consummatory, internal concerns); similarly, the values undergirding the consensual perspective (instrumental, internal concerns) are distinct from those undergirding the rational perspective (consummatory, external concerns). For this reason, individual evaluators of group decision process effectiveness might be expected to emphasize performance criteria that reflect their own values.

Evaluators of collective decision processes who take a rational perspective (primarily focused on external, consummatory concerns) emphasize clear thinking as the primary ingredient for effective decision making. From this very task-oriented perspective (particularly common in the management sciences), any decision process should be directed by explicit recognition of organizational goals and objectives. Methods that efficiently assist decision makers with improving the consistency and coherency of their logic and reasoning would be highly valued.

Evaluators of collective decision processes who take a political perspective (primarily focused on external, instrumental concerns) encourage flexibility and creativity in approaches to problems. Idea generation (brainstorming) would be judged on how attuned participants were to shifts in the problem environment and on how well the standing of the group was maintained or enhanced. The search for legitimacy of the decision (i.e., its acceptability to outside interest groups and external stakeholders) would be notable through a fully adaptable process.

Evaluators of collective decision processes who take a consensual perspective (primarily focused on internal, instrumental concerns) expect full participation in meetings that allow open expression of individual feelings and sentiments. Extended discussion and debate about conflicting concerns should lead to collective agreement on a mutually satisfactory solution. As a result, the likelihood of support for the decision during implementation would be increased through such team building. This very interpersonally oriented perspective is dominant in the field of organization development.

Evaluators of collective decision processes who take an empirical perspective (primarily focused on internal, consummatory concerns) would stress the importance of evidence in a decision process. Particular attention should be directed to securing relevant information and developing large and reliable data bases to provide decision support. Proponents of this perspective, typically trained in the physical and social sciences (especially management information systems), believe that to be effective a decision process should allow thorough documentation and full accountability.

The recognition of four distinct perspectives concerning effective decision processes is not unique to CVA. Churchman (1971), for example, suggested four basic forms of inquiring systems: formal-deductive (Leibnizian), synthetic-representational (Kantian), dialectical-conflictual (Hegelian), and empirical-inductive (Lockean). In a similar vein, Mitroff and Mason (1982) contrasted four aspects of group policy-making: rational, interpretive, existential, and empirical. Drawing on Jung's (1959) identification of cognitive functions, Taggart and Robey (1981) noted four dominant decision-making styles: a logical (intuition/thinking), insightful (intuition/feeling), sympathetic (sensation/feeling), and matter of fact (sensation/thinking). Zakay (1984) even offered initial evidence of these perspectives with a factor analysis of 25 items making up his Decisions' Goodness Questionnaire. He reported that 4 factors explained about two-thirds of the variance in the evaluation of decision processes by 145 industrial managers, and he labeled the factors subjective rationality, realism and resources, feelings and social compromise, and information utilization. These distinctions are summarized within the CVA framework shown in Figure 18-6.

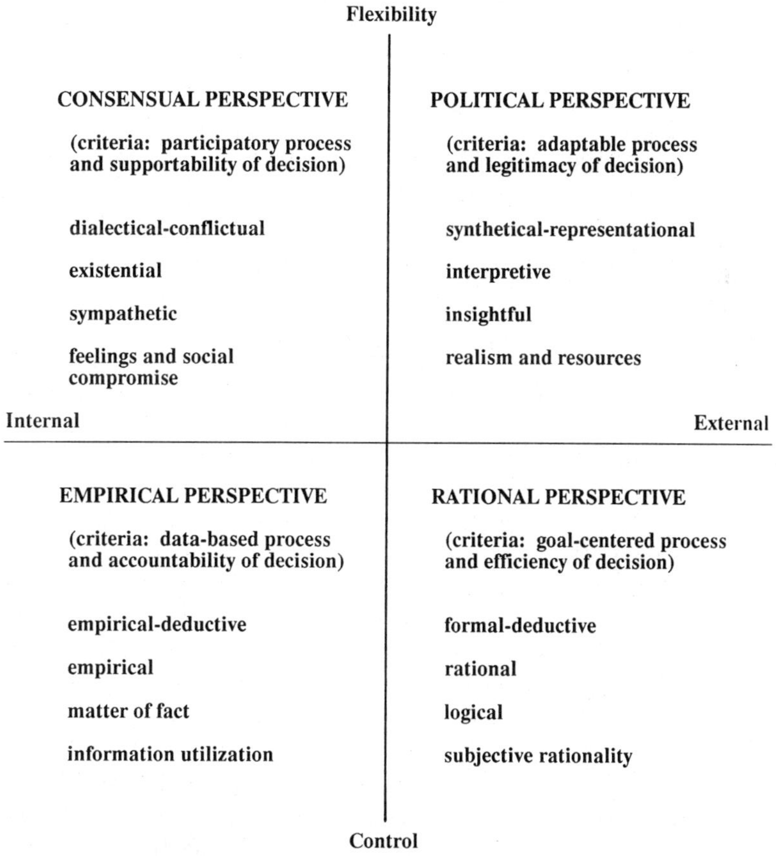

Flexibility

CONSENSUAL PERSPECTIVE

(criteria: participatory process
and supportability of decision)

dialectical-conflictual

existential

sympathetic

feelings and social
compromise

POLITICAL PERSPECTIVE

(criteria: adaptable process
and legitimacy of decision)

synthetical-representational

interpretive

insightful

realism and resources

Internal   External

EMPIRICAL PERSPECTIVE

(criteria: data-based process
and accountability of decision)

empirical-deductive

empirical

matter of fact

information utilization

RATIONAL PERSPECTIVE

(criteria: goal-centered process
and efficiency of decision)

formal-deductive

rational

logical

subjective rationality

Control

FIGURE 18-6.   Four Perspectives of Effective Decision Making for the Competing Values Approach

The Measurement of Group Decision Process Effectiveness

It can be argued, consistent with the CVA framework, that there are individual differences in perspective concerning the assessment of group decision process effectiveness. For example, the overall performance of a particular decision-making group reported from a consensual perspective (i.e., in which a participatory process and supportability of the decision would be most highly valued) might be rated differently if observed from a rational perspective (i.e., in which a goal-centered process and efficiency of the decision would be most highly valued). One of the potential contributions of the CVA framework is to encourage the use of a larger array of evaluative criteria that do not implicitly favor one set of organizational or group values over another.

Each of the four perspectives has been identified with at least two dominant criteria (one more oriented toward means, the other toward ends) by which group decision processes typically are evaluated. Eight valid and reliable scales have been developed to measure group members' self-reported assessments about specific facets of their collective work: (1) a goal-centered process and (2) efficiency of decision (as if from a rational perspective); (3) an adaptable process and (4) legitimacy of decision (as if from a political perspective); (5) a participatory process and (6) supportability of decision (as if from a consensual perspective); and (7) a data-based process and (8) accountability of decision (as if from an empirical perspective). Decision process profiles can be created by plotting scale scores for the eight effectiveness criteria on the axes as shown in Figure 18-6. When perceptions of a decision process are more positive, the profile is extended outward on the axis. Concavities in the profile indicate aspects of decision process effectiveness that are perceived as being comparatively more negative.

Profiles of group decision process effectiveness criteria as illustrated in Figure 18-7 have been used for a variety of purposes. As a diagnostic tool, for example, such profiles indicate how group members agree (or disagree) about the strengths and weaknesses of the decision processes they commonly experience. For the purpose of design, an "ideal" profile is drawn to elicit specific goals and objectives for incrementally adjusting or completely restructuring the form of collaborative work. By redrawing profiles for the same group across an extended period of time (or at least across multiple decision-making situations), unwanted shifts in effectiveness can be uncovered and explicitly addressed (e.g., trends toward greater inefficiency or less access to data). Perhaps the most common application of the profiles is to assess the added value of specific interventions (such as a decision conference) in the routine decision making of a management group or executive team: On what dimensions of process effectiveness are self-reports more or less positive?

One clear finding in evaluating the DTG demonstration experiment in this manner is that decision conferencing is perceived by most management groups and executive teams as both a highly participatory and highly goal-centered process. This is a particularly noteworthy result since the CVA framework would predict considerable difficulty in simultaneously achieving both. Groups and organizations repeatedly have

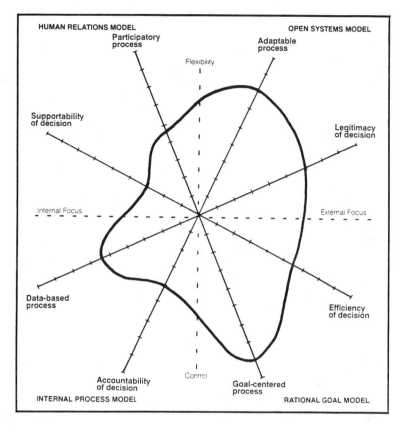

FIGURE 18-7.   Profiles of Group Decision Process Effectiveness Criteria

found that the tensions in value between the *flexibility structure/internal focus* of the consensual quadrant and the *control structure/external focus* of the rational quadrant are extremely difficult to resolve. In designing a group decision intervention that provides contemporaneously for participation and goal-centeredness, the DTG demonstration experiment has indicated that certain forms of computer-augmented teamwork may be able to meet one of the more difficult organizational challenges: producing a succulent broth in a kitchen full of gratified cooks.

ACKNOWLEDGEMENT

The contributions of my colleagues David Andersen, David Brinberg, James Jaccard, Jeryl Mumpower, George Richardson, Thomas Stewart, and Anna Vari are gratefully acknowledged. I apologize to them for being unable to document in this chapter the full magnitude and quality of their scholarship.

APPENDIX 18–A[1]
EXPERT ESTIMATION AND FORECASTING

Lusk, D. M., T. R. Stewart, K. R. Hammond, and R. I. Potts (1990).

Moninger, W. R., J. Bullas, B. deLorenzis, E. Ellison, J. Flueck, J. C. McLeod, C. Lusk, P. D. Lampru, W. F. Roberts, R. Shaw, T. R. Stewart, J. Weaver, K. C. Young, and S. H. Zubrick.

Mumpower, J. L. (1985).

Mumpower, J. L. (1987).

Mumpower, J. L., S. Livingston, and P. Lee (1987).

Mumpower, J. L., L. Phillips, O. Renn, and V. R. R. Uppuluri, (1987).

Stewart, T. R. (1991).

Stewart, T. R. (1990).

Stewart, T. R., and M. Glantz (1985).

Stewart, T. R., and C. R. B. Joyce (1988).

Stewart, T. R., and C. McMillan, Jr. (1987).

Stewart, T. R., W. R. Moninger, J., Grassia, R. H. Brady, and F. H. Merrem (1989).

Vari, A., and J. Vecsenyi (1984).

Vari, A., and J. Vecsenyi (1988).

MULTIPARTY CONFLICT MANAGEMENT AND ANALYTICAL MEDIATION

Darling, T. A., and J. L. Mumpower (1990).

Darling, T. A., and G. P. Richardson (1990).

Farago, K., A. Oldfield, and A. Vari (1988).

Farago, K., A. Vari, and J. Vecsenyi (1989).

Mumpower, J. L. (1988).

Mumpower, J. L., and T. A. Darling (1991).

Mumpower, J. L., S. P. Schuman and A. Zumbolo (1988).

Rohrbaugh, J., McClelland, G., and R. Quinn (1986).

Vari, A. (1991).

Vari, A. (1988).

Vari, A. and K. Fargo (1991).

Vari, A., J. Vecsenyi and Z. Paprika (1986).

SIMULATION AND SYSTEM DYNAMICS

Andersen, D. F. (1982).

Andersen, D. F. (1990).

Andersen, D. F., I. J., Chung, T. R. Stewart, G. P. Richardson (1990).

Aderson, D. and J. Rohrbaugh (in press).

---

[1]See the Bibliography at the back of the book for full details for each citation.

Richardson, G. P. (1986).

Richardson, G. P. (1991)

Richardson, G. (1991b).

Richardson, G. P. and R. E. Lamitie (1989).

Richardson, G. and A. Pugh (1981).

Richardson, G. P., and J. Rohrbaugh, (1990).

Richardson, G. and P. Senge (1989).

Richardson, G. P., J. A. M. Vennix, E. F., Andersen, J., Rohrbaugh, and W. A. Wallace (1989).

Rohrbaugh, J. and D. F. Andersen (1983).

Vennix, J. D. Anderson, G. Richardson & J. Rohrbaugh (in press).

MODELING OF JUDGMENT AND CHOICE

Balzer, W. X., J. Rohrbaugh, and K. R. Murphy (1983).

Brinberg, D. (1981).

Brinberg, D. and V. Cummings (1984).

Brinberg, D., and J. Durand (1983).

Jaccard, J., and M. Becker (1985).

Jaccard, J., D. Brinberg and L. J. Ackerman (1986).

Jaccard, J., and D. Sheng (1984).

Jaccard, J., and C. Wan (1986).

Jaccard, J., C. Wan and G. Wood (1988).

Jaccard, J., and G. Wood (1988).

McCartt, A. T. (1986).

Mumpower, J. L., and B. F. Anderson (1983).

Stewart, T. R. (1988).

Stewart, T. R., and T. Leschine (1986).

Stewart, T. R., P. Middleton, and O. Ely (1983).

SMALL GROUP INTERACTION PROCESSES

Brinberg, D., and J. Jaccard (1989).

Brinberg, D., and N. Schwenk (1985).

Eden, C. F., and J. Rohrbaugh (1990).

Harmon, J., and J. Rohrbaugh (1990).

Jaccard, J., D. Brinberg, and P. Dittus (1989).

Reagan-Cirincione, P. (1992).

Reagan, P., and J. Rohrbaugh (1990).

Rohrbaugh, J. (1981).

Rohrbaugh, J. (1987).

Rohrbaugh, J. (1988).

Rohrbaugh, J. (1984).

Stewart, T. R. (1987).

DECISION CONFERENCING

McCartt, A. T., and J. Rohrbaugh (1989).

Milter, R. G. (1986).

Milter, R. G., and J. Rohrbaugh (1985).

Milter, R. G., and J. Rohrbaugh (1988).

Quinn, R. E., J. Rohrbaugh, and M. R. McGrath (1985).

Reagan-Cirincione, P., and J. Rohrbaugh (1991).

Reagan-Cirincione, P., S. Schuman, S. Richardson, and S. Dorf (1991).

Rohrbaugh, J. (1989a).

Rohrbaugh, J. (1989b).

Schuman, S., and J. Rohrbaugh (1991).

Vari, A., and J. Vecsenyi (in press).

Vari, A., and J. Vecsenyi (1990).

Vari, A., and J. Vecsenyi (1986).

Chapter 19

Strategy Development and Implementation—The Role of a Group Decision Support System

Colin Eden and Fran Ackermann

University of Strathclyde

I believe...that in deciding where you would like to be, as opposed to where you are probably going to end up, you need a great deal of discussion and a great deal of development of new thinking and new processes. The idea of doing this through the planning department, or through a paper on strategy presented to the board, seems to me to be quite inadequate. This process involves large amounts of time and constant discussion with those involved lower down the line who will actually execute the strategies on which the whole picture relies. This sort of circular debate, frequently widening out to involve others within and without the company, goes on until all are satisfied that the result is as good as they are going to get. (John Harvey-Jones, 1988, until recently chief executive of Imperial Chemical Industries or ICI).

This chapter is about the role of computers and special-purpose computer software in facilitating the type of discussion Harvey-Jones talks about. The role of the computer is twofold—to help groups in the organization with the discussion of strategy through the provision of a group decision support system (GDSS) and to provide members of an executive team with a sort of executive information system (EIS), which can help with the implementation of strategy.

One of the greatest difficulties facing chief executives in creating a sound strategy for their organization is not the development of the strategy but rather making the strategy have any real impact throughout the organization. The resolution of the difficulty rarely lies in making the strategy more correct from the point of view of its content, but in gaining commitment, ownership, and appropriate strategic control. The key lies in being able fundamentally to change strategic *thinking* in the organization. Indeed "strategic planning often gets in the way of strategic thinking" (Bryson, 1988). Decision conferencing (Phillips, 1990) and other group decision support systems, such as the one reported here, are making progress by locking together the *processes* of strategy development *and* implementation. That is, computer *and* facilitator-aided group processes are allowing more data to be carefully managed within the context of the sort of group activities that promote higher levels of ownership (Eden, 1992). The strategy is more robust because it has absorbed more of the experience, wisdom, and judgments of a wider cross section of the organization.

A number of recent projects, in both public and private sector organizations, that are using the GDSS method discussed here have involved up to 200 managers in a direct input to the development of the strategy for their organization. Their participation in an overtly analytical process for dealing with their wisdom, and the consequent belief that they have had an opportunity to *influence* the strategy, generates high levels of ownership. By bringing to the surface the realities as seen by those further down in the organization, it not only provides ownership but also counters the risks of locked-in perspectives that derive from the mind of the organization at the top.

> One reason why you should try to develop the direction in which you think the company should go from both ends of the company at once is that in the process you gain the commitment of those who will have to follow the direction—and "make it happen"—and in a free society you are unlikely to get this commitment without a high degree of involvement and understanding of both where the ultimate goal is, and the process by which the decisions regarding that goal have been reached. (Harvey-Jones, 1988).

Returning to the introductory quotation, we will now consider some of the characteristics of strategy development. In the light of these characteristics we will consider the role of computer assistance (group decision support)—specifically the role of a *methodology* known as Strategic Options Development and Analysis (SODA) (Ackermann, 1990; Eden, 1989a) and special purpose *software* (COPE) (Cropper, Eden, and Ackermann, 1990), which allows a group to play with ideas about strategy through the real-time interaction with graphic computer representations and analyses of the data. In addition we will consider how the computer model constructed to support groups becomes an executive support system to the process of strategic control. We will also discuss some of the prerequisites for the successful use of group decision support systems and executive information systems in organizations.

THE NATURE OF STRATEGY DEVELOPMENT

Strategy development usually involves some or all of the following activities, which can be usefully undertaken with a group:

- Articulating *strategic vision*
- Identifying major *strategic issues* facing the organization
- Generating *options* and building *scenarios*
- Identifying *stakeholders* and their possible response in relation to their own goals

These activities represent the groundwork of strategy building, followed by the following:

- Developing an appropriate *goal system* for the organization
- Setting *strategies* within the context of the goal system
- Establishing a series of *strategic programs* related to the strategies and representing an action package
- Creating a *mission statement* in relation to the above
- Developing a *strategic control system* involving a review of strategic performance and the performance of strategy

If attention is paid to the major problems of implementing strategy—making it work for the organization—these processes may advantageously involve large numbers of staff within the organization. Indeed it is typical for our own work with organizations, in both the private and public sector, to use a cascading series of strategy workshops that usually involve between 40 and 200 staff members. At several stages during these "bottom-up" group workshops, the senior executive team will meet to evaluate and analyze the content generated. Sometimes the executive team may work with the output of 10 to 20 workshops: on other occasions they may work only with the content generated by the executive team members themselves.

This continuing process of strategy development and review is depicted by Figures 19-1 and 19-2. Figure 19-1 shows the conceptual relationship among the different parts of the strategy; the mission statement is at the center of a hierarchy of supporting strategies, each of which contains a system of strategic objectives or goals, which are in turn supported by a system of strategic programs that locate portfolios of actions. The strategy is thus a hierarchical system of interacting and interrelating means and ends, where each means may affect multiple ends. Some ends can be conceptualized as a strategy or key goal ("Take risks with people earlier"); a strategic objective, or goal ("Ensure acquisitions match staff expectations"); or a strategic program ("Reduce risks of jeopardizing careers").

Figure 19-2 shows how the process of strategy development and review typically involves a combination of workshops both across and down the organization. Workshops that identify strategic issues and establish strategic programs tend to involve a group selected from across the organization (horizontal cut) and involve key actors in relation to the issues to be addressed. Workshops that are more concerned with collecting the wisdom and experience of staff lower down the line tend to involve a team associated with particular products or tasks (vertical cut).

The executive team members are central to whatever processes are used for strategy development, and it is they who are likely to gain the most significant benefit from computer-aided group decision support. This chapter describes some aspects of the use of SODA and COPE to provide such support. The approach has been used in a wide variety of different formats, depending on the nature of the organization—culture,

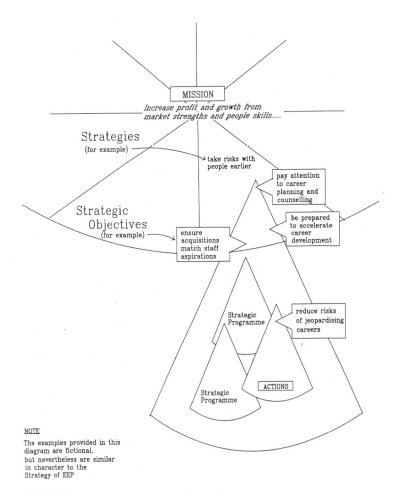

FIGURE 19-1.   Schematic Representing the Relationship Among Mission, Strategies, Strategic Objectives, and Strategic Programs

personal style of the chief executive, level of sophistication in strategic management, and time and money available. The support system has been used in such organizations as Reed International (Eden, Ackermann, and Timm, 1990), Shell (Eden, 1990a), and British Telecom Prison Service (Eden and Cropper, 1991); in government departments such as the Northern Ireland Office and National Health Service (Telford, Ackermann, and Cropper, 1990); and in multiorganizational settings (Pizey and Huxham, 1991).

SODA (THE METHOD) AND COPE (THE SOFTWARE) AS A GDSS AND EIS

The conceptual framework described above is founded on the notion that strategy development concerns the discovery of how to *manage and control the future*. It involves

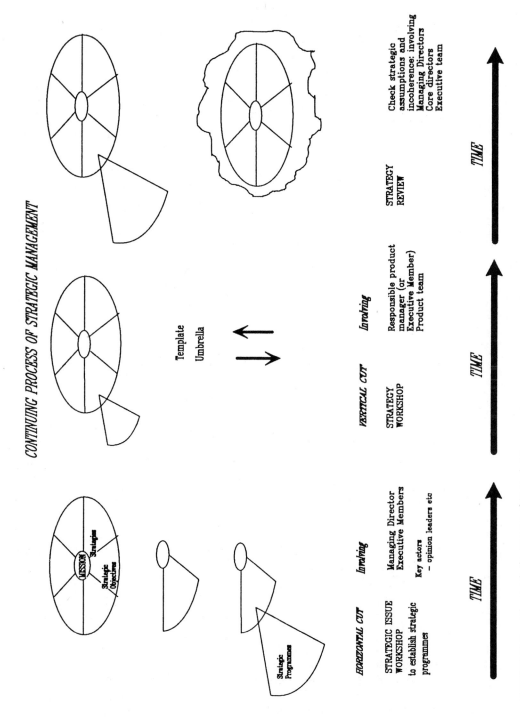

CONTINUING PROCESS OF STRATEGIC MANAGEMENT

HORIZONTAL CUT	Involving	VERTICAL CUT	Involving
STRATEGIC ISSUE WORKSHOP to establish strategic programmes	Managing Director Executive Members Key actors – opinion leaders etc	STRATEGY WORKSHOP	Responsible product manager (or Executive Member) Product team

STRATEGY REVIEW — Check strategic assumptions and incoherence: involving Managing Directors Core directors Executive team

Template
Umbrella

MISSION
Strategies
Strategic Objectives
Strategic Programmes

TIME   TIME   TIME

FIGURE 19-2.   The Continuing Process of Strategic Management

329

capturing the experience and wisdom of organizational members about how they believe an attractive vision of the future can be attained. Strategic thinking is thus action-oriented and concerned with identifying how to intervene in the incrementalism of the organization itself and its relationship with the environment. It is about discovering the means that can create desired ends. The data are the outcome of managers thinking about the future, and thinking about the future involves creating new knowledge about the relationship between the organization and its environment and questioning the underlying "industry recipe" (Spender, 1989) that is implicitly guiding emerging strategy (Mintzberg and Waters, 1985). These theories are based on experience and wisdom rather than precise forecasts or quantitative analyses. Judgments are made about how the market and the organization *will* be working.

The data of strategic thinking therefore, will be dominated by a qualitative belief system that represents theories about why the world works and thus how it can be changed. The need to recognize the complex interaction among the multiple beliefs of organizational members reflects the reality of every goal being qualified by others and every strategy being constrained and enhanced by a network of other strategies.

SODA and the Discovery of a Strategic Belief System

As indicated, the process of collecting experience and wisdom involves a series of workshops. Usually each workshop includes between 6 and 24 people who will be invited to *influence* the strategy of the organization through the identification of strategic issues and emerging goals.

The group decision support *system* (GDSS) is generally a combination of "nominal group techniques" (Delbecq, Van de Ven, and Dustafson, 1975); "dominos/sno-cards" (Backoff and Nutt, 1988; Eden, Jones, and Sims, 1983), and the specially designed graphics-based software (COPE) for recording, analysis, and display. Participants work in groups of six to ten people and are encouraged to use "dominos" (20 by 10-cm cards shaped as ellipses) to record and display their own views of the strategic issues facing the organization in the context of the views of other members of the group.

As participants display their ellipses on the wall in front of them, they are continuously structured by the facilitator, with help from participants, into clusters of related statements. They are also implicitly arranged by the facilitator into a hierarchically arranged means-ends structure so that the most superordinate end is at the top and the most detailed means or option is at the bottom. Each cluster of statements represents an *emerging strategic issue* identified by the group. The group members are encouraged to elaborate and contradict the emerging view of issues that are being created on the wall. Figure 19–3 shows an example of a developing cluster.

The clusters, their content, and the interrelationship between content within clusters and among clusters are recorded by the computer software. This is simply a record of a means-ends hierarchy—assertions about the future and their consequences. In practice the recorder will modify what is written on the ellipses so that each assertion indicates an intervention to change the world, that is, suggests a call to action. The software records each statement as a numbered concept and records the linkage among concepts in the

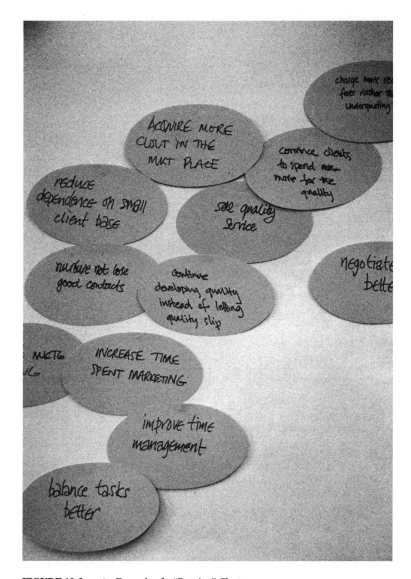

FIGURE 19-3.   An Example of a "Domino" Cluster

form of a directed graph or cause map (Huff, 1990)—concepts as nodes linked together by arrows. Figure 19-4 shows a cluster being recorded and represented on the computer screen. The record of material generated during this early stage of issue identification is not classified into goals, strategies, actions, and so on but rather remains as raw data (the computer record is in the default typeface and color—yellow).

The request to focus on issues is designed to grab the attention of participants by allowing them to express "firefighting" concerns (Eden, 1990b) they each have about the

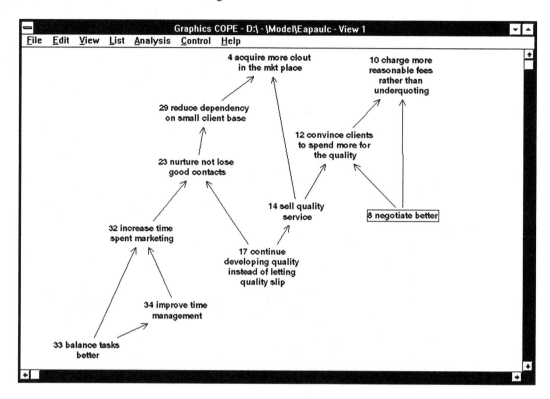

FIGURE 19-4.   A Cluster Recorded by COPE

future. This practice may promote a temptation to refer continually to the present (and thus past) nature of the world as it is expressed by the "corporate rain dance" of the annual planning process rather than to build explicit theories that are genuinely prospective. However, the use of dominos to record discussion is aimed at encouraging individuality while developing creativity and synergy alongside synthesis and reducing the probability of group-think (Eden, 1992).

Focusing on strategic issues rather than the development of idealized scenarios or preferred goals is deliberately designed to ensure that strategy becomes something more than "motherhood and apple pie." The clusters are specific theories that apply to the world of the participants' specific organization rather than to any organization. It also reduces the possibility of participants discussing "espoused theories," derived from attendance at management courses, rather than the theories of action that will drive future decision making (Argyris, 1983; Bartunek and Moch, 1987).

Emerging Strategic Goals

The second stage of work is focused on the identification of emerging strategic goals. Participants are encouraged to take a holistic view of each cluster and consider the goals that are implicit through the identification of a cluster as a strategic issue. When members of the group have emotionally and psychologically envisioned issues that must be resolved, they will be implicitly or subconsciously presuming a desired direction for the organization. This stage of the workshop is designed to make explicit these assumptions about direction; hence they are the *emerging strategic goals of the organization.*

These goals are usually written onto Post-its (to differentiate them from the issue content) and are organized hierarchically in relation to each cluster in turn. It is at this stage that the clusters become explicitly related to one another, for each goal informs others, some of which are superordinate and thus are relating to several clusters. The software is used to record these goals (which are coded differently within COPE: usually colored white, made bold, and given a larger typeface compared with issue statements). Through the large amount of material generated and the cross linkages being collated into a single model, the group will now become increasingly dependent on COPE and the computer display to manage the complexity of strategy development. Thus, the display can be used to focus on any part of the model and show its linkage upward to superordinate ends and downward to subordinate means. Attention of the group gradually shifts from material on the wall to the aggregated model on the computer display. Thus, the group absorbs the use of computer-aided group support in a natural rather than directed manner. The use of the computer appears obvious and transparent.

Completing the Groundwork of Strategy Development in Groups

The stages listed at the beginning of the chapter continue but with greater emphasis on direct recording of the discussion into the computer software. Thus the group is encouraged to consider those statements that are most subordinate, within the strategic issues, as possible strategic options. The software is used to help locate potential options that might be particularly significant. For example, not all of the most subordinate concepts need to be considered in the first instance; those that have a single chain of ramifications are likely to be less important than those with many ramifications. The software finds those potential options that are either potent or key (potent options are those that have ramifications for a large number of goals; key options are those that are most subordinate within the model and have more than one consequence). As the group addresses these possible options they are encouraged to develop actionable means to resolve the strategic issue being considered and so add new concepts to the model. As possible strategic options are identified, they are given a typeface or color that will clearly indicate them on the computer display, on a printout, and as an analyzable set within the model. Similarly, the possible reaction of stakeholders to key options are noted within the model, both as responses that could damage or support the strategy and as stakeholder goals that might encourage them to respond in the manner predicted.

Refining Strategy

These stages may be undertaken many times with a variety of groups in the organization. When working with any specific group a choice will be made about whether they are to build their own model of issues, goals, options, and stakeholder responses or whether it is appropriate to aggregate their views with those recorded from previous groups. The choice is mostly resolved by considering the time available to work with the increased complexity of an aggregated model set against the potential for increased ownership of a broad organizational perspective on strategic issues.

Although it is possible for the executive team to consider the model after the backroom work of aggregating the material has been carried out, it is not possible for the groups generating the material to work with it all unless the software can be used in real time. This is especially true if a series of groups are working on the material because they will want to be able not only to review what previous groups have contributed but also to add their own comments and insights directly to it. Thus using real-time software will enable them to grasp the direction of other groups while adding their own. This facility also enables the executive team to work on the material interactively if it should so choose.

Whichever route has been chosen, the executive team will meet to consider a large amount of qualitative data—typically 1,000 to 1,500 concepts made up of 40 to 50 issues, 80 to 90 potential goals, and 200 to 300 potential strategic options. Its task, with the help of two facilitators and the computer support, is to refine the goal system, agree on appropriate strategies to meet these goals, evaluate options, and create a program of action to support the strategies—and so write a mission statement that will act as an inspiration to members of the organization.

Two facilitators are used so that one facilitator can act mostly as a process manager in front of the group and the second facilitator can act predominantly as a content manager in front of two computer screens (one screen working as a preview for the main screen refresh or for exploratory analysis). The large screen used by the group is either the display from a three-color projector or a large 37 inch color VGA monitor. The process manager is seen to deal with the relational processes and aids the group through flexible interventions into the group's interaction. The content manager works on supporting the task undertaken by the group by capturing the data interactively (Bostrom, Clawson, and Anson, 1993), relating these new data with existing material when appropriate through extensive knowledge of the model and displaying relevant material when the group's attention is transferred from one issue to another. Thus it is possible for the content manager to control to some extent the direction of the workshop through the material displayed.,

With one facilitator paying attention to process and the other to content, it becomes possible to allow the analysis of content to be contingent on the social processes of the group and the social processes of the group to be contingent on the analysis of content (Eden, 1990c). The facilitators are able to act in concert, and the social needs of the group and content of the issue are also able to be in concert with one another so that effective negotiation occurs (Eden 1989b).

The GDSS's task in relation to the executive team is to provide help in the management of complexity. COPE, embedded within the SODA methodology, is designed to provide this help in a number of ways (see Eden, Ackermann, and Cropper, in press 1990) for a fuller description of analyses of cause maps):

- Each of the different *categories* of data, or all of the data, can be identified and displayed separately.
- Clusters can be formed where concepts are grouped so that there is a minimum number of bridging links to other clusters, thus *identifying manageable parts* of the model and suggesting *emerging features* of the strategy.
- Clusters can be based on *hierarchical analysis* of the model; thus sets can be formed that relate to particular parts of the goal system, allowing the exploration of possible strategic programs.
- Particular parts of the model can be chosen to depict an *overview* by "collapsing" the overall model down to, for example, the relationship between key options and certain goals.
- *Central concepts* can be isolated through a sequence of analyses that identify those concepts with a dense domain of other concepts or, alternatively highly elaborated support (subordinate chains of means to a selected end).
- *Potent strategic options* can be identified and automatically recoded as those options that have the most ramifications for the full range of goals.

These analyses allow the structure of the strategy model to be explored so that the emerging characteristics of the data can be identified. It is through the playful use of the model in this way that the executive team is able to get an analytical feel for the model as a whole.

Subsequently the team is able to focus on the task of reducing the goal system to a manageable size—about 10 to 12 core strategic goals (strategies) supported by 15 to 20 other goals (strategic objectives). The process is a combination of analyzing goal centrality with the merging of goal statements to capture the essential features, of maybe 4 adjacent goal statements, into 1 goal (this merging process is easily managed with the help of the software, so that all interrelationships are maintained). The process is cyclical, involving various analyses to provide an agenda of displays. These displays are focusing on central concepts and subsequent rewording, merging, and "deleting" (concepts are never deleted in practice but rather reduced in typeface size and colored deep blue so they become insignificant; sometimes they resurface as significant as the cycle proceeds).

Executive teams seem able to use the support system with remarkable ease. They quickly become accustomed to the power of the software so that facilitation shifts from highly directed conceptual and technical guidance to collaborative support. The use of the computer mouse in a Windows environment allows members of an executive team to grab control of the software so that the GDSS is transparent rather than technical magic. Figure 19-5 shows an executive team at work.

Gradually the model is refined so that its form follows the conceptual categories shown by Figure 19-1, and the model typically is reduced to 250 to 300 concepts. The model contains the strategy of the organization, which may be presented as 10 to 12 interlocked strategic programs. It is not unusual for the launch and presentation of the strategy to all participating managers to be made by projecting COPE onto a large screen, although it is usually necessary for a printed version of the core elements to be issued as an overview.

FIGURE 19-5.   An Executive Team Working with COPE

COPE Acting as an EIS

The strategy model developed by multiple groups and refined by the executive team is the agenda for strategic action. For it to be successfully implemented, an effective strategic control system is absolutely essential (Goold and Quinn, 1990). Although a significant element of strategic control is the process of strategy review on a regular 6-month and 12-month basis (Eden, Ackermann, and Timm, 1990), a fundamental element is the problem-solving support the strategy framework is expected to provide executives on a day-to-day basis. In this respect the model is used in a variety of forms as a type of EIS.

First, the model resides on the personal computer of senior staff as the basis for problem setting (Rein, 1976); resource acquisition; acquisition, mergers and takeovers; and new product evaluation. It is also used as the basis for vertical cut workshops in relation to strategy implementation task groups (Figure 19-2). Strategic control is established through the requirement that all requests for major decisions must be made by direct reference to the strategy model; by so doing, decisions are more likely to be coherent in relation to the detail of strategy and in relation to one another. This corresponds with Turban's (1988) view that "EIS's principle use is in tracking and control." A strategy that cannot be referred to in its full complexity allows decisions to be justified against strategy statements that are superordinate and "motherhood" statements, which are open to multiple interpretations to suit the needs of the manager who is requesting resources.

Second, the model becomes the basis for the review of all subordinate staff. Agreed-on strategic actions are recorded in the model with respect to the manager responsible for delivery and the date of delivery, thus meeting another suggested EIS characteristic—that the "current state of performance in each area should be continually measured" (Rockart, 1979).

All managers are able to use COPE to search for all actions designated to a particular individual or team, and not only to check on progress but also, and much more important, to check that progress is being designed to achieve the ends that the strategy originally established. It is common for individual managers to claim successful implementation of a particular strategic action without undertaking the task in such a manner that the strategic aims of the action are achieved. COPE forces such considerations simply because all displays of actions show the supporting actions and expected consequences (Figure 19-6): The manager is expected to demonstrate the attainment of consequences as well as the action itself.

The review process is not restricted to the use of the model to check implementation

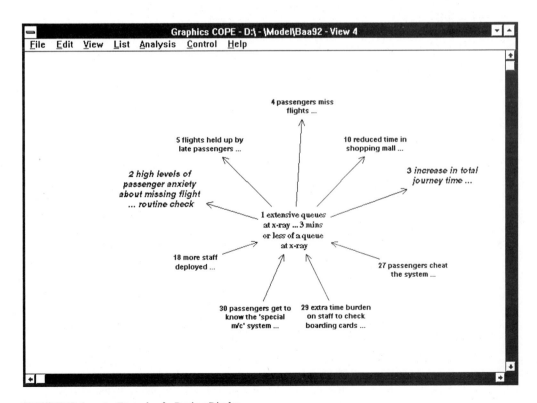

FIGURE 19-6.   An Example of a Review Display

of detailed actions; it is also a part of the annual performance review of senior staff. Here the model becomes a structured prompt for asking staff members to explain their performance and the performance of their subordinates in building the strategic future of the organization.

Another characteristic of EIS, suggested not only by Turban (1988) but also by Harvey and Meiklejohn (1988), is that an EIS should be a "system tailored to the specific industry in which the company operates and to the specific strategies it has adopted" (Anthony, Dearden, and Vancil, 1972). COPE achieves this tailoring because its content comprises strategies generated from specific theories applying only to that particular organization rather than to organizations in general. Furthermore, the strategic content has been refined by the executive team, thus ensuring that the EIS relates directly to the strategies being pursued by that team. Closely related to this feature is the combination of the system's ease of use and ability to tailor the display to match the decision maker's style—both acknowledged requirements for a usable EIS. Decision makers are able to examine the content of the system through a variety of different means, thus gaining different perspectives on the content. The multifarious forms of analysis and display ensure that the system can produce either textual or graphic output, depending on the organizational or personal requirement.

Additionally, COPE, through its use of color and graphics, not only adds clarity to the model during the GDSS stage but also provides extensive graphic support on the manager's desk Harvey and Meiklejohn, 1988; Turban, 1988). Executives are able to use the graphic ability of COPE to view specific information in a variety of ways, thus helping them to understand why they agreed to a particular strategic objective and how to achieve it.

PREREQUISITES FOR EFFECTIVE GROUP DECISION SUPPORT

Effective group decision support depends on being able to meet two straightforward and necessary but not sufficient conditions. The first is the demand for real-time working, thus requiring a very fast response from the software. This feature in turn ensures that input can be made at close to the speed of commentary of the group and that analyses can be made while the group is working. In practice this requirement means that "on-the-hoof" analyses must take no longer than about 30 seconds. For the group to be supported effectively it must gain support at the time when the group is thinking rather than as the result of backroom work. This prerequisite not only depends on the design and demands of the software but also on the processing speed of the hardware. It is this second condition that has changed in recent years; the processing speed of the 80386 chip and its availability in personal computers that has created new opportunities for on-the-hoof work.

The second important prerequisite for a GDSS is that it should meet the *social needs* of a working group. The group is actively seeking to reward itself with progress as a workshop continues. It is used to providing this reward through summaries from the "chair" and through an awareness that analytical progress is being made toward a conclusion. Individuals "finish" tasks rather than "solve" them (Eden, 1987a), which may result in one member finishing a task before other members of the group. Thus members of the group can become disinterested, feel they have arrived at robust conclusions, and become more interested in another issue before decision support software is ready to perform its analytical purpose. Many decision support software packages demand that the user completes 100 percent of data entry before any analyses can be undertaken. In GDSS it is vital that the group can gain rewards from the decision support system with incomplete data. Thus, GDSS should be highly interactive by showing the group that the system is continually providing support.

The group must see that progress is being made and added value is generated. GDSS should, therefore, provide the group with a history (Eden, 1990d) in a similar way to that which is provided by the large sheets of paper progressively filling wall space during low-tech strategy workshops (Friend and Hickling, 1987).

A group problem-solving activity usually works well when it is fun and entertaining. In GDSS this facet can be expressed by providing a system that makes active use of colorful graphics and so attracts the attention of participants. GDSS may also provide entertainment through cross-linkages, as members are able to see how new ideas inter-relate with previous ideas and begin to understand the views and problems of other members.

When a group is using GDSS, the support system itself is usually designed to facilitate the workshop by providing structure to the discussion. To this extent the GDSS is replacing the role of the traditional chair and, some would claim, enabling greater democracy (Watson, DeSanctis, and Poole, 1988) among the group. However, there is a great danger that the support system will focus too much on the content aspects of group problem solving and too little on the social process (Phillips, 1990). An important prerequisite of GDSS design is that it balances the social management role of a facilitator and the problem-structuring and analytical role of formal model building.

Finally, the physical environment of GDSS needs to be carefully thought through (Eden, 1990c; Hickling, 1990). It is interesting how firm Harvey-Jones (1988) is about this topic: "One area of concern which top management tends to neglect is that of the environment in which discussions are held...this can have a very substantial effect on the type and quality of the discussion." High-tech environments such as the POD (Austin, 1987) do not necessarily support a group in positive ways. Our own experience and research with senior management groups suggest that a balance between a high-tech core, which is visible in the sense of providing computer support but is as invisible as possible with respect to overall environment, is important (Ackermann and Eden, 1989). Figure 19-5 depicts a typical environment for work with senior management teams, where the setting is a hotel room with all the computing equipment hired from local rental organizations.

Most of these prerequisites affect the probability of executives making effective use of COPE as an EIS as well as their being receptive to a computer-aided GDSS. Those that are especially important are the prerequisites of speed, color, and the lack of reliance on backroom work. The prerequisites of speed lies in the power of the hardware, and "it has only been in the past few years that technology has become sufficiently flexible and powerful to make EIS a practical proposition" (Harvey and Meiklejohn, 1988). This speed enables the executives not only to manage the large amounts of information available but also, if they should desire, to carry out a quick analysis on the information without having to wait for long periods of time. This waiting is coupled with the need to have a system that does not require backroom work. If executives have to ask for the information, it is likely to arrive later than they need and may no longer be relevant. Graphics and color, as mentioned earlier, are also prerequisites.

THE EFFECTIVENESS OF SODA AS A GDSS

Implicit in many of the discussions about the effectiveness of GDSS is the belief that organizations should be more democratic and that GDSS will contribute to this aim. A criterion such as this is not necessary to the success of GDSS but rather reflects the values of the evaluators (Ackermann and Eden, 1989; Eden, 1987b). The notion that democracy is a good thing is a matter for debate; what is more relevant to the type of GDSS environments in which SODA is used is the way in which the power base of the participants changes with computer-based GDSS and the way in which specific factors that are often correlated with democracy change. It may be the wish of the manager to "buy into" the process to ensure that participants feel that they have had more airtime so that greater consensus and commitment occur. But the manager may also hesitate to demand that this result actually happens because he or she may lose control of the ability to mobilize bias (Schattsneider, 1960) and manage meaning (Pettigrew, 1977) in relation to his or her own views about the politics of implementation—views that necessarily cannot be made public. The political feasibility of a strategy is perhaps the ultimate test of its robustness (Eden, 1992).

Similarly a wish to reduce the role of social approval in contributing to problem solving is an important characteristic to study, but it is never going to be removed by the imposition of GDSS; rather it is likely to be changed. Factors such as the skills that participants demonstrate in the use of, for example, keyboards may become significant features in the influence process (Eden, Williams, and Smithin, 1986; Mantei, 1988). Such skills are still unlikely to be related to the quality of ideas. Nevertheless, some research seems to be indicating that if all members of a group are given the opportunity to participate (actively or passively) in problem solving (through GDSS), there is less likelihood that the participants will involve themselves in settling other (hidden) agenda items that will generate dysfunctional social dynamics (Applegate, Konsynski, and Nunamaker, 1987). The aim with SODA is to maintain participation by demonstrating to those using the airtime that they have been heard (not just the words but the meaning by collecting concepts or crucial chunks of data and setting them in the context of other concepts) and so release them from the requirement to repeat themselves (Huber, 1984a). If members of a group do not repeat themselves, it is possible for others to participate and/or for the meeting time to be reduced. If a group becomes aware of increased productivity, it develops a more positive attitude to the meeting.

If GDSS does provide a more efficient forum, it is likely that the extra airtime will mean that views expressed will be deeper and more subtle than would have otherwise been the case. It is a common experience of meetings that there is little time to express views that are beyond motherhood and apple pie. However, the expression and visual record of deeper views inevitably cause more conflict, albeit at a more subtle level, than can occur otherwise. Thus, when COPE and SODA are used as a GDSS, conflict is not necessarily decreased in the first instance. Conflict is allowed to surface rather than remain as potential sabotage after the workshop. The GDSS is designed as a structured way to manage conflict toward consensus that is lasting.

Many of those who are concerned to measure the effectiveness of GDSS have done so through experiments with student groups working on relatively well-structured problems. Such research is clearly important and useful. However, descriptions of work with senior management groups cannot be so easily validated. To discover how groups, working on highly confidential and very messy issues, have responded to GDSS is a complex research problem. Such research is particularly complicated by the need to recognize and account for the political and social history of the group and the extent to which the group addresses strategic issues in the full knowledge that it has a future together. Typically, a student group has no relevant history, no important future together, and can only be set to work on well-structured problems.

Our own studies of the effectiveness of SODA have been based on the chaotic and opportunistic interviews that can be undertaken with senior executives when they are prepared to reflect and talk about their experiences. This usually means discussions in the bar after workshops, walking the corridors, gentle persuasion toward interviews in a sequence of time gaps after workshops, and so on. The data elicited are qualitative, not amenable to statistical analysis, and inevitably lead to powerful qualitative insights that cannot be verified directly by other researchers. The richness of the data depends on the trust that develops between ourselves as helpful and useful facilitators of GDSS and yet is biased because of such relationships. It is not surprising that we use COPE as a technique for the analysis of qualitative research data of this sort. However the outcome these last ten years of research into many different versions of SODA and COPE has simply led to the considered theoretical and conceptual developments that have produced the current GDSS method known as SODA and to the confidence we have in the content of this chapter. The issues raised by this research are tackled in greater depth elsewhere (see Ackermann, 1990; Eden, 1992).

SUCCESS IN EIS

Success in using systems in general may be measured by the level at which the decision maker uses the system, and EIS appears to be no exception. If a system is seen as a useful way of being able to review the agreed-on direction, to be able to go back to the basics rather than get caught up with day-to-day tasks, it is providing *support* to the executive. Certainly it is important to be sure that the system is easy to use, thus preventing a waste of time, and that attractive graphics to facilitate use are incorporated. However, as with all information systems, the success of its use appears to lie mainly in the information it contains and how it can be exploited. It has been interesting to note that when systems provide sufficient incentives, senior executives are prepared to struggle through reasonably archaic user interfaces as long as, in their opinion, *the benefits of the system outweigh the effort in accessing them.*

SODA and COPE—although it is the software that is more in focus in the context of EIS—do not fit within the traditional view of such systems. COPE does not utilize quantitative data and does not provide trend determination or exception reporting—three requirements stated by Finlay (1989). What it does do, nevertheless, is to support executive work. Executives have used the resultant model, created through the group processes, to monitor their strategic progress. This goal has been achieved by attaching names and in some cases time scales to the action portfolios to increase the likelihood of implementation and control of the strategy. Furthermore, executives have established complex color codings to determine the state of progress on the actions in question. They have used the model as a sophisticated "look-up" facility to brief them before meetings and presentations.

As can be seen, then, the system is capable of use in a manner that matches the style of the decision maker, and thus it does conform to one of the more traditional EIS characteristics (Turban, 1988). Furthermore, the system may well encapsulate the properties encompassed in the belief that there is a need for "strategic scanning capabilities in an EIS, as well as 'executive thought support' rather than decision support" (Zmud, 1986). After all, COPE enables executives to play with the model by exploring different options and supporting thought and thus to act opportunistically (Eden, Ackermann, and Timm, 1990) in relation to external events.

The difficulties in getting EIS accepted in the company are still largely unresolved, and the information needs of executives still have to be explored and understood better before EIS will be accepted. Therefore, likely sets of characteristics for such systems perhaps should remain flexible and adaptable, borrowing from those systems that are being used by executives rather than those fitting the stated characteristics. As a consequence, it may be those EIS that base their information on contributions from members throughout the organization and that help executives in the practical control and implementation of strategy that provide indicators for other EISs to follow.

CONCLUDING REMARKS

Our work in the public sector has led to a drawing together of research on public sector strategy making with our own research on strategy development through group decision support. Specifically, joint projects with John Bryson at the University of Minnesota have enabled us to lock together our own conceptualization of the strategy development process with the framework developed by Bryson (1988). A recent action research project with the Northern Ireland Office and a current project undertaken by Bryson and a Schools Board have enabled the synthesis of the two approaches to permit both conceptual and methodological development.

In the private sector, we have always taken stakeholder analysis to be an important element of work with groups. However it has always been dominated by competitor analysis, in which the cognitive mapping element of SODA has helped to evaluate the goal systems and strategic responses of competitors to devise possible strategies. Thus each workshop has included activities designed to raise consciousness about competitor dynamics through the explicit use of competitor data revealed throughout the workshop (Eden and Huxham, 1988). These activities have been mostly informed by a hypergame analysis of competitor interactions (Bennett and Huxham, 1982).

In the public sector framework provided by Bryson, there is due emphasis on stakeholder analysis, but it is informed by the role of mandates and implicitly by collaboration rather than competition. This shift of emphasis has led to our conceptualizing this part of the strategy development process in terms of collaborative advantage (B. Gray, 1989; Huxham, 1991, 1992). Thus activities throughout the process—in the workshop, in the methods of analysis of the COPE model, and in the development of implementation strategies—are influenced by the need to see collaboration with stakeholders as the dominant outcome that can be achieved through effective strategy development. Seeking opportunities for collaborative advantage usually requires a significant shift in the mental set of managers in the organization as well as the top management team: a group decision support system approach encourages this shift.

As the parallel project undertaken by Bryson unfolds, we expect to see further developments from the synthesis of the two interlinked approaches. Unfortunately, strategy development projects of this sort demand long-term immersion in the organization (18 to 24 months, and in some cases several years) for the research to monitor strategic change. Conceptual and methodological developments of GDSS used for strategy work are not likely to occur as the result of large n studies of short duration.

Although most of our work is aimed at high levels of staff involvement, some recent projects with only the chief executive officer (CEO) have revealed the extent to which a COPE model of the emerging strategy of the organization allows the CEO to explore its coherence and shifting balance (Eden and Cropper, 1991). Mintzberg has argued for attention to the emerging strategy of an organization (Mintzberg and Waters, 1985) and for "crafting" strategy (Mintzberg, 1987). However, he has had little to say about the practical issues in the discovery of an emergent strategy, which can emerge through so many aspects of the organization that it is not practicable to collect *the* emergent strategy. Clearly the approach we have reported, which involves a cross section of the organization, reveals one form of the emergent strategy. Another form is that which is revealed by the strategy statements on control documents that permeate the organization and on bid statements that aim to raise additional resources.

The project with the Prison Service of England and Wales sought to discover the emergent strategy in the second way by looking at control statements and statements made in the bid for public money and to Parliament. A COPE model was constructed to represent the collection of these statements (a model of about 1,000 concepts). The model was then used as a GDSS for the CEO and two of his close colleagues so that they could evaluate the coherence of their emergent strategy and redevelop it. In addition they wished to evaluate the shifting balance over time of their strategic intent. This type of long-term GDSS with a constant group of executives seems to us to have enormous potential if we are able to develop a GDSS that can be used in real time and can provide significant added value from analytical tools. The requirements set out above for the use of EIS seem to apply equally to the use of GDSS for this more cerebral activity.

Bibliography

Abel, M. (1990). Experiences in an exploratory distributed organization. In *Intellectual teamwork: the social and technological foundations of cooperative work,* ed. J. Galegher, R. Kraut, and C. Egido. Hillsdale, NJ: Lawrence Erlbaum.

Acker, S., and S. Levitt. (1987). Designing videoconference facilities for improved eye contact. *Journal of Broadcasting and Electronic Media* 31, no. 2:181–191.

Ackermann, F. (1990). The role of computers in group decision support. In *Tackling strategic problems: The role of group decision support,* ed. C. Eden and J. Radford. London: Sage.

Ackermann, F., and C. Eden. (1989). Issues in computer and non-computer supported GDSS's. Paper presented at the Operational Research Society Conference, Southampton, England.

Ackerman, M. S., and T. Malone. (1990). Answer garden: A tool for growing organizational memory. *ACM Conference on Office Information Systems*, pp. 12–13 Cambridge, MA: ACM Press.

Adelman, L. (1984). Real-time computer support for decision analysis in a group setting: Another class of decision support systems. *Interfaces* 14:75–83.

Ahuja, S., R. Ensor, J. Koszarek, and M. Pack. (1989). Supporting multi-phase groupware over long distance. Paper presented at the IEEE Global Telecommunications Conference, Dallas, TX.

Ajzen, I., and M. Fishbein. (1990). *Understanding attitudes and predicting social behavior.* Englewood Cliffs, NJ: Prentice-Hall.

Alexander, M. B. (1989). The adoption and implementation of computer technology in organizations: The example of database machines. Ph.D. dissertation, Indiana University, Bloomington.

Allen, T., and P. Gerstberger. (1973). A field experiment to improve communications in a product engineering department: The nonterritorial office. *Human Factors* 15:487–498.

American National Standards Insititute (1988). Human factors engineering of visual display terminal workstations. ANS1/HFS100-1988.

Andersen, D. F. (1990). Analyzing who gains and who loses: The case of school finance reforms in New York State. *System Dynamics Review* 6:21–43.

Andersen, D. F. (1982). *Introduction to computer simulation: The system dynamics modeling approach.* Reading, MA: Addison-Wesley.

Anderson, D. and J. Rohrbaugh (In press). Some conceptual and technical problems in integrating models of judgement with simulation models. *IEEE Transactions on Systems, Man, and Cybernetics.*

Andersen, D. F., I. J. Chung, G. P. Richardson, and T. R. Stewart. Issues in designing interactive games based on system dynamics models. *Proceedings of the 1990 International Systems Dynamics Conference,* Chesnut Hill, MA.

Anson, R. G. (1990). Effects of computer support and facilitation support on group processes. Ph.D. dissertation, Indiana University, Bloomington.

Anson, R. G., R. P. Bostrom, and B. E. Wynne. (1991). *Effects of computer and facilitator support on group processes and outcomes: An experimental assessment.* Working paper, University of Georgia, Athens.

Anthony, R. N., J. Dearden, and R. F. Vancil. (1972). *Management controls system.* Homewood, IL: Irwin.

Applegate, L. (1991) Technology support for cooperative work: A framework for studying introduction and assimilation in organizations. *Journal of Organizational Computing* 1:11–39.

Applegate, L. M., B. R. Konsynski, and J. F. Nunamaker. (1987). A group decision support systems for idea generation and issue analysis in organizational planning. *Journal of Management Information Systems* 3:5–19.

Applegate, L., and N. Wishart. (1988). *The Prudential: Organizing for technology innovation.* Boston: Harvard Business School Case Services.

Argyris, C. (1983). Action science and intervention. *The Journal of Applied Behavioral Science* 19:115–140.

Araujo, R. B., Coulouris, G. F. Onions, J. P. and Smith, H., (April, 1988). The Architecture of the Prototype COSMOS Messaging System, In *Proceedings of the European Teleinformatics Conference—Euteco '88,* Vienna, Austria. (September, 1988).

Austin, N. C. (1987). A management support environment. In *ICL Technical Bulletin.* Oxford. International Computers.

Backoff, R. W., and P. C. Nutt. (1988). A process for strategic management with specific application for the nonprofit organization. In *Strategic planning: Threats and opportunities for planners,* ed. J. M. Bryson and R. C. Einsweiler. Chicago: Planners Press.

Bahgat, A. (1986). A decision support system for zero-base capital budgeting: A case study. Ph.D. dissertation, Rutgers Graduate School of Management, New Brunswick, NJ.

Bales, R. (1950). *Interaction process analysis: A method for the study of small groups.* Reading, MA: Addison-Wesley.

Bales, R. F., and S. P. Cohen. (1979). *SYMLOG: A system for the observation of groups.* New York: Free Press.

Balzer, W. K., J. Rohrbaugh, and K. R. Murphy. (1983). Reliability of actual and predicted judgments across time. *Organizational Behavior and Human Performance* 32:109-123.

Bartunek, J. M., and M. K. Moch. (1987). First-order, second-order, and third-order change and organization development interventions: A cognitive approach. *The Journal of Applied Behavioral Science* 23: 483-500.

BBN Software Products Corp. (1989) *BBN/Slate Multi-media Document Communication System Reference Manual*: Author.

Beauclair, R. A. (1987). An experimental study of the effects of GDSS process support applications on small group decision making. Ph.D. dissertation, Indiana University, Bloomington.

Begeman, M., P. Cook, C. Ellis, M. Graf, G. Rein, and T. Smith. (1986). PROJECT NICK: Meetings augmentation and analysis. Paper presented at the Conference on Computer-Supported Cooperative Work, Austin, TX.

Bennett, P., and C. Huxham. (1982). Hypergames and what they do: A "soft OR" approach. *Journal of the Operational Research Society* 33: 41-50.

Bennis, W. G., and P. E. Slater. (1968). *The temporary society*. New York: Harper & Row.

Billingsley, J. (1989). Small group appropriation of decision structures in a computer-assisted group decision support environment. International Communication Association.

Blackman, B. (1983). Toward a grounded theory for intercultural communication. In *International and Intercultural Communication: Current Perspectives*, ed. W. B. Gudykunst. Beverly Hills, CA: Sage.

Bostrom, R. P. (1989). Successful application of communication techniques to improve the systems development process. *Information & Management* 16: 279-295.

Bostrom, R. P., and R. G. Anson (1993) *Electronic meeting agenda design: Mapping technology to tasks*, Working paper, University of Georgia, Athens.

Bostrom, R. P., R. G. Anson, and V. K. Clawson. (1991). Group facilitation and group support systems. In *Group support systems: New perspectives*, ed. L. M. Jessup and J. S. Valacich. New York: Van Nostrand Reinhold.

Bostrom, R. P., and R. G. Anson. (1988b). A new member of your management team: Collaborative work support systems. *Information Executive 1*, no. 1:43-46.

Bostrom, R. P., V. K. Clawson, and R. G. Anson. (1991). *Training people to facilitate electronic environments*. Working paper 70, University of Georgia, Athens.

Bouton, C., and R. Y. Garth. (1983). *Learning in groups*. San Francisco: Jossey-Bass.

Bowers, John and Churcher, John. *Local and global Structuring of computer mediated communication:* Developing linguistic perspectives on CSCW in *COSMOS*, in Proc. of the conference on Computer-Supported Cooperative Work. Portland, OR.

Boyacigiller, N. A., and N. J. Adler. (1991). The parochial dinosaur: Organizational science in a global context. *Academy of Management Review* 16, no. 2:262-289.

Brinberg, D. (1981). A comparison of two behavioral intention models. *Advances in Consumer Research* 8:48-52.

Brinberg, D., and V. Cummings. (1984). Purchasing generic prescription drugs: An analysis using two behavioral intention models. *Advances in Consumer Research* 11:229-234.

Brinberg, D., and J. Durand. (1983). Eating at fast-food restaurants: An analysis using two behavioral intention models. *Journal of Applied Social Psychology* 13, no. 6:459-472.

Brinberg, D., and J. Jaccard. (1989). Multiple perspective on dyadic decision making. In *Dyadic decision making*, ed. D. Brinberg and J. Jaccard. New York: Springer-Verlag.

Brinberg, D., and N. Schwenk. (1985). Husband-wife decision making: An exploratory study of the interaction process. *Advances in Consumer Research* 12:487–491.

Brookes, C. H. P. (1985). A corporate intelligence system for soft information exchange. In *Knowledge representation for decision support systems*, ed. L. B. Methlie and R. H. Sprague. Amsterdam: North-Holland.

Brooks, F. P. (1975). *The mythical man month: Essays on software engineering.* Reading, MA: Addison-Wesley.

Bryson, J. (1988). *Strategic planning for public and nonprofit organizations.* San Francisco: Jossey-Bass.

Bulick, S., M. Abel, D. Corey, J. Schmidt, and S. Coffin. (1989). The U.S. WEST advanced technologies prototype multi-media communications system. *Globecom '89: Proceedings of the IEEE Global Telecommunications Conference*, Dallas, TX.

Carbaugh, D. (1984). Cultural communication and organizing. In *International and intercultural annual*, ed. W. B. Gudykunst and Y. Y. Kim. Beverly Hills, CA: Sage.

Carper, W. B., and T. A. Bresnick. (1989, September). Strategic planning conferences. *Business Horizons*, pp. 34–40.

Cash, J., W. McFarland, and J. McKenney (1988). *Corporate information systems management: The issues facing senior executives.* Homewood: Dow Jones Irmin.

Cash, J., and P. McLeod. (1985). Managing the introduction of information systems in strategically dependent companies. *Journal of Management Information Systems* 1, no. 4:5–23.

Cassidy, M. F. (1988). Decision conferencing for strategic decision making. Paper presented at AT&T Behavioral Science Days '88, Holmdel, NJ.

Cassidy, M. F., M. J. Conway, and J. A. Rodriguez. (1988). Electronically supported meetings for collaborative decision making. Paper presented at AT&T Behavioral Science Days '88, Holmdel, NJ.

Chidambaram, L. (1989). An empirical investigation of the impact of computer support on group development and decision making performance. Ph.D. dissertation, Indiana University, Bloomington.

Chidambaram, L., and R. P. Bostrom. (1989). *The issue of group development: Implications for group decision support system research and design.* Working paper, University of Georgia, Athens.

Chidambaram, L., and R. P. Bostrom. (1992). An empirical investigation of the impact of GDSS on group performance overtime. Working Paper #60, University of Georgia, Athens.

Chidambaram, L., R. P. Bostrom, and B. E. Wynne. (1991). A longitudinal study of the impact of group decision support systems on group development. *Journal of Management Information Systems* 7, no. 3:7–25.

Chidambaram, L., and B. H. Jones. (1991). Impact of communication medium and computer support on group behavior and performance. Paper presented at the TIMS/ORSA Conference, Nashville, TN.

Churchman, C. W. (1971). *The design of inquiring systems: Basic concepts of systems and organizations.* New York: Basic Books.

Collaros, P. A., and L. R. Anderson. (1969). Effect of perceived expertness upon creativity of members of brainstorming groups. *Journal of Applied Psychology* 53:319–322.

Collier, K. G. (1980). Peer group learning in higher education: The development of higher order skills. *Studies in Higher Education* 5, no. 1:55–62.

Conklin, J., and M. L. Begeman. (1988). The right tool for the right job. *Byte* 13, no. 10:255–262.

Connolly, T., L. M. Jessup, and J. S. Valacich. (1990). Idea generation using a GDSS: Effects of anonymity and evaluative tone. *Management Science* 36, no. 6:689-703.

Cooper, R., and R. Zmud. (1990). Information technology implementation research: A technological diffusion approach. *Management Science* 36, no. 2:128-139.

Cornell, P., and R. Luchetti. (1989). Ergonomic and environmental aspects of computer supported cooperative work. Paper presented at the Annual Meeting of the Human Factors Society, Denver, CO.

Coxon, A. P. M. (1979). Perspectives on social networks. *Perspectives on social network research*, pp. 489-500, ed. P. W. Holland and S. Leinhardt. New York: Academic Press.

Cropper, S., C. Eden & F. Ackerman. (1990). Keeping sense of accounts using computer-based cognitive maps. *Social Science Computer Review* 8:345-366.

Crowley, T., and H. Forsdick. (1989). MMConf: The diamond multimedia conferencing system. Paper presented at the Groupware Technology Workshop.

Darling, T. A., and J. L. Mumpower. (1990). Modeling cognitive influences on the dynamics of negotiations. Proceedings of the 23rd Annual *Hawaii International Conference on System Sciences*, 3, pp. 22-30. Los Alamitos, CA.

Darling, T. A., and G. P. Richardson. (1990). A behavioral simulation model of single and iterative negotiations. *Proceedings of the 1990 International System Dynamics Conference*, Cambridge, MA.

Delbecq, A. L., A. H. Van de Ven, and D. H. Gustafson. (1975). *Group techniques for program planning*. Glenview, IL: Scott, Foresman.

DeMarco, T., and T. Lister. (1985). Programmer performance and the effects of the workplace. *Proceedings of the IEEE*, pp. 268-272.

Dennis, A. R., J. F. George, L. M. Jessup, J. F. Nunamaker, and D. R. Vogel. (1988, December). Information technology to support electronic meetings. *MIS Quarterly* 12, no. 4:591-624.

Dennis, A. R., A. R. Heminger, J. F. Nunamaker, and D. R. Vogel. (1990). Bringing automated support to large groups: The Burr-Brown experience. *Information & Management* 18:111-121.

Dennis, A. R., C. K. Tyran, D. R. Vogel, and J. F. Nunamaker. (1990). An evaluation of electronic meeting systems to support strategic management. Paper presented at the International Conference of Information Systems, Copenhagen, Denmark.

Dennis, A. R., J. S. Valacich, and J. F. Nunamaker. (1990). An experimental investigation of group size in an electronic meeting system environment. *IEEE Transactions on Systems, Man, and Cybernetics* 20, no. 5:1049-1057.

Dennis, A. R., J. S. Valacich, and J. F. Nunamaker. (1991). Group, sub-group, and nominal group idea generation in an electronic meeting environment. Proceedings of the 24th Annual Hawaiian International Conference on Systems Science, 3, pp. 573-579. Los Alamitos, CA: IEEE Computer Society Press.

DeSanctis, G. (1984). Computer graphics as decision aids: Directions for research. *Decision Sciences* 15, no. 4:463-487.

DeSanctis, G., G. W. Dickson, B. Jackson, and M. S. Poole. (1991). Using computing in the face-to-face meeting: Some initial observations from the Texaco-Minnesota Project. Paper presented at the Annual Meeting of the Academy of Management, Miami. FL.

DeSanctis, G., M. D'Onofrio, V. Sambamurthy, and M. S. Poole. (1989). Comprehensiveness and restrictiveness in group decision heuristics: Effects of computer support on consensus decision making. Paper presented at the International Conference on Information Systems, Boston, MA.

Desanctis, G., and R. B. Gallupe, (1985). Group decision support systems: A new frontier. *Database* 16, no. 2:3-10.

DeSanctis, G., and R. B. Gallupe. (1987). A foundation for the study of group decision support systems. *Management Science* 33, no. 5. 589-609.

DeSanctis, G., M. S. Poole, G. Desharnais, and H. Lewis (In press). Using computing to facilitate the quality improvement process: The IRS-Minnesota project. *TIMS Interfaces.*

DeSanctis, G., M. S. Poole, G. Desharnais, and H. Lewis. (1992). Using computing in quality team meetings: Some inital observations from the IRS-Minnesota Project. *Journal of Management Information Systems.* 3, no. 8:7-26.

DeSanctis, G., V. Sambamurthy, and R. T. Watson. (In Press). Building a software environment for GDSS research. In *Readings in decision support and executive information systems*, ed. P. Gray. Englewood Cliffs, NJ: Prentice Hall.

Dickson, G. W., G. DeSanctis, and D. J. McBride. (1988). Understanding the effectiveness of computer graphics for decision support: A cumulative experimental approach. *Communications of the ACM* 29, no. 1:40-47.

Dickson, G. W., L. Robinson, R. Heath, and J. E. Lee. (1989). Observations on GDSS interaction: Chauffeured, facilitated, and user-driven systems. Proceedings of the 22nd Annual Hawaii International Conference on System Sciences, 3, pp. 337-343. Los Alamitos, CA: IEEE Computer Society Press.

Diehl, M., and W. Stroebe. (1987). Productivity loss in brainstorming groups: Toward the solution of a riddle. *Personality and Social Psychology* 53, no. 3:497-509.

Dollimore J, Wilbur S. (September, 1989). *Experiences in Building a Configurable CSCW System,* in Proc. of First European Conf. on Computer Supported Cooperative Work, London.

Dollimore J. (April, 1988). *The design of an Object Server as a storage module for the COSMOS Messaging System,* European Teleinformatics Conference—In *Proceedings of the European Teleinformatics Conference*—Euteco '88, Vienna, Austria.

Dollimore, Roberts and Coulouris. (March, 1989). *Towards a Language for Defining Structure in Message-based Cooperative Working,* Cosmos report 69.1.

Doran, P. M. (1991). A repeated measures experimental analysis of the effects of group decision support systems on decision making, decision implementation and stress. Ph.D. dissertation University of Georgia, Athens.

Doyle, M., and D. Strauss. (1976). *How to make meetings work.* New York: Jove.

Drexler, A. B., D. Sibbet, and R. H. Forrester. (1988). The team performance model. In *Team building,* ed. W. B. Reddy and K. Jamison. Alexandria, VA: NTL Institute for Applied Behavioral Science.

Drucker, P. F. (1988). The coming of the new organization. *Harvard Business Review 66,* no. 1:45-53.

Drunkel, T. (1989, December). A fiber-linked futuristic world. *INSIGHT,* pp. 39-49.

Dufner, D., and S. R. Hiltz. (1991). Distributed group support systems: Experimental design and pilot study, Proceedings of the 20th Annual Hawaii International Conference on System Sciences, 3, pp. 386-393. Los Alamitos, CA: IEEE Computer Society Press.

Eden, C. (1987a). Letter to Marshall Scott Poole.

Eden, C. (1987b). Problem solving or problem finishing? In *New directions in management science,* ed. M. C. Jackson and P. Keys. Hants, England: Gower.

Eden, C. (1989a). Strategy options development and analysis—SODA. In *Rational analysis in a problematic world,* ed. J. Rosenhead. London: Wiley.

Eden, C. (1989b). Operational research as negotiation. In *Operational research and the social sciences,* ed. M. C. Jackson, P. Keys, and S. A. Cropper. New York: Plenum.

Eden, C. (1990a). Strategic thinking with computers. Long Range Planning, in press.

Eden, C. (1990b). Cognitive maps as a visionary tool: strategy embedded in issue management. In *Strategic planning: models and analytical techniques,* ed. R. G. Dyson. London: Wiley.

Eden, C. (1990c). The unfolding nature of group decision support—Two dimensions of skill. In *Tackling strategic problems: The role of group decision support,* ed. C. Eden, and J. Radford. London: Sage.

Eden, C. (1990d) Managing the environment as a means to managing complexity. In *Tackling strategic problems: The role of group decision support,* ed. C. Eden and J. Radford. London: Sage.

Eden, C. (1992). A framework for thinking about group decision support systems (GDSS). In *Operational research and the management of complexity,* ed. C. Eden, M. Jackson, J. Rosenhead, and R. Tomlinson. London: Sage.

Eden, C., F. Ackermann, and S. Cropper. (1990). The analysis of causal maps. *Journal of Management Studies.*

Eden, C., F. Ackermann, and S. Timm. (1990). Strategy performance and the performance of strategy. Paper presented at the British Academy of Management Conference, Glasgow.

Eden. C., and S. Cropper. (1991). Coherence and balance in strategies for the management of public services: Two confidence tests for strategy development, review and renewal. Paper presented at the British Academy of Management Conference, Bath.

Eden, C., and C. Huxham. (1988). Action oriented strategic management. *Journal of the Operational Research Society* 39:889–899.

Eden, C., S. Jones, and D. Sims. (1983). *Messing about in problems.* Oxford: Pergamon.

Eden, C. F., and J. Rohrbaugh. (1990). Using the competing values approach to explore ways of working. In *Tackling strategic problems: The role of group decision support,* ed. C. F. Eden and J. Radford. Newbury Park, CA: Sage.

Eden, C., T. Williams, and T. Smithin. (1986). Synthetic wisdom: The design of a mixed mode modelling system for organizational decision making. *Journal of the Operational Research Society* 37, no. 3:233–241.

Ellis, C. A., S. J. Gibbs, and G. L. Rein. (1991). Groupware: Some issues and experiences. *Communications of the ACM* 34, no. 1:38–58.

Elwart-Keyes, J., D. Halonen, J. Horton, R. Kass, and R. Scott. (1990). User interface requirements for face to face groupware. Paper presented at CHI'90 Human Factors in Computing Systems, Seattle, WA.

Engelbart, D. C. (1973). Coordinated information services for a discipline or mission oriented community. Paper presented at the Computer Communications Conference, San Jose, CA.

Engelbart, D. C. (1990). Knowledge-domain interoperability and an open hyperdocument system. Proceedings of the Conference on Computer-Supported Cooperative Work, Los Angeles. pp. 143–156.

Engelbart, D. C., R. W. Watson, and Norton J. C. (1976). The augmented knowledge workshop. Paper presented at AFIPS National Conference.

Epplie, J. E. (1984). Organization strategy and structural difference for radical versus incremental innovation. *Management Science* 30, no. 6:682–695.

Faerman, S. R., R. E. Quinn, and M. P. Thompson. (1987). Bridging management practice and theory: New York State's public service training program. *Public Administration Review* 47:310-319.

Farago, K., A. Oldfield, and A. Vari. (1988). Conflicting perspectives in multi-stakeholder problems: A comparative study. In *Hazardous waste: Detection, control, treatment,* ed. A. Abbou, pp. 1769-1780. Amsterdam: Elsevier.

Farago, K., A. Vari, and J. Vecsenyi. (1989). Not in my backyard! Conflicting views on the siting of a hazardous waste incinerator. *Risk Analysis* 9:463-471.

Farallon Computing. (1991). Timbuktu 4.0.

Farn, C. K., and K. Sung. (1988). Collective decision making behavior in the Chinese society and its implications in group decision support systems. Paper presented at GDSS Workshop, Kona, HI.

Fellers, J. W. (1989). The effect of group size and computer support on group idea generation for creativity task: An experimental evaluation using a repeated measures design. Ph.D. dissertation, Indiana University, Bloomington.

Fellers, J. W., and B. E. Wynne. (1988). An exploratory investigation of critical success factors for knowledge acquisition in expert systems development. Paper presented at the 1988 Conference on the Impact of Artificial Intelligence on Business and Industry, Denton, TX.

Ferwanger, T., Y. Wang, H. Lewe, and H. Krcmar. (1989). Experiences in designing the Hohenheim CATeam Room, pp. 87-101. Proceedings of the First European Conference on CSCW, EC-CSCW'89.

Fikes, R., and T. Kehler. (1985). The role of frame-based representation in reasoning. *Communications of the ACM* 28, no. 9:904-920.

Finlay, P. (1989). *Introducing decision support systems.* Manchester, England: NCC Blackwell.

Fishbein, M., and I. Ajzen. (1975). *Belief, attitude, intention, and behavior: An introduction to theory and research.* Reading, MA: Addison-Wesley.

Fisher, B. A. (1970). Decision emergence: Phases in group decision making. *Speech Monographs* 37:53-66.

Flowers, B. E. ed. (1988). Joseph Campbell, *The Power of Myth with Bill Moyers.* New York, NY: Doubleday.

Foroughi, A. (1990). An empirical study of an interactive, session-oriented computerized negotiation support system (NSS). Ph.D. dissertation Indiana University, Bloomington.

Friend, J., and A. Hickling. (1987). *Planning under pressure.* Oxford: Pergamon.

Gallupe, R. B. (1988). Case analysis in the 1990's: Using a GDSS to support small group case analysis. pp. 32-41. Proceeding of Administrative Sciences Association of Canada—Management Education Division, Halifax.

Gallupe, R. B., L. Bastianutti, and W. Cooper. (1991). Unblocking brainstorms. *Journal of Applied Psychology* 76, no. 1:137-142.

Gallupe, R. B., A. Dennis, K. W. Cooper, J. Valacich, L. Bastianutti, and J. F. Nunamaker. (In press), Electronic brainstorming and group size. *Academy of Management Journal.*

Gallupe, R. B., G. DeSanctis, and G. W. Dickson. (1988). The impact of computer support on group problem finding: An experimental approach. *MIS Quarterly* 12, no. 2:276-296.

Gladstein, D., and D. Caldwell. (1985). Boundary management in new product teams. Academy of Management Proceedings. Ada, Ohio: Academy of Management.

Goodman, G., and M. Abel. (1986). Collaboration research in SCL. *CSCW'86: Proceedings of the First Conference on Computer-Supported Cooperative Work,* Austin, TX.

Goodman, G., and M. Abel. (1987). Communication and collaboration: Facilitating cooperative work through communication. *Office: Technology and People* 3, no. 3

Goold, M., and J. J. Quinn. (1990). The paradox of strategic controls. *Strategic Management Journal* 11:43-57.

Gopal, A. (1991). The effects of technology support level and task type on group outcomes in a group decision support system environment. Ph.D. dissertation, University of Georgia, Athens.

Gopal, A., R. P. Bostrom, and W. Chin. (1992). Modeling the process of GSS use: An adaptive structuration perspective. Proceedings of the 24th Annual *Hawaii International Conference on Systems Sciences.* Los Alamitos, CA: IEEE Society Press.

Gouran, D. S., and R. Y. Hirokawa. (1986). Counteractive functions of communication in effective group decision making. In *Communication and group decision making,* pp. 81-92. ed. R. Y. Hirokawa and M. S. Poole, Beverly Hills, CA: Sage.

Gray, B. (1989). *Collaborating.* San Francisco: Jossey-Bass.

Gray, P. (1983). Initial observations from the decision room project. Paper presented at the International Conference on Decision Support Systems, Boston. pp. 135-138.

Gray, P. (1987). Group decision support systems. *Decision Support Systems* 3, no. 3:233-242.

Gray, P., M. Mandviwalla, L. Olfman, and J. Satzinger. (1993). The user interface in group support systems. In Group support systems, ed. L. M. Jessup and J. S. Valacich, pp. 192-213. NY: Macmillan Publishing Company

Gray, P., and L. Olfman. (1989). The user interface in group decision support systems. *Decision Support Systems* 5, no. 2:119-137.

Grohowski, R., C. McGoff, D. R. Vogel, B. Martz, and J. F. Nunamaker. (1990). Implementing electronic meeting systems at IBM: Lessons learned and success factors. *MIS Quarterly* 14, no. 4:369-382.

Group Technologies. (1990). *Aspects 1.0.* Arlington, VA.

Gustafson, D. H., R. K. Shukla, A. Delbecq, and G. W. Walster. (1973). A comparative study of differences in subjective likelihood estimates made by individuals, interacting groups, Delphi groups, and nominal groups. *Organizational Behavior and Human Performance* 9:280-291.

Hackman, J. R., and C. G. Morris. (1975). Group tasks, group interaction process, and group performance effectiveness: A review and proposed integration. In *Advances in experimental social psychology,* ed. L. Berkowitz. New York: Academic Press.

Hall, E. (1966). *The hidden dimension.* New York: Doubleday.

Hannan, M. T., and J. Freeman. (1977). Obstacles to comparative studies. In *New perspectives on organizational effectiveness,* ed. P. S. Goodman and J. M. Pennings. pp. 106-131. San Francisco: Jossey-Bass.

Hare, A. P. (1976). Handbook of small group research, 2nd ed. New York: Free Press.

Harmon, J., and J. Rohrbaugh. (1990). Social judgement analysis and small group decision making: Cognitive feedback effects on individual and collective performance. *Organizational Behavior and Human Decision Processes* 46:34-54.

Harvey, D., and I. Meiklejohn. (1988). *The executive information systems report.* London: Business Intelligence Ltd.

Harvey-Jones, J. (1988). *Making it happen.* London: Collins.

Hatvany, N., and V. Pucik. (1981). An integrated management system: Lessons from the Japanese experience. *Academy of Management Review* 6, no. 3:469-480.

Hayne, S. (1990). The application of computer supported collaborative work and knowledge-based technology to the view modeling and integration problems: A multiuser view integration system. Ph.D. dissertation, University of Arizona, Tucson.

Hayne, S. and S. Ram. (1990). Multi-user view integration system: An expert system for view integration. Proceedings of the International Conference on Data Engineering. 402-409.

Heminger, A. R., and J. S. Valacich. (1991). Comments: A system to support distributed group meetings. Paper presented at the Annual Meeting of the Midwest Decision Sciences Institute, Indianapolis, IN.

Herschel, R. (1991). An assessment of the effects of varying group gender composition on group performance and group member attitudes in an EMS environment. Ph.D. dissertation, Indiana University, Bloomington.

Hickling, A. (1990). Decision spaces: A scenario about designing appropriate rooms for group decision management. In *Tackling strategic problems: The role of group decision support,* ed. C. Eden and J. Radford. C. Eden, and Radford J. London: Sage.

Hill, G. W. (1982). Group vs. individual performance: Are n + 1 heads better than one? *Psychological Bulletin* 91, no. 3:517-539.

Hiltz, S. R. (1979, December). Using computerized conferencing to conduct opinion research. *Public Opinion Quarterly.*

Hiltz, S. R. (1984). *On-line communities: A case study of the office of the future.* Norwood, NJ: Ablex.

Hiltz, S. R. (1986). The virtual classroom: Building the foundations. Research report 23, Computerized Conferencing and Communications Center at the New Jersey Institute of Technology, Newark.

Hiltz, S. R. (1988). Productivity enhancement from computer-mediated communication: A systems contingency approach. *Communications of the ACM* 31, no. 12: 1438-1454.

Hiltz, S. R. (1992). *The virtual classroom: A new option for learning.* Norwood, NJ: Ablex.

Hiltz, S. R., M. Holmes, D. Dufner, and M. S. Poole. (1991). Distributed group support systems: Social dynamics and design dilemmas. *Journal of Organizational Computing* 2, no. 1:135-159.

Hiltz, S. R., K. J. Johnson, and M. Turoff. (1986). Experiments in group decision making, 1: Communication process and outcome in face-to-face vs. computerized conferences. *Human Communication Research* 13, no. 2:225-253.

Hiltz, S. R., K. Johnson, and M. Turoff. (1991). Experiments in group decision making, 2: The effects of designated human leaders and statistical feedback in computerized conferences. *Journal of Management Information Systems,* 8, no. 1, pp. 81-108.

Hiltz, S. R., K. Johnson, C. Aronovitch, and M. Turoff. (1981). Face to face vs. computerized conferences: A controlled experiment. Research report 12, Computerized Conferencing and Communications Center at the New Jersey Institute of Technology, Newark.

Hiltz, S. R., K. Johnson, and M. Turoff. (1985). Mode of communication and the "risky shift": Controlled experiments with computerized conferencing and anonymity in a large corporation. Research report 21, Computerized Conferencing and Communications Center at the New Jersey Institute of Technology, Newark.

Hiltz, S. R., and K. Johnson. (1990). User satisfaction with computer-mediated communication systems. *Management Science* 36, no. 6:739-764.

Hiltz, S. R., M. Turoff, and K. Johnson. (1982a). The effects of formal human leadership and computer-mediated decision aids on group problem solving via computer: A controlled experiment. Research report 18, Computerized Conferencing and Communications Center at the New Jersey Institute of Technology, Newark.

Hiltz, S. R., and M. Turoff. (1981). The evolution of user behavior in a computerized conferencing system. *Communications of the ACM* 24, no. 11

Hiltz, S. R., M. Turoff, and K. Johnson. (1989). Experiments in group decision making, 3: Disinhibition, deindividuation, and group processes in pen name and real name computer conferences. *Decision Support Systems* 5, no. 2:217-232.

Hiltz, S. R., and M. Turoff. (1978). *The network nation: Human communication via computer.* Reading, MA: Addison-Wesley.

Hiltz, S. R., and M. Turoff. (1985). Structuring computer-mediated communication systems to avoid information overload. *Communications of the ACM* 28, no. 7:680-689.

Hiltz, S. R., M. Turoff, and K. Johnson. (1982b). Using a computerized conferencing system as a laboratory tool. *SIGSOC Bulletin* 13, no. 4:5-9.

Ho, T. H., and K. S. Raman. (1991). Effect of GDSS and elected leadership on small group meetings. *Journal of Management Information Systems* 8, no. 2:109-133.

Ho, T. H., K. S. Raman, and R. T. Watson. (1989). Group decision support systems: The cultural factor, pp. 119-129. Paper presented at the International Conference on Information Systems, Boston.

Hoffer, J., S. Michalle, R. G. Anson, and R. P. Bostrom. (1990). Identifying the root causes of data and systems planning problems: An application of PLEXSYS electronic meeting support system. Proceedings of the 23rd Annual Hawaiian International Conference on Systems Science, 3. Los Alamitos, CA: IEEE Computer Society Press.

Hoffman, L. R., (1965). Group problem solving. In *Advanced in experimental social psychology,* ed. L. Berkowitz, pp. 99-132. New York: Academic Press.

Hofstede, G. (1980). *Culture's consequences: International differences in work-related values.* Beverly Hills, CA: Sage.

Hofstede, G. (1984). Cultural dimensions in management and planning. *Asia-Pacific Journal of Management* 1, no. 2:81-99.

Hofstede, G. (1985). The interaction between national and organizational value system. *Journal of Management Studies* 22, no. 4:347-357.

Houdeshel, G., and H. J. Watson. (1987). The management information and decision support (MIDS). *MIS Quarterly* 11, no. 1:127-140.

Howell, J., Dorfman, and S. Kerr. (1986). Moderator variables in leadership research. *Academy of Management Review* 11, no. 1:127-140.

Howell, J., P. Dorfman, and S. Kerr. (1986). Moderator variables in leadership research. *Academy of Management Review* 11, no. 1:88-102.

Hsu, E. (1992). Management games for management education: A case study. Working Paper. Rutgers University, Rutgers.

Huber, G. P. (1981). The nature of organizational decision making and the design of decision support systems. *MIS Quarterly* 5, no. 5:1-10.

Huber, G. P. (1984a). Issues in the design of group decision support systems. *MIS Quarterly* 8, no. 3:195-204.

Huber, G. P. (1984b). The nature and design of post-industrial organizations. *Management Science* 30, no. 8:928-951.

Huber G. P. (1990). A theory of the effects of advanced information technology on organizational design, intelligence, and decision making. *Academy of Management Review* 15, no. 1:47-71.

Huff, A. S. (1990). *Mapping strategic thought.* New York: Wiley.

Huseman, R. C., and E. W. Miles. (1988). Organizational communication in the information age: Implications for computer-based systems. *Journal of Management* 14, no. 2:181–204.

Huxham, C. (1991). Practising collaborative advantage. Paper presented at the Association for Public Policy Analysis and Management Research Conference, Bethesda, MD.

Huxham, C. (1992). Pursuing collaborative advantage. In *Operational Research and the Management of Complexity,* ed. C. Eden, M. Jackson, J. Rosenhead, and R. Tomlinson. London: Sage.

ISDD Lab Vita: ISDD Collaborative Work Support System Research Laboratory. (1991, July). Bloomington: Institute for the Study of Developmental Disabilities, Indiana University.

Ishii, H. (1990, October). Teamworkstation: Towards a seamless shared workspace. Paper presented at the Conference on Computer-Supported Cooperative Work, Los Angeles.

Jablin, F. M., and D. R. Siebold. (1978). Implications for problem-solving groups of individual and group problem solving. *Southern Speech Communication Journal* 43:327–356.

Jaccard, J., and M. Becker. (1985). Attitudes and behavior: An information integration perspective. *Journal of Experimental Social Psychology* 21:440–465.

Jaccard, J., D. Brinberg, and L. J. Ackerman. (1986). Assessing attribute importance: A comparison of six methods. *Journal of Consumer Research* 12, no. 4:463–468.

Jaccard, J., D. Brinberg, and P. Dittus. (1989). Dyadic decision making: Individual and dyadic level analysis. In *Dyadic decision making,* ed. D. Brinberg and J. Jaccard. New York: Springer-Verlag.

Jaccard, J., and D. Sheng. (1984). A comparison of six methods for assessing the importance of perceived consequences in behavioral descriptions: Applications from attitude research. *Journal of Experiment Social Psychology* 32:1–23.

Jaccard, J., and C. Wan. (1986). Cross-cultural analysis of behavioral decision making. *Journal of Cross Cultural Psychology* 17:123–149.

Jaccard, J., C. Wan, and G. Wood. (1988). Idiothetic methods for the analysis of behavioral decision making: Computer applications. In *Cognition and personal structures: Computer access and analysis,* ed. J. Mancuso and M. Shaw. New York: Praeger.

Jaccard, J., and G. Wood. (1988). The effects of incomplete information on the formation of attitudes toward behavioral alternatives. *Journal of Personality and Social Psychology* 54:580–591.

Janis, I. L. (1972). *Victims of groupthink: A psychological study of foreign policy decisions and fiascoes.* Boston: Houghton Mifflin.

Jarvenpaa, S., V. S. Rao, and G. P. Huber. (1988). Computer support for meetings of groups working on unstructured problems: A field experiment. *MIS Quarterly* 12, no. 4:645–666.

Jessup, L. M., T. Connolly, and J. Galegher. (1990). The effects of anonymity on group process in automated group problem solving. *MIS Quarterly* 14, no. 3:313–321.

Jessup, L. M., and D. A. Tansik. (1991). Group problem solving in an automated environment: The effects of anonymity and proximity on group process and outcome with a GDSS. *Decision Sciences*: 22, no. 2:226–279.

Johansen, R. (1988). *Groupware: Computer support for business teams.* New York: Free Press.

Johansen, R., A. Martin, R. Mittman, D. Saffo, D. Sibbert, and S. Benson. (1991). *Leading business teams: How teams can use technology and group process tools to enhance performance.* Reading, MA: Addison-Wesley.

Johansen, R., J. Vallee, and K. Spangler. (1979). *Electronic meetings: Technical alternatives and social choices.* Reading, MA: Addison-Wesley.

Johnson-Lenz, P., and T. Johnson-Lenz. (1981). The evolution of a tailored communications structure: The TOPICS system. Research report 14, Computerized Conferencing and Communications Center at the New Jersey Institute of Technology, Newark.

Johnson-Lenz, P., and T. Johnson-Lenz. (1982). Groupware: The process and impacts of design choices. In *Computer-mediated communication: Status and evaluation,* ed. E. B. Kerr, and S. R. Hiltz, pp. 45–55. New York: Academic Press.

Johnson-Lenz, P., T. Johnson-Lenz, and J. F. Hessman. (1980). JEDEC/EIES computer conferencing for standardization activities. In *Electronic Communication: Technology and Impacts, AAAS Selected Symposium 52,* ed. M. M. Henderson and M. J. MacNaughton. Boulder, CO: Westview.

Jones, B. H., and T. Hill. (1990). Negotiation support systems. Paper presented at the IFIP Conference, Budapest.

Jones, E. H. (1988). Analytical mediation: An empirical investigation of the effects of computer support for different levels of conflict in two-party negotiation. Ph.D., Indiana University, Bloomington.

Jung, C. G. (1959). *Psychological types.* New York: Pantheon.

Kanter, R. (1988). When a thousand flowers bloom: Structural, collective and social conditions for innovation in organizations. In *Research in organizational behavior,* ed. B. M. Staw and L. L. Cummings, pp. 169–211. Greenwich, CT: JAI Press.

Kayser, T. A. (1990). *Mining group gold.* El Segundo, CA: Serif.

Keen, P. G. W. (1988). Telecommunications: Organizational advantage. Paper presented at the Society for Information Management Conference, Minneapolis, MN.

Kerr, E. B. and S. R. Hiltz. (1982). *Computer-mediated communication: Status & evaluation.* New York: Academic Press.

Kinney, S. T. and R. Watson. (1992). The effect of medium and task on dyadic communication. Proceedings of the International Conference on Information Systems, Forthcoming. Baltimore, MD:ACM.

Konsynski, B. R. (1976). A model of computer-aided definition and analysis of information system requirements. Ph.D. dissertation, Department of Computer Sciences, Purdue University, West Lafayette, IN.

Konsynski, B., J. Kottemann, J. F. Nunamaker, and J. Scott. (1984). PLEXSYS-84: An integrated development environment for information systems. *Journal of Management Information Systems 1,* no. 3:64–104.

Konsynski, B. R., and J. F. Nunamaker. (1982). PLEXSYS: A systems development system. In *Advanced system development/feasibility techniques,* ed. J. D. Couger, M. A. Colter, and R. W. Knapp. New York: Wiley.

Kraemer, K. L., and J. L. King. (1988, June). Computer-based systems for cooperative work and group decision making. *ACM Computing Surveys 20,* no. 2:115–146.

Krauss, R., C. Garlock, P. Bricker, and L. McMahon. (1977). The role of audible and visible back channel responses in interpersonal communication. *Journal of Personality and Social Psychology 35*:523–529.

Kraut, R. E., and C. Egido. (1988). Patterns of contact and communication in scientific research collaboration. *CSCW'88: Proceedings of the Conference on Computer-Supported Cooperative Work,* Portland, OR.

Lai, K. Y., T. Malone, and K. C. Yu. (1988). Object lens: A "spreadsheet" for cooperative work. *ACM Transactions on Office Information Systems 6,* no. 4:332–353.

Lamm, H., and G. Trommsdorff. (1973). Group versus individual performance on tasks requiring ideational proficiency (brainstorming): A review. *European Journal of Social Psychology*, pp.361–387.

Lantz, K. (1986). An experiment in integrated multi-media conferencing. *Proceedings of the First Conference on Computer-Supported Cooperative Work,* Austin, TX.

Latane, B., K. Williams, and S. Harkins. (1979). Many hands make light work: The causes and consequences of social loafing. *Journal of Personality and Social Psychology* 37; 822–832.

Lawrence, P. R., and J. W. Lorsch. (1967). *Organization and environment.* Homewood, IL: Irwin.

Lee J. (October, 1990). SIBYL, A tool for managing group design rationale, *Strudel-An extensible electronic conversation toolkit*, in Proceedings of CSCW '90, Los Angeles CA.

Lee, J. (1990). Sibyl: A qualitative decision management system. In *Artificial intelligence at MIT: Expanding frontiers*, ed. P. H. Winston. Cambridge, MA: MIT Press.

Lee, J., and Malone T. (1988). How can groups communicate when they use different languages? Translating between partially shared type hierarchies. *ACM Conference on Office Information Systems,* 22–29. Palo Alto, CA: ACM Press.

Leonard-Barton, D. (1988). Implementation as mutual adaptation of technology and organization. Research Policy 17:251–267.

Leonard-Barton, D., and I. Deschamps. (1988). Managerial influence in the implementation of new technology. *Management Science 32:414–438.*

Lewin, A. Y., and J. W. Minton. (1986). Determining organizational effectiveness: Another look and an agenda for research. *Management Science 32 414–438.*

Lim, L. H., K. S. Raman and K. K. Wei. (1990). Does GDSS promote more democratic decision-making? The Singapore experiment. Proceedings of the 23rd Annual Hawaii International Conference on System Sciences, 3, 59–68. Los Alamitos, CA: IEEE Computer Society Press.

Linstone, H., and M. Turoff. (1975). *The Delphi method: Techniques and applications.* Reading, MA: Addison-Wesley.

Lipp, A. (forthcoming). A knowledge-based system built with the aid of collaborative work support software. Ph.D. dissertation, University of Georgia, Athens.

Lohmöller, J. (1989). Latent variable path modeling with partial least squares. Heidelberg, Germany: Physica-Verlag.

Lusk, C. M., T. R. Stewart, K. R. Hammond, and R. J. Potts. (1990). Judgement and decision making in dynamic tasks: The case of forecasting the microburst. *Weather and Forecasting* 6:627–639.

Mack, L. A. (1989) Technology for computer-supported meetings. Paper presented at the Annual Meeting of the Human Factors Society, Denver, CO.

MacKay, W. E. (1988) More than just a communication system: Diversity in the use of electronic mail, pp.26–28. *ACM Conference on Computer-Supported Cooperative Work,* Portland, OR: ACM Press.

MacKay, W. E., T. W. Malone, K. Crowston, R. Rao, D. Rosenblitt, and S. K. Card. (1989). How do experienced information lens users use rules? *ACM Conference on Human Factors in Computing Systems,* Austin, TX: ACM Press.

Malone, T. W., K. R. Grant, K. Y. Lai, R. Rao, and D. A. Rosenblitt. (1989). The information lens: An intelligent system for information sharing and coordination. In *Technological Support for Work Group Collaboration*, ed. M. D. Olson, Hillsdale, NJ: Lawrence Erlbaum.

Malone, T. W., L. R. Grant, F. A. Turbak, S. A. Brobst, and M. D. Cohen. (1987). Intelligent information sharing systems. *Communications of the ACM.* 30, no. 5:390–402.

Malone, T. W., K. R. Grant, K. Y. Lai, R. Rao, and D. Rosenblitt. (1988). Semi-structured messages are surprisingly useful for computer-supported coordination. In *Computer-Supported Cooperative Work: A Book of Readings*, ed. I. Greif, pp.311-331. San Mateo, CA: Morgan Kaufmann.

Mantei, M. (1988). Capturing the capture lab concepts: A case study in the design of computer supported meeting environments. Paper presented at the Conference on Computer-Supported Cooperative Work, Portland, OR.

Markus, L. (1984). *Systems in organizations: Bugs and features*. Marshfield, MA: Pittman.

Mason, R. O. (1989). MIS experiments: A pragmatic perspective. In The information systems research challenge: Experimental research methods, ed. I Benbasat, Boston; Harvard Business School.

McBride, D. J. (1988). An exploration of team information processing in a dynamic group choice task involving uncertainty. Ph. D. dissertation, University of Minnesota, Minneapolis.

McCartt, A. T. (1986). Multi-attribute utility models and tenure process. In *New directions for institutional research: Applying decision support systems in higher education*, ed. J. Rohrbaugh and A. T. McCartt. San Francisco: Jossey-Bass.

McCartt, A. T., and J. Rohrbaugh. (1989). Evaluating group decision support system effectiveness: A performing study of decision conferencing. *Decision Support System* 5:243-253.

McGoff, C. J., and L. Ambrose. (1991). Empirical information from the field: A practitioners' view of using GDSS in business. *Hawaii International Conference on System Sciences*. Los Alamitos, CA: IEEE Society Press.

McGrath, J. E. (1984). *Groups: Interaction and performance*. Englewood Cliffs, NJ:Prentice-Hall.

McGrath, J. E., and I. Altman. (1966). *Small group research: A synthesis and critique of the field*. New York: Holt, Rinehart & Winston.

McLeod, P. L. (1991). An assessment of the experimental literature on electronic support of group work: Results of a meta-analysis. [Working paper,] University of Michigan, Ann Arbor.

Mennecke, B., J. A. Hoffer, and B. Wynne. (1992). Group development and history in GDSS research: A new direction. Proceedings of the 24th Annual Hawaii International Conference on System Sciences. 3, Los Alamitos, CA: IEEE Computer Society Press.

Meyer, N. D., and M. E. Boone. (1987). *The information edge*. New York: Holt, Rinehart & Winston.

Milgram, S. (1963). Behavioral study of obedience. *Journal of Abnormal and Social Psychology* 67:371-378.

Milter, R. G. (1986). Resource allocation models and the budgeting process. In *New directions for the institutional research: Applying decision support systems in higher education*, ed. J. Rohrbaugh and A. T. McCartt. San Francisco: Jossey-Bass.

Milter, R. G., and J. Rohrbaugh. (1988). Judgement analysis and decision conferencing for administrative review. In *Advances in information processing in organizations*, ed. R. L. Cardy, S. M. Puffer, and J. M. Newman. Greenwich, CT: JAI Press.

Milter, R. G., and J. Rohrbaugh. (1985). Microcomputers and strategic decision making. *Public Productivity Review* 9:175-189.

Minski, M. (1968). Semantic information processing. Cambridge: MIT Press.

Mintzberg, H. (1973). *The nature of managerial work*. New York: Harper & Row.

Mintzberg, H. (1987). Crafting strategy. *Harvard Business Review* 65, no. 4:66-75.

Mintzberg, H., and J. A. Waters. (1985) Of strategies, deliberate and emergent. *Strategic Management Journal* 6:257-272.

Miranda, S. M. (1991). Cohesiveness and conflict management in group decision support systems. Ph.D. dissertation, University of Georgia, Athens.

Mitroff, I. I., and R. O. Mason. (1982). Business policy and metaphysics: some philosophical considerations. *Academy of Management Review* 7:361-371.

Monge, P. R., C. McSween, and J. Wyer. (1990). *A profile of meetings in corporate America: Results of the 3M meeting effectiveness study.* Austin, TX: 3M Meeting Management Institute.

Moninger, W. R., J. Bullas, B. deLorenzis, E. Ellison, J. Flueck, J. C. McLeod, C. Lusk, P. D. Lampru, W. F. Roberts, R. Shaw, T. R. Stewart, J. Weaver, D. C. Young, and S. H. Zubrick. (1991). "Shootout-89—A comparative evaluation of knowledge-based systems that forcast severe weather." *Bulletin of the American Meteorological Society,* 72, 1339-1354.

Moore, G. C. (1989). An examination of the implementation of information technology for end users: A diffusion of innovations perspective. Ph.D. dissertation, University of British Colombia, Vancouver.

Mosvick, R. K., and R. B. Nelson. (1987b). *We've got to start meeting like this! A guide to successful business meeting management.* Glenview, IL:SCott, Foresman.

Mumpower, J. (1991). The judgement policies of negotiators and the structure of negotiators and the structure of negotions. Management Science 37; 1304-1324.

Mumpower, J. L. (1988). An analysis of the judgmental components of negotiation and a proposed judgmentally-oriented approach to mediation. In *Human judgment: The social judgment theory approach,* ed. F. Homburger. Amsterdam:North Holland.

Mumpower, J. L. (1985). Expert judgments of risk. In *Safety evaluation and regulation of chemicals,* ed. F. Homburger. Basel: Karger.

Mumpower, J. L. (1987). Very simple expert systems. In *Expert judgment and expert systems,* ed. J. L. Mumpower, L. Phillips, O. Renn, and V. R. R. Uppuluri,. Berlin: Springer-Verlag.

Mumpower, J. L., and B. F. Andersen. (1983). Causes and correctives for errors of judgment. In *Social impact assessment methods,* ed. K. Finsterbush and C. Wolf. Beverly Hills, CA: Sage.

Mumpower, J. L., and T. A. Darling. (1991). A structural analysis of resource allocation negotiations and implications for negotiation support system design. *Hawaii International Conference on System Sciences* pp.641-649. Los Alamitos, CA: IEEE Computer Society Press.

Mumpower, J. L., S. Livingston, and T. Lee (1987). Expert judgements of political riskiness. *Journal of Forecasting* 6:61-65.

Mumpower, J. L., L. Phillips, O. Renn, and V. R. R. Uppuluri, eds. *Expert judgment and expert systems.* Berlin:Springer-Verlag.

Mumpower, J. L., S. P. Schuman, and A. Zumbolo. (1988). Analytical mediations in application in collective bargaining. In *Organizational decision support systems,* ed. R. M. Lee, A. M. McCosh, and P. Kigliarese. Amsterdam:North Holland.

Nadler, D., and M. Tushman. (1980). A model for diagnosing organizational behavior. *Organizational Dynamics (1980).* Autumn, 35-42.

Newman, W., and R. Smith. (1989). Prospects for the use of video to simulate physical presence. Paper presented at the International Workshop on Telematics, Denver, CO.

Niederman0, F. A. (1990). Influence of a computer-based structured procedure on problem formulation activities and outcomes. Ph.D. dissertation, University of Minnesota, Minneapolis.

Nunamaker, J. F. (1981). Educational programs in information systems. *Communications of the ACM* 24, no. 3:124.

Nunamaker J. F., L. M. Applegate, and B. R. Konsynski. (1988, November). Computer-aided deliberation: Model management and group support. *Journal of Operations Research* 36, no.6, 826-848.

Nunamaker, J. F., L. M. Applegate, and B. R. Konsynski. (1987). Facilitating group creativity:

experience with a group decision support system. *Journal of Management Information Systems* 3, no. 4:5-19.

Nunamaker, J. F., A. R. Dennis, J. S. Valacich, and D. R. Vogel. (1991). Information technology for negotiating groups: Generating options for mutual gain. *Management Science* 37, no. 10:1325-1346.

Nunamaker, J. F., A. R. Dennis, J. S. Valacich, D. R. Vogel, and J. F. George. (1991). Electronic meetings to support group work: Therory and practice at the University of Arizona. *Communications of the ACM7*

Nunamaker, J. F., B. R. Konsynski, and C. Singer. (1976). Computer aided analysis and design of information systems. *Communications of the ACM 12.*

Nunamaker, J. F., D. R. Vogel, A. Heminger, B. Martz, R. Grohowski, and C. McGoff. (1989). Experiences at IBM with group support systems: A field study. *Decision Support Systems* 5, no. 2:183-196.

Olfman, L. (1987). A comparison of application-based and construct-based training methods for DSS generator software. Ph.D. dissertation, Indiana University, Bloomington.

Olson, G. M., and J. S. Olson. (1991). User-centered design of collaboration technology. *Journal of Organizational Computing* 1:61-83.

Olson, G. M., J. S. Olson, M. R. Carter, and M. Storrøsten (In press). Small group design meetings: An analysis of collaboration. *Human-Computer Interaction.*

Olson, J. S., G. M. Olson, L. A. Mack, and P. Wellner. (1990). Concurrent editing: The group's interface. Paper presented at INTERACT '90—Third IFIP Conference on Human-Computer Interaction, Elsevier, Holland.

Olson, M. H. (1987). Computer supported cooperative work. *Office Technology and People* 3, no. 2:77-81.

Oppenheim, L. (1987). *Making meetings happen: A report to the 3M Corporation.* Austin, TX: 3M Meeting Management Institute.

Option Technologies. (1990). *OptionFinder Users Reference Manual (Version 3.2).* Mendota Heights, MN

Parsons, T. (1959). General theory in sociology. In *Sociology today: Problems and prospects*, ed. R. Merton, L. Broom, and L. S. Cottrell. New York: Basic Books.

Park, H. (1990). The use of GDSS Facilities for international business negotion. PhD. dissertation, (1989). Claremont Graduate School, Claremont, CA.

Pate, L., and R. Lake. (1989). A network environment for studying multimedia network architecture and control. Paper presented at the IEEE Global Telecommunications Conference, Dallas, TX.

Perkins, R. E. (1991). Spider: An investigation in collaborative technologies and their effects on network performance, Phoenix, Arizona: IEEE Global Telecommunications Conference. *GlobeCom '91:* pp 2074-2080.

Peters, T. J., and R. H. Waterman. (1982) *In search of excellence: Lessons from America's best-run companies.* New York:Harper & Row.

Pettigrew, A. (1977). Strategy formulation as a political process. *International Studies in Management and Organization* 7:78-87.

Phillips, L. D. (1984a). A theory of requisite decision models. *Acta Psychologica*, no. 56:29-48.

Phillips, L. D. (1984b). Decision support for managers. *In The managerial challenge of new office technology*, ed. H. J. Otway and M. Peltu. London:Butterworths.

Phillips, L. D. (1985, April). Systems for solutions. *Datamation Business*, pp 26-29.

Phillips, L. D. (1986, October). Computing to consensus. *Data International*, 68N68-6.

Phillips, L. D. (1988a). People-centered group decision support. In *Knowledge based management support systems*, ed. G. Doukidis, F. Land, and G. Miller. Chichester, England:Harwood.

Phillips, L. D. (1988b). Requisite decision modeling for technological projects. *In Social decision methodology for technological projects*, ed. C. Vlek and G. Cvetkovitch. Amsterdam:North Holland.

Phillips, L. D. (1990). Decisions analysis for group decision support. In *Tackling Strategic problems: The role of group decision support*, ed. C. Eden and J. Radford. London: Sage.

Pinsonneault, A., and K. L. Kraemer. (1989). The impact of technological support on groups: An assessment of empirical research. *Decision Support System* 5, no.2:197-216.

Pinsonneault, A., and K. L. Kraemer. (1990) The effects of electronic meeting on group processes and outcomes: As assessment of the empirical research. *European Journal of Operations Research* 46:143-161.

Pizey, J., and C. Huxham. (1991). 1990 and beyond: Developing a process for group decision support in large scale event planning. *European Journal of Operational Research.*

Pollard, C. (1991). Organizational adoption, diffusion and implementation of group support systems: A case study of OptionFinder. Ph.D. dissertation. University of Pittsburgh.

Poole, M. S. (1986). *Task function coding system.* Technical Manual. Minneapolis: University of Minnesota; Department of Speech.

Poole, M. S., and G. DeSanctis. (1987). *Group decision making and group decision support systems:* A 3-year plan for the GDSS research project. Working paper, Minneapolis. MIS Research Center, University of Minnesota.

Poole, M. S., and G. DeSanctis. (1989). Use of group decision support systems as an appropriation process, paper presented at the Hawaii International Conference on Systems Sciences. pp 149-157.

Poole, M. S., and G. DeSanctis. (1990). Understanding the use of group decisions support systems: The theory of adaptive structuration. *In Organizations and communication technology*, eds. J. Fulk and C. Steinfield, pp. 173-193. Beverley Hills, CA: Sage.

Poole, M. S., M. Holmes, and G. DeSanctis. (1991). Conflict management and a computer supported meeting environment. *Management Science 37,* no. 8:926-953.

Poole, M. S., D. R. Siebold, and R. D. McPhee. (1985). Group decision-making as a structurational process. *Quarterly Journal of Speech* 71:74-102.

Quarterman, J. S. (1990). *The matrix: Computer networks and conferencing systems worldwide.* Bedford, MA:Digital.

Quinn, J. (1986). Innovation and corporate strategy: Managed chaos. *In Technology in the modern corporation: A strategic perspective*, ed. Horwitch. New York, Pergamon.

Quinn, R. E. (1988). *Beyond rational management.* San Francisco:Jossey-Bass.

Quinn, R. E., and J. Rohrbaugh. (1981). A competing values approach to organizational effectiveness. *Public Productivity Review* 5:122-139.

Quinn, R. E., and J. Rohrbaugh. (1983). A spatial model of effectiveness criteria: Towards a competing values approach to organizational analysis. *Management Science* 29:363-377.

Quinn, R. E., J. Rohrbaugh, and M. R. McGrath. (1985). Automated decision conferencing: How it works. *Personnel* 62:49-55.

Raman, K. S., and K. V. Rao. (1988). Group decision support systems for public bodies. Prism working paper 88-013, University of Hawaii, Honolulu.

Raman, K. S., B. C. Y. Tan, and K. K. Wei. (1991). *Effect of communication mode on groups performing intellective versus preference tasks: An empirical investigation.* Working paper. National University of Singapore.

Rao, U. (1991). Hypertext functionality: A theoretical framework. Ph.D., Rutgers Graduate School of Business, New Brunswick, NJ.

Rao, U., and M. Turoff. (1990). Hypertext funcionality: A theoretical framework. *International Journal of Human-Computer Interaction* 4, no. 2:333–358.

Reagan, P., and J. Rohrbaugh. (1990). Group decision process effectiveness: A competing values approach. *Group and Organization Studies* 15:20–43.

Reagan-Cirincione, P. (1992). An experimental evaluation of a group decision support system combining group facilitation, decision modeling, and information technology. In Proceedings of the 25th Annual Hawa International Conference on Systems Science 3. Los Alamitios, CA: IEEE Computer Society Press.

Reagan-Cirincione, P., and J. Rohrbaugh. (1991). Decision conferencing: A behavioral approach to the aggregation of expert judgment. *In Expertise and decision support*, ed. G. Wright and F. Bolcer. New York:Plenum.

Reagan-Cirincione, P., S. Schuman, G. Richardson, and S. Dorf (1991). Decision modeling: Tools for strategic thinking. Interfaces 21:52–65.

Reder, S., and R. Schwab. (1990). The temporal structure of cooperative activity. Paper presented at the Conference on Computer-Supported Cooperative Work, Los Angeles.

Rein, G., and C. Ellis. (1989). The Nick experiments reinterpreted: Implications for developers and evaluators of groupware. *Office: Technology and People*

Rein, M. (1976).*Social science and public policy.* Harmonswort, England:Penguin.

Resnick, P., and M, King. (1990). The rainbow pages: Building community with voice technology. Paper presented at a conference concerning Directions and Implications of Advanced Computing, Boston.

Richardson, G. P. (1986). Problems with causal-loop diagrams *System Dynamics Review* 2:158–170.

Richardson, G. (1991). System dynamics: Simulation for policy analysis from a feedback perspective. In Qualitative simulation modeling and analysis, ed. P. Fishvick and P. Luker. New York:Springer-Verlag.

Richardson, G. P. (1991). *Feedback thought in social science.* Philadelphia: University of Pennsylvania Press.

Richardson, G. P., and M. E. Floyd. (1984). Entrained oscillations in pipon pine. *Dynamica* 10:39–41.

Richardson, G. P., and R. E. Lamitie. (1989). Improving Connecticut school aid: A case study with model-based policy analysis. *Journal of Education Finance*

Richardson, G. and A. Pugh (1981). Introduction to system dynamic DYNAMO. Cambridge:MIT Press.

Richardson, G. P., and J. Rohrbaugh. (1990). Decision making in dynamic environments: Exploring judgments in a system dynamic model-based game. In *Contemporary issues in decision making* ed. K. Borcherding, O. I. Larichev, and C. M. Messick. Amsterdam: North Holland Elsevier.

Richardson, G. and P. Senge (1989). Corporate and statewide perspectives on the liability insurance crisis. In Computer-based management of complex systems, ed. F. Milling and E. Zahn Berlin:Springer-Verlag.

Richardson, G. P., J. D. Sterman, and P. Davidsen. (1988). Modeling the estimation of petroleum resources in the United States. *Technological Forecasting and Social Change* 33:219-249.

Richardson, G. P., J. A. M. Vennix, D. F. Andersen, J. Rohrbaugh, and W. A. Wallace. (1989). Eliciting group knowledge for model-building. *In Computer-based management of complex systems*, ed. P. M. Milling and E. O. K. Zahn. Berlin: Springer-Verlag.

Ring, R. (1980, November). A new way to make decisions. *Graduate Engineer*, pp. 46-49.

Robichaux, B. P. (1990). The effects of conceptual models and presentation methods on group member perceptions and understanding for novice users of a group decision support system. Ph.D. dissertation, University of Georgia, Athens.

Rockart, J. F. (1979, March). Chief executives define their own data needs. *Harvard Business Review*, pp. 81-92.

Rogers, E. M. (1983). Diffusion of innovations. Third Edition. N.Y.: The Free Press.

Rohrbaugh, J. (1981). Improving the quality of group judgment: Social judgment analysis and the nominal group technique. *Organizational Behavior and Human Performance* 28:272-288.

Rohrbaugh, J. (1984). Making decisions about staffing standards: An analytical approach to human resource planning in health administration. *In Decision making in the public sector*, ed. L. G. Nicro. New York (1983). Marcel Dekker.

Rohrbaugh, J. (1987). Assessing the effectiveness of expert teams. *In Expert judgment and expert systems*, ed. J. Mumpower, L. Phillips, O. Renn, and V. R. R. Uppuluri. Berlin:Springer-Verlag.

Rohrbaugh, J. (1988). Cognitive conflict tasks and small group processes. *In Human judgement: The social judgement theory approach*, ed. B. Brehmer and C. R. B. Joyce. Amsterdam:North Holland.

Rohrbaugh, J. (1989a). A competing values approach to the study of group decision support systems. Proceedings of the 22nd Annual *Hawaii International Conference on System Sciences*, pp. 158-166. Los Alamitos, CA:IEEE Computer Society Press.

Rohrbaugh, J. (1989b). Demonstration experiments: Assessing the process, not the outcome, of group decision support. *In The information systems research challenge: Experimental research methods*, ed. I. Benbasat. Cambridge, MA:Harvard Business School.

Rohrbaugh, J., and D. F. Anderson. (1983). Specifying dynamic objective functions: Problems and possibilities. *Dynamica* 3:1-7.

Rohrbaugh, J., G. McCelland, and R. Quinn. (1986). Measuring the importance of utilitarian and egalitarian values: A study of individual differences about fair distribution. *In Judgment and decision making: An interdisciplinary reader*, ed. K. R. Hammond, and L. Arkes. Cambridge University Press.

Rohrbaugh, J., and A. T. McCartt. (1986). *New directions for institutional research*. San Francisco:Jossey-Bass.

Root, T. (1988). Design of a multi-media vehicle for social browsing. *CSCW'88:Proceedings of the Conference on Computer-Supported Cooperative Work*, Portland, OR.

Sambamurthy, V. (1989). A comparison of two levels of computer-based support for communication and conflict management in equivocality reduction during stakeholder analysis. Ph.D. dissertation, University of Minnesota, Minneapolis.

Sambamurthy, V., and M. S. Poole. (1991). The effects of the level of sophistication of computerized support on management of cognitive conflict in groups. Working paper, Florida State University, Information and Management Sciences Department, Tallahassee.

Satzinger, J. (1991). User interface consistency across end-user application programs: Effect on learning and satisfaction. Ph.D. dissertation, Claremont Graduate School, Claremont, CA.

Schattsneider, E. E. (1960) *The semi-sovereign people.* New York:Holt, Reinhard & Winston.

Schein, E. H. (1970). *Organizational psychology.* Englewood Cliffs, NJ: Prentice-Hall.

Schein, E. (1969). Process consultation: Its role in organization development, Reading, MA:Addison-Wesley.

Schmidt, J., D. Corey, M. Abel, S. Bulick, and S. Coffin. (1989) Multi-media communications: The US WEST advanced technologies prototype telecollaboration system. Paper presented at the International Workshop on Telematics, Denver, CO.

Schuman, S. And J. Rohrbaugh. (1991). Decision conferencing for systems planning. Information and management 21:147–159

Sein, M. (1987). Conceptual models in training novice users of computer systems: Effectiveness of abstract vs. analogical models and influence of individual difference. Ph.D. dissertation, Indiana University, Bloomington.

Seward, R. (1988). The Pod: A structural system to support group processes. Presentation at the Center for Information Systems Research, MIT, Cambridge, MA.

Shaw, M. E. (1981). *Group dynamics: The psychology of small group behavior,* 3rd ed. New York:McGraw-Hill.

Shaw, M. E. (1973). Scaling group tasks: A method for dimension analysis. *JSAS Catalog of Selected Documents in Psychology* 3:8.

Shepherd A, Mayer N, and Kuchinsky A *Strudel—An extensible electronic conversation toolkit,* in Proceedings of CSCW '90, Los Angeles. CA.

Sillars, A., S. F. Coletti, and M. A. Rogers. (1982). Coding verbal conflict tactics. *Human Communications Research* 9:73–95.

Simon, H. A. (1960) *The new science of management decision.* New York NY: Harper & Row.

Sims, H. P., and C. M. Manz. (1984) Observing leader verbal behavior: toward reciprocal determinism in leadership theory. *Journal of Applied Psychology* 69: 222–232.

Smoot, L. (1989). VideoWindow teleconferencing. Paper presented at Broadband ComForum, Buena Vista, FL.

Spender, J. C. (1989). *Industry recipes, and enquiry into the nature and sources of managerial judgment.* Oxford, UK: Basil Blackwell.

Steele, F. (1981). *The sense of place.* Boston: CBI.

Stefik, M., G. Foster, D. G. Bobrow, K. Kahn, S. Lanning, and L. Suchman. (1987). Beyond the chalkboard: Computer support for collaboration and problem solving in meetings. *Communications of the ACM* 30, no. 1: 32–47.

Stein, B., and R. Kanter. (1980). Building the parallel organization: Toward mechanisms for permanent quality of work life. *Journal of Applied Behavioral Science* 16:371–388.

Steinbach, C. (1990). *Innovations in state and local government.* New York: Ford Foundation.

Steiner, I. D. (1972). *Group process and productivity.* New York: Academic Press.

Sterman, J. D., and G. P. Richardson. (1985) An experiment to evaluate methods for estimating fossil fuel resources. *Journal of Forecasting* 4:197–226.

Stewart, T. R. (1987). The delphi technique and judgment forecasting. *Climatic Change* 11:97–113.

Stewart, T. R.(1988). Judgment analysis. In *Human judgment: The social judgment theory approach,* ed. B. Brehmer and C. R. B. Joyce. Amsterdam: North Holland.

Stewart, T. R. (1990a). A decomposition of the correlation coefficient and its use in analyzing forecasting skill. *Weather and forecasting Forecasting* 5: 661–666.

Stewart, T. R. (1990b). Scientists' uncertainty and disagreement about global climate change: A psychological perspective. *International Journal of Psychology.*

Stewart, T. R., and M. Glantz. (1985). Expert judgment and climate forecasting: A methodological critique of Climate Change to the Year 2000. *Climatic Change* 7: 159-183.

Stewart, T. R., and C. R. B. Joyce. (1988). Increasing the power of clinical trials through judgment analysis. *Medical Decision Making* 8:33-38.

Stewart, T. R., and T Leschane. (1986). Judgment and analysis in oil spill risk assessment. *Risk Analysis* 6:305-315.

Stewart, T. R., and C. McMillian. (1987). Descriptive and prescriptive models of judgment and decision making: Implications for knowledge engineering. In *Expert judgment and expert systems,* ed J. L. Mumpower, L. Phillips, O. Renn, and V. R. R. Uppuluri. Berlin: Springer-Verlag.

Stewart, T. R., P. Middleton, and D. Ely. (1983). Judgments of visual air quality: Reliability and validity. *Journal of Environmental Psychology* 3:129-145.

Stewart, T. R., W. S. R. Moninger, J. Grassia, R. H. Brady, and F. H. Merrem. (1989). Analysis of expert judgement and skill in a hail forecasting experiment. *Weather and Forecasting* 4:24-34.

Stone, P. (1988). Developing facilities to support group work: Eight mistaken premises. Working Paper 2000, Grand Valley State University:

Sundstrom, E., and I. Altman. (1989). Physical environments and work-group effectiveness. *Organizational Behavior* 11: 175-209.

Swift, C. R. (1989). Audience activity in computer mediated communication. Ph D dissertation, Indiana University, Bloomington.

Symantec Corp. (1990). *MORE 3.0.* Cupertino, CA: Authors.

Taggert, W., and D. Robey. (1981). Minds and managers: On the dual nature of human information processing and management. *Academy of Management Review* 6: 195-197.

Tan, B. C., K. K. Wei and K. S. Raman (1991). Effects of support and task on group decision outcome: A study using SAMM. In Proceedings of the 24th Annual Hawaii International Conference on Systems Sciences 3, Kawai, 537-48.

Teichroew, D., E. A. Hershey, and Y. Yamamoto. (1982). The PSL/PSA approach to computer-aided analysis and documentation. In *Advanced system development/feasibility techniques,* ed. J. D. Cougher, M. A. Colter, and R. W. Knapp. New York. Wiley.

Teichroew, D., and H. Sayani. (1974). Automation of systems building. In *Systems analysis techniques,* ed. J. D. Couger, and R. W. Knapp. New York: Wiley.

Telford, W. A., F. Ackermann, and S. Cropper. (1990). Managing quality. Medical Informatics Europe '90—Proceedings, Glasgow.

Thompson, J. D. (1967). *Organizations in action.* New York: McGraw-Hill.

Toffler, A. (1980). *The third wave.* New York: Morrow.

Trevino, L. K., R. H. Lengel, R. L. Daft. (1987). Media symbolism, media richness, and media choice in organizations. *Communications Research* 14, no. 5: 553-574.

Trevino, L. K., R. H. Lengel, and R. L. Daft. (1987). Media symbolism, media richness, and media choice in organizations. *Communication Research* 14, no. 5: 553-574.

Turban, E. (1988). *Decision support and expert systems—Managerial perspectives.* New York: Macmillan.

Turkle, S. (1984). *The second self: Computers and the human spirit.* New York: Simon & Schuster.

Turoff, M. (1971). Delphi and its potential impact on information systems. *AFIPS Conference Proceedings,* pp. 317-326.

Turoff, M. (1972). Delphi conferencing: Computer based conferencing with anonymity. *Journal of Technological Forecasting and Social Change* 3, no. 2: 159-204.

Turoff, M. (1982). Management issues in human communication via computer. *In Emerging office systems: Proceedings of the Stanford University International Symposium on Office Automation.* Norwood, NJ: Ablex.

Turoff, M. (1985). Information and value: The internal information marketplace. *Journal of Technological Forecasting and Social Change* 27, no. 4: 257-373.

Turoff, M. (1988). The anatomy of a technological innovation: Computer mediated communications. *Journal of Technological Forecasting and Social Change* 36: 107-122.

Turoff, M., J. Foster, S. R. Hiltz, and K. Ng. (1989). The TEIES design and objectives: Computer mediated communications and tailorability, Paper presented at the Hawaii International Conference on System Science, Kona. 403-411.

Turoff, M., and S. R. Hiltz. (1982a). Computer support for group versus individual decisions. *IEEE Transactions on Communications* COM-30, no. 1: 82-90.

Turoff, M., and S. R. Hiltz. (1982b, July). The electronic journal: A progress report. *Journal of the American Society for Information Science* 33, no. 4:195-202.

Turoff, M., U. Rao, and S. R. Hiltz. (1991). Collaborative hypertext in computer-mediated communications. Hawaii International Conference on System Sciences, pp. 357-366. IEEE Computer Society Press.

Valacich, J. S. (1989). "Group size and proximity effects on computer-mediated idea generation: A laboratory experiment." Ph.D. University of Arizona, Tucson.

Valacich, J. S., A. R. Dennis, and J. F. Nunamaker. (In press). Anonymity and group size effects on computer mediated idea generation. *Small Group Research.*

Valacich, J. S., A. R. Dennis, J. F. George, and J. F. Nunamaker. (1990). *Electronic support for group idea generation: Shifting the balance of process gains and losses.* [Working paper,] University of Arizona, Tucson.

Van de Ven, A. H., and A. L. Delbecq. (1971). Nominal versus interacting groups for committee decision-making effectiveness. *Academy of Management Journal* 14:203-212.

Van Over, L. D., and S. T. Kinney. (1992). Dispersed group decision-making. In *JAI research annual on computers and the social sciences,* ed. S. Nagel and D. Garson. Greenwich, CT: JAI Press.

Vari, A. (1988). Supporting negotiations in strategic decisions. In Organizational decision support systems, ed, R. Lee, A. McCosh, and P. Migliarese Amsterdam: North Holland.

Vari, A. (1991). Argumatics: A text analysis procedure for supporting problem formulation. *Quality and Quantity.*

Vari, A., and K. Farago (1991). From open debate to position war: Siting a radioactive waste repository in Hungary. Waste Management 11:173-182.

Vari, A., and J. Vecsenyi. (1984). Decision analysis of industrial R & D problems: Pitfalls and lessons. In *Analyzing and aiding decision processes,* ed. P. C. Humphreys, O. Svenson, and A. Vari, pp. 183-195. Amsterdam: North Holland.

Vari, A. and J. Vecsenyi (in press). Experiences with decision conferencing in Hungary. *Interfaces.*

Vari, A., and J. Vecsenyi. (1986). R & D strategy making in a research institute: A case history. *Journal of Applied Systems Analysis* 10: 118-123.

Vari, A., and J. Vecsenyi. (1988). Concepts and tools of artificial intelligence for human decision making. *Acta Psychologica* 68: 217-236.

Vari, A., J. Vecsenyi and Z. Paprika (1986). Supporting problem structuring in high level decisions:

The case of a hazardous waste incinerator. In New directions in research on decision making, ed. B. Brehmer, H. Jungermann, P. Lourens, and G. Sevon. Amsterdam: North Holland.

Vari, A., and J. Vecsenyi. (1990). Starting a new venture by using decision support systems. *DSS-90 Transactions* pp. 224-231.

Venkatraman, N., and V. Ramanujam. (1987). Planning systems success: A conceptualization and an operational model. *Management Science* 33, no. 6:687-705.

Vennix, J., D. Anderson, G. Richardson, and J. Rohrbaugh (in press). Model-building for group decision support: Issues and alternative in knowledge elicitation. European Journal of Operational Research.

Ventana Corporation. (1991). *GroupSystems Users Manual.* Tucson, AZ.

Vitalari, N. P. (1985). The need for longitudinal designs in the study of computing environments. In *Research methods in information system,* ed. E. Hirschheim, R. Fitzgerald, G. Harper Wood, and T. Mumford, pp. 243-265. Amsterdam: North Holland.

Vogel, D. R. (1986). An experimental investigation of the persuasive impact of computer generated presentation graphics. Ph.D., University of Minnesota, Minneapolis.

Vogel, D. R. (1989). Group decision support systems: Hardware and software developments. Paper presented at the Conference on Information Systems and Decision Processes.

Wagner, G. (1990). *VisionQuest User's Guide.* Austin, TX: Collaborative Technologies Corp.

Walton, R. (1989). *Up and running: Integrating information technology and the organization.* Boston:Harvard Business School Press.

Watson, H. J., R. P. Bostrom, R. H. Huseman, and A. Gopal. (1990). Georgia's End User Computing Research Center: The Executive 2000 project. Proceedings of the 22 Annual *Hawaii International Conference on System Sciences.* Kona: HI IEEE Computer Society, 3.

Watson, R. T. (1987). A study of group decision support system use in three and four-person groups for a preference allocation decision. Ph.D. dissertation. University of Minnesota, Minneapolis.

Watson, R. T., M. B. Alexander, C. Pollard, and R. P. Bostrom. (1991, February 15). *The use and adoption of OptionFinder: A keypad based group decision support system.* Austin, TX: 3M Meeting Management Institute.

Watson, R. T., and R. P. Bostrom. (1991). Enhancing group behavior with keypad based group support systems. *Human Resources Development Quarterly* 2, no. 4:

Watson, R. T., G. DeSanctis, and M. S. Poole. (1988). Using a GDSS to facilitate group consensus: Some intended and unintended consequences. *MIS Quarterly* 12, no. 3: 463-480.

Watson, R. T., and M. J. Dowling. (1991). The effect of a group support system on the case method of teaching. Working paper, University of Georgia, Athens.

Wei, K. K., B. C. Y. Tan, and K. S. Raman. (1992). SAGE: A HyperCard-based GDSS. Paper presented at the Hawaii International Conference on System Sciences, Kauai,

Weick, K. E. (1979). *The social psychology of organizing,* 2nd ed. Reading, MA:Addison-Wesley.

Weinstein, S. (1987, November). Telecommunications in the coming decades. *IEEE Spectrum*24, no. 11:

Weiss, J. J., and G. W. Zwahlen. (1982). The structured decision conference:A case study. *Hospital and Health Services Administration* 27: 90-105.

White, O. (1991). Mind control and the decision process. *Governing* 4:23-24.

Wilbur, S. and Young, R. (April, 1988). The Cosmos Project—*A Multi-Disciplinary Approach to Design for Computer-Supported Group Working.* European Teleinformatics Conference—In *Proceedings of the European Teleinformatics Conference—Euteco '88,* Vienna, Austria, p147-156.

Williamson, J. B., D. A. Karp, J. R. Dalphin, and P. S. Gray. (1982). *The research craft: An introduction to social research methods.* Boston: Little, Brown.

Winograd, T. and F. Flores. (1986). Understanding computers and cognition. Norwood, NJ:Ablex Publishing Corporation.

Wold, H. (1982). Soft modeling: The basic design and some extensions. In *Systems under indirect observation: Causality, structure, prediction,* ed. K. G. Jöreskog and H. Wold, pp.1-54. Amsterdam:North Holland.

Wooler, (1986, September). Letting the computer take the strain. *Financial Weekly* 4.

Wooler, S., and S. Barclay. (1988). Strategy for reducing dependence on a strike-prone production facility. In *Strategic decision support systems,* ed. P. C. Humphrey, A. Vari, J. Vecsenyi, and O. Larichev. Amsterdam:North Holland.

Wynne, B. E., and A. Heminger. (1990). Electronically support communities: Reflections and speculations. Paper presented to the Hawaii International Conference on Systems Sciences, Kona.

Wynne, B. E., and N. J. Robak. (1989). Entrepreneurs enabled: A comparison of Edelman prize-winning papers. *INTERFACES* 19, no. 2: 70-78.

Zajonc, R. B. (1965). Social facilitation. *Science* 149: 269-274.

Zakay, D. (1984). The evaluation of managerial decisions' quality by managers. *Acta Psychologica* 56:49-57.

Zander, A. (1979). The study of group behavior during four decades. *Applied Behavioral Science* 15:272-282.

Zigurs, I., G. DeSanctis, and J. Billingsley. (1989). Attitudinal development in computer-supported meetings: An exploratory study, pp. 353-358. Proceedings of the 21st Annual Hawaii International Conference on System Sciences, 3

Zigurs, I., M. S. Poole, and G. DeSanctis. (1988). A study of influence in computer-mediated group decision making. *MIS Quarterly* 14, no. 4:625-644.

Zigurs, I., T. Smith, and M. Pacanowsky. (1989). Multimedia communication support for distributed groups: An exploratory field study. Paper presented at the Conference of the International Communications Society, San Francisco.

Zmud, R. (1986). Supporting senior executives through decision support technologies: A review and directions for future research. *Decision support systems: A decade in perspective,* ed. E. R. McLean and G. H. Sol. Amsterdam:Elsevier Science.

Zuboff, S. (1988). *In the age of the smart machine.* New York:Basic Books.

Appendix

PRODUCT INDEX

This is an index of the software products mentioned in this book, each of which has been used to support teams. The attributes describing each product are outlined below.

Attribute	Description
Name	Name of software product
Time[1] (See Introduction Chapter 1 for a discussion of this dimension.)	An indication of whether this system supports primarily and same-time (**Same**), different time (**Diff**), or both same- and different-time team interactions (**Both**).
Support (See Introduction for a discussion.)	An indication of whether this system supports primarily team task (**Task**) or communication (**Comm**) or both team task and communication activities (**Both**)

---

[1] The place dimension was not included because of the assumption that most same and different time systems could be used in both same and different places.

Attribute	Description
Type (See Chapter 15 for a discussion.)	**P(WS)**—each participant has a workstation, usually a personal computer, in a network; software coordinates team activities across the network.
Type *(con't)*	**P(KP)**—each participant has a keypad that is connected to a facilitator's personal computer that runs the software. **F(WS)**—Only the facilitator has a workstation that runs software; participants have no input devices.
Technology platform	The hardware-software environment in which the system operates
Chapter described in	Chapter in which the system is described. If this field is blank, the system was only cited. In this case, the reader should contact the vendor or see the references in chapters where cited for more information.
Chapter cited in	Chapter(s) where system is discussed

Let us examine the **Aspects** (product name) entry to illustrate the information contained in the index. **Aspects** supports primarily team communications in a same-time environment where each participant has a Macintosh computer. It is cited in Chapter 10. The reader should contact the vendor, Group Technologies, for more information (see the Vendor Contact Index following this index).

Two sets of software were not included in the table, even though they were used to support teams, because they are well known, commercially available applications that support single users or general network applications:

1. A number of single-user commercially available software packages were used to support group work in decision conferencing/chauffeured mode. These packages include the following (the numbers in parentheses indicate the chapters in which these tools are cited):

Allocate (18)   MORE (10)
Excel (14)   PROPS (16)
Expert Choice (11, 16)   SMLTREE (18)
Harvard Graphics (16)   STATGRAPHICS (16)
HyperCard (10)   Stella (18)
IFPS (14)   STORYBOARD (14)
LINDO (18)   Word (14)
LOTUS 1-2-3 (16, 17)

2. A number of commercially available software packages were also used to provide shared access to single-user software:

CARBON COPY (10)
CLOSE-UP LAN (16)
Timbuktu (10)

Product Index

Name	Focus Time	Support	Type	Platform	Chapter described in	Chapter cited in
1 Answer Garden	Diff	Both	P(WS)	UNIX	5	5
2 Aspects	Same	Comm	P(WS)	Mac		10
3 CGS Environment	Same	Task	P(WS)	Windows	14	14
4 COMMENTS	Both	Both	P(WS)	MS-DOS	11	11
5 Coordinator	Diff	Comm	P(WS)	MS-DOS		5, 6, 17
6 COPE	Same	Task	F(WS)	MS-DOS	19	11, 15, 19
7 Cosmos	Diff	Both	P(WS)	Mac, Sun, UNIX	6	6
8 Co-op	Same	Task	P(WS)	MS-DOS		14
9 Cruiser	Same	Comm	P(WS)		11	7, 11
10 DECAID1	Same	Task	P(WS)	MS-DOS	16	16
11 EIES*	Both	Both	P(WS)	UNIX	4	2, 4, 11
12 Folder	Same	Task	P(WS)	Windows	13	13
13 FREENET	Diff	Comm	P(WS)		11	11
14 Group Issue Analyzer	Same	Task	P(WS)	Windows	13	13
15 Group Scratch Pad	Same	Comm	P(WS)	Windows	13	13
16 Group View Modeling	Same	Task	P(WS)	Windows	13	13
17 GroupSystems	Diff	Task	P(WS)	MS-DOS	8	2, 8, 11, 13, 14, 15, 16, 17
18 HIVIEW	Same	Task	F(WS)	MS-DOS		18
19 Hypervoice	Diff	Comm	P(WS)	Personal Computer	5	5
20 IBMPC	Diff	Comm	P(WS)	IBM Mainframe		3
21 Information Lens	Diff	Comm	P(WS)	Xerox Interlisp	5	1, 5
22 Lotus Notes	Diff	Both	P(WS)	OS/2		17
23 Meeting Chair	Same	Comm	P(WS)	Windows	13	13
24 Object Lens*	Both	Both	P(WS)	Mac	5	1, 5
25 Office Express/grapeVINE	Diff	Comm	P(WS)	DEC VAX		11
26 OptionFinder	Same	Task	P(KP)	MS-DOS		11, 13, 15
27 POLICY PC	Same	Task	F(WS)	MS-DOS		18
28 SAGE	Same	Task	P(WS)	Mac	12	12, 15
29 SAMM	Same	Task	P(WS)	UNIX	9	9, 11, 12, 14, 15
30 ShrEdit	Same	Comm	P(WS)	Mac		10
31 Spider	Same	Comm	P(WS)	Mac		7
32 Sybil	Both	Both	P(WS)	Mac	5	5
33 Synapse	Both	Task	P(WS)	Mac	5	5
34 TeleCollaboration	Same	Comm	P(WS)		7	7
35 VideoWindows	Same	Comm	P(WS)		11	7, 11
36 Virtual Classroom	Both	Both	P(WS)	UNIX	4	4, 11
37 VisionQuest	Both	Task	P(WS)	MS-DOS		2, 11, 13, 14, 15, 16, 17

*These systems provide facilities to develop specific applications. A number of these are discussed in the chapters referenced.

VENDOR CONTACT INDEX

1, 19, 21, 24, 32, 33
Answer Garden, Hypervoice,
    Information Lens,
Object Lens, Sybil, Synapse
Mass. Institute of Technology
Sloan School of Management
Cambridge, MA 02139
Phone: 617-253-6843
Contact: Thomas Malone

2
Aspects
Group Technologies, Inc
1408 N. Filmore St, Suite 10
Arlington VA, 22201
Phone: 703-528-1555
Fax: 703-525-3293
Contact: Dimitri Korahais

3
CGS Environment
Claremont McKenna College
Information Science Department
130 E. 9th Street
Claremont, CA 91711
Contact: Paul Gray

4
Comments
Indiana University
Business School, Bu 560-D
10th and Fee Lanes
Bloomington, IN 47405
Phone: 812-855-9703
Contact: Joseph Valacich

5
Coordinator
Action Technologies, Inc.
1145 Atlantic Ave.
Alameda, CA 94501

6
COPE
University of Strathclyde
Strathclyde Business School
26 Richmond Street
Glasgow, G1 1XH
United Kingdom
Phone: (44)-41-552-4400
Fax: (44)-41-552-6686
Contact: Colin Eden

7
Cosmos
Queen Mary & Westfield College
Dept of Computer Science
Mile End Road
London, E1 4NS
United Kingdom
Phone: (44)-71-975-5555
Fax: (44)-71-975-5500
Contact: Sylvia Wilbur

8
Co-op
Naval Postgraduate School
Code AS/BD
Monterey, CA 93943-5000
Phone: 408-646-2630
Fax: 408-646-3407
Contact: Tung Bui

10
DECAID1
Queen's University
School of Business
Kingston, Ontario K7L 3N6
Canada
Contact: Brent Gallupe

11
EIES, Virtual Classroom
New Jersey Inst. of Technology

CIS
Newark, NJ 07102
Contact: Starr Roxanne Hiltz

12, 14, 15, 16
Folder, Group Issue Analyzer, Group Scratch-
    pad, Group View Modelling
University of Calgary
MIS Area, Faculty of Management
2500 University Drive NW
Calgary, Alberta T2N 1N4
Canada
Contact: Stephen Hayne

17
GroupSystems
Ventana Corp.
1430 E. Fort Lowell Rd. Suite 301
Tucson, AZ 85719
Phone: 602-325-8228

18
HIVIEW
Decision Analysis Unit
London School of Economics
Houghton St.
London WC2A 2AE
United Kingdom

20
IBMPC
Contact Local IBM Representative
Re Computer Conferencing Systems

22
Lotus Notes
Lotus Development Corporation
55 Cambridge Parkway
Cambridge, MA 02142
Phone: 617-693-4437

25
Office Express/grapeVINE

Institute of Information
Technology
Level 15, Tower 1, The Plaza
Bondi Junction, NSW 2022
Australia
Phone: (61)-2-389-3800
Fax: (61)-2-387-858

26
OptionFinder Option Technologies, Inc.
1725 Knollwood Lane
Mendota Heights, MN 55118
Contact: William Flexner

27
Policy PC
Executive Decision Services
P. O. Box 9102
Albany, NY 12209
Phone: 518-465-8872

28
SAGE
National University of Singapore
Dept of Info Sys & Comp Sci
Lower Kent Ridge Road
Singapore 0511
Singapore
Phone: (65)-775-6666
Contact: K S Raman

29
SAMM
Dickson, Anderson & Associates
11301 Fetterly Road, Suite 201
Minnetonka, MN 55343
Phone: 612-546-3248
Academic Contact: Gerry DeSanctis
Industry Contact: Gary Dickson

30
ShrEdit
University of Michigan

Machine Intelligence Lab
701 Tappan Street
Ann Arbor, MI 48109
Contact: Gary Olson

31
Spider
Apple Computer, Inc.
Advanced Technology Group
Applications Technology
20525 Mariani Ave. MS: 76-2C
Cupertino, CA 95104
Contact: Rod Perkins

34
TeleCollaboration
US West Advanced Technologies
4001 Discovery Suite
Boulder, CO 80303

37
VisionQuest
Collaborative Technologies Corp.
8920 Business Park Dr. Suite 100
Austin, TX 78759
Phone: 512-794-8858
Fax: 512-794-8861

GEOGRAPHIC INDEX

The geographic index lists the nations and institutions represented in this book. The chapter is shown following the institution's name.

EDUCATION INDEX

VIDEO INDEX

VisionQuest-$10 10 minutes
Collaborative Technologies Corp.
8920 Business Park Dr. Suite 100
Austin, TX 78759
Phone: 512-794-8858

Together-11 minutes
Coordination Technologies, Inc.
35 Corporate Drive
Trumbull, CT 06611
Phone: 1-800-292-7755
Contact: Richard Zboray

Notes
Lotus Development Corp.
55 Cambridge Parkway
Cambridge, MA 02142
Phone: 617-693-4437
Contact: John Bartlett

Meetings That Work-
Digital Equipment Corporation
Contact your local representative

Aspects-5 minutes
Group Technologies, Inc.
1408 N. Filmore St. Suite 10
Arlington, VA 22201
Phone: 703-528-1555
Contact: Dimitri Korahais

MIS/CMR2-13 minutes
University of Arizona
BPA/Dept. of MIS
Tucson, AZ 85721
Phone: 602-621-2748
Contact: Doug Vogel

GroupSystems-11 mins
Ventana Corp.
1430 E. Fort Lowell Rd., Suite 301
Tucson, AZ 85719
Phone: 602-325-8228
Strategy on the Screen-23 mins
BBC

Index